MW00713807

MEMOIRS

OF

SPAIN

DURING THE REIGNS OF

PHILIP IV. AND CHARLES II.

FROM 1621 TO 1700.

BY

JOHN DUNLOP,

AUTHOR OF THE HISTORY OF FICTION, ETC.

VOL. II.

EDINBURGH,
THOMAS CLARK, 38. GEORGE STREET;
LONDON, WHITTAKER & CO.

MDCCCXXXIV.

3244

PRINTED BY NEILL AND COMPANY, OLD FISHMARKET, EDINBURGH.

CONTENTS

OF

VOLUME SECOND.

MEMOIRS OF SPAIN, &c.

———

CHAPTER I.

ACCESSION OF CHARLES II.

Vagituque locum lugubri complet, ut æquum
Cui tantum in vitâ restat transire malorum.
LUCRETIUS.

On the 8th of October 1665, Charles the Second was proclaimed King by the Duke of Medina de-las-Torres, who, at this ceremony, was mounted on horseback, and was accompanied by all the grandees at that time in the capital. He was richly apparelled in a silk suit, embroidered with gold and silver, and set with diamond buttons. In his right hand he carried the royal standard, and by his left side rode the Corregidors of the city. The cavalcade first proceeded to the Plaça Mayor, in front of the balcony from which the late king had been wont to view the bull-fights. The heralds who went before, ascended a scaffold, which was covered with rich tapestry, and then ranged themselves around the Duke, who lifted up the banner, calling three times, " Castilla for the Catholic King Charles, second of that name," and all the people shouted aloud *Viva*. After the King had been thus proclaimed with due form in the great square, the ceremony was repeated at the Convent of the Descalças Reales,—at the Town-house,—the gate of Guadalaxara,—and the Royal Palace.[1]

Spain, at the period of the accession of Charles II, was truly unhappy. Her finances were deranged,—her industry paralyzed,—her internal resources completely exhausted,—and her arms disgraced abroad. Her throne was ascended by a sickly child, only four years old, who, when he first came into the world, was so small and tender, that he was placed in a box of cotton.[2] A few months before his succession, Sir Richard Fanshawe had written of him during an excursion of the Court to Aranjuez :— " The little prince remains here in the palace, as far as I can learn nothing so lively as his father ; pray God he prove so lasting !"[3] After the proclamation, such was the debility of this royal infant, that his demise was almost daily expected ; and till he was ten years old he was brought up in the arms and on the knees of the ladies of the palace, without having ever been permitted to put his foot on the ground.[4] His ceaseless wailings testified his bodily infirmities and sufferings, and alarmed his anxious subjects with the dread of a war, an interregnum, or subjection to foreign dominion.

By the testament of Philip IV, the Queen-mother was called to the regency, with a council of government consisting of the Cardinal Sandoval, Archbishop of Toledo, the President of Castile, the Vice-Chancellor of Aragon, the Inquisitor-General, and the Marques d'Aytona, as a representative of the Grandees. The Archbishop, however, having died nearly at the same time with the King, his place was supplied by Pascal, Cardinal of Aragon, who succeeded him as Archbishop of Toledo. In fact, however, the whole sovereign power was vested in the Queen, as completely as in France it had been in the

[1] *Memoirs of Lady Fanshawe*, p. 225.   [2] D'Aulnoy, *Voyage*.
[3] *Letters*.   [4] D'Aulnoy, *Voyage d'Espagne*.

hands of Anne of Austria during the minority of her son;
for though the Council had the privilege of advising, they
had no power to control her wishes. Unluckily she had
neither the talents nor temper requisite for government.
It was a still greater misfortune that she was inordinate-
ly fond of power, and jealous of its exercise; and it was
the greatest mishap of all, that she possessed it through a
course of years sufficiently long to subvert the authority
of the crown, to ruin its subjects, and to disable the monarch, even had he been so inclined, from the power of repairing the evils she had occasioned, or at least grievously augmented. The welfare of Spain was to her a matter of indifference, and the inhabitants of Madrid, from
the first moment of her arrival in that capital, had been
the objects of her special aversion. She was entirely devoted to the interests of the Court of Vienna, and was
governed in all things by the instructions she received
from it, except in points that regarded her private inclinations; for in these she would listen to no counsel whatever, but persisted in their gratification against the remonstrances of her wisest advisers.[1] A regency, unless when
exercised by the heir to the monarchy, is almost always
a period of weakness: it is a state of temporary and sometimes not clearly defined authority, which imparts hopes,
and not terror, to the ambitious and turbulent. The
Count of Castriglio and the Duke of Medina de-las-
Torres, continued the factions and animosities which had
divided them towards the close of the last reign, and occasioned the formation of a political party, which was
wholly dependent on the Queen, and subservient to her
wishes. From the commencement of her regency, she
devolved the immediate exercise of authority on her
confessor the Jesuit Nithard, who had accompanied her
to Spain at the period of her marriage, but had been

---

[1] *Universal History*, t. xix. book 1.

wisely kept at a distance from all public affairs during the lifetime of the late king. Soon after assuming the sovereign power, however, the Queen contrived to introduce him into the Council, by engaging the Archbishop of Toledo to resign in his favour the office of Inquisitor-General, which gave him *ex officio* a place in the regency. This low-born stranger, who now engrossed the whole administration of affairs, was a person of the most limited capacity, and though he had now reached the mature age of sixty, was totally inexperienced in the management of public business. Accustomed only to the petty arts of monkish intrigue, he proved himself altogether unequal to the government of a vast but declining monarchy, and he rendered himself at once odious to the grandees, and ridiculous to the people, by affecting to imitate the haughtiness and austerity of the renowned Cardinal Ximenes. The general discontent against his administration was fomented by John of Austria, who often made Nithard the object of his invective and sarcasm.

The Queen, availing herself of the reverses sustained by that Prince in Portugal, had persuaded the late King to exclude his once favoured son from all share in the administration. Though of confessed abilities both as a statesman and a soldier,—though esteemed by the Grandees and adored by the people, he was obliged to continue for the present in exile at Consuegra, and yield to a narrow-minded monk, that share in the government to which he was so justly entitled by his talents.

Such was the situation of Spain, and such the director of its counsels, at a time when the relations of the country with foreign states required, in all branches of the administration, the greatest skill, circumspection, and energy.

The most imminent external danger to which the kingdom lay exposed at the accession of Charles II, was on its western frontier, from the incursions of the victorious Portuguese. At the close of the late reign, negotiations for peace had commenced under the mediation of Sir R. Fanshawe, the English ambassador at the Court of Madrid. But in the mean while, Mareschal Schomberg repeatedly defeated the Spanish Generals, took several strong places without resistance, and ravaged the whole province of Spanish Estremadura.

The Emperor of Germany was the natural and family ally of the King of Spain. Besides the connection of these two potentates as descended from the same ancestors, they were united by the ties of frequent intermarriages in their families, and still more by the bonds of political interest derived from a common dread of France, whose encroachments had reduced their respective dominions, and whose systematic enmity and ambitious designs, furnished continual causes of alarm. At present, however, the Emperor was but inadequately provided with either troops or money, his resources having been recently exhausted in repelling a formidable invasion of the Turks, and in suppressing an insurrection among his Hungarian subjects. The influence possessed in Germany by former Emperors, was now greatly reduced by recent changes which had taken place in the Germanic constitution. Many princes of the empire were overawed by the extension of the French territory towards the Rhine and the occupation of a part of Lorraine; while others, from interest and inclination, were devoted to France, which they regarded as their great support against the despotism and encroachments of their own imperial chief.[1]

At this period, Italy had, in a great measure, lost its weight in the balance of power. Of those states which yet retained a share of their former importance, the Republic of Venice was leagued with France, and the Duke

[1] Coxe, *Hist. of House of Austria*, c. 63.

of Savoy was still held by that power in a humiliating state of subjection, though he was impatient of the yoke imposed on him, and was anxiously watching for an opportunity to rescue himself from bondage.

Charles II. of England held in his hands, at his restoration, the balance of Europe. But that pre-eminence which the British nation had attained during the vigorous sway of Cromwell, was lost in the course of his profuse, voluptuous, and dissipated reign; and by his dishonourable dependence on Louis XIV, he contributed, more than any other prince in Europe, to the humiliation of Spain and the preponderance of France.

The want of other allies was but ill compensated to Spain by the arrival of an ambassador from Alexis Michaelovitz, Czar of Muscovy, who proposed a treaty between the indolent Spaniards and his own barbarous subjects.[1] This embassy, however, excited a greater sensation than any which had arrived in Spain since the beginning of the 15th century, when Tamerlane sent to Henry the Invalid, King of Castile, a Tartarian envoy, who appeared in barbaric splendour at Burgos, and presented the Spanish prince with two gorgeous Hungarian beauties who had been discovered by Tamerlane among the captives of the Sultan Bajazet, and whom he supposed would prove the most acceptable offering he could present to the Castilian Monarch.

While Spain had thus declined in her internal resources and in the power of her government, and while she was altogether destitute of allies who might afford her the protection and support she so much required, France, her ancient hereditary enemy, was daily increasing her native strength as well as her external influence. It is true, that at this moment, a peace, solemnly concluded, and apparently firmly cemented, subsisted between the na-

---

[1] Desormeaux, *Abregé Chronol.* t. v.

tions. But the rainbow of the Pyrenees was already fading away, and various signs on the horizon portended an approaching tempest.

Mazarin, by whom the peace of the Pyrenees was concluded on the part of France, and who regarded that treaty as his master-stroke of policy,—the consummation as it were, of his long and prosperous administration,—had died about a year after the celebration of those royal nuptials which had been the ultimate aim of all his intrigues, and which had raised him to the summit of civil glory. It was regarded as a symptom of the continuance of his pacific disposition, that he bequeathed the Flora of Titian, a picture of prodigious value, to Luis de Haro, and a golden table-clock to the Count of Fuénsaldagna,[1] at that time ambassador to Paris from the Court of Madrid. His death had been therefore considered as a severe misfortune by the Spanish ministry, whose principal object it was to preserve that peace which had been obtained with so much cost and trouble, and which seemed almost essential to the existence of the nation.

A few months after the accession of Charles II. to the throne of Spain, the death of Mazarin was followed by that of the Queen Mother of France, Anne of Austria. Being much attached to her native country, she had always supported its interests at court, and had been instrumental in procuring for Spain, on reasonable terms, the peace of the Pyrenees. As she had great influence over the mind of her son, it is believed that had she survived for some years longer, she might have moderated, or directed to some other channel, that ambition which Louis hastened to gratify at the expense of her country and kindred.

Louis XIV. received the worst possible education, or rather his education had been utterly neglected. The Queen Mother and Mazarin had pursued with him the

<hr/>

[1] Aubery, *Hist. du Cardinal Mazarin*, livre viii.

same self interested system which Olivarez had adopted
with Philip, and which the present Regent of Spain was
now following out with her hapless son. The little attention which had been paid to the improvement of Louis
in his youth, ought always to be taken into account while
estimating the character of that wonderful monarch. On
the death of Mazarin, to whom his proud sovereign had
been so submissive, and to whom all affairs of state had
been implicitly entrusted, Louis suddenly roused from his
youthful dream of indolence and pleasure. He resolved
himself to govern the state, and announced that for the
future he should be his own prime minister. Philip IV.
had made a similar declaration on the disgrace of Olivarez, but he had remained too long supine, to persevere in
the unwonted effort. Louis, on the other hand, maintained his resolution ; and, by his judicious choice of servants, and the spirit which he inspired into his people, he
quickly raised France to that power which enabled her to
crush Spain into atoms, and spread consternation over all
the rest of Europe.

According to the system on which Louis proceeded,
the duties of each minister were prescribed to him, and
each was accountable to the Sovereign for his acts of administration. In consequence of the adoption of this method, and his own discernment in estimating talents and
character, Louis had more able and faithful servants than
had ever yet fallen to the lot of a royal master. Colbert,
who had been bred under Mazarin, directed his attention
to those objects of internal government, which had been
somewhat neglected in France since the days of Sully.
He restored to order the deranged finances of the state,
and thus enabled his sovereign to purchase Dunkirk and
Mardike from the English. The experience and address
of the Marquis de Lionne, who had been also a pupil of
Mazarin, were highly serviceable in negotiations and the

general management of foreign affairs. Louvois proved
a zealous and effective minister in the war department,
and so long as it was under his superintendence, the
troops were regularly paid, the garrisons maintained, and
the magazines adequately supplied. The warlike genius
of Condé, Turenne, and Luxembourg, had now been fostered by long experience, and an host of heroes who had
fought under them were ready for the field. The skill
and science of Vauban were peculiarly useful from the
nature of those wars in which Louis engaged, and which
were chiefly prosecuted in countries studded with fortified towns. Those factions which had distracted the
kingdom during the minority of Louis, disappeared before his dignity and condescension. The turbulent De
Retz—the fiery rebellious Condé, had become the most
submissive and obedient of his subjects. This change,
from the extreme of popular discontent to the most devoted loyalty, is chiefly attributable to the personal qualities of the sovereign. There may have been greater
kings than Louis; but (in the words of Bolingbroke) he
was the best actor of majesty that ever filled a throne.
He was possessed of all those endowments which could
flatter the pride or conciliate the affections of a vain, vo-
latile, and high-spirited people. He was distinguished
for manly beauty, and his majestic deportment was tem-
pered with affability and politeness. Fond of display
and magnificence, he gratified the vanity of his subjects
by the pomp of his public entertainments and the grandeur of his palaces. Though little skilled in military affairs, and for a son of Louis XIII. and grandson of
Henry the Great, not even remarkable for personal courage, he possessed, in a surprising degree, the talent of inspiring his generals and troops with enthusiasm.[1] Though

[1] Louis les animant du feu de son courage,
    Se plaint de sa grandeur, qui l'attache au rivage.
                                        BOILEAU.

illiterate himself, and even, according to some accounts, grossly ignorant, he was a munificent patron of learning, and a founder of academies for the promotion of science and art. But even this liberality was rendered subservient to that system of glory and *eclat* which formed the basis of his empire.

Louis was animated by an ardent love of fame, and he soon showed that he was desirous to be respected by foreign princes as well as by his own subjects. Before the end of the reign of Philip IV, the ambassador of that monarch at the Court of London had, in an evil hour, claimed precedence over the representative of the Majesty of Louis. The French King immediately recalled his ambassador from Madrid, and threatened that unless he received solemn reparation for the injury, hostilities should immediately recommence. He was by that time well prepared for war, and would have been glad of any pretext to declare it. But the Court of Madrid averted his wrath by despatching an envoy extraordinary to Paris, who publicly offered a most submissive apology in presence of all the foreign ministers, as was recorded by a medal expressly struck for the occasion. His treatment of the Pope was still more arrogant. Crequi, the French ambassador at Rome, having met with an affront from the guards of Alexander VII, that pontiff was obliged to punish the offenders, to send his nephew into France to ask pardon, and to allow in Rome itself the erection of a pillar as a monument of his humiliation.

But the lofty spirit of Louis did not confine itself to points of mere ceremony and national honour. His views extended to an enlargement of the territorial limits of France, and he resolved to follow up that system of policy which, planned by Henry IV, and pursued by Richelieu, had humbled the House of Austria in both its branches, and acquired for France that paramount influence in Europe, which was before possessed by her rival. Availing himself of the embarrassments of the Spanish government, and the weakness of the minor, now seated on the throne of Spain, he resolved to appropriate a large portion of the Netherlands, though he had solemnly renounced his right to any part of the succession on his marriage with the Infanta, and had acknowledged the young king (who possessed the strongest claims on his guardianship and protection) as heir to the whole monarchy. He founded his pretensions, on what was called the right of-devolution, by which, according to the local customs in Brabant, Franche Comté and other parts of the ancient Burgundian possessions, a daughter of a first marriage was entitled to succeed in private inheritances, in preference to the sons by a second union. This unusual law of succession, which was applicable only to private families, Louis now contended ought to be followed as the rule in claims to the sovereignty, and of consequence that his Queen Maria Theresa, daughter of Philip IV. by his first marriage, had a preferable right to the King of Spain, who was the offspring of his second nuptials. He justified the breach of his renunciation by the subterfuge, that it was null and void, from the minority of the Infanta, and that it was contrary to the fundamental laws both of Aragon and Castile; and he pretended, that natural rights depending on blood and succession, could not be annihilated by any deed or contract whatever. Besides, he maintained that, as the dowry of the Infanta never had been paid, he was not under any obligation to observe his part of the stipulations.

The appropriation of these territories, which included Brabant, Hainault, Artois, Luxemburgh, and Franche Comté, with the lordships of Namur and Limburgh, had been in the view of Louis before the death of Philip IV; and during the last illness of that monarch, Tu-

renne had, at the request of his royal master, drawn up
a memorial on the best steps to be adopted for securing
these provinces in the event of Philip's decease.

Immediately after the accession of Charles II. to the
throne of Spain, the King of France preferred his claims
to the court of Madrid, but, at the same time, expressed
his anxiety that the matter should be brought to an amicable adjustment. Louis, likewise, caused his rights to be
examined by his ministers and jurisconsults, who found
that they were incontestable. The Queen of Spain, and
her council of regency were far from seeing the matter in
the same light. The lawyers of both nations maintained
the claims of their respective crowns. Louis was always
anxious to give to his ambitious projects the appearances
of justice, and the pretensions of France were discussed
in various political writings which were disseminated all
over Europe. A manifesto from the King himself set
forth his rights, and detailed his endeavours to obtain them
without having recourse to arms. The Spaniards, in their
publications on the subject, placed in the strongest light
the efficacy of the renunciation, and showed that the law
of inheritance, for which Louis contended, was applicable
only to a private inheritance, and not to the royal succession.[1]

Spain had the best of the argument; and Louis, though
desirous to cover his claims with specious pretences, was
no doubt aware that they were less fit to be adjusted by
reasoning than by arms, and in this sort of disputation he
was abundantly sensible of his superiority. While the
controversy was proceeding, and his title was under

---

[1] Of the publications on the Spanish side, the best was written
by a celebrated Neapolitan jurisconsult, Francisco d'Andrea, who
employed his pen in the controversy at the request of the Viceroy of Naples, Don Pedro d'Aragon. (Giannone, *Storia Civile di
Napol.* lib. xxxix. c. 1.)

discussion at Madrid, he was busily preparing for the meditated aggression. His army was placed on its fullest
establishment, and he reviewed his troops at Compiegne,
where they appeared in full array, in presence of his whole
court, who assembled in the utmost magnificence. He
deemed himself secure, at present, from any opposition on
the part of the Dutch, who were at this time occupied by
their naval war with England, and whom the Marques of
Castel-Rodrigo, the governor of the Spanish Netherlands,
had been at no pains to conciliate, but had, on the contrary, provoked, by an injudicious attempt to wrest from
them the town of Williamstadt in name of the Bishop of
Munster. In England, the intrigues of Louis had proved
eminently successful. Sweden he bound to his interests by a subsidiary treaty; and, by threats or promises,
he gained the neutrality or acquiescence of the German
principalities. He even opened negotiations with the
Court of Vienna, and it has been suspected that he concluded a secret treaty with the Emperor, by which that
potentate agreed to permit Louis to occupy the Netherlands, on condition that the sovereignty of Spain should
pass into the Imperial family, in the event of the sickly
child who now held its sceptre dying without issue.[1]

The Queen-regent of Spain, and her minister Father
Nithard, had left the Netherlands defenceless in every
quarter; but even if the towns in the Low Countries
had been more strongly garrisoned than they were, and
the fortifications in a better state, the French King was
prepared to overcome all difficulties. He entered Flanders at the head of an army of 35,000 men, with Turenne
under him as Lieutenant-General; while a corps of 5000
troops invaded Luxemburg, and another of 8000 advanced
to take post in Dunkirk. Louvois, the French war minister, had placed large magazines in all the frontier towns:

[1] Voltaire, *Siècle de Louis XIV.*

Wherever the army turned, supplies were at hand; and
it was chiefly this new improvement in the war-department
that contributed to the rapid success of this brilliant
campaign.

On thus entering Flanders, in the most hostile attitude,
Louis' published no declaration of war. He even dis-
avowed any design to violate the peace of the Pyrenees,
and merely notified in a letter to the Regent of Spain,
his intention to take possession of the territories which
were unjustly withheld from his Queen, or to secure an
equivalent for them.

The Spaniards in the Netherlands, though they had
been long apprized of their danger, were in no condition
to resist such a force as was now brought against them;
and Louis quickly possessed himself of the ill defended
provinces of a crushed and fallen monarchy.[1] He entered Charleroy as if it had been his own capital. Aeth,
Tournay, and Douai surrendered in a few days at discretion to the King in person; while Courtrai and Oudenarde were taken by Marshal d'Aumont, who commanded the corps which had marched to Dunkirk. The King
next meditated the siege of Lisle, which was the best
fortified town in the Netherlands, and was defended by
a garrison of 3000 regular troops, besides the armed bur-
gesses. This enterprise appeared so difficult and hazardous in the present conjuncture, that both Louvois, the
war minister, and Turenne, attempted to dissuade the
King from undertaking it. The French army had been
diminished by the garrisons which required to be left in
the captured towns, and the largest force which the Spaniards had in the field lay in the neighbourhood, with
the intention of affording it succour. This army was led
by the Count Marsin, who began his treasonable career
by withdrawing from Barcelona the French garrison

[1] Ibid.

which he commanded. Subsequently to that period, his hostility to the Court of France had been so active and persevering, that he was exempted from the general amnesty extended to the other adherents of Condé. He had latterly served the King of Spain against Portugal, and he now commanded the Spanish forces in the Netherlands, which were opposed to the French arms. Louis, in spite of all obstacles, made his preparations for investing Lisle. When he arrived before it, the Governor sent to inquire in what part of the lines were the King's quarters, that he might not fire in that direction. But his Majesty, who perhaps doubted the Governor's good faith, returned for answer, that they would be in every station in the camp of his army.[1] Lisle presented the only resistance which the French arms had yet encountered. It held out nearly a month from the time of its first investment, and its garrison, after having made some vigorous but ineffectual sallies, surrendered on terms of capitulation. As soon as the King had entered Lisle, he received information that Marsin, who was yet ignorant of its capture, was advancing to its relief at the head of 6000 men. Mareschal Crequi was sent out against him with a superior force, and the Count, now learning the fate of Lisle, attempted to avoid an engagement. He was, however, brought to action by Crequi, and defeated with the loss of 1500 prisoners.[2] Thus, in a

[1] De Quincy, *Hist. Militaire de Louis le Grand*, t. i. p. 284.

[2] Jean Gaspar Ferdinand Count de Marsin, who has been so frequently mentioned, (see above, vol. i. p. 497, &c.), was never pardoned by the French King, and spent the remainder of his life in the Spanish service. When, in 1657, Charles II. of England raised some troops in Flanders to aid in re-establishing him on his throne, Count Marsin was appointed, as we have seen, Lieutenant-General. Charles, who seems to have always entertained a grateful recollection of those foreigners from whom he had received any service or kindness while in Flanders or Spain, particularly recommended him

period of less than three months, Louis vanquished the
only army which the Spaniards brought into the field
against him, and rendered himself master of all the principal fortresses between the Scheldt and the English
Channel. These the celebrated Vauban was employed to fortify on a new system, and the citadel of Lisle
was the first stronghold constructed according to his improved principles. The Queen, and the greater part of
the Parisian court who had followed in her train, visited
the cities which had been captured. She was received
by the inhabitants as their sovereign, and she confirmed
to them as her subjects, all the immunities and privileges which they had ever enjoyed from the House of
Burgundy.[1]

After this campaign, which resembled a pleasant summer excursion, and which a French writer terms a *promenade militaire*, the king returned to Versailles; but
it was only for a short while, to make preparations for the
conquest of Franche Comté, which was invaded in the
most inclement season of the year. Twenty thousand

to the notice and attention of Sir Richard Fanshawe, who was his
ambassador in 1664 at Madrid, where the Count at that time
resided, (Fanshawe's *Memoirs*). He died there in 1673. After
his death, his son, whom Condé succeeded in introducing to the
French service, was created a Mareschal of France, and made a
considerable figure during the war of the succession.

[1] Rapid as the conquests had been in this campaign, the Marquis de Feuquiere maintains, that it was a great mistake in the
King of France to have wasted so much time in the siege of se-
condary fortresses,—that he ought at once to have pushed on with
his whole army to Brussels, which, not being in a condition to sustain a siege, would have opened its gates, and this possession of the
seat of government would have insured the speedy surrender of
all the other towns in the Netherlands. Had this plan been adopted,
Louis, he says, would never have been compelled to accept the
terms of peace dictated to him, by the Triple Alliance, at Aix-
la-Chapelle. (*Mémoires*, c. 50.)

troops, secretly drawn together from different quarters, were assembled in the neighbourhood of Besançon, with Condé at their head. That prince was now restored to a full share of his sovereign's favour and confidence. His name, once so proud, had indeed been tarnished by disloyalty and deserved disaster ; but he had still the lion heart and the eagle eye ; and his rebellion is a stain which his subsequent victories, at least have sweetened, if they have not washed away.

Franche Comté was a province of inestimable value to France, as it secured its frontier towards the Rhine, and gave it Switzerland and Mount Jura for a barrier. But though a fertile district, and inhabited by a brave intelligent population, it now added little to the power or wealth of Spain. It was far separated from her other dominions, and the inhabitants, who were extremely jealous of their ancient privileges, contributed nothing to the general support of the empire. In fact, the kings of Spain were rather the protectors and nominal sovereigns of Franche Comté than its actual masters, and though included within the government of Flanders, it had, in reality, little dependence on that province,—its administration being conducted by its own parliament, with a due regard to the privileges of the people. As its government thus formed a species of republic, the province was of course distracted by parties. One of these factions, being gained over by the French, facilitated the capture of Besançon, which surrendered the day after it had been invested by Condé. It insisted on no other terms of capitulation than to be left in possession of a consecrated handkerchief, which was held in great reverence in the city, and this condition was very readily granted. Louis in person besieged Dôle, which was carried in four days ; and in less than three weeks from the time of its invasion, the

whole of Franche Comté submitted to the victors.[1]
The Spanish Council, surprised and incensed at the little
resistance which had been made, wrote to the governor of
Franche Comté that Louis should have sent his valets
to take possession of the province, instead of marching
against it in person.

The Queen Regent of Spain appealed to the German
Diet against the invasion of territories which formed part
of the Circle of Burgundy ; and, in particular, solicited assistance from the Emperor Leopold, both as a member of
the Austrian family, and as head of the empire.[2]   But,
whether in consequence of his embarrassed situation,
or the secret treaty which it has been suspected he had
concluded with France, the appeal was totally disregarded.
Fortunately, however, for Spain, the successful aggressions of Louis excited the greatest apprehension in many
of the States of Europe.   Another campaign, it was believed, would put him in possession of the whole of the
Netherlands.   The Dutch were particularly alarmed at
the prospect of their frontier being thus exposed to the
ambition of such an aspiring and encroaching neighbour.
The Peace of Breda had recently terminated the fierce
naval war which they had carried on with England, and
whatever might be the disposition of the unprincipled
monarch of that kingdom to act in subserviency to the
designs of Louis, the spirit of the nation compelled him
to join in a confederacy for setting bounds to the aggran-

---

[1] Voltaire, *Siècle de Louis XIV.*   Amelot de la Houssaie in his
Epistle Dedicatory to Louis XIV. prefixed to a translation of a
work of Gracian, which the French writer calls *L'Homme de Cour,*
says that he conquered Franche Comté *en plein Carnaval.*   Sir
William Temple, in one of his letters, talks " of the foul and
shameless treason by which Franche Comté was lost, and of which
the Marquis d'Yonne the governor, and his son the Count St Amour,
have the chief *honour.*"

[2] Coxe's *Hist. of House of Austria,* c. lxiii.

dizement of France. About the same time Louis had also given umbrage to Sweden, by withholding the stipulated subsidies. The feelings of dread and animosity experienced by these three powers gave rise to the Triple Alliance, of which the object was to arrest the progress of the French arms, and preserve the Netherlands to Spain. Turenne, who knew thoroughly the resources of France, advised Louis to prosecute the war. But Louvois, and the other ministers, who were jealous of that Mareschal's influence with the King, and who knew that it would be increased by the prolongation of hostilities, persuaded him. to propose terms of accommodation.[1] Louis, accordingly, sent a declaration to the States-General, announcing that he was willing to grant peace to Spain, on condition of being allowed either to keep Franche Comté, with Cambray and St Omers, in the Netherlands, or to retain all the fortresses lately conquered by him in the Low Countries—relinquishing Franche Comté. The Triple League accepted this proposal as the basis of all future proceedings, it being understood that Spain was to have her choice of the alternative. The allies agreed that they should grant the contending parties their mediation, and bound themselves that they should oblige France to adhere to this proposal, and Spain to accept one or other of the alternatives offered. " This project," said De Witt, in a letter to Temple, " gives a certain way of obtaining peace, or a war wherein all the states of Christendom will support us, or at least commend our conduct."

This alliance, founded on the principle of extorting the consent of the recusant party, was concluded at the Hague, by De Witt, Sir William Temple, and Count Dohna the Swedish minister, with the rapidity which the exigency of affairs required,—the Swedes having acceded to it, on condition of some pecuniary claims against Spain.

[1] Reboulet, *Hist. de Louis XIV.* t. i. p. 666.

and the Emperor being adjusted within a definite time.
It was then fixed by these three diplomatists, that a congress for the final settlement of terms of peace should be
held at Aix-la-Chapelle. The Court of Madrid, however, was most unwilling to relinquish any part of its hereditary possessions, in satisfaction of claims which were
so manifestly unjust, and which had been urged with so
much violence; and the Marques of Castel-Rodrigo, the
governor of the Spanish Netherlands, instead of accepting
the mortifying alternative submitted for his choice, used
every effort to engage the United Provinces and England in a war against France, for compelling the restitution both of Franche Comté, and the recent usurpations in the Netherlands. He even threatened that the
Spaniards would entirely abandon the Low Countries rather than submit to so cruel a humiliation. Sir William
Temple seemed at first inclined to listen to the proposal
of Spain, and to form an offensive league between England and Holland, in order to oblige Louis to give up all
his late acquisitions; but he at length concurred with De
Witt's more moderate views, and Spain, instead of procuring their assistance, was threatened with war by the
three allied powers if she refused to acquiesce in this partial dismemberment of her territories. Louis, at the same
time, marched, towards the frontiers of the Netherlands,
an army of not less than 100,000 men, which he divided
into three corps. One, under Condé, entered Luxemburg; the second, under the Duke of Orleans, took the
direction of Ostend; and Louis himself, at the head of
the most considerable force, threatened Brussels.[1] Being thus pressed on all hands, the Governor of the Netherlands intimated that he would agree to one or other
of the alternatives offered. The Dutch were anxious that
Spain should relinquish Franche Comté, and retain her

[1] Reboulet, *Hist. de Louis XIV.* t. i. p. 667.

towns in the Netherlands, which they hoped might prove a barrier to the farther encroachments of Louis in their own vicinity. The Marques of Castel-Rodrigo, however, to whose judgment and discretion the hard choice was ultimately left by the Court of Madrid, made his election to recover the province of Franche Comté, and to abandon to the French all the towns conquered by them in Flanders during the last campaign. This choice was considered by Sir William Temple as highly injudicious. Franche Comté was in itself but a poor province, and the authority of the King of Spain within its circle was very limited. However important it might have been in the days of Spanish glory, as opening an entrance to the heart of France, it was useless to a monarchy which could not preserve its own territories, far less invade its more powerful neighbours. On the other hand, by relinquishing the fortresses in the Netherlands, the Spaniards allowed their enemy to extend his garrisons into the heart of that country, and preserved but a feeble barrier for the remaining provinces, which, if lost, would totally cut off the strongest bond of connexion between Spain and the other European Powers. But the Marques of Castel-Rodrigo, who was incensed at the Dutch, because they had not demanded better terms in behalf of his country, was not displeased to leave them in some anxiety concerning the safety of their frontier. Besides, as he felt reluctance to the peace, and was ever looking forward to a more prosperous renewal of the war, he judged that if France were once possessed of the fortresses in the Netherlands, which were now to be delivered up to her, she could not long resist the temptation of seizing the others, and then Spain might hope to engage her hereditary enemy with all that aid which the joint forces of Holland and England could supply.[1]   Meanwhile, however, Spain was forced to ac-

[1] Temple's *Memoirs*, t. iii. p. 205, &c.

quiesce in the terms of pacification dictated to her by the allies. She ceded Courtrai, Bergues, Furnes, and the whole of that territory which has been subsequently called French Flanders, and soon afterwards the possession of her remaining provinces was guaranteed to her by England and Holland.

Louis was as much displeased as Spain at the treaty of Aix-la-Chapelle. He was enraged to find limits thus set to his ambition, and he already meditated for Holland a long and severe retribution. His own offer, indeed, was made the basis of the league: but he had always inclined rather to the opinion of Turenne, in favour of a prosecution of the war, than to that of his ministers. In fact, his proposal had been made merely with the view of allaying the jealousy of the neighbouring powers, and detaining them in a state of inaction till he had either subdued the whole Netherlands, or found in the reluctance of Spain a pretext for eluding his offer without incurring the vengeance of the Triple Alliance. He contrived, however, to evade any farther renunciation of his claims to the Spanish succession; and it appears surprising that the confederacy which had been concerted to put a stop to the conquests of Louis, did not also devise means to preclude his grasping this ulterior and most important object of his ambition. But the Dutch, always fluctuating between their jealousy of the House of Bourbon, and their ancient hatred to that of Austria, would take no decisive measures against either; and Charles of England had placed himself at the head of the triple alliance, not so much from general views of policy, or a desire to curb the ambition of Louis, as from a wish to obtain supplies by acquiring a temporary popularity among his subjects.

On all points not specially provided for by the peace of Aix-la-Chapelle, the treaty of the Pyrenees continued

to be the measure of the rights of France and Spain, and
tranquillity was apparently as firmly settled as before the
last brief campaign.   But Louis was not at rest, and the
Congress of Aix-la-Chapelle, so far from having terminated farther competition, or put an end to national antipathies, gave rise, in fact, and that at no distant period,
to all those warlike events which marked the close of the
17th century.

Nearly at the same time with the treaty of Aix-la-
Chapelle, peace was concluded between Spain and Portugal.   The King of England had engaged by his articles
of marriage with the Princess Catherine of Portugal, to
mediate an arrangement between these powers ; and Sir R.
Fanshawe, who was ambassador from London to the
Court of Madrid at the accession of the present king, had
received instructions to adjust, if possible, the terms of
agreement betwixt the two crowns.   For some time, however, the exertions of Sir Richard had availed little to
dispose the Spaniards to any terms whatever of accommodation with Portugal,—their bad success in the war seeming only to exasperate them, and to engage them, as it
were in honour, to prosecute the contest.   One of the
chief obstacles, and it appeared to be almost insurmountable, was the refusal of Spain to recognise the actual sovereign of Portugal by the title of King, on which the
Portuguese government insisted as essential to any treaty
whatever.   But, at length, when France began to follow
up its demands, founded on the pretended right of devo-
lution, by active preparations for the invasion of the Netherlands and Franche Comté, the Court of Madrid lent
a more favourable ear to the solicitations of Sir R. Fanshawe.   That ambassador, accordingly, succeeded in adjusting some preliminary articles with the Spanish ministers ; and in the year 1666, he made an expedition to
Lisbon, in order to promote this design.   Power was at

the same time given by the Queen-Regent of Spain to
the Marques of Liche, then a prisoner of war in Portugal, to arrange the terms of accommodation. Fanshawe
met at Lisbon with Sir Robert Southwell, who had been
sent from London to Portugal for the double purpose of
accelerating the negotiations, and claiming payment of
the Queen's dowry.[1] England was, at this time, particularly desirous to cement a peace in the Peninsula, as it
was the only means by which Portugal could afford to
pay the stipulated sum. Besides, she had now become a
party in the formation of the triple alliance, of which the
main object was to set bounds to the ambition of France :
and Sir William Temple being convinced that Spain
could never oppose any effectual resistance to the French
arms in Flanders, while distracted by a war on her western frontier with Portugal, declares, in one of his letters
from Brussels, " that a truce between Spain and Portugal
is the hinge of all affairs at this time in Christendom."
The endeavours of Sir R. Southwell and Fanshawe were
constantly impeded by the difficulties concerning the
title of king, and were also counteracted by the arrival of
two French agents at Lisbon, whose express purpose
it was to divert the Court from any agreement whatever.
Sir R. Fanshawe, however, returned to Madrid with a
projet, signed by himself and Sir R. Southwell, in order
to present and enforce it there.[2] Soon after his arrival,
he was superseded in his embassy by the Earl of Sand-
wich, who was chosen by both parties as mediator and
guarantee in his master's name for the treaty of peace
which was to follow. The prospects, however, of its ultimate conclusion seemed still at a distance. The news
of the formation of the triple alliance had anew excited
the hopes of Spain ; and the Count of Castel-Melhor, the
Portuguese minister, who was justly proud of the recent

---

[1] Southwell's *Letters*.   [2] Ibid.

triumphs of his country, and eager to prosecute the war, had entered into an alliance, offensive and defensive, with France for ten years, by which he engaged to maintain four French regiments in Portugal,—to pay besides, the sum of L.100,000 annually,—to keep 17,000 native troops on foot during two campaigns, and neither to listen, directly or indirectly, during the years of the league, to any proposals of accommodation with Spain : On the other hand, France bound herself ultimately to procure a peace for Portugal, on favourable conditions, and to compel Spain to give her sovereign the title of King.[1] This league, however, was never carried into effect, owing to that celebrated revolution which took place in the government of Portugal, by which both his crown and his wife were wrested at once from the imbecile Alfonso, and his brother Pedro installed in the possession of both. A convocation of the Cortes, which was to take place in consequence of these important events, was seized as an opportunity for the renewal of the treaty with Spain. It was apprehended, indeed, that the Queen, who was a Princess of Nemours, might still be inclined to support the French interests ; but the popular clamour was at present in favour of peace with Spain, and the prudent Pedro, who as yet held only a precarious and usurped authority, did not venture to oppose the wishes of his subjects. A treaty was at length concluded, on condition that both crowns should restore all places taken during the war which either of them now possessed, except Ceuta, on the coast of Africa, which was reserved to Spain ;—that all confiscations should be void, and the prisoners on both sides set at liberty without ransom ;—that trade and commerce should be free between the two nations ;—that the Portuguese should have the right of passage through all the dominions of the Catholic King, and enjoy in Spain similar

[1] Southwell's *Letters.*

privileges with those possessed by the English; while, on the other hand, the Spaniards should be entitled in Portugal to the same rights or immunities which they had possessed in the time of Sebastian;—that, finally, his Catholic Majesty should recognise the title of King in the House of Braganza, and that the arms of Portugal should be immediately erased from the escutcheon of the Spanish monarchy. These terms were not unfavourable to Spain, considering that she had sustained such reverses during the late campaigns with Portugal, and that both France and England were inclined to support the cause of her rival. But it was a severe humiliation to have been foiled by this petty kingdom, and to be compelled at length, after a warfare of thirty years, to acknowledge the right of the House of Braganza to the throne of Portugal.

When the mother country was thus drooping, the colonies could not possibly thrive; and, accordingly, whilst affairs in Europe were in this unfortunate state, the foreign possessions of Spain presented prospects equally inauspicious. It is manifest there must have existed some glaring error in government, when a monarch, who possessed such an extensive territory, everywhere filled with mines of gold and silver or with the most valuable commodities, was thus reduced to abject poverty and insignificance.

The Spanish colonies, being founded in an earlier and less enlightened age than those of France or England, were regulated with inferior political wisdom. All the settlements of the Spaniards were managed conformably to those maxims of policy which prevailed in their administration at home. Tyranny was the principle of their government,—bigotry of their religion, and monopoly of their trade.

The conquerors of Mexico had deprived the Indians

of liberty and property. Their avarice and cruelty had
at length nearly stripped the land of its natives; but
the preference shewn by the government to Spaniards
born in Europe, soon reduced the descendants of the
companions of Cortez to a situation not much better than
that of the original inhabitants. They were always placed
in the degradation of an inferior caste. Their commerce,
when at all allowed, was checked by grievous restrictions;
and their industry was discouraged by excessive and injudicious taxation, as also by the exorbitant exactions of
the clergy; yet after all, the sovereign drew comparative-
ly but a small annual revenue from Mexico, the finances
being absorbed by the expenses of their collection, or dissipated by the malversation of officers. Almost all employments were filled by native Spaniards, and with the
view that they might not obtain too extensive an influence by a prolonged continuance of power, they held their
situations but for a brief and limited period. Hence each
officer was possessed with the avidity which a new and
lucrative post inspires. Rapacious, because his time was
short, he oppressed the people and defrauded the crown.
Another with the same dispositions succeeded him; and
no one was anxious to establish what might prove useful
in the department entrusted to him, because he knew
that his successor would annul every regulation which he
did not conceive to be subservient to his own immediate
interests. The viceroys in particular, lest they should
by their intrigues render themselves formidable or independent, were only permitted to retain their governments
during three years; and, in consequence, the successive
viceroys, though there were a few remarkable exceptions,
became imbued with the spirit which actuated the Roman
proconsuls in the later ages of the republic, and entertained no object but to enrich themselves to as great an
extent as the limited duration of their government would
allow. They were also engaged in frequent disputes with

the clergy, concerning their respective rights of extortion ; and their mutual oppression of the people was constantly exciting the most serious alarms of tumults and insurrections.

Those Spaniards who conquered Peru, being for the most part adventurers, without birth, education, or principle, and being removed farther from the inspection or control of government, committed still greater enormities than those perpetrated by their countrymen in Mexico. From the execrable era of those civil commotions that followed the murder of Pizarro, the system which had been at first established, continued to be practised with unabating rigour. The native Peruvians, like the Mexicans, were stripped of their property, and became the slaves of the government or of individual masters. Without property or freedom, they naturally fell into a state of apathy and listless indifference. The land they inhabited was gradually converted into a desert, and was at length so much depopulated, that it required to be supplied by a foreign race.[1]

In short, the immense fabric of this western empire seemed on the eve of crumbling into dust : the most important fortresses mouldered away,—the country was left without arms or magazines—the soldiers, who were neither disciplined nor clothed, turned beggars or thieves,— the principles of war and navigation were forgotten, and even the instruments employed in these arts became unknown,—the treasures, which should have filled the royal coffers, were continually pilfered,—commerce was conducted on a system of fraud, and the hatred which commenced between the Spaniards born in America and those who came from Europe, and which the government had injudiciously fomented, completed the ruin of the colonies.

[1] Raynal, *Hist. Philosophique*, t. ii.

Such, for many years previous to the accession of Charles II, had been the melancholy state of the chief Spanish possessions in America. But at the commencement of this reign, the engrossing policy pursued by the Spaniards in their colonies, created a new evil, which threatened the total annihilation of their commerce in the West Indies, and the loss of whatever wealth they still derived from their Mexican and Peruvian empires.

It was at this time that a number of daring and enterprising bands, the outcasts of different European nations, but chiefly of France and England, being disappointed by accident or the enmity of the Spaniards in their more pacific pursuits in America, embodied themselves under naval leaders of their own choice, and, instigated at once by desire of vengeance and thirst of plunder, waged against Spain a predatory war, which they were allowed to prosecute, if not with the support, at least with the connivance, of the other maritime states of Europe.

From the period of the first discovery of America, the Spaniards had been particularly jealous of the interference of other powers with their exclusive rights in the West Indies, which they regarded as their peculiar possessions. " It is very observable," says De Witt in his Political Maxims, which were written about the commencement of the present reign, " that all the welfare of Spain depends on its trade to the West Indies." [1] Of this the Spaniards themselves had been in all ages sufficiently convinced. Hence the appearance of a strange sail in these regions was always viewed by Spaniards with suspicion and hostility. Though unable to people such extensive countries themselves, they were resolved that no other nation should hold them, and waged incessant war on all who attempted to settle either on

[1] Part ii. c. viii.

the greater Antilles or Caribbee Islands.   When they
encountered any such intruders at sea, they captured the
vessels if able to master them, and treated the mariners
as pirates.   The continental conquests, indeed, of the
Spaniards caused some diminution in the importance they
attached to the West Indies.   None of the mines in the
islands were comparable in riches to those of the main
land, and from want of labourers many of them were left
unwrought.   The colonists, however, in Hispaniola, applied themselves to the cultivation of the sugar-cane and
the hunting of cattle, in which that enormous island
abounded.   But they did not long enjoy even this right
exclusively.   The earliest intruders were French and
English mariners, who first began to hunt beeves in
order to victual their ships, and afterwards established
factories on the island for this purpose.   The employment
was commenced by the crews of wrecked vessels, or by
seamen who had mutinied against their commanders; but
the freedom from all restraint or subordination enjoyed in
such a life, soon allured others to leave their ships in order to join in these occupations.   Towards the close of
the 16th century, Drake, " the scourge of Spain," sacked
the city of St Domingo, and soon after that period the
numbers of the French and English increased so much
in the West Indies, that the Spaniards found themselves compelled to abandon all the northern and western
parts of Hispaniola.   Early in the following century, the
two nations who were their chief maritime rivals, founded
a joint colony on St Christophers, one of the Caribbee
Islands, which the Spaniards had not thought it worth
while to occupy.   This settlement gave great encouragement to the hunters on the north-west coast of Hispaniola.   Their factories for drying the skins and curing
the flesh of beeves, daily multiplied ; and, as their value
increased, they bethought themselves of providing for

their farther security, by seizing on the small island of
Tortuga, near the north-west point of Hispaniola, where
the Spaniards had placed a garrison which was too weak
to resist them. The occupation of this island gave a degree of stability to the association of the Buccaneers, and
Tortuga became in time a real mart and colony.[1] A number of French emigrants, too, who had settled in Marti-
nique and others of the Caribbee Islands, being reduced
to despair from the necessity they were under of submit-
ting to exclusive privileges, abandoned their settlements,
and fled to the northern coast of Hispaniola, which had
now for many years been considered as a place of refuge
for their adventurous countrymen.

It was about this period that these hunters and provision merchants began to be known by the name of
Buccaneers, an appellation derived from Boucan, an Indian word for the hut in which the flesh of beeves was
smoked and dried according to a peculiar process derived
from the Caribbees.

From residing constantly near the sea,—from their excursions to neighbouring islands,—and their frequent
communication with mariners, whose ships resorted to
Tortuga from all parts of the West Indies, many of the
Buccaneers began to quit, at least for a time, their hunting employments, and to embark in their small vessels on
some tempting cruise. Their numbers were daily augmented by deserters from French, English, or Dutch
ships, which came on the American coast,—by criminals who were banished from France, and adjudged to
three years service in the colonies, and by those seafarers
who frequented the shores of Hispaniola or Mexico, and
softened the name of Pirate under that of " Brethren of

[1] Burney's *History of the Buccaneers of America*, c. 3. and 4. Ed.
1816, 4to.

the Coast." [1]   A mixed assemblage was thus formed of
French, English, Dutch and Portuguese, who were united by one common interest—*plunder*. Spaniards alone,
whose treasures formed the chief object of cupidity,
were excluded from the favour of admission into their
armed associations.   The name of Flibustiers was given
to these freebooters by the French, but that of Buccaneer
continued to be assigned them by the English, though it
had been originally applied to those who exercised an occupation on land.[2]

   The free and lawless life they had led on shore prepared them to be rovers on the main. For some time
the Buccaneers were amphibious characters, uniting the
double employments of hunting and cruising ; but, from
early success at sea, the former soon became a subordinate
occupation, and the more sober calling of the hunter or
curer was soon lost in the daring vocation of the pirate.
The Spaniards, too, wishing to root them out from Hispaniola, destroyed the horned cattle, the chace of which
formed their occupation on shore, so that they were compelled to betake themselves entirely to sea for their subsistence. Hearing that a French adventurer called Pierre
le Grand, had captured, with only one boat and twenty-
eight men, the vice-admiral of the Spanish flotilla, near
the western coast of Hispaniola, they were encouraged to
follow the example.

   In the beginning of their adventures, they had only a
few small sloops, without decks, wretchedly supplied with
provisions, or some barks and canoes, where, piled on each
other, they lay down to sleep, and where they were exposed, night and day, to all the inclemency of the sky,
and all the dangers of the sea. But, at length, in order
that they might exercise piracy on a larger scale, they

[1] Archenholtz, *History of the Pirates of America*, c. ii.
[2] Burney, *Hist. of Buccaneers.*

were induced to procure somewhat larger vessels than those fragile barks in which they had first tempted the western main. Being unable, however, to purchase or build them at Tortuga, they set forth in canoes to seek them elsewhere. They cruised for some time near Cape Alvarez, where the Spaniards were wont to trade, from one town to another, in small ships loaded with hides, tobacco, and other commodities. Having succeeded in capturing a great number of these vessels, they carried them to Tortuga, and having sold the cargoes to the merchant-ships which occasionally touched there, they were soon enabled to provide themselves with all things necessary for undertaking a piratical voyage.[1]

It was then that the Buccaneers entered into a species of association, and bound themselves to each other by certain laws and regulations. A general right of participation in various articles, particularly provisions for present consumption, was acknowledged among them. Bolts, locks, and all other safeguards, were strictly prohibited, it being held that the employment of such securities would have impeached the honour of their calling. While on actual service, they obeyed the chief they had chosen, but they had conceived lofty ideas of their independence, and at all other times followed their own caprice or pleasure.

---

[1] Esquemeling, *History of the Buccaneers.* Esquemeling, the author of this history, was a Dutchman, and was himself an associate of Brasiliano, Lollonois, and other pirates. He published his account of the Buccaneers in the Dutch language in 1678, under the title *de Americaensche Zee Roovers.* His work has been translated into French, Spanish, and English, but with various additions and interpolations. The English version, along with the narrative by Rhingrose of some piratic expeditions of Davis in the South Sea, and the journal of the French *Flibustier,* Ravenau de Lussan, forms the common and popular book entitled *History of the Buccaneers,* ed. in two vols. 12mo.

The proportions of prize-money were regulated, as also the amount of the compensation for wounds, or loss of limbs, and the rewards for illustrious actions.[1] On commencing the trade of a Buccaneer, it was customary with those who were of respectable lineage, to relinquish their family name, and assume some other, borrowed from terms of war, or of their native country, as Lollonois and Brasiliano. Anecdotes are preserved concerning them, which show, that amid all their wild enormities, many of them preserved a regard to a certain code of honour, and were strongly under the influence of religion, or at least of superstition. When they had taken a city, they often sang *Te Deum* in the churches, before proceeding to plunder them.[2]

In their naval enterprises, they generally formed themselves into small companies, consisting of 50 or 100 men, who were sometimes bound together by a subscribed written agreement, resembling a charter-party. Before they went to sea, they gave notice to all concerned, of the day on which they were to embark, obliging each man to bring as much powder and ball as was thought necessary. Having come on board, their first care was to supply themselves with provisions, and for this purpose they made short excursions along the coast, in order to rob the Spaniards of their hogs, which, with tortoises, formed the chief article of their consumption. The ship being victualled, they then deliberated where they should proceed to seek their desperate fortunes, and agreed on certain conditions with regard to the division of the expected booty.[3] The captain whom they had chosen was allowed a larger share of the spoil than the rest of the crew. But his authority over them being confined to is-

[1] Archenholtz, *History of the Pirates*, c. iii.
[2] Ravenau de Lussan, *Journal*, &c. ap. *History of Buccaneers*.
[3] Esquemeling, *Hist. of Buccan.*

suing orders in battle, they lived in the greatest disorder. As they neither felt the apprehension of want, nor
paid due attention to preserve the necessaries of life, they
were frequently exposed, during their voyages, to the severest extremities of thirst and hunger. But deriving,
even from such hardships, a courage superior to every
danger, the sight of a sail transported them almost to a
degree of phrensy. They never deliberated on the attack, but boarded the ship as quickly as possible. When
they threw out their grappling, the largest vessel seldom
escaped them. The smallness of their own barks, and
the skill they showed in their management, saved them
from the shot of their superior foes, to whom they presented only the prows of their vessels, occupied by fu-
sileers, whose aim was taken with so much exactness,
that it amazed the most experienced gunners. In cases
of extreme necessity, they attacked the sails of every country, but they fell on the Spaniards at all times. They
were exasperated against that nation, in consequence of
the disappointments they had often experienced in finding themselves precluded from the privilege of hunting
and fishing, which they considered as natural rights; and
they pretended that the cruelties which the Spaniards
had exercised on the inhabitants of the New World, fully
justified the implacable hostility they had sworn against
them.[1]

The seas which surrounded the West Indian islands
were peculiarly well adapted for the pirates' vocation.
The numerous uninhabited isles of these regions, presented them with secure harbours, and with bays or in-
lets, which abounded in fish, tortoise, and water fowl,
while they also served as shelter for themselves, or
places of concealment for their plunder. Nor could

[1] Raynal, *Hist. Philosoph.* t. iii.

they be easily discovered or pursued by ships of war, in the harbours and lagoons of these solitary isles, that, formed for them at all times a natural protection and a refuge, where they might lie in wait for those rich prizes which were the objects of their avidity. They seldom attacked the vessels which sailed from Europe to America, as the merchandize they contained would not have been easily sold, nor have proved very profitable to them in these early times. But, lurking in the creeks of the islands, they sedulously watched for those ships which, on their return, were laden with gold, silver, and precious stones, and all the valuable productions of the New World. If they met with a single vessel, they never failed instantly to attack and board it. When they descried a fleet, they followed at a distance till it sailed out of the Gulf of Bahama, and as soon as they observed that any one of the convoy was separated from the rest, they overtook and grappled it. The Spaniards, who trembled at the very approach of the Buccaneers, seldom made an effectual resistance. Quarter was granted after the ship had struck, if its cargo proved a rich one, and they had experienced little resistance. If otherwise, all the prisoners were frequently thrown into the sea.[1] When they had obtained a valuable prize, they proceeded to some place of rendezvous to divide the spoil. This station was, at first, Tortuga, but afterwards the French pirates resorted to St Domingo, and the English to Jamaica. Sometimes they refreshed themselves at the small islands to the south of Cuba, where their vessels were careened. It was at these times, and after the division of the booty, that they indulged in all kinds of profusion : Stained at one moment with blood, and loaded with spoil, they were plunged at the next in sensuality. They deemed, like more refined voluptuaries, that the danger and death, by

[1] Raynal, *Hist. Philosoph.* t. iii.

which they were so closely surrounded, should but urge
them on to the speediness of enjoyment. They seemed
scarcely able to devour or destroy with sufficient rapidity
the rich produce of their piracies. As soon as they had
landed, their table groaned under strong liquors and provisions; gaming, music, and dancing succeeded each other
without intermission. Women, attracted by gold, resorted to the rendezvous of the pirates, from all the American islands, and added a dangerous zest to their tumultuous orgies. They arrayed themselves also in the most
costly garbs, overloaded with lace and embroidery, and they
exhausted for expensive wares the repositories of the Caribbees and Antilles. Their extravagance and debauchery, which in every form was carried to the utmost excess,
knew no limit but the want and indigence which their
lavish profusion produced. Men who had been the owners of millions, were in a brief space of time totally ruined, and finding themselves destitute even of raiment and
provisions, returned again to sea.[1]

As the hostility of the Buccaneers had hitherto been
almost exclusively directed against the Spaniards, the other
Europeans in the West Indies regarded them as cham-
pions in a common cause, and their numbers were constantly recruited from all quarters by French, Dutch, and English volunteers. The governors of the islands belonging
to these nations, being influenced by similar feelings, gave
frequent encouragement, either openly or by connivance,
to the Buccaneers; and whenever it happened that Spain
was at open and declared war with any of the maritime
powers of Europe, those freebooters, who were natives of
that country which was engaged in hostilities with her,
obtained commissions, that rendered the vessels in which
they cruised regular privateers.[2]

[1] Ibid. and Archenholtz, *Hist. of Pirates*.
[2] Burney's *Hist. of the Buccaneers*.

A pirate who, from being a native of Portugal, was called Bartholomew Portugues, and his contemporary, named Brasiliano, from his long residence in Brazil, were distinguished by their numerous and successful captures at sea, —their perilous adventures and hair-breadth escapes. The former, with a vessel manned by only thirty sailors, and armed with four small guns, took a large ship provided with twenty cannon and seventy men, bound from Carthagena to the Havannah. Having become notorious by his numerous piracies and murders, Portugues was placed at the head of a band of Buccaneers, who equipped for him a vessel, with which he proceeded to Campeachy, and by his skill and undaunted courage, succeeded in cutting out a richly laden carac from the river which forms its harbour.[1]

Brasiliano being chosen the leader of a crew of pirates who had mutinied against their captain, began his audacious career by the capture of a galleon from Mexico, with a quantity of plate on board, which he carried to Jamaica. The coast near Campeachy was his usual rendezvous, and Jamaica the place where he spent, with the utmost profusion, the wealth he had gained by his piracies on the Mexican shore. His course was everywhere marked by the most atrocious cruelties. Towards the Spanish nation he entertained an inveterate hatred; and it is said that he commanded several of them, when taken prisoners, to be roasted alive on spits.[2]

Montbar, who was by birth a gentleman of Languedoc, was distinguished by a similar abhorrence of the Spaniards. Having read in his youth a circumstantial, and probably exaggerated account of the cruelties practised by them in the conquest of the Western World, he conceived an animosity, which he carried to a degree of phrenzy, against a nation that had committed such

[1] Esquemeling, *Hist.*   [2] Ibid.

enormities. He had also heard some account of the Buccaneers, who were said to be the most deadly enemies of
the Spanish name; and being animated with a desire to
avenge the innocent blood that had been shed, he embarked on board a ship in order to join them. Having arrived
on the coast of Hispaniola, the Buccaneers quickly perceived that he was such a leader as they required. Opportunities soon occurred that enabled him to exercise his
spirit of detestation and revenge against the Spaniards,
without satiating or extinguishing it. His life was devoted to the gratification of this enmity, more than to the
acquisition of plunder; and so much did the Spaniards
suffer from his unrelenting animosity, that they bestowed
on him the name of the Exterminator.[1]

The depredations of these pirates had made much noise
in Spain towards the close of the reign of Philip IV.
They had occasioned that monarch great displeasure, and
were the subject of frequent complaints from him to the
English government.[2] But little attention was paid to
his remonstrances, and nothing effectual was done on the
part of Spain herself to repress the evil under which her
western colonies groaned.

The number and enormities of the Buccaneers had
reached their height at the accession of Charles II. to the
throne of Spain. The savage disposition of Montbar and
that of the other freebooters who followed his example,
disgusted the Spanish colonists with navigation, and induced them to confine themselves, in a great measure, within their own settlements. In despair at finding that their
merchandise became the perpetual prey of these spoilers,
they sent out no more trading vessels,—they gave up all
the advantages which their mercantile connexions or spe-
culations afforded them; and though much chagrined at

---

[1] Raynal, *Hist. Philosoph.* t. iii.
[2] Fanshawe's *Letters*, p. 155.

the loss and inconvenience which they thus suffered, yet
the dread of falling into the hands of bloody and rapacious
pirates prevailed over their long habits of commercial policy, and their desire of gain.   Their terror and despondency served only to increase the boldness of the Buccaneers.
Hitherto they had merely landed on the Spanish settlements in order to carry off provisions, or other necessaries
of life, when in absolute want of them.   But they no
sooner found their captures at sea begin to diminish from
the late caution of the colonists, than they determined to
recover on shore what they had lost on the main.   They
now attacked and plundered the most wealthy seaports
and the continental capitals of South America,—

> And Chili heard them through her States,
> And Lima ope'd her silver gates.

So much had the descendants of the conquerors of the
New World degenerated from the valour of their ancestors,—the companions of Cortez and Pizarro,—that 2000
American Spaniards often fled before 200 of these audacious freebooters. The richest towns were thus sacked, and
the most populous districts laid waste. The culture of
lands began to be neglected equally with navigation; and
the Spaniards durst now no more appear in their harbours or roads than venture to sail in the latitudes where
cruised the Buccaneers.[1]

This method of conducting the war which was newly
adopted by the freebooters, required superior forces, more
numerous associations, and leaders of more extensive views
and more daring enterprise.

The first pirate who began these invasions was Lewis
Scot, who sacked the town of Campeachy,—carrying off
all the treasure, and exacting an enormous ransom to save
the houses from destruction. On the other side of the
continent, Davies landed near Nicaragua; and, availing

[1] Raynal, *Hist. Philosoph.*

himself of the darkness of the night, he and his companions sailed up the river which leads to the vicinity of
that town. They encountered a sentinel, to whom they
spoke Spanish and passed for fishermen. They afterwards disembarked without meeting any obstacles, and
massacred the soldiers who had peaceably witnessed their
landing. Having thus penetrated into the middle of
Nicaragua without discovery, they dispersed themselves
throughout the town, pillaging the churches and rifling
the houses of the chief inhabitants.[1] They then hastily
regained their barks, and set sail with their plunder, consisting of silver and precious stones. Arriving at Jamaica
with the booty he had thus acquired, Davies was chosen
admiral of seven or eight piratic vessels, in the command
of which he performed many naval exploits, and also pillaged the city of St Augustine in the Floridas.[2]

Among the various leaders of the Buccaneers, a Frenchman called L'Olonnois was particularly signalized by his
ferocity, astonishing exploits, and singular fate. His
name was derived from the sands of Olonne on the coast
of Poitou, of which he was supposed to be a native. He
was transported in his youth, as a bondsman, to the Caribbee Islands, but soon raised himself from this abject
state to the command of a piratic vessel, and in that capacity he formed more extensive associations than had
been hitherto known among the Buccaneers. Having
united with another pirate called Michel le Basque, these
two commanders assembled 700 men, the largest force the
freebooters had yet been able to muster, and landed on
Terra Firma, where they entered the towns of Maracaibo and Gibraltar situated on the Bay of Venezuela.
The booty they obtained by the plunder and ransom of
these places, was estimated at half a million of crowns.

[1] Archenholtz, *Hist. of Pirates*, c. 4.
[2] Esquemeling, *Hist. of Buccan.*

The barbarities which L'Olonnois is said to have been in
the custom of practising on the unfortunate prisoners who
fell into his hands, exceeded the cruelties of all his predecessors, and indeed surpass belief. Sometimes he allowed them to perish with hunger; at other times he put
them to the most frightful tortures in order to compel
them to disclose where treasures were concealed, and when
they would not, or could not, confess, he tore out their
tongues. On one occasion, it is reported that he put the
whole crew of a Spanish ship, consisting of ninety men, to
death, himself performing the office of executioner, by be-
heading them with his sabre, from which he afterwards
licked the trickling blood. He caused the crews of four
other vessels to be thrown into the sea; and, more than
once, in his phrensy, he tore out the hearts of his victims
and devoured them. His ultimate fate corresponded to
his life, and was such as his atrocious cruelties merited.
Having been abandoned by most of his followers in consequence of a difference of opinion concerning an expedition
which he projected against Guatemala, he incautiously disembarked with a small band on the Isthmus of Darien,
where he was taken prisoner by a horde of savage Indians,
who tore him in pieces alive, throwing his carcass, limb
by limb, into the fire, and then scattering the ashes to
the air.[1]

The Buccaneers now landed on the continent and
islands in such formidable numbers, that several Spanish
towns in South America and the West Indies submitted
to pay them contributions in order to escape from being
plundered. At this time, also, a piratic leader named
Mansvelt, more provident and more ambitious in his
views than any who had preceded him, formed a project
of founding an independent Buccaneer establishment. So
popular was he among the freebooters, that both French

[1] Burney's *History*. Esquemeling, *Hist.*

and English gladly followed him as their commander;
but as he fitted out his fleet from Jamaica, it may be in-
ferred that the English constituted the greater proportion of his associates in his attempt to fix a colony. The
spot designed by him for this purpose, was an island
named Santa Katalina (St Catherine's) or Providence,
lying about forty leagues to the eastward of the Mosquito
shore.   At the time when Mansvelt commenced his
scheme of settlement, this island was occupied by a Spanish garrison.   Having sailed thither from Jamaica with
not fewer than fifteen vessels and 500 men, he assaulted
and took the fort, which he garrisoned with 100 Buccaneers and the slaves he had made prisoners.   Leaving
the command to a Frenchman called Simon, he returned
to Jamaica with the intention of procuring recruits and farther supplies for his new establishment. But the Governor
of Jamaica, however friendly to the Buccaneers so long
as they made that island their rendezvous and emporium,
saw many reasons for disliking Mansvelt's plan, and
would not consent to his raising levies within his government. In consequence of this opposition, Mansvelt sailed
for Tortuga, to try what assistance he could procure in
that seminary of thieves and pirates. But he died suddenly during the passage, and Simon, after waiting for
some time in expectation of his arrival, at length surrendered to a large Spanish force which had landed and laid
siege to his fortress.[1]

Morgan, who, by his reach of mind, the extent and
duration of his adventures, and his wonderful success,
has surpassed all the pirates, had sailed with Mansvelt,
as second in command, on his voyage to Santa Katalina.   He was a native of Wales, and the son of a
wealthy yeoman in that principality. When a boy he
quitted his father's house, and hastening to the nearest

[1] Burney's *Hist. of the Buccaneers*, c. 5.

seaport, he embarked in a vessel bound for Barbadoes, where, on his arrival, he was sold as a slave. Having obtained his liberty after serving the due time in that island, he went to Jamaica, where he engaged himself with a pirate vessel,[1] and having gained a little money in three or four cruizes, he agreed with some of his comrades to unite their stock in order to purchase a ship. With this vessel he performed some voyages so successfully to the Bay of Campeachy, that he was chosen as second in command to Mansvelt, and on the death of that pirate a body of several hundred of his followers, who now regarded Morgan as the most capable and fortunate of the Buccaneer leaders, placed themselves under his orders. His first enterprise was directed against Port du Prince in Cuba. The Spaniards, however, being apprized of his approach concealed their treasures, and though the town fell easily into his hands, the wealth obtained by pillage was not so great as had been expected.

To compensate for this disappointment, Morgan next resolved on an expedition against Porto-bello, one of the richest and most strongly fortified sea-ports belonging to the Spaniards in America. Two castles, considered as almost impregnable, and situated at the entrance to the harbour, defended the city, so that no ship or boat could pass without permission. Morgan had not communicated to any one his design against Porto-bello, in order to prevent the Spaniards from obtaining any information concerning his intentions. When the project was announced to the pirates, the most intrepid among their small band were daunted, and declared it to be impossible that so few could take so strong and extensive a city. But a brief address of Morgan at once inflamed their cupidity, and roused their courage. " What boots it," he exclaimed, " how small be our number, if our hearts be great ! The

---

[1] Johnson's *Lives of Pirates*, &c.

fewer we are the closer will be our union, and the larger our shares of plunder."[1]. So ably were Morgan's operations contrived, and his designs so well concealed, that he surprised and blew up one of the castles, and then advanced to the town before its garrison or inhabitants were in any degree ready to oppose him. The citizens, amid the confusion, threw their treasures into wells and cisterns,[2] and the governor, with the garrison, abandoning the town, fled to the other castle. Here the Spaniards made a gallant resistance, but were, at length, compelled to yield to the furious assault of the pirates. The conquest of this town, which was achieved by a force of only 500 men against a numerous and regular garrison, and in spite of almost insuperable obstacles, was an exploit of which the ablest general might have boasted, if performed in more legitimate warfare. But Morgan tarnished the fame which he might have acquired from his capacity and valour, by the shocking barbarities which he exercised on the vanquished. After the town and castle had capitulated, they were given up to indiscriminate plunder,—the prisoners were shut up in churches or convents, where they were burned alive; and for several days after the capture of this ill-fated city, the pirates gave themselves up to every excess of debauchery.

Having divided their booty in the Isle of Cuba, and lavished in Jamaica, with their usual riot, the immense wealth they had acquired, their captain, by a kind of circular note, appointed a rendezvous at Isla de Vaca, where a number of new French Buccaneers, attracted by the report of his recent successes, placed themselves under his command. From this island Morgan sailed with his fleet to Maracaibo and Gibraltar, and, availing himself of the local knowledge of a Frenchman who had been present

[1] Archenholtz, *Hist. of Pirates*, c. 7.
[2] Johnson, *Lives of Pirates*.

with L'Olonnois at their former capture, he again sack-ed these unfortunate towns. Here he renewed his prac-tice of shutting up his prisoners in churches, and tortur-ing or starving them to death, while their merciless vic-tors were rioting in the plunder of their homes.

Morgan remained so long at Gibraltar, that the Spa-niards had time to take measures for cutting him off on his return to Maracaibo. But he extricated his fleet and prizes with consummate skill from the difficulties by which they were environed, and sailed clear off with a booty of not less than 250,000 pieces of eight.

Soon after the return of the pirates to the West In-dies from this prosperous expedition, a treaty was con-cluded between Great Britain and Spain, which was chiefly devised with a view of terminating the career of the freebooters, whose atrocities now began to excite the indignation of the civilized world. It was expressly sti-pulated that all depredations should cease between the subjects of the respective monarchs, who pledged them-selves that those who owed them allegiance should for-bear from future acts of hostility.

So far from being deterred by the articles of this treaty, the Buccaneers immediately, as with one accord, resolved to undertake some grand expedition. Morgan's reputa-tion as a piratical leader now stood so high, that adven-turers from all quarters rallied under his command. A fleet of not fewer than thirty-seven vessels and 2000 men, assembled, by his appointment, at Cape Tuberon, on the west of Hispaniola. Having collected so large a force, he held a council with its chiefs, and proposed for their determination whether they should attempt Vera Cruz, Carthagena, or Panama. After due deliberation, the choice fell on Panama, which was believed to be the rich-est of the three. Indeed, it was at that time accounted one of the greatest, as well as one of the most opulent, cities of America. It contained 2000 large houses, which were fine piles of building, and 5000 smaller dwellings, but all three stories in height. Of these, a considerable number were erected of stone, and the rest of cedar wood, very elegantly constructed, and magnificently furnished. The city was the emporium for the silver of Mexico, and gold of Peru; whence those valuable metals were brought on the backs of mules (2000 of which were kept for that purpose alone) towards the coast of the South Sea, near the shore of which this magnificent city stood. Its merchants lived in great opulence. Not only were their houses loaded with gold and silver, but were filled with beautiful paintings, and other masterpieces of art, which had been accumulated from the intense desire of being surrounded with every species of luxury. Many of them had also country-houses and gardens, alike embellished by art and nature, on some small islands at a short distance from the walls. The churches of Panama were decorated with peculiar magnificence. The cathedral was built in the Italian style, surmounted with a large cupola, and enriched with gold and silver ornaments, as were also the eight convents which this city comprised.[1]

Such was Panama in 1670, when the freebooters selected it as the object of their bold attempt, and the victim of their insatiable cupidity. Before embarking on this exploit, specific articles of agreement were drawn up and subscribed, in order to regulate the distribution of the anticipated plunder. Morgan, as commander-in-chief, was to receive one hundredth part of the whole, and each captain was to have eight shares: adequate provision was stipulated for the maimed and wounded, as also rewards for those who should particularly distinguish themselves. Morgan having retaken the Island of Santa Katalina,

[1] Archenholtz, *Hist. of Pirates.*

despatched, from that ancient settlement of pirates, a detachment of 400 men to seize the Fort of St Laurence, at the mouth of the River Chagre, which he considered an essential preliminary to the expedition against Panama. As soon as he had received intelligence of the successful attack on this castle, he proceeded with the remainder of his force to the entrance of the Chagre, and thence set forth for the city. Sometimes marching by land, and sometimes sailing up the serpentine course of the river, he at length, at the end of eight days, during which his troops had suffered the severest hardships, and overcome almost incredible difficulties, came in sight of the South Sea, and the spires of Panama. By the advice of one of his guides, he did not take the direct road to the town, and, in consequence, escaped the ambuscades which had been laid for him.

This city was not defended by regular fortifications. Some works had been lately raised, but it lay open in various quarters, and was to be protected or won by battle in the plain. The Spaniards having assembled about 2000 infantry and 400 cavalry, well equipped, came out to meet the Buccaneers on their advance to the walls. It is said[1] that, in this combat, they employed wild bulls, under the conduct of Indians and Negroes, which they drove, to the number of upwards of 2000, upon the freebooters, to disorder their lines. But this device does not appear to have been attended with success. Among the ranks of the Buccaneers there were many who had been accustomed to the chace of wild cattle, and who now, by their shouts, and by waving party-coloured flags before them, intimidated the bulls, and threw them back on their own lines, which they disordered, like the elephants of old. After an engagement which lasted two hours, the Spaniards were routed, and the greater part

[1] Archenholtz, *Hist. of Pirates.*

were either slain or taken prisoners. A Spanish captain, who was among the latter, informed Morgan concerning the strength and position of the town. Though open in many places, Morgan and his men were twice gallantly repulsed, and suffered much from the great guns which were placed in every direction. But in defiance of all opposition and danger, the pirates in three hours carried the city. Thus victorious, they, as usual, refused quarter, and slew all whom they encountered. Morgan, aware of the dissolute habits of his followers, and apprehensive that the Spaniards might fall on them while they were in a state of intoxication, called them together, and prohibited them from tasting the wine, which, he alleged, the enemy had mixed with poison.[1] Ere the freebooters had well fixed their quarters in Panama, several quarters of it burst out in flames, which spread so rapidly, that in a short time many magnificent edifices, built of cedar, and a great number of inferior houses, were burned to the ground.[2] The churches, convents, hospitals, and 200 warehouses, filled with valuable merchandize, were all reduced to ashes. Whether these fires, which continued burning during four weeks, were raised by the directions of Morgan, or happened accidentally, owing to the consternation of the inhabitants during the assault, has been disputed; but there can be no doubt of the cruelty, rapacity, and licentiousness of the pirates in their pillage of Panama, both during this conflagration and after it had been extinguished. Immense treasures were found in the wells and caves, and many valuable commodities were taken in the vessels which had been left aground at low water. But not satisfied with these acquisitions, Morgan sent out detachments to scour the neighbouring country for plunder, and to bring in as prisoners all from whom a

[1] Johnson's *Lives of Pirates, &c.*
[2] Burney, *Hist. of Buccaneers,* c. 6.

ransom might be extorted. By the infliction of torture, several rich deposits of treasure were discovered in the surrounding forests, and the fugitive inhabitants were driven back as captives to the town, with exception of a few who escaped with their treasures by sea, and went for shelter to the islands in the Bay of Panama. One galleon also was almost miraculously saved, after being laden with the king's plate and jewels, and with other precious articles belonging to the church and some of the richest inhabitants. Morgan fitted out a fast-sailing ship, in the hope of intercepting her, but she had got too much ahead to be overtaken.

Having remained a month amid the ruins of Panama, Morgan and his followers at length departed, taking with them 175 mules loaded with spoil, and 600 prisoners, some of them carrying burdens, and others for whose release a ransom was expected. When they had returned to the mouth of the Chagre, a division commenced of the spoil. But Morgan suspected that his followers had not brought the whole plunder into the common stock, and the pirates, on the other hand, believed that their commander had already appropriated more than his share of the treasure to himself. Morgan was a man capable of forming vast designs, and showed consummate skill, perseverance, and intrepidity in their execution : he possessed the art of inspiring his followers with confidence by his words, and of stimulating them to the most audacious enterprises ; but none of his tribe had been ever so beset by the sordid lust of lucre, and he held in little respect the maxim with regard to the observance of honour among thieves. Perceiving that the suspicions entertained concerning his undue appropriation of the spoil, and an ignominious search to which he subjected his associates, had diminished his authority and popularity, he fraudulently resolved to withdraw from the command. Before the dawn of that day which had been appointed for the final division of the booty, while the other pirates were in a deep sleep, Morgan, accompanied by a few of the principal Buccaneers of his own country, set sail for Jamaica, in a vessel he had filled with the rich spoils of a city which had long served as the staple or mart of commerce between the old and new world.[1] This instance of a treachery unheard of before, excited an indescribable rage in the breasts of the pirates, who thus saw themselves deprived of the greater part of that wealth which they had acquired with so much risk and suffering. The English pursued the robber in the hope of wresting from him the booty of which he had disappointed their avidity : the French, though equal sharers in the loss, sullenly retired to Tortuga.

Morgan arrived safe at Jamaica, where he began to levy men, with the view of colonizing the Island of Santa Katalina, which he intended to hold as his own, and make it a common place of refuge for pirates : but the injury his character had sustained among his own class, in consequence of his recent act of treachery, and the arrival of a new governor at Jamaica, with more strict orders to enforce the late treaty with Spain, compelled him to abandon his design. Having afterwards contrived to find favour with Charles II. of England, or some of his ministers, he was knighted, and appointed a Commissioner of the Admiralty Court in Jamaica ; and when the governor of that island returned to England, on account of bad health, he left him to act as a deputy during his absence. In this capacity his administration was distinguished by extreme severity towards his old associates, several of whom suffered the provoking hardship of being tried and executed under his authority. One whole crew of Buccaneers who fell into his hands, were sent by him to be delivered up to the Spaniards at Carthagena. Though soon super-

[1] Raynal, t. iii.

seded by the arrival of a new governor from England, he
continued in the office of a Commissioner of Admiralty
during the remainder of the reign of Charles II. But in
the time of James II, the Court of Spain unjustly complained of his connivance with the freebooters, and he was
in consequence sent a prisoner to England, where he was
detained three years in confinement, without any regular
charge being brought against him.[1]

The enforcement of the treaty between Spain and
England, and the secession of Morgan with some of his
chief associates from the ranks of the Buccaneers, gave a
temporary respite to the Spaniards. But fresh adven-
turers renewed the depredations, which were continued
without intermission, during the whole of the present
reign. Since the sack of Panama by Morgan, the ima-
ginations of the Freebooters had continually dwelt on
expeditions to the South Sea, and there were sad fore-
bodings in Peru of attacks both by sea and land. As
the numbers of the Buccaneers increased, neither the
West Indies nor the eastern coasts of America furnished
plunder sufficient to satisfy so many rapacious adventurers, whose modes of expenditure were not less lavish or
profligate than their means of acquisition were violent
and iniquitous. The towns in Cuba and Terra Firma
had been repeatedly rifled, and were now completely despoiled. The Buccaneers were thus urged by a species
of necessity to extend their enterprises. Some sailed
through the Straits of Magellan to the South Sea.
Others, having formed alliances with the Indians, reached that ocean by crossing the Isthmus of Darien; and,
having seized the first vessels they found, ravaged the
coasts of Peru and western shores of Mexico. In these
excursions they continued to display the same furious and
irresistible valour, the same thirst of spoil, and the same

[1] Burney, _Hist. of Buccan._ c. 11.

brutal inhumanity to their captives, that had characterised their more early expeditions.   Leon in Mexico,
though situated twenty miles from the coast, was taken,
sacked, and burned, by the freebooters under Davies ; a
similar fate was also experienced by Guayaquil in Peru,
which was the port of Quito, and by the magnificent city
of New Grenada, on the Lake of Nicaragua.

At length, towards the close of the present reign, and
during a war between France and Spain, the French
Flibustiers were often united with their countrymen in
regular hostilities, and frequently contributed greatly to
the success of their arms, particularly in the attack on
Carthagena.   Their junction with regular troops, served
in some degree to reclaim them from their predatory habits, and to check their barbarous outrages on humanity.
The expedition against Carthagena was the last transac-
tion in which the Buccaneers made a conspicuous figure.
Shortly after the termination of that enterprise, an end
was put to the war between France and Spain, by the
treaty of Ryswick.   Peace, in former times, by releasing
the Buccaneers from public demands on their services,
left them free to pursue their own projects, with an understood license or privilege to cruise against the Spaniards without the danger of being subjected to inquiry.
But now the Kings, both of Great Britain and France,
were earnestly desirous to give satisfaction to Spain, as
its succession depended on the will of its monarch, who
was then in declining health, and without issue.   Louis
XIV. sent back from France to Carthagena the silver
ornaments of which its churches had been stripped.   Fresh
prohibitions and proclamations against the Buccaneers
were issued both by the French and English governors in
the West Indies.   Their expeditions of late had not
been accompanied with the uniform success which attended their earlier adventures, and the coasts became so

strictly guarded, that it was more difficult than formerly
to effect disembarkations on the Spanish dominions. Encouragement was at the same time held out to them to
settle as planters.[1]   Most of the freebooters, accordingly,
adopted this occupation, or followed in merchant ships
the trade of mariners, or retired among their old allies,
the Darien Indians.   Ancient habits, indeed, led a few
to persist in their early courses.   But they dispersed
over the world, and did not limit themselves as formerly
to plundering the Spaniards.   Little is heard of them
subsequent to the peace of Ryswick in 1697; and after
the accession of Philip V. to the throne of Spain, the race
became entirely extinct.

But the piracies of the Buccaneers at sea, and their depredations on land, had endured for more than thirty
years ere their singular associations were dissolved ; and
it has often excited astonishment, that, without any regular system,—without laws or any species of subordination except in the moment of action, and destitute
even of any fixed revenue, their numbers should have
so increased, and all their enterprises have been crowned with such marvellous success.   During the same period in which they flourished, the most powerful European
nations frequently sent considerable fleets to the New
World.   But the intemperance of the climate, the want
of subsistence, and the dejection of the troops, occasioned
the failure of the best concerted expeditions.   On the
very scene of their misfortunes, and on the spots where
they were repulsed, a small body of adventurers, who had
no resources to enable them to carry on war except what
their depredations supplied, triumphed over all such obstacles, and successfully accomplished the most difficult and
hazardous enterprises.   But the Buccaneers were endued
with that vigour of mind, and possessed of that energy of ac-

[1] Id. c. 27.

tion, which often compensates for the want of regular discipline or of skilful combinations. Besides, they were
countenanced and protected by those maritime nations
which were at enmity with the Spaniards; and the Spanish Americans themselves were so far degenerated from
the military spirit of their ancestors, that they had lost
all knowledge of the art of war, and had even become un-
acquainted with the use of fire arms.[1] They had conceived an almost superstitious horror at the Buccaneers,
whom they figured as monsters of supernatural strength
and cruelty. Hence, even with the greatest advantage
in point of numbers, they seldom ventured to defend themselves, but fled with precipitation at the approach of those
demons in human form.

In such circumstances, it was fortunate for the Spaniards, and perhaps for the other maritime nations of
Europe, that piracy, and not permanent conquest, was the
object of the Buccaneers. Had they formed for themselves any regular mode of government, they might have
become a powerful and independent state. Yet, among
their chiefs, Mansvelt and Morgan alone appear to have
contemplated any scheme of a regular settlement, uncon-
nected with the European governments. In these higher
designs they were not seconded by their restless followers, who acted from momentary impulse, and were always
impatient to abandon a conquest as soon as they had
rifled it of its riches.

Though bound in a species of association and regulated
by the same principles of action, their plans were destitute
of unity, and there was no chief to preside over the whole,
or combine, for the formation of a system, the diversity
of characters and objects among so many different nations. Hence, the Buccaneers had no decided or permanent influence on the destinies of the West Indies or

[1] Raynal, *Hist. Philosoph.*

America. But had their enterprises been systematically conducted, had their bands been duly organized, and had a leader of talents and genius directed their energies, and claimed their obedience, it is impossible to tell what results might have been produced by the constancy, indefatigable activity, and dauntless courage of the Buccaneers.

It was often the mere love of danger and excitement that drove these wild and lawless rovers across the main. But long years of crime obliterated the feelings of humanity, and having outraged society in all its received forms and maxims, the hardened Buccaneer could never again look for shelter within its sanctuary. Hence his life became one of daring guilt and reckless adventure—of lavish profusion—of impetuous and almost phrensied passion. His death was often that so gloriously typified in the lines of the poet——

> And now my race of terror run,
> Mine be the eve of tropic sun:
> No pale gradations quench his ray,
> No twilight dews his wrath allay;
> With disk like battle-target red,
> He rushes to his burning bed,
> Dyes the wide wave with bloody light,
> Then sinks at once, and all is night.

CHAPTER II.

Quos inter medius venit furor.

VIRGIL, *Æneid.*

DURING the course of the troubles and disasters which marked the commencement of the new reign, Father Nithard exercised the supreme authority in the State. But his talents, it was soon discovered, were not such as enabled him to contend with the difficulties by which he was on every side surrounded, or to avert the dangers of a declining monarchy. His knowledge of the world, and of public business, was extremely limited ; and his good qualities were confined to that species of disinterestedness by which a Jesuit prefers the aggrandizement of his order to his own personal advantage. The Grandees, who, since the death of Olivarez, had again become powerful and turbulent, declared against Nithard ; and, ranging themselves, along with the people, on the side of John of Austria, insisted that he should be recalled and employed. At first Nithard displayed some pride, or rather insolence, telling the grandees, that they owed more respect to one who had daily their God in his hands and their Queen at his feet. But he soon found how much more easy it is to govern a weak devotee than a proud discontented nobility.

At this time Don John was still at Consuegra, his residence as Prior of Castile, about fourteen leagues north-

east from Madrid. He was unquestionably the favourite
of the nation; and their voice proclaimed him to be the
only person fit to support the sinking fortunes of the monarchy. While commanding in Portugal, during the
last reign, the Queen, who was envious of his popularity,
had diverted the supplies which were intended for his
use, and left him no other alternative than that of retiring from the service. This was the origin of the dissensions between them which now distracted the state. The
Queen-regent was averse to his recall, from the apprehension that he might succeed in dismissing her ecclesiastical
favourite from the Council, or at least in circumscribing his
authority. She, accordingly, formed a design of removing
Don John from the kingdom on pretence of sending
him to his government of the Low Countries, which had
recently been overrun by the French arms. The Peace
of Aix-la-Chapelle was not yet finally concluded, and the
Queen engaged that he should carry with him a large
auxiliary force, and ample pecuniary supplies, to enable
him to regain those important towns which had been occupied by the French. Don John, however, was aware,
that, as in the Portuguese campaign, he should be left
without resources; and that, in the event of a renewal of
the war, the disgrace of failure would, at court, be attributed to him alone. He, therefore, never seriously intended to leave Spain, but he at first appeared to accept
the proposal, and actually proceeded to Corunna, as if
about to embark for Flanders, where his arrival was for
some time daily expected.[1] He remained a considerable
time in Galicia; but, on various pretexts, he always deferred sailing, till at length, being informed of the sudden
death of an Aragoneze gentleman called Don Joseph
Malladas, who was one of his most attached and faithful
followers, he immediately conceived a suspicion (which in

---

[1] Sir William Temple's *Correspondence.*

fact appears to have been but too well founded), that he
had been privately put to death by orders of the Queen
or her unworthy favourite. Accordingly, on receiving this
intelligence, he threw off the mask, and refused to accept
of the appointment to the Netherlands. He did not, indeed, charge the Queen with the murder of Malladas;
but he excused himself to her, and the Council of Regency, on the score of a defluxion which had attacked his
breast, while, to his friends, he complained, that her Majesty had only sought to disgrace him by a nomination to
the government of Flanders, as neither troops nor money
had been provided to enable him to act with a vigour worthy of his rank and character. Don John, however, humbly requested permission to pay his respects to the Queen
at the Court of Madrid, on his way back from Corunna
to his former residence at Consuegra. This favour, however, was refused him, and the Queen issued a document,
to be circulated among the chief tribunals and councils of
the kingdom, wherein she accused Don John of a dere-
liction of duty, in declining to embark for the government
of the Netherlands, and she maintained that, on her part,
she had assembled at Corunna, by her exertions, a fleet
and army superior to any which had been fitted out in
Spain since the time of Charles V. By the refusal, however, of Don John to embark, the Queen, though she
prohibited his appearance at Madrid, was compelled to
permit him to remain in Spain, where he daily fomented
the popular discontents, by throwing the blame of every
misfortune on the Jesuit, and, in particular, by inveigh-
ing against the treaty of Aix-la-Chapelle, which abandoned to the French some of the most important of the
Spanish possessions in the Netherlands.

A design at length, it is alleged, was formed by the
adherents of Don John, for seizing on the person of
the Jesuit, and, by his death, delivering the kingdom

from its thraldom. Whether this deed of blood was
actually meditated, or whether the charge was a stratagem of the Queen and her party to throw odium on
her enemies, it enabled her to act with more vigour
than formerly. She confiscated all the revenues of Don
John, and despatched the Marques of Salinas, Captain
of the Spanish guard, with an adequate civil and military
force, to arrest him at Consuegra, and to conduct him prisoner to the Alcazar of Toledo. That prince, however,
being apprized of the danger, fled, accompanied by an
escort of thirty horsemen, to the valley of Aranda in
Aragon, and thence to Catalonia, where he found refuge
in the fortress of Flix. From this retreat he addressed
a long expostulatory letter to the Queen, in which he
urged the necessity of the immediate departure of Nithard
from the kingdom, or at least his exclusion from the council of regency. Nithard now became alarmed, and wished
to quit Spain, but the Queen reassured him, and by her
directions, the council prepared a long memorial, in which
several heads of accusation were brought forward against
Don John; and his trial, on the following charges, was
suggested. 1. His refusal to embark for the Netherlands.
2. His attempt to seize the person of Nithard. 3. His
treasonable letter to the Queen. Mutual written recriminations now passed between Nithard and Don John,
in which each charged his enemy with designs of assassination. The kingdom was filled with satires and party
libels, and the whole court and capital became divided
into factions, which favoured one or other of these rivals.
- Among other machinations of the Jesuit against Don
John, he suborned persons to denounce him to the Inquisition as a suspected Lutheran, and an enemy to the
ecclesiastical institutions of his country, particularly to
the order of Jesus. The information lodged against him
presented only some vague and general propositions; but

the Inquisitor-General produced a copy of a letter of Don John in which he said, that having consulted several eminent theologians, he had been advised by them, that it would be an allowable, and even laudable action, to put the Father Nithard to death, as his removal would prove conducive to the benefit of the State,—adding, that he was merely prevented from carrying this recommendation into execution, from his reluctance to have any share in the future condemnation of his Reverence, who, he was fully convinced, was, at this period, in a state of impenitence and mortal sin. This epistle, (which certainly was not authentic), was stigmatized by the inquisitorial censors whom Nithard had employed for its revision, as scandalous, heretical, and offensive to pious ears. The usual secrecy observed in the proceedings of the Inquisition was in this case violated, and some Jesuits declaimed from the pulpit on the danger to which the kingdom must be exposed under the government of a heretical prince, who thus persecuted the Catholic religion in the person of its ministers. But before the proceedings in the Inquisition could be brought to a termination, they were arrested by the farther progress of political events.[1]

Aragon and Catalonia having declared in favour of Don John, he made a sort of triumphal progress through these provinces, with an escort of 300 horse, granted to him by the Duke d'Ossuna, Viceroy of Catalonia. On his entrance into Aragon, the Duke of Terranuova, who was Governor of that kingdom, divested himself of his authority in favour of Don John, who now assumed the administration of affairs in that quarter. Having been joined by many of the principal inhabitants of the province, he at length advanced from Saragossa with 700 resolute followers to Torrejon de Ardoz, within three leagues of Madrid. Here he was met by the Papal

---

[1] Llorente, *Hist. de la Inquisicion d'España*, c. 27.

Nuncio, who had been charged by the Court with the task of mediation. To the request that he should remain four days at Torrejon to give time for satisfying his demands, "he replied that Nithard must quit the capital in two days, and the kingdom as quickly as possible." Don John professed, however, that as soon as the Jesuit had taken his departure, he would dismiss his followers, and if he entered Madrid, it should be but for the purpose of throwing himself at the feet of her Majesty. The Queen and her minister, though they had foreseen this insurrection, had not provided any means to quell it. The orders which they issued for placing the city in a state of defence on the near approach of Don John, were not obeyed. Tumults arose in every street, and the people complained that the town was about to be sacked for the sake of a foreign Jesuit. In this situation the Duke d'Infantado and the Marques of Liche, who were among the foremost adherents of Don John, being unable to obtain a personal interview with the Queen, unceremoniously communicated to her, through one of her secretaries, the absolute necessity of consenting to the immediate departure of Nithard. The Council of Regency, at which, on this occasion, the minister was not present, then assembled, and its members were unanimously of opinion that, in order to preserve the city from commotion, the obnoxious favourite must quit Madrid in the course of three hours. This resolution was straightway communicated to the Queen, and a document, which in fact was intended as a sentence of banishment from the kingdom, (though in form it merely granted him permission to retire wherever he chose), was presented to her Majesty for signature. Perceiving that his fate was inevitable, she consented, apparently with a good grace, declaring, that she never had any object in view but the welfare of the State. Nithard was informed of his dismissal and banishment, at

which he had no reason to be surprised, by the Admiral
of Castile, who took the opportunity of recalling to his
recollection all the acts of misgovernment, by which he
had merited this disgrace.   The upstart favourite was
much irritated by reprimands to which he had been little
accustomed, and complained bitterly of the affront thus
offered in his person to the Inquisition of Spain.   He also
was deeply affected by the necessity of quitting Madrid,
without being permitted to take leave of his royal mistress.
Before his departure, she sent to offer him considerable
sums of money, and pecuniary assistance was also tendered by different individuals; but he declined all recompense, saying, " that he had come a poor monk into Spain,
and as such would leave it."   Nithard, accordingly, departed on that evening on which the order for his exile
had been communicated to him, taking nothing with him
but the habit which he wore and his breviary.   He set
out, attended by the Archbishop of Toledo and several
officers of the inquisition.   As soon as the crowd, which
had been all day collecting, saw the Father, they threw
stones, loading him at the same time with reproaches and
maledictions; and it is believed that he might probably
have fallen a victim to the popular fury, had he not been
accompanied by the Cardinal Archbishop. The unhappy
Exile was sensibly affected by the treatment which he received from the multitude; but he endured it with pa-
tience and resignation.   When he had proceeded but a
short way on his journey from Madrid, the Queen sent
after him an order for a sum of 2000 ducats, to be distributed among his domestics, and another grant to defray
his expenses.   From Spain he went to Rome in the
character of ambassador, with which the Queen invested
him.   Her influence some years afterwards, procured for
him a Cardinal's hat; but all her endeavours to obtain
permission for his return to Madrid proved ineffectual.

Having thus got rid of the Father Nithard, the grandees waited on Don John, who now addressed a letter of thanks and congratulation to the Queen on her patriotic conduct; and in order to show that the dismissal of an unpopular minister had been the sole object of his advance to Madrid, he retired, as soon as that was accomplished, to Guadalaxara, about ten leagues distant, there to await, as he said, her Majesty's farther orders. The Queen, however, was fully aware that his chief desire was to enter the capital, and seize on the authority left vacant by the absence of Nithard. Little conciliated by his show of moderation, she wrote, commanding him, on pain of rebellion, to dismiss his guards, and to retire from the place where he then was to a greater distance from Court. Don John, however, was not disposed to yield much farther to the Queen, whom he had so severely humbled. Though he dismissed his guards, he continued at Guadalaxara, whence he opened a negotiation with her Majesty, which terminated in his obtaining all that he now required. For himself, he only asked a recall of the decrees and sentences which had been recently pronounced against him: but he procured an ample pardon for all his friends and confederates, and also the establishment of a new council of state, for the express purpose of devising means to diminish taxation, and alleviate the sufferings of the people. This apparent disinterestedness, and the care which he showed for the welfare of the nation, greatly increased the popularity which Don John had hitherto enjoyed: but the Queen, as soon as she learned that he had dismissed his guards, and given his friends leave to depart, began to forget many of the stipulations of the treaty. In order, indeed, to give some temporary satisfaction to the people, the *junta* appointed for the diminution of taxation and the reform of abuses, was called together, and the President of the Council of Finance, along with the President of Castile, and the Archbishop of Toledo, were now placed at its head. This assembly received various memorials and representations from the most intelligent persons in the kingdom. But their labours proved in a great measure nugatory, since the sole result of the inquiries and deliberations of the Junta was a decree which totally disappointed the expectations of the public. Its provisions with regard to the reductions of salaries and the sale of offices, were either altogether insignificant, or were never carried into effect.[1] The delusion thus practised on the people, occasioned great murmurs and dissatisfaction. But the Queen, instead of applying herself to obtain from the Junta a more effectual decree, or to carry that which had been promulgated, such as it was, into execution, was now wholly occupied with a project of raising a formidable body of Life guards, to be constantly stationed in the capital, by whose means she expected to repress in future any popular commotions, and to resist any renewed attempts against her authority on the part of John of Austria. This regiment, when levied, she placed under the command of the Marques d'Aytona, the declared enemy of Don John, and the successor of Father Nithard, in her favour and confidence. The citizens of Madrid, who had hitherto accounted themselves the loyal guards of their king, and were accustomed to see him preceded or attended only by a few halberdiers, were much disgusted at this innovation; and their dislike to the newly raised corps was increased by its insubordination and frequent outrages. Its soldiers often extended their depredations to the neighbourhood of the city,

[1] Quegli (says Gregorio Leti, in his Life of John of Austria) chiebbero qualche favore ed intrico furono ristabiliti ne' loro uficii, e salarie, la vita loro durante; e questo decreto non venne eseguito, che à prejudicio delle vedove, e di qualche misero, senza che il popolo in generale ne ricevesse il preteso ed aspettato sollievo.

and committed violence in open day. On one occasion, a
party of them sallied forth to rob the garden of a *venta* or
posada, about half a league from Madrid. The host and
one of his servants having attempted to prevent the pillage, were murdered by these ruffians, and the inn itself
was afterwards plundered. Some officers of justice who
repaired to the spot, in order to take cognizance of this
atrocious act, were assaulted by the comrades of the de-
linquents, and would have been slain, had it not been for
the assistance of the neighbouring villagers. Scarcely a
night passed at Madrid, in which there was not blood-
shed, owing to the quarrels which arose between these
soldiers and the inhabitants. Robbers and assassins, too,
from all quarters of Spain, availing themselves of this
state of disorder, flocked to Madrid, and perpetrated
crimes which they knew would be universally attributed
to the obnoxious guards. Little inquiry being made by
government concerning the offences of the soldiery, and
no punishment being inflicted, even when the perpetrators
of the most heinous crimes were discovered, the Corregidors of Madrid laid a formal complaint before the Queen,
and required that the regiment should either be altogether disbanded, or steps taken to preserve it in better discipline. The Council of Castile also remonstrated on the
evils resulting from the unwonted measure of maintain-
ing a force of this description in the capital. But the
Queen turned a deaf ear to all these representations,—
being persuaded it was necessary that such a corps should
be constantly quartered at Madrid, in order to hold the
populace in subjection, and preserve the kingdom from
those disturbances so usual during the minority of princes.

The people, thus disappointed in their hopes of some
relief from the burdens to which they had been so long
subjected, and daily irritated by the insolence and unre-
pressed outrages of the soldiery, had again recourse to Don

John, who still continued to reside at Guadalaxara, though under a strict prohibition from shewing himself at Court, or even approaching nearer to the capital. This prince, who, notwithstanding his assumed moderation, was most desirous to displace the Regent, or, at least, to share with her the government of the State, willingly listened to the complaints of the malecontents, and menaced the queen with a civil war unless the regiment of guards was disbanded, and some measures were devised to alleviate the public distresses. The ferment, too, began to spread from the capital to the provinces. Grenada took arms in support of Don John; Aragon and Catalonia sent him 1200 Miquelets, and engaged to furnish as many more troops as he might think necessary towards the accomplishment of his plans for the regeneration of the kingdom. The Queen, who perceived that both grandees and people waited only a signal from Don John to break into open rebellion, and who also knew that she was not in a condition to resist any general revolt, now hastened to allay the approaching tumult by some apparent concessions. In a new treaty, negotiated by the Nuncio, she consented to share the government of the monarchy with Don John, who was, in consequence, declared Vicar-General of the Crown, in Aragon, Catalonia, Valencia, the Balearic Isles, and Sardinia. His friend, the Duke d'Ossuna, also obtained the government of Milan. The other provinces remained under the regency of the Queen, who was now permitted, without farther molestation from Don John, to retain her regiment of Life Guards. Notwithstanding the sacrifice she had made, her Majesty felt much relieved by the removal of her formidable rival to such a distance, and she now used every means to accelerate his departure for the eastern provinces of Spain. Don John established his court at Saragossa, where he fixed his residence in one of the quarters of the Archiepiscopal palace within the city. The ancient seat of the kings of Aragon, called the Aljaferia, which was situated on the Ebro, about a mile beyond the walls of Saragossa, had been converted, since the time of Ferdinand and Isabella, into a residence for the officials of the inquisition; and in consequence, Philip IV, in his frequent visits to Saragossa, had usually taken up his abode in the archiepiscopal palace. This gigantic pile had been founded by an archbishop of Saragossa, who was nephew of King Ferdinand the Catholic; it was surrounded by delightful gardens, which the rapid Ebro skirted, and it commanded a view over the city and adjacent country, as far as the cliffs of the Pyrenees. The building was enlarged and beautified by Don John, and the interior was ornamented with many exquisite productions of art, particularly Raphael's designs for the victories and triumphs of Scipio Africanus.[1]

Here Don John resided for some years in great splendour, assuming in every respect the state and demeanour of a monarch. He ruled over Aragon with an authority superior to that which had been exercised by its ancient kings; and for this power he was in a great measure indebted to his own excellent conduct. The good of the people formed the chief object of his administration, and he found the ancient constitution of the kingdom well adapted for its promotion. By rigidly adhering himself to the laws, he taught the people to obey them without murmuring. But though strict in the execution of justice, he never failed, when a due opportunity offered, to temper it with mercy. By these means, he soon brought the affairs of his viceroyalty into order, while confusion prevailed in every other quarter of the monarchy.

But though deservedly popular in Aragon, and the other provinces which composed his government, the Cas-

---

[1] F. Bremundan, *Viage de Carlos II.*

tilians, and particularly the citizens of Madrid, were high-ly exasperated at the conduct of Don John, and alleged, that, for the gratification of his personal ambition, he had sacrificed the interests of the people of which he had so long stood forth as the zealous protector.

This appears to have been the age in Spain of party-writing, and acrimonious political pamphlets. Persons at the head of affairs addressed to each other long epistles of expostulation and reproach. These were circulated among the people, and their respective adherents then took up the theme. This sort of warfare had been long carried on between Don John and Father Nithard; and at present the conduct of the new Vicar-General of Aragon was subjected to much scrutiny and censure, in various publications. Nor, on the other hand, were writings in his vindication awanting. In one of these, which was written with considerable address, and circulated through Madrid, two days after his departure from Guadalaxara to Saragossa, the question is propounded (and in such a monarchy as Spain it seems a bold one) whether Don John acted right in accepting an employment which held him at a distance from Madrid, instead of entering the capital at the head of his friends and the soldiery, in order to displace a profligate ministry, or compel them to diminish the national imposts, and afford some relief from the public burdens. It was argued, in defence of the line of conduct which Don John adopted,—That nothing had been omitted on his part, in so far as representations or remonstrances might avail; but that he could not have followed more violent courses, without forfeiting his allegiance to his young sovereign, and occasioning far greater disorders than those which he sought to remedy: that, in the temper in which the populace then were, a general confusion must have been the consequence of Don John's advance to Madrid at the head of an armed force, and such disorders in the capital might have proved dangerous to the royal person, if the report which prevailed was true, that the Queen had declared that, in the event of any serious commotion, she would come forth from the palace to the streets, with the infant king in her arms: that, though this Queen had shown that she entertained towards him a bitter enmity, and had offered him many injuries, Don John nevertheless owed her much reverence as the mother of his sovereign, and the relict of his late father: that such an enterprise as the one which it was so generally thought Don John ought to have undertaken, did not resemble his attempt for the removal of Nithard —the one concerning only the expulsion of a foreign Jesuit—the other the safety of Spain. It was farther argued, that it was a mistake to suppose Don John could have obtained all he wished, without any farther disturbance, by his mere approach to the capital. In that event, the people of Madrid must either have risen or not: a popular insurrection would have been attended with evils sufficiently manifest; and, without a rising of the inhabitants, any force which Don John could have brought with him to the capital, must have proved inadequate to overthrow the present evil government, which would only have been strengthened in consequence of his failure. Finally, supposing that he had succeeded in all his designs,—that he had forced the Regent to retire to a convent,—secured the person of the King, and assumed the reins of government, —little permanent advantage would have resulted, since the partizans of the Queen, who were still powerful and numerous, would have exerted themselves to reinstate her in the former authority she enjoyed, and the country would have become the prey of two factions, whose ceaseless contentions would have left but little leisure for any statesman to watch or labour for the public good; and if, amid these dissensions, the death of the King had unfortunately occurred, Don John could never have been able to escape the imputations which his enemies would have been eager to cast on his motives and actions. On the whole, therefore, as the expulsion of Nithard had not been attended with those advantages which were anticipated, but, on the contrary, a new set of evil advisers had, hydra-like, sprung up in his place, the wisest course which Don John had to follow, both for the national interests and his own, was to retire from the rage of his enemies to a distant government, where, since he could not contribute to the happiness of the whole empire, he might at least benefit those provinces which were entrusted to his own peculiar care.

This justification made a considerable impression on many of the inhabitants of Madrid; but the enemies of Don John, while they rejoiced at his absence, still continued to render it the subject of their censure, and to represent him to the people as having forsaken them from the most self-interested motives. Meanwhile, the Queen availed herself of the distance to which she had succeeded in removing Don John, and of his temporary unpopularity, to consolidate her own power, and take precautions against the dangers to which she was exposed, from the enmity of the citizens of Madrid. Among other measures, she prohibited its inhabitants, whom, it is said, she had always detested, from carrying fire-arms, or having them in their houses, under pain of death. This interdiction, however, which gave deep offence, was not complied with; and so little was the viceregal authority respected in Madrid, that, on more than one occasion, bands of the young nobility forced the public prisons in open day, and released state-criminals.

The tumults and outcries of the populace, who conceived that they had been abandoned by their favourite, Don John, and that no legal or pacific means of redress now remained to them, seriously alarmed the Queen. The people complained, apparently with justice, that they were as much oppressed by taxes, though the nation was in perfect peace, as if it had been still in a state of warfare, and that all those abuses which the Court had repeatedly promised to remedy and repress, were allowed to subsist as formerly. In order that they might not be exasperated beyond endurance, the Queen appointed a new Council or Junta, whose attention was to be exclusively devoted to the re-establishment of due order in the finances, and a retrenchment in the superfluous expenses of the crown. But this institution, like many others of a similar description which had preceded it, soon became useless or rather burdensome to the state. The members who composed this tribunal obtained lucrative appointments for themselves and families. They grasped at valuable presents from those who required their forbearance, and shut their eyes on the robberies committed by financiers, and on the illegal appropriation of the royal domains. The Junta thus became itself an abuse, like the other supreme councils, all of which were filled with an useless number of officers, who absorbed the public revenues, and never brought any thing to a termination. One may judge of the expense of such establishments from the salary enjoyed by the Chancellor of the Council for the Indies, which amounted, it is said, to not less than 100,000 ducats.

While the Queen was thus alternately irritating the inhabitants of Madrid by tyrannical regulations, and then attempting to soothe them by delusive pretences of a reformation of abuses, Don John remained quiet in Aragon. Though an attentive observer of all the occurrences at Court, he did not apparently interfere in politics, except that he had been carrying on a negotiation with the Pope, in order to compel Nithard to resign the office which he still retained of Inquisitor-General of Spain. That in-

triguing Jesuit had not relinquished all hopes of his recall
to Madrid; and it was dreaded, that if he ever accomplished this object, his situation as Inquisitor might still
give him much influence in the State, and ready access
at all times to the Queen. Don John, however, succeeded in obtaining his renunciation of that dignity, and the
President of Castile was appointed in his room. Nithard
survived till the year 1681; but he continued to reside
constantly at Rome, and interfered no farther in Spanish
affairs.

There seems no good reason for supposing that Don
John at this time entertained any treasonable designs of
seizing the crown to the prejudice of his infant brother.
But there can be no doubt that he had long indulged in
dreams of sovereignty; for the Duke of York, in his Memoirs, informs us, that the Earl of Bristol ingratiated
himself with Don John when he was in the Netherlands,
" by feeding his humour, by casting his nativity, and talking perpetually to him of crowns and sceptres. "[1] The
feeble and precarious state of the young king's health,
disclosed to his view the most ambitious prospects.
With Charles II. would terminate the present dynasty;
and the Spanish succession would then open either to the
German branch of the House of Austria, or the family
of Bourbon. But the misconduct of the Queen had rendered the former odious in Spain, and it was not probable
that the powers of Europe, so jealous of the aggrandizement of Louis XIV, would permit a prince of the race of
Bourbon to ascend the Spanish throne. In these peculiar circumstances, Don John, notwithstanding his illegi-
timacy, hoped that he might step in between the claim-
ants. Singular stories also, concerning his birth were propagated at this time, and readily believed in Spain. Don
John was the reputed child of Philip IV. and the actress

[1] *Life of James II*, t. i. p. 293.

Calderona. His enemies maintained that he was the son of the Duke of Medina de-las-Torres, who was a favoured lover of his mother, and to whom, as they alleged, he bore a striking personal resemblance. But, on the other hand, the friends of Don John gave out, that he was the legitimate son of King Philip and of his first Queen, Isabella of Bourbon. The Queen and Calderona having each given birth to a male child nearly at the same period, the King, they said, was at that time so infatuated with his love for the actress, that he consented, on her solicitation, to allow her son to be privately substituted for the royal infant. In consequence of this exchange, the illegitimate offspring of Calderona was brought up at Court, as successor to the monarchy, by the name of Prince Balthazar; and the true heir was privately educated at Ocana, under the bastard appellation of John of Austria.[1] This improbable story was countenanced by Don John, and in the event of the young king's death, would have been publicly promulgated. His partizans would at least have feigned to believe it—the public would have asserted it,—evidence of it, whether true or false, could have been easily procured, and Don John would in all likelihood have ascended the throne, as the legitimate son of Philip IV. and Isabella of Bourbon.

In this very year, the young king was attacked by an illness which had nearly proved fatal, and the utmost alarm pervaded not only the Spanish empire, but the whole of Europe, at the danger of a life so precious. It is probable that the sickness of the king, and the immediate prospect of his dissolution, induced Don John to remain in his viceroyalty, which comprehended some of the most important provinces in the monarchy, in order that he might cultivate the friendship of the grandees of Aragon, and ingratiate himself with the hardy popula-

[1] D'Aulnoy, *Mém. Secrets de la Cour d'Espagne*, t. i.

tion of Catalonia. He also judged it expedient to ab-
stain at present from any factious interference with the
proceedings of the court at Madrid, which might have
proved prejudicial to his future prospects. Accordingly,
four years afterwards, when the Count de Monterey, one
of his firmest adherents, while passing through Saragossa,
on his way to Madrid from his government of the Netherlands, attempted to persuade him to take a more prominent
part in the management of affairs—depicting the dangers
to which the monarchy was exposed, particularly in the
provinces he had just quitted, Don John refused to listen to
his suggestions. But neither was he disposed altogether to
quit the kingdom; and he, accordingly, declined the government of the Low Countries, which the Queen-regent
at this period anew pressed on his acceptance. The king,
indeed, to the great joy of his subjects, and the relief of
all the potentates of Europe, recovered from his dangerous illness. But Don John still remained at Saragossa,
and continued there, with little interruption, during the
greater part of the protracted and perilous contest in
which his country was now about to be involved.[1]

[1] For the disputes between the Queen-regent and John of Austria, I have chiefly consulted Ortiz, *Compendio*, t. vi.; Gregorio
Leti, *Vita di Don Giovanni d'Austria*; D'Aulnoy, *Mémoires de la
Cour d'Espagne*; and Desormeaux, *Abregé Chronologique de l'His-
toire d'Espagne*.

CHAPTER III.

WAR WITH FRANCE.

Nova prælia tentant.
VIRGIL, *Æneid.*

WE have seen that, soon after the commencement of the present reign, Louis XIV. had violently possessed himself of a great part of the Spanish Netherlands, and that England, Holland, and Sweden, alarmed at this increase of his power, had formed an alliance, offensive and defensive, in order to preserve for Spain the remainder of her provinces—an object which was accomplished by the Peace of Aix-la-Chapelle.

But that treaty afforded a vain and feeble hope of tranquillity to Europe. Louis had only employed the interval of repose in preparing for a new war. Although he had obtained a considerable accession of territory in the Netherlands, he was not satisfied with a part, however valuable, when he had aspired to the possession of the whole; and he was aware, that he could not accomplish his schemes of universal monarchy so long as Holland formed a point of union for the European States. Louis, too, was fearful that the enterprising Dutch might injure the manufactures and commerce of his kingdom. It was farther alleged that they were exciting the monarchies of Europe to throw off the yoke of their despots; and this report increased the jealousy with which free governments are always viewed by arbitrary princes. He was also eager to avenge himself for those obstacles which the

Dutch Republic had opposed to his entire subjugation of the Spanish provinces. Political circumstances, he perceived, were peculiarly favourable to the accomplishment of his designs. He was aware that the Triple Alliance of England, Sweden, and Holland, to which Spain had afterwards acceded, was founded on such discordant principles, and was connected by so feeble a bond of union, that it could not long subsist, or oppose a permanent barrier to the consolidated power of France. As a preliminary to his invasion of Holland, he employed all his arts to break up this confederacy. He soon recovered the ancient national influence with the Swedish government, and, by means of the Dutchess of Orleans, he easily gained her brother, the King of England, whose profusion and love of pleasure reduced him to the humiliating necessity of becoming a pensioner of France.

While Louis thus disarmed the confederacy which had been formed against him, he secured the alliance of the Bishop of Munster and Elector of Cologne, who alone could open to him the gates of Holland on the Meuse and Rhine, and preserve for him a safe retreat in the event of disaster. After some negotiation, the Emperor of Germany agreed not to afford assistance to the Dutch, provided the French king abstained from any attack on the Austrian dominions.

In the year 1671, Louis also opened a negotiation with the Queen-regent of Spain, in order to detach her from the league which she had formed with Holland, and tempted her with a scheme for the partition of the Seven United Provinces; but every principle, both of gratitude and policy, concurred in determining the queen to maintain her faith towards Holland. The arts and eloquence of the Marquis de Villars, the French ambassador at the court of Madrid, were exhausted in vain on the Regency, and the impolitic example of England and Sweden, which had deserted the Dutch Republic, and abandoned it to the vengeance of Louis, did not influence the determination of the Spanish counsels.

The immense preparations, however, of France, seriously alarmed the Queen. Fearing, and with much reason, that Louis, incensed at her refusal to renounce the alliance of the Dutch, might again invade the Spanish provinces, and involve the whole Netherlands in one common destruction, she hastily despatched orders into Flanders, to prepare for a vigorous defence; and she at the same time sent about 8000 troops to Ostend, with orders to Count Monterey, the governor of the Netherlands, to employ them for the service of the Dutch. Thus France and England, which had both contributed so much to the creation of the Republic of Holland, were now conspiring its ruin; and Spain, which had so long attempted to crush its freedom, became its chief support. Since the death of the late Prince William of Orange, about twenty years before, Holland had enjoyed a more free and popular government than in the time of its four successive Stadtholders; and the political wisdom of the Pensioner De Witt, had raised his country to an enviable height of mercantile prosperity. But twenty years of peace had also rendered the Dutch more fit for commerce than for war. The old troops were now worn out, and the new levies were unable to cope with the veterans of France. No commander existed who knew ought of military tactics, and it is even said that the stores of ammunition had been recently delivered over, in the way of traffic, to the enemy. The present constitution, though it might be admirably adapted to maintain civic prosperity, was not so well calculated for repelling the attacks of an enemy as the former government. De Witt was severely, and most justly blamed, for having thus left his country (while he could not be ignorant of the grasping ambition of Louis) in a situation utterly defenceless. The people, alarmed at the prospect of a foreign invasion in their present unprepared state, wished to be as the other nations, and demanded, like the tribes of Israel, a ruler who should go out before them to fight their battles.

At this time the young Prince of Orange, afterwards William III. of England, had just attained majority, and was already eager to grasp the power which had been possessed by his ancestors. His partizans procured his election as Captain-General and High Admiral, but the friends of De Witt and the republican party prevented for some time longer, his elevation to the dignity of Stadtholder, which, it had been declared by the edict 1667, styled Perpetual, should never be conferred on an individual.

After his appointment to the command of the army, the Prince assembled a force of 25,000 men on the banks of the Issel, to oppose the threatened invasion by the French; while the Spanish commander, persuaded that the enemy would make the first attack on Maestricht, sent the chief part of his troops to garrison that city.

Meanwhile, the French monarch invaded the Netherlands, both by the Meuse and Rhine,[1] at the head of an army of upwards of 100,000 men, divided into three corps, which were commanded by the most skilful and experienced generals of Europe. The advantageous position and promptitude of Louis, baffled the tardy combinations of two powers who were so ill fitted to coalesce as the Spaniards and the Dutch. The intestine divisions which existed in Holland between the republican party and the partizans of the House of Orange, prevented any effectual resistance to the French arms. It was these dissensions which

[1] The celebrated passage of the Rhine by Louis, near the spot of its junction with the Issel, forms the subject of one of Boileau's laudatory Epistles to the King.

spread that terror and confusion which everywhere appeared on this formidable invasion, and occasioned, in a few
days, the loss of places, each of which might have withstood the enemy for many months. In the course of some
weeks, the armies of Louis, being aided by the dryness
of the season, took forty strong citadels, and overran two-
thirds of the whole Dutch territories. One corps, having
marched through the Province of Holland with little resistance, advanced within five leagues of Amsterdam,
when, in order to preserve their remaining independence,
the inhabitants were reduced to the last and desperate
expedient of opening the sluices, and inundating the country. It was then that the people, seeing no safety for
their country but in the force and unity of sovereign
power, conferred on the young Prince of Orange the dignity of Stadtholder, in addition to that of Captain-General which he already held. Irritated and incensed by
their late disasters, they soon afterwards sacrificed to popular vengeance the two brothers De Witt, who were
known to be the opponents of the House of Orange, and
were believed to be engaged in an amicable correspondence with France.

The unprovoked and unprincipled invasion of the
United Provinces, excited, as soon as it had proved successful, universal alarm and indignation among the powers
of Europe. They regarded the subjection of Holland as
a step towards their own slavery, and retained no hopes
of defending themselves should such a vast accession be
permanently made to the dominions of France. The
Emperor of Germany, though his territories lay at a distance, and though he was usually slow in his proceedings,
at length appealed to arms; and before the close of this
season, a new alliance cemented the union between the
Emperor and Spain, for the protection of the United
Provinces. The Dutch, encouraged by this support, and

by the spirit of their young leader the Prince of Orange, began to gather courage behind their inundations. Groningen was the first place that arrested the progress of the enemy, and no sooner had he paused, than the allies commenced offensive operations in the field. Turenne, who had commanded in chief under the King of France, recommended to him to raze all the fortresses which were not necessary for preserving his conquests, but the war-minister Louvois, being of a different opinion, the army was drained and diminished by garrisons for nearly forty citadels.[1] Montecuculi, who led the Imperialists and Spaniards on the Upper Rhine, eluded the vigilance of Turenne, and, after a sudden march, sat down before Bonn. The siege and capture of Naërden by the Prince of Orange, afforded his country reason to expect the successful issue of still more important enterprises. Nor were their hopes disappointed. William, who was the fourth in a family sequence of military renown unparalleled in the annals of Europe, early showed himself worthy of his heroic descent, and the high trust confided to him. Evading all the French Generals, and leaving them behind him, the Prince, by a series of masterly manœuvres, joined his army to that of the Imperialists. Bonn surrendered in a few days after this junction, and several other places in the Electorate of Cologne fell into the hands of the allies. The communication being thus nearly cut off between France and the United Provinces, Louis was obliged to recall his forces, and abandon all his conquests, with even more celerity than he had achieved them.[2] Utrecht, Gueldres, and Overissel, which he had occupied, were thus relieved from the presence of a foe, and the horrors of war were thereafter transferred from the United Provinces to the Spanish Netherlands.

Soon after the evacuation of Holland, the King of Eng-

[1] Ramsay, *Hist. de Turenne.*   [2] Russell's *Modern Europe.*

land, urged by his Parliament, and threatened by Spain
with a war, which would have destroyed the English trade
in the Mediterranean, found himself compelled to renounce that alliance with France which was so odious to
his people, and to conclude a peace with the Dutch.
Louis was at the same time deserted by many of his German allies; and the diet of the empire, provoked by his various aggressions, and stimulated by the representations of
its imperial head, declared war against him, and menaced
his hereditary dominions with an invasion by the whole
forces of the empire.

Having been foiled in this enterprise, the French
monarch directed his attention, with his usual promptitude, to other conquests; and his decision again turned
even failure to advantage. He had been highly exasperated at the assistance which the Spaniards had afforded
to the Dutch; and a war, which, in fact, already subsisted
between the two nations, was now formally declared. This
contest, which raged for many years in Flanders, Roussillon, Alsace, and Sicily, was one of the most unfortunate
in which Spain had ever been engaged, though the Emperor and many of the German states, as we have shewn,
had espoused along with her the cause of Holland. The
King of France, indeed, being assailed by so many enemies, was forced to relinquish his conquests in the United
Provinces. But the weight of his power was, in consequence, more severely felt by Spain, against which he now
directed his chief efforts, and he proved uniformly successful
in whatever quarter of her dominions these were exerted.
Whether from total want of resources in the State, or
from the incapacity of the Queen, few attempts were made
to withstand the enemy. The Spanish grandees and
hidalgos were now reluctant to quit the pleasures of the
theatre and the Prado to assume arms, the use of which
they had almost forgotten. " In the various states of

society," says Gibbon, " armies are recruited from very different motives. Barbarians are urged by the love of war; the citizens of a free republic may be prompted by a principle of duty; the subjects, or at least the nobles, of a monarchy are animated by a sentiment of honour; but the timid and luxurious inhabitants of a declining empire must be allured into the service by the hopes of profit, or compelled by the dread of punishment."[1] At this period, however, the resources of the Spanish treasury were exhausted, and the government had no inducements to offer, which could compensate for the hardships and dangers of a military life. The inhabitants of Madrid would scarcely have discovered that the nation was at war, if they had not successively received intelligence of the loss of Franche Comté, of nearly the whole Spanish Netherlands and Sicily, as also of the total annihilation of their marine.

At the opening of the campaign in 1674, Louis astonished all Europe by the vigour of his exertions. Before the allies could assemble their forces, he had not less than four great armies in the field; and, placing himself at the head of one, he entered Franche Comté, which, it will be recollected, he had conquered from the Spaniards about seven years before, but had restored, in conformity with the terms of the treaty of Aix-la-Chapelle. The Swiss had been not only reconciled to this new aggression, but had been persuaded to shut the passage against any succours which might attempt to march through their territories to Franche Comté, either from Germany or Italy: And the Duke de Navailles, who was stationed in the Dutchy of Burgundy to watch the motions of the Spaniards, had already prepared for this invasion, by the capture of the town of Gray. Louis then advanced in person to the siege of Besançon, which was at that time defended by the Prince de Vaudemont, a son of Duke

---

[1] *Decline and Fall of the Rom. Emp.*, c. 17.

Charles of Lorraine, who was at present engaged on the side of the Spaniards. The Duke had undertaken to relieve Besançon should it be attacked; and, accordingly, on the first intelligence of these hostilities, he began his march from Germany, with the intention of entering Franche Comté through Switzerland. But a passage being refused him by the Swiss, in consequence of their compact with the French monarch, of which the Duke had not been apprized, he found himself obliged to make a circuitous march to Rheinfelds, where he intended to pass the river which gives that town its name. So much time, however, was thus consumed, that before he crossed, the King of France had already made himself master of Besançon. The town was easily taken, but the citadel, which the Spaniards accounted impregnable, made some resistance, and might have held out much longer, had it not been commanded by a rock, which was neither defended nor fortified, because it was esteemed inaccessible to an enemy. By their skill and exertions, however, the French contrived to mount on it forty pieces of cannon, which they directed with such effect against the citadel, that it was soon obliged to capitulate. The capture of Besançon, which was a subject of great triumph to the French monarch, was followed by that of Dole, Salins and some other places, which completed the conquest of Franche Comté; and this ancient appanage of the House of Burgundy, which, by the marriage of the heiress of that Dutchy with the Emperor Maximilian, had passed into the Austrian family, was severed from the Crown of Spain, and henceforth united to France. The province, as its name imports, being exempted from every species of tax or tribute, had of late years been rather a burden to the Spanish monarchy, though in former times, and under enterprising sovereigns, it was accounted an invaluable possession, by opening a way to the heart of the

French dominions. On the present occasion, it was subdued even in a shorter time than in the campaign of 1668;
and it was the facility with which the former enterprise
had been achieved, that induced Louis to appear on a
field where laurels were so easily gained. He is also said
to have been fond of undertaking sieges, and to have well
understood that department in the science of war; but he
seldom invested a town in person, without being absolutely certain of taking it. His minister, Louvois, prepared
all things so effectually—the troops were so well equipped,
and Vauban, who conducted most of the sieges, was so
great a master in fortification, that the King's glory was
always safe, and never more so than at the siege of Besançon.

Franche Comté being thus speedily reduced, the King
of France despatched the troops which had achieved its
conquest to reinforce his army under the Prince of Condé
in Flanders.   Still, the French forces were so much
divided, that, even after this accession, they did not there
exceed 50,000 men, while the allies, consisting of Spaniards, Imperialists, and Dutch, all commanded by the
Prince of Orange, amounted to at least 70,000, of whom
about 15,000 were Spaniards.[1] Those jealousies, however,
which existed among the Spanish troops and their old
enemies the Dutch, as also the frequent differences which
arose between the Prince of Orange and the Count de
Monterey, governor of the Netherlands, prevented the
allied army from executing any project with the success
which might have been anticipated from its numerical superiority.

The Prince of Orange, indeed, had the nominal command, but his plans were often counteracted by the Spanish and Austrian generals, who, being responsible to
their sovereigns, wished every thing to be regulated by a

[1] Beaurain, *Campagne de Condé en 1774.*

majority in a council of war. In consequence, the allies remained inactive during a great part of the summer, in their quarters at Brussels, Louvain, and Mechline. Monterey and the Prince of Orange earnestly pressed the Austrian General, Count Souches, to pass the Meuse along with them, but it was only after long persuasion, and many councils of war, that this commander could be induced to cross that river at Namur. The allies then advanced in a body towards the French camp at Pieton in Hainault, which had been strongly fortified by Condé, whose chief object in this campaign was to protect the frontiers of France, and preserve the recent acquisitions made in Flanders during the previous war in 1667.[1]

The confederates were baffled in all their attempts to penetrate into France, and Condé long avoided that general engagement to which they endeavoured to force him. The Prince of Orange being at length satisfied that there was no way of bringing on a battle but by the siege of some fortress, which it might be thought of importance for the enemy to relieve, determined to invest Tournay, and with this design marched towards Seneff, on the borders between Hainault and Brabant. His army was in three divisions—the Germans leading the van—the Dutch forming the main body—and the Spaniards the rear—all protected by a rear-guard of 4000 cavalry, under the Prince de Vaudemont. Condé observing their march, as they deployed through a narrow defile in the vicinity of Seneff, judged that the opportunity which he had so long watched, of assailing them with advantage, had at length arrived. Having waited till the vanguard and centre had crossed the narrow passes, he attacked the rear just as it entered them. The Spaniards were quickly thrown into confusion, and a great part of their artillery and baggage, with many prisoners,

[1] Beaurain, *Campagne de Condé.*

was taken. The Prince of Orange, who had somewhat incautiously exposed his army to this attack, amply
compensated for his imprudence, by his subsequent conduct. On receiving notice of the assault, he had sent
back with all promptitude, three squadrons to support
his rear; but the Spanish troops, already broken, soon
brought the Dutch into disorder, and the French pursu-
ing their success with vigour, cut this reinforcement to
pieces. Had the Prince of Condé been content with this
advantage, he would have gained an incontestable claim
to a victory, but, lured on by the hopes of a still more
complete success, he advanced till he encountered the
whole army of the Prince of Orange returning to the succour of the fugitives. One of the fiercest and most obstinate engagements then commenced which had been fought
in the whole course of the war; and such was the impe-
tuosity of the charges made by the Prince of Orange, that
Condé, it is said, was obliged to employ greater efforts,
and to hazard his person more, than in any action where,
even during the heat of youth, he had commanded. The
combat was several times renewed, and, after sunset, it
was continued by the light of the moon. At length, the
allies were obliged to abandon their positions; but they
continued their march in good order towards Arras, and
the French, at the same time, returned to their camp at
Pieton. The slaughter on both sides was great, but, by
most accounts, the loss of the allies exceeded that of the
French.[1] Condé bore testimony to the conduct of his

---

[1] The accounts given of the results of this action are very different. Sir William Temple says, that when darkness at length
parted the armies, the French retired to their former quarters, and
next morning the confederates occupied the positions which they
had designed to take up when they commenced their march the day
before. Reboulet, on the other hand (*Hist. de Louis XIV.*) asserts
that the allies left the field of battle before midnight, and retreated under the cannon of Arras, instead of encamping between

youthful rival during this action, by declaring that the
Prince of Orange had acted in all respects like an experienced captain, except in venturing his life like a young
soldier.

After the battle of Seneff, the allies abandoned all
thoughts of an invasion of the French frontiers; yet, in
order to give an appearance of superiority to the confederates, and to bring the French to a new engagement, the
Prince of Orange next invested Oudenarde. But the Imperial generals not being disposed to hazard a battle, he
raised the siege on the approach of the Prince of Condé.
Before the close of the campaign, however, he took Grave,

Marimont and Bains as they had proposed. Beaurain says both
parties quitted the last scene of action nearly at the same moment,
but that the victory was due to the French, as the allies had been
attacked successfully all along their line of march. Temple states
the loss on each side at six or seven thousand men. De Quincy
and Reboulet estimate the French loss at this number; but rate
that of the allies as high as 17,000; and the Marquis de Feuquiere nearly at the same amount. Captain Carleton, who was
present at the battle accompanied by some English volunteers, and
was posted in the rear along with the Spaniards, says that 18,000
were slain on each side: The French quitted the field first, and
the confederates in two hours followed their example. " Though
common vogue," he adds, " has given this engagement the name of a
battle, in my weak opinion it might rather deserve that of a confused skirmish—all things having been forcibly carried on, without
regularity or even design enough to allow it a higher denomina-
tion" (*Memoirs*). It certainly was not what the French call *batailes*
rangées, having been a series of attacks by the French along the
marching-line of the confederates. " Je le mets," says the Marquis
de Feuquiere, " au nombre des combats, et non des batailles ; parce
que les armées n'eurent jamais assez de terrain pour se mettre en
bataille, que les fronts par lesquels on combattit furent toujours
fort petits, et qu' à proprement parler, l'action de Senef se passa
contre la colonne presque entière de l'armée ennemie qui marchoit,
et non pas contre une armée qui se fût mise en disposition de com-
battre." (*Mémoires*, c. 80.)

the only town of importance which remained to the French in any of the United Provinces. After this event, the allied armies in the Netherlands broke up for the season, with mutual reproaches and great discontent on all sides. The Prince of Orange, indeed, was so disgusted with the conduct of the Imperialists, and of their general Count Souches, that he threatened to leave the army, but was at length prevailed on by the Count de Monterey to continue in the command. There seems little doubt that the Austrian general, who was at the head of 25,000 men, had on all occasions preferred the safety, and, what he supposed to be the interests of his master, to the common cause; and, to his irresolution and selfish policy, all the delays of the allies, and the many favourable opportunities they lost, were universally attributed.

The third French army, under Turenne, had assembled in Alsace, to oppose the Imperialists, whom he routed in all directions, and, after multiplied defeats, compelled them with disgrace to repass the Rhine.

Nothing of much importance was accomplished by the fourth French army, which had been collected in Roussillon. The Duke of San-German, who commanded the Spanish forces, having penetrated into that province, gained, near Baños, a considerable advantage over the enemy's troops, under the orders of Maréchal Schomberg, who had been in the French service since the peace between Spain and Portugal. The French lost upwards of 2000 men, and Maréchal Schomberg's son was taken prisoner.[1] Had the Duke of San-German followed up this victory, he might have driven the enemy entirely out of Roussillon. But intelligence having reached Madrid, about this time, of the revolt at Messina, the Duke received orders to spare his troops, in order that they might be sent to Sicily. In compliance with this in-

[1] Ortiz, *Compend. Cronol.*

junction, the Spanish General retired into Catalonia, and large bands of his soldiers having been embarked on this destination, he was obliged to remain merely on the defensive, with the diminished force which was now left under his command.

This revolt of Messina greatly alarmed the Court of Madrid, and, towards the close of the present year, occupied its whole attention. The avarice and oppression of the Spanish Government, which had occasioned the revolution of Portugal, and the commotions at Naples in the time of Masaniello, produced also the insurrection at Messina. That city was distinguished from the other towns of Sicily by a government of its own, which resembled an independent republic rather than a municipality. It had a Senate chosen from the citizens, and the Spanish Governor, who was styled the *Estratico*, exercised over it a very limited authority. This liberal form of administration had secured to Messina a degree of prosperity, such as was rarely exemplified in the territories ruled by the House of Austria. But though the city had been long distinguished for loyalty, and had maintained its fidelity during the tumults which agitated Naples and Palermo in 1647, the Spaniards, unfortunately, entertained some degree of jealousy at its flourishing condition, which they foresaw would afford an alluring example of the blessings of independence to neighbouring states, whose privileges were more restricted.

Luis de Hoyo, the Spanish Governor of Messina, had been bred up in the political school of the Count d'Oñate, and had served during the commotions of Naples under that cruel and crafty Viceroy.[1] This governor, or *Estratico*, as he was styled by the Spaniards, conceived, soon after

[1] Lancina, *Historia de las Revoluciones del Senado de Messina,* lib. i.

his appointment, the design of overthrowing the power of the Senate, and rendering the Spanish authority absolute.[1] With this view, he associated to himself the lowest rabble in Messina; and, availing himself of the distresses occasioned by a scarcity of provisions, which was at that time severely felt, he instigated the mob against the senatorial order, and all the more respectable class of citizens. The houses of the nobility were burned, and a species of revolution effected, which deprived the citizens of most of their privileges, and placed the supreme power in the hands of the Vice-regent of Spain. Then arose in the city the two factions of the Merli[2] and the Malvizzi, the former of whom, consisting of the rabble, and a very few leaders from the higher ranks, supported the royal prerogative, while the latter defended, or wished to restore, the ancient privileges and immunities of the Senate and city. The Prince de Ligne, who was at that time Viceroy of Sicily, was uncertain what part to take; but at length, on arriving at Messina, he not only declared against the Governor, but expelled him from the city, and restored the exiled nobility.[3] The obnoxious Luis de Hoyo was succeeded by Diego de Soria, Marques of Crespano, who was received with much joy and congratulation by the Senate, and their followers the Malvizzi. This new governor affected for a time to hold the ba-

[1] The Spanish and Italian authors differ considerably in their details of the revolt of Messina, particularly in what relates to the conduct of the Estratico and Viceroy. Of all the Italian writers, Brusoni is the fullest on the topic of the insurrection at Messina. The huge Spanish folio of Lancina, dedicated to Charles II, and published in 1692, is entirely devoted to that subject.

[2] They so styled themselves, because a blackbird was the crest in the arms of Luis de Hoyo. Lancina, *Revol. del Senado de Messina*, lib. iii.

[3] Brusoni, *Hist. d'Italia*, lib. xxxix.

lance between the opposite factions of the Merli and Malvizzi.[1]   But it soon appeared, that he was imbued with the political maxims of his predecessor, and that he intended, by exciting divisions among the citizens, to arrogate the sole authority to himself,—a design which the people, on good grounds, believed to be not unacceptable either to the Viceroy or Court of Madrid.   Crespano, in order to obtain possession of the persons of the senators, sent for them to the palace, on pretence of consulting them concerning some affairs of importance. But as soon as they arrived and had entered its walls, the gates were closed on them.   This stratagem, however, had not been contrived with such secrecy but that the Malvizzi faction conceived some suspicion of the treacherous design. They had followed the senators to the palace in vast numbers, and rose in tumult when they found that they were arrested.[2]   Nor were they appeased by obtaining the freedom of the prisoners.   They attacked Crespano and the Spanish garrison, who were obliged to shut themselves up in the palace, which was of great strength, and in the fortresses by which Messina is surrounded.   The Viceroy (now the Marques of Bayona), who had approached the town, apparently with conciliatory views, was not permitted by the citizens to enter it.   After much fighting and subsequent negotiation, the palace and some of the fortresses surrendered, and the obnoxious governor was obliged to fly for safety to Palermo.[3]

The Queen-regent, instigated, it is supposed, by Luis de Hoyo, who, though disgraced in Sicily, still retained some influence in Spain, refused, at first, to listen to the complaints of the deputies whom the inhabitants of Mes-

---

[1] Lancina, *Revoluciones*, lib. iii.
[2] Reboulet, *Hist. de Louis XIV.* t. ii.
[3] Id. and Brusoni, *Hist. d'Italia.*

sina had sent to Madrid, in order to claim a redress of grievances, and the preservation of their ancient privileges.[1]
But being now alarmed lest the other towns in the island
should follow the example of Messina, she weakly granted to the citizens all that they had previously required.
This concession, however, now came too late. Of the
two popular factions into which the town was at this time
divided, that called the Merli wished, indeed, to accept
the offers made by the Spanish Court: but the more
powerful Malvizzi, headed by Caffaro, a son of one of the
senators, having prevailed, it was resolved to place the
city under the protection of France, and to demand succour from that kingdom.[2] Deputies were accordingly
despatched to Mareschal d'Estrées, ambassador from
Louis XIV. to the Vatican, offering that monarch possession of Messina, and the sovereignty of Sicily. These
envoys being directed by him to proceed to France, soon
afterwards arrived in Paris, and there laid their case before the King and his advisers. Various opinions were
entertained on the subject in the French counsels. Some,
mindful of the Sicilian Vespers, and of ancient national
antipathies, dissuaded all interposition in the affairs of
the island. But the proposals and offers of the deputation were ultimately accepted.[3]

Meanwhile the Viceroy of Sicily, supported by the
troops which had been detached from the army of the
Duke of San-German in Catalonia, blockaded Messina,
both by sea and land ; and, before the expected foreign assistance could arrive, he had nearly obliged it to capitulate for want of provisions. At length, however, a French
fleet, under Valbelle, loaded with grain, and bearing also
some troops and ammunition, entered the harbour in spite
of the blockade.[4] The French commander refused, how-

[1] Brusoni, c. 41. [2] Desormeaux, *Abregé Chronol.*
[3] Giannone, *Histor. de Nap.* lib. xxxix. c. 3. [4] Id.

ever, to co-operate with the citizens of Messina, till they had placed the principal posts in his hands, and formally acknowledged allegiance to the French monarch. These conditions being complied with, he joined them in an attack on the Spanish lines, which proved completely successful, and relieved Messina, for a time, from the blockade of its former masters. A more powerful succour, both in troops and provisions, under the Duke de Vivonne, brother of Madame Montespan, and the celebrated naval officer Du Quesne, subsequently appeared before Messina. The Spanish admiral La Cueva (afterwards Duke of Albuquerque), though commanding a superior squadron, was defeated, without much resistance, and the French fleet, in consequence, entered the harbour of Messina.[1] The Queen-regent, indignant at his pusilanimity and bad success, ordered him, with several of his principal officers, to be laid under arrest; he was confined for some time afterwards in the fortress of Gaeta, and the Marques of Montesarchio was appointed in his room.[2] But this severity did not restore courage either to the Spanish soldiers

[1] Boileau addressed two letters to the Duke de Vivonne, " Sur son Entrée dans le Fare de Messine," written as from the Elysian fields, in name of Balzac and Voiture, in which he has happily imitated the hyperboles and antitheses of these celebrated *Bel Esprits* of the preceding reign. Balzac says, " Vous avez redonné le pain à une ville qui a accoutumé de le fournir à toutes les autres. Vous avez nourri la mere nourrice de l'Italie. * * * Sans châtier la mer, comme Xerxes, vous l'avez rendue disciplinable. Vous avez plus fait encore,—vous avez rendu l'Espagnol humble." Voiture writes in a tone somewhat more familiar. " Il est venu ici un bon nombre d'Espagnols qui y étoient et qui nous en ont appris le détail. Je ne sais pas pourquoi on veut faire passer les gens de leur nation pour fanfarons. Ce sont, je vous assure, de fort bonnes gens; et le Roi, depuis quelque tems, nous les envoie ici fort humbles et fort honnêtes. A voir de quel air vous courez la mer Méditeranée, il semble qu'elle vous appartienne toute entière."

[2] Giannone, lib. xxxix. c. 3. Lancina says in the fortress of Castel-Uovo at Naples.

or sailors. Those commanders who were sent to replace
La Cueva, were still more unfortunate than their predecessor. The provinces, and other towns in the island,
had not yet declared in favour of the French; but in the
course of this season, Du Quesne and the Duke de Vivonne undertook at once the defence of Messina, and the
conquest of the remainder of the island. Augousta was
taken, Palermo and Syracuse were threatened, and the
whole coast of Sicily kept in constant alarm.

Being now fully convinced that her vessels could not
hold the sea against the French, the Queen-regent, on
payment of a certain sum, obtained the promise of a fleet,
for six months, from Holland, in order to drive them from
the coasts of Sicily and the Mediterranean. The Prince
of Orange, having devoted his attention chiefly to the
army, there had not been, since the death of De Witt,
the same activity as formerly in the naval-yards and arsenals of Holland. A fleet, however, was at length equipped, and placed under the command of De Ruyter, who,
at that time, was accounted the greatest naval officer in
Europe. Having anchored at Cadiz in 1675, he there
received some title of Spanish dignity, with other distinctions, on which he set little value. But while the Queen-
regent loaded him with superfluous honours, she failed in
fulfilling all the essential articles of her agreement with
the Dutch. The Spanish vessels which were joined to
his own force, were so worn out, that they were nearly
unfit for service, and the Spaniards treated him with such
haughtiness, and gave him such disgust, particularly by
compelling him to lower his flag before that of their own
admiral, that he wished most earnestly to return to his
own country. Having sailed from Cadiz to Palermo, the
Viceroy of Sicily proposed to him that he should cruise
about, in order to prevent farther supplies from entering
Messina. While engaged in this service, he fell in with

the French fleet, which he brought to action near the
Island of Stromboli. Du Quesne, who commanded it,
was an antagonist in every way worthy of De Ruyter,
being the most skilful and distinguished naval officer who
had as yet appeared in the French service. The fight,
which was obstinately contested for twelve hours, terminated only with night, and at the conclusion, it was doubtful which side was best entitled to claim the victory.
Soon after this action, the Dutch Admiral was joined by
nine Spanish ships, under the Prince of Montesarchio.
But even with this accession, it was not considered prudent to renew the combat. The combined fleet withdrew
to the neighbourhood of Melazzo, and, in consequence of
its position on that coast, Du Quesne was unable to enter
the harbour of Messina by the old tower called the Pha-
ros, and, therefore, making a wide circuit of the whole
island, he at length succeeded in getting in by the straits
to the south.

In consequence of having lost some vessels during a
storm in the Straits of Messina, and other charges preferred against him by the Viceroy of Sicily, the Spanish
Admiral was recalled, and sent a prisoner to the Castle
of Pampeluna. He was succeeded by Don Diego de
Ibarra, an old and experienced officer, who immediately
assumed the command at Palermo.[1]

About three months after the action near Stromboli,
De Ruyter, having received a prolongation of his command, sailed along with the Spanish Admiral for Augousta, and presented himself before that town in the design
of attacking it by sea, while the Viceroy of Sicily besieged it by land. Du Quesne, who still remained at
Messina, was no sooner informed of this project, than he
set sail for Augousta, in order to frustrate the plans of
his rival. When De Ruyter was aware of his approach,

[1] Lancina, *Revoluciones de Messina*, lib. viii.

he relinquished his attack on the town, and advanced with
his whole fleet to meet him.   The Dutch Admiral led
the van in person, and commenced the action with a fury
which astonished his Spanish allies.   But he was unfortunately wounded in both legs by a cannon-ball, in less
than an hour after the battle began.   He continued, however, to give his orders, and the fight was kept up, under
his directions, till night put an end to the conflict.   As
in the former naval engagement between these two distinguished seamen, both parties claimed the advantage.
The French squadron was driven off, and chased for nearly
an hour,[1] but it ultimately gained its main object of relieving Augousta ;[2] for the allied fleet, being so broken and
shattered that it could no longer continue offensive operations against that town, sailed to refit at Syracuse, where
De Ruyter died of his wounds, ten days after the combat
in which they had been received.

In consequence of this loss, the command was taken by
the Dutch Admiral Van-Häen, who now sailed to Palermo, where, while he was occupied in repairing his ships,
and recruiting their respective crews, Du Quesne, accompanied by the Duke de Vivonne, arrived with twenty-
eight men-of-war, twenty-five gallies, and nine fireships,
before the harbour.   On their advance, the combined
fleets of Spain and Holland, consisting of twenty-nine
war-ships, nineteen gallies, and four fireships, formed in a
crescent at the entrance to the port,—covered on the left
by the batteries on the mole, and protected on the right
by the bastions of the town.   In this strong position, after being reconnoitred three or four days by the French,
they were at length attacked.   The combined squadron
fought with great spirit, till the Spanish Vice-Admiral
cut out of the line and ran ashore, to avoid being burned

[1] Richer, *Vie de Ruyter.*
[2] Reboulet, *Hist. de Louis XIV.* t. ii.

by a fireship. The French improved this advantage, and having the wind in their favour, bore down on the Dutch, and set one of their largest ships on fire. The flames speedily communicated to two others, on which, after destroying their own fireships, the Dutch vessels retired within the port. But even there they were not in safety. Four French fireships being driven by the gales into the harbour of Palermo, set fire to eight sail which had sought refuge within its shelter. Most of these having blown up, their explosion destroyed the port of Palermo, and a number of houses which were built in the vicinity. On the whole, the combined squadron lost seven men of war, six gallies, and seven fireships. Not fewer than 5000 sailors were killed or drowned, and among the slain were the Dutch Admiral Van-Haën,[1] and the Spanish Admiral Ibarra.

Such was now the want of naval talent among the Spanish grandees, that after Ibarra's death the Queen was obliged to confer on a land officer, named Fernando Carriglio, the command of the miserable remains of her marine. Montesarchio, however, after being detained for some time at Pampeluna, succeeded in justifying himself from the charges of the Viceroy of Sicily, and was, in consequence, reinstated in his former command.

Nor were the Spaniards more fortunate by land, in Sicily, than they had been on the seas by which that island is surrounded. A Spanish army of 7000 men, under the Count de Buquoi, having attempted, about the time of these naval disasters, to invest Messina, was attacked by the Duke de Vivonne, and was totally routed, with the loss of its General, who was slain during the action.

It seems extraordinary that such a succession of victories did not secure to the French the complete and per-

[1] Richer, *Vies de Du Quesne et Ruyter.* *Universal History*, vol. xxi. 19. 1.

manent possession of Sicily. But the Duke de Vivonne, who was now nominated Viceroy of the island, though a commander of some spirit and courage in the field, was totally deficient in talents for civil government.[1] Presuming on the favour enjoyed by his sister, Madame de Montespan, he studied only the means of speedily enriching himself, and in his avidity plundered the people whom he should have protected. The insolence of the French soldiery, and their dissolute habits, which their General was at no pains to repress, completely alienated the minds of the inhabitants of Messina, and even led them to regret their former government. Had the French marched their troops to Palermo immediately after their great naval victory and the defeat of Buquoy, they might probably have obtained possession of that city; but the commotions which arose in Messina, and the conspiracies which were daily discovered, rendered it unsafe to withdraw any of their forces. Their acquisitions were thus confined to Messina, Augousta, and a few unimportant places on the coast, while the Spaniards were still enabled to preserve their footing in the other parts of the island. The Dutch, however, by retiring to their own harbours with the wreck of their fleet, left the French undisputed masters of the shores of Sicily and the Mediterranean.

In the Netherlands, meanwhile, the campaign of 1675 proved less unfortunate for the allies than that by which it had been preceded. But nothing decisive or even important was achieved on either part. It was later of commencing on the French side than usual, in consequence of some

---

[1] " Cette Révolte," says the Marquis de Feuquiere, " auroit été suivie de la perte entiere de ce royaume pour les Espagnols, si le commandement de l'armée du Roi en ce pays-là avoit été commis à un autre homme que le Maréchal de Vivonne, dont la pesanteur et la paresse naturelle donna le tems aux Espagnols, et à leurs alliés, de pourvoir à la conservation du reste de l'Isle." (Mémoires, c. 50.)

commotions in Guyenne and Brittany, which drew many
of their forces into these quarters. As soon, however, as
the tumults were appeased, every imaginable effort was
employed in France to prepare for the campaign. Louis
intended this year to make an inroad into the Spanish
Netherlands with the flower of his troops, and with all
possible vigour and energy. Condé was nominated to the
supreme command, and the King affected to serve under
him as a volunteer in the army. The first important
operation was the siege of Limbourg, which was invested with a part of the army, while Louis lay encamped with the remainder in the position most favourable for opposing any attempts which might be made
to relieve it by the Prince of Orange, who was then
on his march for that purpose. After a brief and feeble
resistance, Limbourg was taken before the Prince could
approach it. All his operations at this time were much
retarded by the slow and uncertain marches of the German horse, and the weakness and disorder of the Spanish
infantry.[1]

. After the capture of Limbourg, the French and the
confederate armies in Flanders remained in a great measure inactive. Neither party dared to besiege any place
of strength, while the other was in waiting to relieve it;
and neither army was willing, without some peculiarly
favourable circumstances, to hazard a general engagement,
which might be followed by the total loss of Flanders, if
victory should declare for the French, and by an invasion
of France in the event of its king being defeated. Louis,
who had no great perseverance, and did not relish a military life except when bearing all before him, returned to
Versailles early in the season, and nothing memorable
occurred in the Low Countries after his departure.

The campaign of 1676 was somewhat more fertile in

[1] Temple's *Memoirs*, part ii. c. 1.

important events. The ministers of the King of France, by preparing magazines during the winter, enabled him to take the field in Flanders at the head of 50,000 men, early in spring, and before forage could be found in the open country. On the other hand, the want of arrangement, and deficiency of pecuniary supplies among the Spaniards, rendered their troops in Flanders incapable of acting by themselves, on any sudden attack by the enemy, or of supplying with provisions, on their march, those Dutch or German troops which might come to their assistance. Their towns, now ill fortified, and worse garrisoned, were capable of opposing but a feeble resistance to the formidable army which Louis commanded in person. It was besides uncertain, where he might first direct his attack; and the Duke of Villahermosa, who was the successor of the Count de Monterey in the government of the Netherlands, had not sufficient forces to station in every quarter, or sufficient activity to march those he possessed, with due celerity, to the relief of the besieged fortresses. Before any of the confederates were in the field, the King of France laid siege to Condé, which he took by storm in five days. He then crossed the Scheldt, and encamped at Sebourg, whence he detached his brother, the Duke of Orleans, to besiege Bouchain, a small but strong fortress, and, from its situation, of much importance for the defence of the Spanish Netherlands. Meanwhile, Louis posted himself so advantageously with his main army, as to compel the confederates either to give up all attempts to relieve Bouchain, or to fight at great disadvantage. Struggling with the difficulties of the season, and the want of provisions, the Prince of Orange came in sight of the French army, which was drawn up to receive him, in the expectation of a general engagement. In spite of his inferiority of numbers, and disadvantages of position, the Prince was inclined to ha-

zard a battle, but he was prevented by the Duke of Villahermosa, who foresaw that a defeat, of which there was
imminent risk, would be followed by the loss of the whole
of Flanders.   Thus the activity of the Prince of Orange
served no other purpose than to render him a spectator of
the surrender of Bouchain, which capitulated eight days
after it had been invested, and the two armies having
then faced each other for some time, withdrew as if by
mutual consent, to a greater distance.   Louis being disposed to rest contented, for this campaign, with the advantages he had so early and so easily obtained, retired
to Versailles, leaving the command of his army to Mareschal Schomberg.   After his departure, the Dutch and
Spaniards laid siege to Maestricht, which, at the time
when it had been last taken by the French, was accounted the strongest place on the frontiers, and since
they possessed it, had been still more strongly fortified,
with all the advantages that could be provided by art or
skill.   It was abundantly supplied with ammunition and
provisions, and was defended by a garrison of 7000 chosen men, under Calvo, an old Catalan officer, who had
been in the service of France ever since the rebellion of
his native province against the Spanish government, and
now commanded at Maestricht in the absence of the governor, Mareschal d'Estrades, who was then at Nimeguen.
The siege was carried on with great spirit, and with
many desperate assaults, by the Prince of Orange and the
Landgrave of Hesse, while the Duke of Villahermosa
was stationed in the vicinity, to watch the motions of the
main French army.   The Prince of Orange had hoped
to carry Maestricht before its approach, as it was at present
occupied, under Mareschal Schomberg, with the siege
of Aire.   But a severe sickness falling on the Prince's
army, weakened it more than all his assaults on the town.
The Germans came not up with the supplies they had

promised, and on the faith of which the siege had been undertaken. The Landgrave of Hesse, who was designed as governor of the place when it should be reduced, and who was ever at the head of the attacks, was wounded in one of them, and being forced to leave the camp, died at a castle in the neighbourhood. In consequence of these events, the united armies became disheartened, and the siege was prosecuted with less energy. Meanwhile, Schomberg, who had trusted to a vigorous defence by Maestricht, had taken Aire; and after the Prince's army had been weakened by sickness, and the casualties of the siege, he marched with all the French forces, through the heart of the Spanish Netherlands, to the relief of Maestricht. On his approach, a council of war, held in the Prince's camp, resolved that the siege should be immediately raised; and, with these operations, the campaign terminated in the Dutch and Spanish provinces. From this time the Prince of Orange, though himself sufficiently firm under misfortune, began to doubt of ultimate success in the war, foreseeing that the weakness of the Spanish forces, and uncertainty of the German counsels, which he had now so long experienced, could only lead to an unfortunate issue.[1] But those allies, particularly the Spaniards, who contributed so little to the success of the war, still urged its continuance. Even the Dutch, though their commerce languished, and though they were loaded with debts and taxes, were yet disposed to try whether another campaign might not procure more favourable terms of peace than they could at present expect, and secure for them a stronger frontier on the side of Flanders. The Prince of Orange, though not without his misgivings, being still prompted by motives of ambition, and inveterate animosity towards the King of France, endeavoured with all his influence to confirm them in this resolution.[2]

[1] Temple's *Memoirs*.   [2] Hume's *Hist. of England*.

The event, however, of the following campaign in 1677
by no means justified the hopes entertained by the Spaniards and the Dutch. Louis recommenced hostilities
before the usual season, by the siege of Valenciennes.
The capture in the preceding years of Condé and Bouchain, where he had formed large magazines, paved the
way for this enterprise. Valenciennes had been long celebrated in history for the sieges which it had sustained. It
was accounted one of the strongest places in the Spanish
Netherlands, and was at this time provided with every
thing necessary for a long resistance. The preparations,
too, of the French were on a scale that bespoke their anticipations of a protracted defence. But in consequence
of the judicious plans of Vauban, and his recommendation of an assault in the day-time, instead of the night
when attacks were usually made, and garrisons were of
course on the watch, the place was carried in a week
from the time when the French army had sat down before it.

After the capture of Valenciennes, the King of France
divided his forces. He himself, with one part, invested
Cambray, while the Duke of Orleans marched with the
other to the siege of St Omers. The Duke, however, had
no sooner opened the trenches before that town, than the
Prince of Orange, who knew by experience that it would
be in vain to await the majestic motions of the Spaniards, hastily assembled an army of 35,000 men, all in
the Dutch pay, and marched with as much expedition as
possible to its relief.[1] When Orleans heard of his approach, he set out to meet him with his whole troops, except a few which were left to guard the works that had
been raised before the besieged city. On his march, he
was joined by a considerable reinforcement under Mares-
chalLuxembourg. The two hostile armies met at Mont-

[1] Carleton's *Memoirs.*

Cassel, where an obstinate battle ensued, which, in consequence of the superior movements of Luxembourg, ended in the defeat of the Prince of Orange. He retreated in good order to Ypres; but the garrison of St Omers, discouraged by the result of this action, and seeing no farther prospect of relief, surrendered a few days subsequent to the engagement. The town of Cambray had already capitulated, and the citadel soon afterwards followed its example.

The loss of the three towns, which had been taken from the Spaniards during this campaign, with the former acquisitions of the French, laid Brabant and Flanders completely open to the incursions of the enemy, and left Spain only Namur and Mons as frontier fortresses. The remainder of the Austrian Netherlands consisted only of large open cities, from which no resistance could be hoped, and which would fall at once into the hands of the French, whenever they chose to occupy them. The Spaniards, however, were but little alarmed at a posture of affairs apparently so desperate. They had found, indeed, by experience, that their Dutch and German allies were unable to protect them; but they confidently trusted that England, whatever might be the present politics of its worthless king, would not ultimately permit its natural enemy to obtain such an acquisition as the whole Spanish Netherlands, which must inevitably lead to the subjugation of the Seven United Provinces. In this belief they were encouraged by Bernard de Salinas, their ambassador at the Court of London, who at this time most industriously fomented the alarm and agitation which now began to appear in the English Parliament, on account of the French successes both in Sicily and Flanders.[1] It was partly in consequence of his intrigues, that addresses were presented by both Houses to Charles II.

[1] Temple's *Memoirs.*

representing the danger to which the kingdom was exposed from the increasing power of France, and praying that his Majesty, by such alliances as he might think fit, should both secure his own territories and the Spanish Netherlands, and thereby allay the just apprehensions of his people. Charles, in the mean while, evaded these remonstrances, by replying in general terms, that he would use all those means for the preservation of Flanders which were consistent with the peace and safety of his dominions.[1]

The King of France, however, paid so much regard to the fear excited in England, of his intentions to make an entire conquest of Flanders, that he resolved to put a limit for this season to his progress. He accordingly dispersed his army, and having returned to Versailles, he wrote to assure the King of England, that he had no design of conquering Flanders—that he was only desirous to procure a lasting peace, and that, notwithstanding the numerous forces he had at present on foot, and the successes he had recently obtained, he was willing to agree to a general truce, provided his allies the Swedes would also consent to it.[2]

During the rapid progress of the French arms in Flanders, the misfortunes of Spain had accumulated in other quarters. The Duke of San-German had been so much weakened by the loss of those troops which he was obliged to despatch to Sicily, that he could no longer make head against the French on the frontiers of Catalonia. Mareschal Schomberg having been recalled from that province in order to assume the command in Flanders, was succeeded by the Duke de Navailles, who found himself at the head of 15,000 men. The Spaniards, at his approach, retired to Girona, and durst not venture on a general engagement, though their Miquelets frequently ha-

[1] Hume's *Hist. of England*, c. 66.   [2] Temple's *Memoirs*.

rassed the French army, by cutting off their detached corps, and intercepting their convoys.

In former times, while the arms of Spain were unsuccessful, the nation had been often consoled by the triumphs of their German allies. But during the late campaigns 'in Alsace and the Upper Rhine, which were the theatres of war between the French and Austrians, there was little subject of congratulation for the Spaniards. The caution of Montecuculi, and the genius of Turenne, were for some time so nicely balanced, that the contest produced no permanent advantage on either side. After the retreat, however, and subsequent retirement of Montecuculi, the war began to assume a new aspect. The Swedes, co-operating in favour of France, drew the troops of Brandenburgh and Munster to the north of Germany, and the French Generals were thus enabled to gain a complete ascendency on the Rhine.

CHAPTER IV.

RISE AND FALL OF VALENZUELA.

Ambition this shall tempt to rise,
 Then whirl the wretch from high,
To bitter Scorn a sacrifice,
 And grinning Infamy.

GRAY's *Eton College.*

AMIDST those disasters by which Spain was afflicted and overwhelmed in almost every quarter of the globe, its young King, having reached the age of fifteen, took possession of the government, as had been appointed by the testament of his father. His subjects felt the highest satisfaction at the termination of his minority, as they hoped for a favourable change in the administration, by a diminution in the influence of the unpopular Queen-regent. Though always feeble in bodily health, Charles had been a child of precocious intellect : But his mother, in order that she might the longer possess the regal authority, systematically neglected his education, and did all in her power to prevent him from having a turn towards ought but amusements and diversions. A few days after he became of age, the Queen presented to him, for signature an act, declaring that, on account of his tender years and want of experience, he left the government to her and the council which had assisted her during his minority : but he refused to subscribe this document, saying, with much spirit, that he hoped God who had made him a King, would enable him to become the Father of his people. Unfortunately, however, none of his future words or actions corresponded to this commencement; and he early betrayed the most manifest imbecility in all transactions. It was reported and believed, though the rumour seems almost incredible, that the rapid change to the worse which took place in his mind and disposition, had been produced by some noxious ingredients which his mother mixed with his chocolate; and it was supposed that the Marchioness de Los Velez, who had been his governess in infancy, alluded to this diabolical act, when she cautioned him to beware of one who, from her fondness of being a queen, might possibly forget that she was a mother.[1]

Don John, who was now weary of his residence at Saragossa, and longed to revisit the capital, had always looked forward to the King's majority as the time when he might possibly deprive the Queen-regent of power, and confine her to a monastery. Notwithstanding his unpopular partition of the government with her Majesty, Don John still continued the favourite alike of the grandees and people, who were all zealously attached to his interests. Both the preceptor and confessor of the young King betrayed the interests of the Regent, to whom they were indebted for their appointments, and urged to their sovereign the expediency of committing the reins of government to his brother.[2] Whilst Don John awaited with impatience at Saragossa the effect of his intrigues, he received an order from the Regent to embark for Sicily, in order to assume the command in that island, and to wrest Messina, if possible, from the hands of the French. This appointment he haughtily and peremptorily refused, and the very day on which the King assumed the government, he presented himself at court. His sudden and unexpected appearance seemed to announce the disgrace

[1] *Universal History*, vol. xxi. book 19. c. 1.
[2] Ortiz, *Compend.* t. vi. lib. 21. c. 3.

and exile of the Queen. But she was not wanting in presence of mind at this dangerous crisis. Summoning all her resolution, she immediately sought the King: she shed many tears, and uniting the most tender blandishments to her marks of overwhelming grief, she prevailed over her formidable enemy. The young monarch, influenced partly by the entreaties of his mother, and partly by his dread of the ambition of Don John, whose frequent demands of the title of Infant led him to believe that he aimed at the crown,[1] issued a peremptory order that he should return immediately to Saragossa. Don John received this mandate, with much surprise and mortification, at the very moment when he was accepting the congratulations of his friends and the court; and, in consequence of it, he was obliged to depart precipitately from Madrid. His partizans, the Count of Monterey, Francisco Ramos, the King's preceptor, and Father Montenegro, his confessor, were involved in Don John's disgrace, and banished from the capital.[2]

The Queen might now have long preserved her authority, had she acted with ordinary prudence and discretion. But before this period she had become totally devoted to a favourite equally obnoxious, and still more unworthy than the Father Nithard. It was said at the time, that the Count of Monterey, second son of Luis de Haro, might have been, (if he had chosen), both minister and favourite. But, having declined some advances which were made to him by the Queen, she fixed her regard on an inferior and less deserving object. Fernando Valenzuela, who had now, in fact, become prime minister of Spain, was a low though dexterous adventurer from the kingdom of Grenada. In early youth he had accompanied, as a page, the Duke d'Infantado when Spanish ambassa-

[1] Ortiz, *Compend. Cronol.* t. vi. lib. 21. c. 3.
[2] Desormeaux, *Abregé Chronol.*

dor at Rome, and on his return was recompensed with the order of St Iago. After the death of his patron, who left him no permanent provision, he was reduced to great difficulties, and was obliged to support himself by those various devices to which unprincipled men, who are possessed of some talents and artifice, frequently resort. His handsome figure—his prepossessing manners, and his turn for poetry, procured him a few friends. He was at length introduced by one of them to Father Nithard, to whose interests he entirely and submissively devoted himself. The Jesuit, perceiving that he was master of considerable address, and finding that his secrecy could be relied on, confided to him the management of some state affairs, and particularly employed him as a spy on the proceedings of Don John and his party. He soon became so useful to his powerful patron, that Nithard gave him at all times free access to the palace, in order that he might have constant opportunities of communicating the success of the various negotiations with which he was entrusted.

Valenzuela was no sooner introduced into the palace, than he contrived to become acquainted with all the secrets and mysteries of the court. Among other matters, he learned that Donna Eugenia, one of the Queen's German attendants, was chiefly possessed of the favour and confidence of her mistress. He soon took means to be remarked by this lady of the household, and had not long obtained her acquaintance, when he received her hand in marriage, by permission of the Queen, who had already observed and been much pleased with Valenzuela. She even conferred on him the post of one of her equerries; and as the dissensions between her Majesty and Don John were at this time daily augmenting, he omitted nothing which could render him in any way serviceable to his royal mistress. She was highly pleased with his zeal, and felt so much indebted to him for his exertions, that she was ever bestowing on him new proofs of her regard.[1]

After the banishment of Nithard, though the Marques d'Aytona was the public and ostensible minister of the Queen, she selected Valenzuela as the person to be entrusted with her most private and confidential concerns. She, accordingly, commanded Donna Eugenia to bring her husband secretly to the royal apartments in the evening, that she might speak with him alone. The first time he was introduced into the chamber of the Queen, the night was far advanced. Instead of a bundle of papers, he carried a sort of buckler in his hand, which at that time was usually borne in Spain, by those who expected to encounter perils or adventures. His hair, which was uncommonly fine, was tied up with a ribbon ; and in the adjustment of his dress he had omitted nothing which might captivate the fancy of the Queen who, on her part, appeared in an elegant deshabille, which she believed to be more becoming than the widow's garb, resembling the dress of a nun, which she usually wore. Valenzuela threw himself at her feet, and, after having thanked her for the distinguished honour she had conferred on him, vowed that the remainder of his life should be faithfully devoted to her service.

The graceful person, agreeable manners, and lively conversation of Valenzuela, improved those favourable sentiments which his zeal and fidelity had originally inspired. From the period of this first interview, scarcely an evening passed that he did not come privately to the Regent's apartments. Donna Eugenia, however, for the sake of decorum, and to avoid scandal, remained during the whole interview. On these occasions Valenzuela informed the Queen concerning the most secret transactions in the court and city, particularly with regard to

---

[1] Desormeaux, *Abregé Chronol.*

the designs of Don John, and the movements of those grandees who were supposed to·be attached to his interests. The Queen was thus apprized of all the secret machinations in the capital. But as she made no inquiries at any one but Valenzuela, and as the retired life she·led appeared to preclude her from obtaining such intelligence, it was commonly said that a *duendo* or familiar Spirit favoured her with these communications; and when it came to be at length discovered that it was Valenzuela who carried to her all this information, he was nicknamed the Queen's *duendo*.[1]

Valenzuela was now known as the regent's favourite, and was generally suspected to be her lover. Her attachment to him daily increased, and was more openly declared. She appeared with him occasionally in public. He wrote, professedly for her entertainment, some dramatic pieces, which were not without merit, and were represented in the theatre at the palace. He was already flattered, as the distributers of royal favours are wont to·be, and the courtiers used every effort to obtain his good graces, as the surest and quickest access to preferment. With rapid steps he rose to the highest employments in the realm. He was appointed master of the horse, and was elevated to the rank of a grandee of the first class, with the title of Marques de Villa Sierra. The apartments in the palace, formerly occupied by the Prince Balthazar, were allotted to him, and he was finally declared·the ostensible prime minister of the state.

But though a man of lively parts and of some accomplishments, Valenzuela neither possessed the judgment nor acquirements requisite for the difficult situation in which he was placed; and while he soon became as absolute as Father Nithard, he was at the same time not less hated. The Grandees were disgusted at finding themselves com-

[1] Ibid.

pelled to apply to a needy adventurer as their channel to honours and emoluments which they regarded as their birthright : The presidents of the different boards were particularly offended at an order from her Majesty, that they should attend on the minister whenever required by him ; and the lower orders, who are always jealous of the promotion of any one from their own ranks, regarded him with contempt and detestation. Madrid resounded with pasquinades and satires, in which the new minister and the Queen were treated with little ceremony ; and caricatures, expressive of the supposed passion of the Queen, and corrupt power of Valenzuela, were hung up, by night, on the walls of the palace, or in its immediate vicinity.

Nevertheless, the minister seems to have been anxious for popularity, and desirous, if possible, to ingratiate himself with his indignant countrymen. He did not, indeed, adopt any measures for restoring the strength and reputation of the Spanish monarchy or bringing its finances into order, for which he was altogether unqualified. But he projected a number of useful public works; and, among other edifices, he rebuilt the Plaça Mayor, the greater part of which had been consumed by fire. He also constructed, at the gate of Toledo, a bridge over the Mançanares, which cost half a million of ducats, and another over the same river near the Pardo, one of the king's hunting seats. By his order, the front of the royal palace at Madrid was completed, and the tower, which contained the apartments of the Queen, was raised to its proper height. During the administration of Valenzuela, the capital was likewise cheaply supplied with the necessaries of life, which had previously risen to an enormous price. He exhibited, also, a variety of spectacles and entertainments, for which the Spaniards, in those days, had almost as great a rage as the Romans towards the close of the Republic. But in these displays he often rendered himself odious and ridiculous by his puerile vanity, and he confirmed the imputations which had been cast on the Queen, by affecting the air of a successful lover as well as of a favourite minister. At the bull-fights, which he often exhibited, he was always dressed in black garments embroidered with silver, and carried dark plumes in his hat, as wearing half mourning because the Queen appeared in public in her widowed garb. As soon as he entered the square where the bull-fights were to be held, he was wont to approach under the royal balcony, to make his obeisance, and ask permission to engage in the combats (*Torear*). This request was invariably refused by the Queen, on account of the danger to which, if granted, it might have exposed him. On one of these occasions it was remarked, that he wore a scarf of black silk with the device embroidered in gold of an eagle gazing intently at the sun, and the presumptuous motto, *Tengo solo licencia*. Some days afterwards he appeared at the cane play (Juego de Cañas), a species of tournament derived from the Moors, bearing a buckler, on which was the ensign of an eagle armed with the thunder of Jupiter, and the same arrogant ill-timed motto. As there was no personal risk in this amusement, her Majesty always permitted him to display his dexterity and address, and he usually carried off from the young grandees who contended with him, the most valuable prizes, one of which, bestowed by the hand of the Queen, was a diamond hilted sword.[1]

In every action and amusement, this upstart minion exhibited all that presumption and pretence of which men who rise by fortune rather than merit are often so justly accused. His vanity, and design of casting the whole court into shade, were always apparent; while his rashness and

[1] Desormeaux, *Abregé Chronol.* Coxe's *Memoirs of Kings of House of Bourbon*, vol. i. sect. 2. *Mémoires de la Cour d'Espagne.*

conceit never allowed him for a moment to suppose, that any merit could equal the influence of his own personal accomplishments. In some respects he had a considerable resemblance to the favourite, Godoy, Prince of the Peace, who so grossly misgoverned Spain a century afterwards. Low birth, a handsome person, some specious exterior accomplishments, an overweening self-confidence, a flimsy patronage of literature, and utter ignorance of the real arts of government, constituted a striking similarity between these two worthless favourites of intriguing queens.

As soon as the king became of age, Valenzuela also assiduously strove to ingratiate himself with the young monarch, by forming pleasure parties for his amusement at Aranjuez, the Escurial, and other royal residences. One day, when the whole court was present at a chace which was held in the vicinity of the Escurial, the King, while aiming at a stag, accidentally wounded Valenzuela on the thigh. The Queen, uttering a shriek, immediately fell senseless into the arms of her attendants. The vehement emotion which she betrayed on this occasion, confirmed the suspicions which had been previously entertained by the public, concerning the nature of her attachment to this favourite.

When the royal household was formed, after the King had assumed the reins of government, Valenzuela, on his own authority, nominated all its officers, of whom the chief were the Admiral of Castile, the Dukes of Albuquerque and Medina Celi. He obtained few friends, however, by his appointments. Those who most earnestly solicited them from him, felt indignant that they should have owed them to his patronage; and he created many new enemies among others, whose claims were rejected, but who conceived themselves entitled to a preference.

Don John, as we have seen, had presented himself at Court on the majority of the King, but had been obliged

weak. Charles vowed that he would now burst the chain
which had been imposed on him; and though the Queen
kept him almost constantly in sight, lest he should be induced to listen to evil counsels, he left the palace one
night privately on foot, accompanied only by the Duke
of Medina Celi and two attendants, and betook himself
to Buenretiro. He thence forthwith despatched an order
to the Queen, that she should confine herself closely to the
palace, and he peremptorily refused all the earnest solicitations which she used to obtain an interview. He also
banished her obnoxious favourite Valenzuela from the capital, and with his own hand he addressed a letter to Don
John of Austria, inviting him to return to Court, in order that he might aid in re-establishing the affairs of the
monarchy.[1]

The news of the King's emancipation from the thraldom
of his mother, who was universally detested, were hailed with gladness at Madrid. On the following day, he
received valuable presents from the grandees, who all
waited on him. The populace flocked to Buenretiro, and
greeted him with acclamations of joy, and there were
general illuminations in the evening. Count Monterey,
who had quitted the government of the Netherlands,
and some other partizans of Don John, who had been
banished from Madrid on account of their adherence to his
faction, now returned to the Capital, and began to make
due preparations for his reception. They assembled a
band of troops, whom they despatched under command of
the Count of Monterey, to escort him in his progress;
and several of their number set out for Aragon, in order
to pay him their respects, and attend him on his journey.[2]

Don John, who was impatiently awaiting at Saragossa
the effects of his intrigues, had no sooner received the
letter from the King, and intelligence of the revolu-

[1] Ibid.   Leti, *Vita di Giovanni d'Austria.*   [2] Ibid.

tion, which had taken place, than he set out for Madrid. His progress was extremely slow, partly on account of the great concourse of people by whom he was attended, and partly in order to afford time for matters being in some degree arranged previously to his appearance at Court. He at length stopped near Guadalaxara, where he awaited the arrival of the Archbishop of Toledo, who was sent there by the King to adjust with him the conditions of his entrance into the capital. It was stipulated that the new regiment of guards which had been raised by the Queen should be sent to serve in Sicily,—that her Majesty should henceforth reside in one of the four cities assigned to her by the testament of the late King,—that the Admiral of Castile, and other adherents of Valenzuela, should be banished from Court,—and that Valenzuela himself should be arrested, and compelled to give an account of his past administration.[1] When he at length arrived, Don John was favourably received by the King at Buenretiro, though he could not accomplish his great object of obtaining the title of Infant, which, he supposed, might pave his way to the throne, in the event of Charles's demise without issue. The conditions arranged at Guadalaxara were scrupulously fulfilled. Her Majesty was ordered to reside in future at Toledo, and on no pretext to quit that city ; and the adherents of Don John who had been banished from court during the regency, were recalled.

The unfortunate Valenzuela, when exiled from Madrid, had sought refuge in the Escurial, by the express orders of the Queen. As soon as it was known that he was somewhere concealed among its extensive buildings, the King despatched a party of 300 horse, headed by Don Antonio de Toledo, son of the Duke of Alva, to arrest the fallen minister. On their arrival at the Escurial,

---

[1] Brusoni, *Hist. d'Italia*, lib. xlv.

Valenzuela was enjoying the pleasures of the chase in an
adjacent forest. But hearing the noise and clamour occasioned by the approach of cavalry, he returned forthwith to the Escurial, and hastened to the convent which
is included within its precincts. Having privately sought
the Prior, he briefly explained to him the danger to which
he was exposed, and begged to be conducted to some place
of security. The Prior, touched with his misfortunes,
concealed him in a niche formed in the wall of one of the
cells. As it was known, however, that he had retired into
the monastery, hardly a corner of it was exempted from
the scrutiny of Antonio de Toledo, and those by whom
he was accompanied. Several days had been consumed
in fruitless search, and Don Antonio was beginning to
suspect that Valenzuela had effected his escape, when, in
consequence of terror or long confinement in a damp and
airless hole, he fell dangerously ill, and the surgeon of the
convent, after being strictly enjoined to secrecy by the
Prior, was brought to the cell in order to bleed him. But
in less than half an hour, this wretch, in the hope of a
pecuniary reward, betrayed his trust, by disclosing the
whole to the emissaries of government.[1] A panel of the
recess in which Valenzuela lurked having been taken
down, he was discovered, in a sound sleep, with his sword
and fire-arms by his side. Being arrested in name of the
King, he was immediately conducted to Consuegra,[2] one
of the dependencies of Don John as Prior of Castile; and,
though still dangerously ill, he was there put in chains,
in order to compel him to make discoveries of all that
concerned him, particularly of his concealed treasures;
for it was reported that, besides the gold found in his
house at Madrid, he had embezzled immense sums belonging to the state: And, in fact, on a farther search,
hoards of money, with large quantities of jewels, were dis-

---

[1] Ortiz, *Compend. Cronol.* t. vi. lib. 21. c. 4.   [2] Id.

covered in the palace of the Escurial, and in his residence at Villa Sierra.[1] It was generally supposed that Valenzuela would have now perished on a scaffold, had it not been for the dread of farther incensing the Pope, who excommunicated all those who had violated the sanctity of a convent by his seizure in a cell of the Escurial.

As soon as the fallen favourite had in some degree recovered from the illness by which he was afflicted, he was removed to Cadiz, and there placed in close confinement till a vessel could be procured for conveying him to the Philippine Islands, where, at this time, criminals were usually sent to work in the mines. He was informed, before his departure, that his wealth had been confiscated, —that he had been deprived of all his employments, and degraded from all his honours, particularly that of a grandee of Spain, in order (as it was expressed in a royal decree) that those who held this high rank might not be contaminated by one so unworthy of it.[2] " I am then," said he, on receiving this intelligence, " more wretched than when I first came to court, or even than when the Duke d'Infantado took me for his page." He was not even informed concerning the destiny of the Queen, as to which he expressed great anxiety : Nor could he learn what had become of his wife and children, who had, in fact, been shut up in a convent at Talavera de la Reyna, with strict injunctions to the abbess not to allow them to quit it, or hold communication with any one beyond its walls.[3]

From the shores of Spain, once the theatre of his splendour and honours, Valenzuela was conveyed to Manilla, the capital of the Philippines, and confined to the Castle of St Philip, in a wooden house, erected on purpose. His

---

[1] Brusoni, *Hist. d'Italia*, lib. xlv.

[2] Ortiz, *Compend. Cronol.* t. vi. lib. 21. c. 4.

[3] Desormeaux, *Abregé Chronol.* Leti, *Vita di Giovanni d'Austria.*

imprisonment, which was at first severe, was afterwards
mitigated.   Those accomplishments and agreeable manners which had originally procured his political elevation,
still continued in exile to alleviate his lot.   Having conciliated the favour of the governor, he was permitted to
amuse himself with theatrical representations of his own
comedies.   About two years after his banishment, when
his enemy Don John was no more, and the Queen-dowager was permitted to return to Court, one of the first
favours which she begged of the King was the recall of
Valenzuela, and a vessel was in consequence despatched
to the Philippine Islands to convey him to Spain.   But
Eguya, who was then chief minister, contrived, by a private communication with the governor, to frustrate the
intentions of the Queen ; and he, in fact, never returned.
In the year 1689, however, he was permitted to remove
to Mexico, where he experienced a kind reception from
the Viceroy, the Count of Galva, who was brother to his
original patron the Duke d'Infantado, and who bestowed
on him an yearly pension of 1200 pesos. We are informed, in the travels of Gemelli Carreri, that his chief amusement at Mexico consisted in training horses, and that,
while engaged in this occupation, he received a kick from
one of them, which occasioned his death.[1]

    While Valenzuela was degraded and expelled his coun-
try, under circumstances of peculiar severity, the Queen,
who had been ordered to quit Madrid, set out for Aranjuez, where she was allowed to remain for a short while
till the apartments were fitted up which were destined for
her, in the Alcazar of Toledo.   That city had long been
the capital of the Gothic monarchs of Castile, and its
Alcazar their favourite palace.   It was built on a rock of
prodigious height, and commanded, from its windows, a
vast prospect of the surrounding country and of the Ta-

    [1] Coxe, *Memoirs of House of Bourbon*, Introduction, sec. 2.

gus; which flows beneath. The Countess d'Aulnoy gives us an amusing and graphic picture of the old queen, and of the life which she led during her banishment at Toledo. After passing through a court 160 feet long by 130 broad, and ascending a magnificent stair-case, " we went through a great gallery and vast apartments, but saw in them so few people, that it did not look as if one could have there met with the Queen-mother of Spain. We found her seated in a great hall, of which the windows were all open, and had a prospect to the valleys and the river. The hangings, cushions, carpets and canopies, were all of gray cloth. The Queen was leaning on a balcony, having in her hand a great pair of beads. When she saw us, she turned towards us, and received us with a countenance merry enough. We had the honour to kiss her hand, which is little, lean, and white. She is very pale, her complexion pure, her face rather long and flat. Her looks are agreeable, and her stature is of a middle size. She was dressed, like all the widows of Spain, in the habit of a nun, without so much as one hair appearing. And there are many (though she is not of that number) who cause all their hair to be cut off when they lose their husbands, for a greater expression of their grief. I observed that her gown was tucked up quite round, that so it might be let down as it wears out : yet I do not believe that she practises this; but such is the fashion of the country. She asked me how long it was since I left France, and inquired if there was any discourse when I quitted it of a marriage between her son and Mademoiselle d'Orleans, and I told her no. Then she said she would show me Mademoiselle's picture, which was drawn from that possessed by the King, and she bade one of her ladies, who was an old duenna, and very ugly, bring it. A box, covered with black satin, and lined with green velvet, contained this portrait, which was about the size of one's hand, and painted in water colours. Do you find, says she, that it is like her? I assured her that none of her features were portrayed; for, indeed, it seemed to squint, the face was awry, and nothing could less resemble a princess so perfect as Mademoiselle. She asked me whether she was more or less handsome than this picture; and when I told her she was handsomer beyond comparison,—'the king, my son, then,' said she, ' will be pleasantly deceived, for he believes this picture is just like her, and yet nobody can be better satisfied.' A little dwarf, but thick as a tun, and no taller than a good big mushroom, all clothed in gold and silver brocade, with long hair hanging down to her feet, then came in, and kneeling before the Queen, asked her if she would please to have supper. On hearing this, we offered to withdraw, but she told us we might follow her, and she went into a parlour, all of marble. She sat down to table alone, and her maids of honour, with the Camerata-Mayor, who looked very sad, came to wait on her. Some of them appeared to me very handsome. They talked to the Marchioness de Palacios, and told her they were horribly tired of the sort of life they passed, and that they dwelt in Toledo as if they were in a desert. There were several dishes placed before the Queen. The first were melons, cooled with ice, and some salads and milk, of which she eat plentifully before she touched any of the flesh, which looked ill enough. She does not want a stomach, and she drank a little pure wine, saying that was to digest her fruit. When she called for drink, one of the *Menines*, who are children of the highest quality, brought her a covered cup on a salver, and kneeling, gave it to the Camerara, who also kneeled when the Queen took it from her hands, and on the other side a lady of the palace presented, on her knees, a napkin to the Queen to wipe her mouth. She gave some dried sweetmeats to Donna Marguereta de Palacios, and to my daughter, saying to them they must not eat much of such things, because they soiled the teeth of young girls. She asked me divers times how the most Christian Queen did, and how she diverted herself; and said that she had lately sent her some boxes of amber pastels, some gloves, and some chocolate. She was above an hour and a half at table, speaking little, but seemed cheerful enough. We desired to know her commands for Madrid; whereon she expressed a great deal of kindness and civility, and after that we took our leave. It cannot be denied that this queen has abundance of understanding, as well as courage and virtue, in bearing, in the way she does, so tedious a banishment."[1]

Thus terminated the unfortunate regency of Mary-Anne of Austria. "She was more desirous of power," says a modern writer, "than capable of wielding it : her regency, however, was not disgraced by any of the bloody episodes which so frequently have characterized such epochs in other monarchies : and, on the whole, minorities in Spain, though they cannot be considered as exempt from calamities and cruelties, have not been stained by so much blood as in many European countries; nor has the temporary enjoyment of the sovereign power been the object of so much ambition, or the cause of such destructive contests, as in France."[2]

Not satisfied with the exile of the Queen and Valenzuela, Don John drove to a distance from the Court and Capital, all persons of distinction who had enjoyed any degree of favour during the regency; and, among others, the Admiral of Castile, though he had been one of the first to pay his court to Don John, was commanded to retire to his estates, which lay at the distance of forty

[1] D'Aulnoy, *Voyage en Espagne.*
[2] Chenevix *on National Character.*

leagues from Madrid, and he was also deprived of the office which he held of Grand Equerry. After his enemies had been all expelled, Don John entered Madrid from Buenretiro, and the King again fixed his residence at his palace within the walls of the city.[1]

The first step taken by Don John in his new administration was, to persuade the King to hold the Cortes of Aragon in person at Saragossa, where he had himself so long resided, and had been so deservedly popular. Don John accompanied his sovereign in this excursion, and during their progress through the province, as also in its capital, the King and his new minister were received by the inhabitants, with every demonstration of loyalty.[2] Indeed, the nation in general testified the highest satisfaction at beholding Don John enter on the unrestrained administration of the government. He had long been pronounced, by the united voice of the people, to be the only person capable of sustaining the sinking monarchy; and, as he possessed considerable natural talents, improved by long experience both in civil and military affairs, and had of late persisted in an incessant clamour concerning the abuses of the state, it was confidently expected that he would speedily apply a remedy to every evil. He suppressed, indeed, the Council of the Indies, which had been kept up at an enormous expense, and he reduced one half of the members who composed the *Hacienda* or Board of Finance. But these were trifling reformations compared with those which were required. He did little for the encouragement of arts, agriculture, commerce, or manufactures, and made not the smallest attempt to excite the industry or arouse the dormant energies of the Spanish nation. Whether it was that the evils of the

---

[1] Leti, *Vita di Giovanni d'Austria.*

[2] Fabro Bremundan, *Viage del Rey Carlos II. al Reyno d'Aragon.*

State were incapable of remedy, or that Don John, having now attained the great object of his ambition, was
little anxious to remove them, or that the public had
formed too high expectations and were too impatient for
their fulfilment, certain it is, that he had not long entered
on the administration, when all the lofty ideas which had
been entertained concerning him vanished as a dream.
The envy, too, attendant on greatness, and the impossibility of recompensing all who had assisted in his elevation,
according to their own estimate of their services, soon
raised a formidable party against Don John, who quickly found how much easier it is to awaken than gratify
public expectation.

It is somewhat amusing to learn, that one of the first
popular accusations against Don John was, his severity
towards the Queen-Dowager; and the harshness he had
manifested in refusing to enter the Capital from Buenretiro till she had departed for Toledo.   The reports that
his ambition reached even a wish to ascend the throne
were revived; and these were confirmed by some new customs which had never yet been introduced by any prime
minister of Spain.   One of those innovations which excited the most remark was, that in his chamber of audience he did not allow seats to be placed for the foreign
ambassadors.   The partizans of the Queen made more
noise on this subject than the envoys who were chiefly interested; and whether they expressed their opinions too
openly, or whether Don John was glad of a new pretext
for vengeance, an additional number of Grandees, among
whom were the Prince of Stigliano and the Marques of
Mondexar, were forbidden to appear at Court.   They
avenged themselves by circulating bitter lampoons, which
they found means to scatter even in different corners of
Don John's apartments,—reflecting on his illegitimate
and dubious birth,—his inordinate ambition,—his bad

success in those wars in which he had commanded during
the late reign, and the disappointment of public expectation. The Duke of Medina del Rio Seco, Admiral of
Castile, did not disdain to employ his pen in these satirical compositions.[1]

This unexpected burst of unpopularity, and the obloquy
which was so suddenly heaped on him, instead of the
public favour he had so long enjoyed, seems to have materially injured Don John's temper and disposition. He
became harsh, distrustful, and vindictive. The Count of
Monterey, who had been persecuted by the Queen because,
as is said, he refused to return her passion, and had prin-
cipally aided Don John to reach his present elevation,
suddenly became to him an object of suspicion. Perceiving that the King was pleased and entertained by the
Count's conversation, he began to fear that he might supplant him in the royal favour, and, in consequence, contrived to remove him from Court, by appointing him to a
command in Catalonia.

The selfish policy of Don John, also induced him to
keep the mind of the young King in the darkest ignorance. Like his deceased brother, Prince Balthazar, he
had received a wretched education; and Don John was
careful that he should obtain no light concerning affairs
of state, or instructions in the art of government. He
never allowed him to quit the palace except in his own
company, and supplied him in its interior with trifling
amusements, which rendered him childish, indolent, and
useless. It was thus that he hoped to make himself indispensable to his nominal master, and to confirm his sway
over him. Don John had also a number of spies in his
pay, distributed through the capital and different parts
of the kingdom, who informed him of every step taken

[1] Pelicer, *Tratado sobre el Origen de la Comedia en España*,
parte ii. p. 93.

to his prejudice by his enemies, who, in spite of all his vigilance, made their way to the King, and carried on court intrigues for the recall of the queen-mother.[1]

From the commencement of his administration, the attention of Don John was claimed by the urgent and unfortunate war with France. The expectations formed of him by the allies in Flanders had been as high as those of his own countrymen, and the Prince of Orange declared to Sir William Temple, that " on Don John coming to the head of Spanish affairs there would be a new world there."[2] But he did not in any degree compensate for the defects of his internal government by the splendour or success of his warlike measures. He was, on the contrary, as unfortunate, at least in Catalonia and the Netherlands, as the ministers who had preceded him.

The French invasion of the frontiers of Catalonia demanded the most immediate measures, and the Count of Monterey (as we have seen) was sent to command the army assembled in that quarter, consisting of 12,000 regular troops, and 5000 Miquelets. As the French force under the Duke de Navailles was inferior in number, that commander was obliged to abandon the siege of Rosas, which he had undertaken, and to commence a retreat beyond the mountains. On his march, the Duke was much harassed by the Spanish troops, who, on one occasion, approached so near, that he found it necessary to hazard an action. This engagement, which took place near the village of Espouilles, was begun with great confidence on the part of the Spaniards; but it terminated completely to the advantage of the French. The former lost near 4000 men in killed and wounded, besides 600 prisoners. Two Grandees of Spain were found among the captives, and two others among the slain. The Count

---

[1] Desormeaux, *Abregé Chronol. Mém. de la Cour d'Espagne.*
[2] Temple's *Memoirs*, c. ii.

of Monterey, indeed, claimed the victory, as his opponents continued their retreat.   But a retreat had been previously their object, and they now accomplished their march into Roussillon without farther molestation.[1]   In the following spring (1678) the Duke de Navailles having been reinforced, again menaced Rosas, and then suddenly laid siege to the strong town of Puycerda, the capital of Cerdagne, which was very gallantly defended.   Monterey assembled his troops, and took such measures as he thought most expedient for its relief; but, whether he wanted sufficient force, or was in reality inferior in military skill to the French Mareschal, who was accounted one of the best officers of that age, his design entirely failed.   He approached the place, indeed, with the greater part of his army, but his opponent was so completely on his guard, that he could neither find an opportunity of throwing succours into the town, nor of attacking the French lines with advantage; and after remaining for some time in sight of Puycerda, he was at length obliged to decamp for want of forage and provisions.   On his departure, the garrison, seeing no farther hope of relief, surrendered on terms, and its capitulation secured to the French general the whole territory of the Cerdagne for the subsistence of his troops, and put him in possession of a key which opened the access between the French and Spanish provinces on the frontiers.[2]   This misfortune formed the pretext for the disgrace and exile of Monterey, against whom proceedings, on account of misconduct, were instituted by order of Don John.   That prince, who had not himself been a very fortunate commander, would have pardoned want of military success to his former friend; but he could not excuse the favour which the Count had acquired with the

[1] Reboulet, *Hist. de Louis XIV.* t. ii. ; Daniel, *Hist. de France.*
[2] Quincy, *Hist. Militaire de Louis le Grand,* t. i.

young king, and which, notwithstanding his disgrace and absence, he still in a great measure retained.

In the Netherlands, the French monarch again took the field, in person, early in spring, and after threatening Luxemburg, Mons, and Namur, in order to throw the allies into uncertainty concerning his intentions, he suddenly sat down before Ghent, which he seized in some measure by surprise; for so little did the Duke of Villahermosa, the Spanish governor of the Netherlands, suspect his design, that he had drawn off the garrison from Ghent, and placed it in Ypres, on which he apprehended an attack. By the capture of Ghent, Louis dismembered the states of the King of Spain in the Low Countries, as he cut off the communication between the maritime towns and the rest of Flanders; he deprived the Spaniards of the command of a district to which they chiefly looked for the subsistence of their armies, and opened to the French a direct road to Antwerp.

Immediately after this important acquisition, Louis in person invested Ypres. The Spanish garrison, consisting of 3000 men, was commanded by the Marquis de Conflans, who made a gallant resistance; but having sustained several severe assaults, he was at length obliged to capitulate, ten days after the trenches had been opened before his fortifications. This conquest was scarcely less important than that of Ghent, as it protected St Omers, and the whole county of Artois, and preserved a communication among all the places between the Lis and the sea.

It was in Sicily alone that the course of events proved favourable to the Spanish nation. Don John had withdrawn from that island the troops which had been formerly sent there from Catalonia—foreseeing that the enormities practised by the French at Messina would quickly lead to their expulsion. The event, in some mea-

sure, justified his policy. Such was the rapacity of the
Duke de Vivonne and his soldiery, that they were held
in the utmost abhorrence, and so far were the French
from making farther progress in Sicily, that they found
it extremely difficult any longer to keep Messina in subjection. Louis had now become aware of the impossibility of establishing the French supremacy in Sicily, or of
continuing to retain Messina without possession of the
whole island. He also foresaw, that in any treaty of
peace which might be hereafter concluded, one of the articles infallibly forced on his acceptance, would be the
surrender of Messina. Had he, indeed, permitted its
cession to become an article of treaty, he might easily
have secured an amnesty for its unfortunate citizens, who
had entrusted themselves to his protection, or he might,
perhaps, have even obtained for them a confirmation of
their ancient privileges. But Louis conceived that his
political pride would suffer less by a voluntary and un-
conditional evacuation of the city, than by yielding to di-
plomatic compulsion. In these circumstances, the French
monarch, preferring the gratification of his false notions
of punctilio, both to the dictates of humanity and the
preservation of true honour, resolved to withdraw his
forces entirely from Sicily ; and he accordingly despatched M. de Feuillade with a powerful squadron to carry
this plan into execution. It required to be conducted
with the utmost secrecy, for it could not be doubted, that
if the design were once suspected, the inhabitants of Messina, disgusted at the previous conduct of their allies,
and now farther exasperated by the treacherous abandonment of them to the vengeance of the Spaniards, would
rise in commotion, and massacre the French, or sink the
vessels destined for their embarkation. Feuillade, on his
arrival, having assumed the character of successor to the
Duke de Vivonne, gave out that he meditated an expe-

dition against a certain quarter of the island, which would require for its success the whole French force at that time in Messina.   Thus, without any suspicion being entertained of his real intentions, he embarked all the troops, and great part of the treasure plundered from the citizens, on board his squadron, which was lying in the harbour.[1]   When ready to sail, he called together the principal inhabitants, and informed them of the orders he had received.   But he, at the same time, offered to suspend his departure for four hours, in order to carry those along with him who feared that they could not remain in safety at Messina.   The utmost consternation prevailed at this cruel and unexpected intelligence.   A number of the inhabitants[2] availed themselves of the Frenchman's proposal, and fled with him from their native country;[3] but they embarked with such precipitation, that the same families were separated in different vessels, and they had no proper means of securing the few effects which they were permitted to convey along with them.   At length the French commander, perceiving that his ships were becoming crowded to a perilous degree, ordered them to sail, while 2000 miserable wretches on the shore still implored, with outstretched arms, to be received on board the departing fleet.

The Sicilian emigrants, who had calculated on the protection and favour of the King of France, being landed in Provence, were dispersed throughout the different cities of the kingdom, where they were, for a time, maintained by the bounty of Louis.   But on some sudden suggestion they were afterwards driven from their asylums and commanded to quit the realm.   Most of them wandered, in

---

[1] Lancina, *Revol. de Messina*, c. x.

[2] The accounts as to the numbers are various : some say only 500 : Brusoni swells the amount to 8000.

[3] Quincy, *Hist. Milit. de Louis le Grand*, t. i.

the last stage of destitution, to the different cities in the
north of Italy; and, being deprived of all means of support, Sicilian nobles, of the highest class, were seen beg-
ging their subsistence, while others, congregating in
troops, betook themselves as banditti to the high way.
Fifteen hundred of these unfortunate and desperate men
passed into Turkey, where they were induced to renounce
their faith, and ally themselves with the enemy of Christendom.[1]

Nor was the fate of those who remained behind at
Messina less deplorable. At first, an amnesty was passed
by the Viceroy, Vincenzo Gonzaga, but this was soon re-
voked by an edict from Madrid, and the resentment of
the Spanish government was manifested in acts of the
most atrocious vengeance. The Marques de las Navas,[2]
being sent from Naples to Messina as Viceroy in place
of Gonzaga, immediately issued an order, by which the
King of Spain completely changed the government of
that city, and deprived it of all its revenues. Its charter
of privileges was burned by the hands of the common
executioner. Its Town-house was razed to the ground,
and on the spot was erected a galling monument of the
degradation of the city,—a pyramid surmounted by a sta-
tue of the King of Spain, cast with the metal of the great
bell which had formerly summoned the people to the deliberations of their free senate.[3] The citizens were all
compelled to deliver up their arms at the Viceroy's palace,
and many of the public functionaries and other principal
inhabitants, perished on the scaffold, or were sent for life
to the gallies.[4] About 500 exiles, who had obtained leave

---

[1] Percival's *Hist. of Italy*, c. x.   *Historical Traveller*, vol. i.
[2] He is called by Lancina and other writers the Count of Santis-
tevan, which was one of his titles.
[3] Percival's *Hist. of Italy*, c. x.
[4] D'Aulnoy, *Voyage d'Espagne.*

from the Spanish ambassador at Paris, ventured to return
to Sicily ; but the Viceroy seized them at the moment of
their disembarkation, and condemned them to immediate
death.   On the whole, by this insurrection of Messina
and its consequences, the population of the city was reduced from 60,000 to 12,000 inhabitants, and it never
recovered the effects of this great disaster. The purposes
of Spanish tyranny, and of vengeance for the late insurrection, were thus fully accomplished, and the future obedience of the city was secured by its insignificance and de-
solation.

The pretext alleged by the King of France for thus
abandoning Sicily and leaving Messina to its fate was,
that his longer occupation of the island would oppose almost insurmountable obstacles to the conclusion of that
treaty of peace, the terms of which were now adjusting in
the congress held at Nimeguen.

It was the usual custom in those times to blend negotiations with war, and articles of peace were always under
consideration by plenipotentiaries, while the hostile armies
were combating in the field.   This system proved little
conducive to a pacific conclusion.   Without at least a suspension of arms, the belligerent powers protract the conferences, that they may see the issue of each campaign.
A battle won, or a fortress lost, changes the views of
parties, and all the preliminaries agreed on require to be
altered and revised.

As early, however, as the year 1674, in the very heat
of the war, and without any cessation of hostilities, negotiations for peace had been formally opened under the
mediation of the King of England.   That monarch having been compelled by his parliament and the nation to
conclude, in 1674, a treaty with the Dutch, offered his
amicable interposition to effect an accommodation among
the other contending powers.   For this purpose he de-

spatched Sir William Temple to the Hague, as a person
well known both to the Spaniards and Dutch, from the
successful manner in which he had concluded the treaty
of Aix-la-Chapelle. On his arrival, however, at Brussels,
he found the Governor of the Spanish Netherlands so little inclined to peace, that he even interposed every possible obstacle to prevent his journey to the head-quarters
of the Prince of Orange. The English envoy also learned
that, in spite of all the reverses they had sustained, the
Spaniards still insisted, that the treaty of the Pyrenees
should be the basis of the pacification. At the formation,
indeed, of the alliance between them and the Dutch it
had been stipulated, that peace should not be concluded
by either of the contracting parties on worse conditions
than that treaty provided; and the Prince of Orange,
whose power had been created by the dangers of the republic, and, in a great measure, depended on a state of
warfare, supported his allies in the full extent of their
pretensions. The French, on the other hand, insisted
on retaining Franche Comté, and all the acquisitions
they had made in Flanders during the present contest.
Sir William Temple, as mediator, was of opinion, that
the King of England could not propose any other conditions for the acceptance of France than those that had
been ratified, in 1668, at Aix-la-Chapelle, by which the
Spaniards were deprived of many towns in Flanders they
had been allowed to retain by the treaty of the Pyrenees.
Though the parties chiefly interested thus widely differed
as to their respective claims, the King of England's mediation still continued; and at length, about the close of
the year 1676, his envoy and the plenipotentiaries of the
belligerent powers met at Nimeguen. None of them were
much inclined to peace, but their military ardour was
moderated by want of means to carry on the war. The
Marques of Balbases, who was the chief Spanish ambas-

sador, and the descendant of the famous Spinola, appeared with great splendour, and eclipsed the envoys of the other powers by the magnificence of his equipages and liveries. When this celebrated congress opened, all parties directed their attention to the events of the campaign, by which they had resolved, that their proposals should be regulated. The great object of the Spaniards was, to protract any final adjustment of differences, in the hope that the King of England might yet be compelled by his parliament to change his character of mediator, for that of a party, and to form a league with themselves and the Dutch for the restitution of the whole of Flanders, and the conclusion of a peace founded on that of the Pyrenees.   The plan of the French, on the other hand, during the whole of the conferences, which were conducted by those able negotiators, Mareschal d'Estrades and the Count d'Avaux was, to break the union of the confederacy, by making separate advances and proposals to the different parties.   They were encouraged in this policy by the success with which the Spaniards had detached the Dutch from their allies during the negotiations at Munster: and according to the testimony of Sir William Temple, they conducted all their machinations with consummate address.   Though the Prince of Orange was averse to a pacification, the Pensioner, and the remnant of the old Barneveldt or De Witt actions, being alarmed at the military preponderance of the House of Orange, were disposed to listen to the overtures of Louis, who, availing himself of this disunion, at length succeeded in enticing the States into a separate peace.   They, however, stipulated in behalf of their Spanish allies, that the French should restore to them, in order to form a protection for Brabant, and Flanders, the towns of Charleroi, Courtrai, Oudenarde, Aeth, Ghent, and Limbourg; and on the side of Roussillon, Puycerda, with all their conquests in that district. The French, on the other hand, were to retain Franche Comté and some of the most important of their recent acquisitions in the Netherlands, as Cambray, Aire, St Omer, Ypres, and Valenciennes, which consolidated their frontier from the Channel to the Sambre.

At the time when this treaty was adjusting, Mons was blockaded by the French; and the Prince of Orange was making preparations to relieve it. These preparatives brought on the battle of St Denis between his army and that of Marshal Luxembourg—a combat which, it has been alleged,[1] the Prince of Orange fought after he had heard of the treaty being concluded between France and the States. The Prince succeeded in driving Luxembourg from his strong entrenchments; but he withdrew his troops immediately subsequent to the engagement, and returned to the Hague, leaving the Dutch plenipotentiaries, who now acted the part of mediators, to finish the treaty which they had commenced between France and Spain.

The Spanish ambassadors were both astounded and exasperated at the defection of the Dutch, and vented their reproaches against them, for thus having first deserted a contest, which, on the part of Spain, had been commenced chiefly for their protection. They started many objections both to the style and substance of those articles which Holland had mediated in behalf of their country.

---

[1] Ancillon, *Tableau des Revolutions de l'Europe*, t. iv. c. 48. Captain Carleton, who was present at the battle, says, "it was whispered in the army, two days before the march of St Denis, that peace had been actually concluded; and when the troops were ordered out, they supposed it was to fire a feu de joie." (*Memoirs.*) The Marquis de Feuquiere, who was also present at this battle in the army of Luxembourg, says, "that the Prince was aware of the treaty, but wished to disturb it by an untoward event, being prompted to give battle by his own chagrin, or the persuasion of the Spaniards." (*Mémoires*, c. 80.)

But, after much discussion and remonstrance, they were at length obliged to accept the terms which the Dutch had negotiated for them. They, however, so long deferred giving their ratification, that the period fixed for adhibiting it was twice prolonged by France at the desire of the States. During this interval the French troops made incursions into the richest parts of Flanders, and there exacted such contributions, and committed such depredations when these levies were withheld, that the Spanish Netherlands were more destroyed between the signing of the peace and the exchange of the ratifications, than they had been in an equal portion of time during the whole course of the war. The calamities and outcries of the Flemings at length induced the Spaniards to give in their ratification; and the Emperor, who was still carrying on an unsuccessful war, soon after followed their example, by concluding a disadvantageous peace with France.[1]

When it was known at Madrid that the King of France was to swear at Fontainbleau to the observance of the articles of the treaty, it was resolved that the same ceremony should be performed by the King of Spain in the Gilded Saloon of the palace at Madrid. This hall was magnificently fitted up for the occasion. At one end there was an alcove raised three steps from the floor, and covered with Persian carpets and cloth of gold. In this recess stood the throne, ornamented by immense pearls and precious stones of the most brilliant lustre. As soon as the King, supported by the Constable of Castile and the Cardinal Porto-carrero, had taken his seat, the French ambassador, who had been received by all the Mayordomos of the palace, and conducted by them through its magnificent and tapestried apartments, was introduced into this saloon. Don Pedro Coloma, Secretary of State, then read aloud the power which the King

[1] Temple, *Memoirs*, c. 3.

of France had conferred on his ambassador, to represent
him at this ceremony. A small silver table, on which
lay a crucifix and the books of the Evangelists, was next
placed before the King. His Majesty, kneeling down,
laid his right hand on the Gospels, while the Cardinal read
out the royal oath to preserve peace with France, and
to fulfil all the articles of the treaty. When this part of
the ceremonial was concluded, the French ambassador
approached the foot of the throne, and delivered a compli-
mental address to the King, who replied briefly, according to his usual custom, and then hastily retired into his
private apartments.

. Though tranquillity was thus restored to Europe, the
allies had separated with mutual dissatisfaction, and the
Spaniards were particularly exasperated at the Dutch,
who, by their selfish desertion of the common cause, had
compelled them to accept of a peace which deprived them
of one of their most ancient provinces, and humbled them
so severely in the eyes of Europe. The haughtiness, too,
with which the terms were prescribed by Louis, revolted
the feelings of national pride as much as the hardness of
the conditions themselves.

This disgraceful, though perhaps necessary peace, was
little favourable to the popularity of Don John, particularly among those who recollected how bitterly he had
inveighed against the far-less ignominious treaty of Aix-
la-Chapelle. After a time, however, the Spanish nation,
though severely disappointed in the expectations which
they had formed of Don John, again began to indulge a
hope, that, being now relieved from the pressure of a dis-
astrous war, he would turn his attention to regulations of
domestic utility, and that good order and abundance might
yet arise in Spain. But the situation of affairs had in
fact now become almost irretrievable. The debts which
had been incurred by the last war, and during a long period

of preceding disaster, with the difficulty of procuring funds
for defraying the ordinary expenses of the civil list, compelled Don John to set up for sale those employments
and dignities which had been formerly conferred as the
reward of merit, or as distinctions due to dignity of birth.
This new venality of the government, as also the lofty
bearing of Don John, contrasted with the humiliating
peace which he had compelled the Spanish nation to accept, and, above all, the dearness of provisions, which Valenzuela for a time had contrived to cheapen, led the public to regret the days of the regency of the exiled Queen-
mother. The whole efforts of Don John were directed
to the maintenance of his own influence and authority.
All affairs of state which did not tend to this selfish object were utterly neglected. The good of the nation,
and the long-promised reform of abuses, were entirely
overlooked amid the factions of a turbulent nobility, the
ceaseless intrigues which agitated the Court, and the cabals which the enemies of Don John were continually
forming against him.

Of these cabals and intrigues, by far the most important were those relating to the marriage of the young
King, which, from the present state of the succession to
the crown, had become a subject of the deepest interest,
not only to the Spanish nation, but to the whole of
Europe.

CHAPTER V.

MARRIAGE OF THE KING.

Jam vincla jugalia curæ.
                    VIRGIL, *Æneid.*

NEVER were the nuptials of any monarch of such importance as those of Charles II, King of Spain. Having
been but a sickly boy, the Spanish nation, and, indeed,
the whole of Europe, looked with apprehension to the
probability of the sceptre passing into the hands of the
Bourbons,—an alarm which was daily heightened by the
increasing power and dominion of the ruler of France.
Though a feeble and imbecile monarch, the life of Charles
was perhaps more highly valued than that of any prince
who had ever worn a crown. When he had reached, however, the age of sixteen or seventeen, his strength and constitution apparently became more confirmed ; and the nation, anxious to avert the calamity of a foreign succession,
seemed resolved to precipitate his marriage. The Queen-
mother, with a view of confirming her own power and ascendency, had proposed for his choice her niece, the daughter of Leopold, Emperor of Germany. By her intervention, the contract was speedily concluded, and the young
princess assumed the title of Queen of Spain. But when
Don John was recalled to Court, and entrusted with the
administration, one of his first measures was to break off
this alliance, which he dreaded might restore the influence of his enemies. The rejected princess soon after-

wards married the Elector of Bavaria, by whom she had an only son, who died at the moment when he was called to the throne of Spain by the testament of Charles II.

The Emperor of Germany felt much indignation at the double affront offered at this time to his family, by the rejection of his daughter, and the banishment of his sister, the Queen-mother, to Toledo. Count Harrach, the Austrian ambassador at Madrid, and the King's confessor, who had now become the enemy of Don John, entered into an intrigue for the purpose of renewing the German matrimonial alliance. But Don John triumphed over all the machinations of his foes. The confessor was excluded from the royal presence, and the Austrian ambassador was recalled.

It seems more than probable that Don John did not wish the King to enter into any matrimonial union whatever. His Majesty's nuptials would, in all likelihood, terminate the expectations he had fondly cherished of one day ascending the throne; and, at all events, the fascinations of a youthful queen would counteract the influence he at present exercised over the mind of the King. But any opposition, even on his part, would have been ineffectual in retarding a measure on which the whole nation was bent, and which in itself was so expedient. He was therefore obliged to be contented with having accomplished his great object of preventing the German match, and having gained some time to secure a princess who might prove favourable to his views and interests. He first made proposals for the Infanta of Portugal, who was at that time heiress to the throne. But the national antipathy of the Portuguese to the Spaniards, and their dread of again falling under the Castilian yoke, occasioned the rejection of this union by the Court of Lisbon.

The treaty of peace which had recently been concluded at Nimeguen, suggested Louisa d'Orleans, commonly called Mademoiselle, as a fit person to be the future Queen of Spain. This princess was the daughter of the Duke of Orleans, only brother to the King of France, and of the charming Henrietta of England, who has been immortalized in the funeral oration of Bossuet. About the year 1675, at the commencement of the negotiations which terminated with the peace of Nimeguen, the Prince of Orange, in his discussions with Sir William Temple, had proposed that a match should be concluded between Mademoiselle and the King of Spain, who should receive, as his Queen's dowry, all the places lately taken from him in the Netherlands, by which means the frontiers of Flanders would be secured, and the honour of Louis be at the same time preserved, as he would thus part with the conquered towns only as a portion to a princess of France.[1] This proposal was communicated to the King of England and to Louis ; but it does not appear that it was brought under the consideration of the Court of Spain ; and, indeed, the parties chiefly interested were at that time of very tender age. When the peace, however, had been at length concluded, they were allotted to each other by the general voice both of the French and Spanish nations. Louisa d'Orleans, as she grew up, had proved handsome, amiable, and prepossessing in her manners, and she was nearly of the same age with the King of Spain, being now in her eighteenth year.

It was feared, however, that some obstacle might be interposed to this, or indeed any other marriage, from the temper and disposition of the King. From the delicacy of his health, he had been consigned in his boyhood to the care of dowagers and duennas, who reprehending him too sharply for his faults, he conceived towards them such an aversion, that as soon as he had notice that a lady waited for him in any place where he was to pass,

---

[1] Temple's *Memoirs*, part ii. c. 1.

he stole away in another direction, or kept himself shut
up all day in his chamber; and when chance unavoidably
brought any of the court ladies in his path, he took their
written requests from their hands, but turned his head
another way that he might not see them. The Marchioness de Los-Velez, who had been his *Aya* or governess,
waited full six months before she could find an opportunity to speak with him;[1] and as every woman believes
that the man by whom she is slighted dislikes her whole
sex, Charles early acquired the character of a determined
woman-hater. As soon, however, as the idea of a marriage with Louisa d'Orleans was started, the King showed
an unexpected zeal and alacrity on the subject. Those
Spanish Grandees, who had been at the Court of France
since the conclusion of peace, spoke of her as a prodigy
of beauty, and the King had seen some portraits of this
Princess which, though not very well executed, were
yet sufficient to excite his imagination. Like a prince
in a fairy tale, he became enamoured of her picture;
he wore it constantly at his breast, and addressed to it
long amatory discourses. The Court was much astonished at this change in the King's disposition, but the
nation was overjoyed at the tidings; and as the memory
of Elizabeth, the first Queen of Philip IV., was embalmed in the recollection of every Spaniard, his subjects
were sufficiently pleased that a French princess should
be the object of their sovereign's choice.

As for Don John, he was obliged to assent to the
united wishes of the king and people. He accordingly
ordered the Marques of Balbases to proceed from Nimeguen to Paris, and demand for his master the hand of
Mademoiselle. The proposal was favourably received by
Louis; but the Princess herself, accustomed to the gaieties
of Paris and amusements of Versailles, looked forward with

[1] D'Aulnoy, *Voyage d'Espagne.*

horror to the rigid formalities of Madrid and the gloom
of the Escurial. She aspired, it is said, to a marriage
with her cousin the Dauphin; and when Louis XIV.,
to console and encourage her, declared that he could have
obtained nothing better than this Spanish match for his
own daughter, she archly replied, " Ah! Sire, but you
might have got something better for your niece."

The King of Spain, before he had even heard of the
consent of Louis, filled up the household of his expected
bride. The Dutchess of Terranueva was nominated Camarera-Mayor, or first lady of honour, to the Queen.
She was Dutchess of Terranueva in her own right, and
widow of the Duke of Monteleone.[1] By her father,
she was descended from the royal House of Aragon,
and by her mother, from the celebrated Fernando Cortez, through whom she had inherited immense wealth,
and a principality in Mexico. At this period she had
reached the age of threescore; her person was emaciated,
—her countenance long, pale, and wrinkled,—her eyes
sharp and small,—her voice harsh,—her temper austere
and imperious. Every movement was regulated with the
most rigid formality; she spoke little, but it was ap-
palling to hear her declare, I chuse it or I chuse it not.
Her cousin, Don Carlos of Aragon, had been assassinated
by bravoes, whom she hired for the express purpose from
Valencia, because he had asserted a claim to the Dutchy
of Terranueva. This summary mode of adjusting the
rights of parties, attracted so much notice in the capital, that she was obliged to retire to Saragossa, where
Don John at that time resided. By complaining to each
other of their unfortunate situations, a species of sympathy
was produced between them. Don John perceived the
ambitious temper of the Dutchess, but as her evil dispositions were veiled by an exterior of the most rigid for-

---

[1] Vayrac, *Etat de l'Espagne.*

mality and decorum, he did not discover all her dark and malignant qualities.[1]   On the recall of Don John, she so far triumphed over calumny, that she was permitted to reside at Madrid, where she dwelt along with her daughter-in-law, the Dowager-dutchess of Monteleone, in one of the most magnificent mansions in that city, which was furnished with cushions of crimson velvet, and tapestry embroidered with gold, and tables of silver, and cabinets inlaid with gems, and beds of green damask, lined with silver brocade and trimmed with lace.   When it became necessary to form the new household on occasion of the projected nuptials, Don John recommended this morose dowager as a suitable attendant for the young and amiable Queen ; and her austere demeanour, her shrewd judgment, and piercing inquisitiveness, gave her unrivalled claims to the situation to which she aspired.

The Marques of Astorga, who had been successively Ambassador at Rome and Viceroy of Naples during the important period of the insurrection at Messina, and had exerted himself in raising funds and fitting out expeditions[2] on that occasion, was appointed Mayor-domo-Mayor, or Master of the household.   This nobleman, now in his 68th year, had amassed great wealth during his viceroyalty at Naples, and he procured his new situation by relieving the necessities of Don John with large pecuniary supplies.   On the whole, Don John took special care that all the offices of the household should be filled by persons who were completely devoted to his interests, and who would study to prepossess the mind of the young Queen in his favour.

[1] *Mém. de la Cour d'Espagne.*

[2] Giannone, *Stor. Civile,* lib. xxxix. c. 3. Madame D'Aulnoy has related an atrocious and almost incredible occurrence in the domestic history of the Marques of Astorga, which equals in horror the mythological fable of Atreus and Thyestes,—the story of the

At the same time that he arranged her household, the King ordered the apartments in the royal palace, destined for the Queen, to be fitted up with all expedition. Being now the month of April, the season had arrived, in which, according to the established ceremonial of the court, the King should have proceeded to Aranjuez. But Don John would not permit him, as he dreaded its vicinity to Toledo, the residence of the Queen-mother, who, he feared, might find some opportunity of throwing herself in the way of her son. His Majesty, therefore, resided chiefly at Buenretiro, and spent his time at the chase or the opera, and in excursions to his pleasure houses of the Pardo and Zarzuela. There were also, occasionally, bull-fights and cane-plays *(juego de cañas)*; and the court became extremely crowded by the nobility who thronged to it from every part of Spain, in expectation of the approaching nuptials.

The Marquis de Villars, who had been well known in Spain as French ambassador about six years before, was now again sent to Madrid. He arrived there on the 17th of June, and after various discussions with Don John on points of precedence and form, he had an audience of the King on the interesting subject of his em-

---

Provençal poet Cabestan, or Boccaccio's tale of Guardastagno. (Decameron, day iv. 9.) " Sa femme ayant pris une implacable jalousie contre une fille admirablement belle qu'il aimoit, elle fut chez elle bien accompagnée, elle la tua, elle lui arracha le cœur et le fit accommoder en ragout ; lorsque son mari en eut mangé, elle lui demanda si cela lui sembloit bien ; et dit que oui : Je n'en suis pas surprise, dit elle, c'est le cœur de la mâitresse que tu as tant aimé ; et aussitôt elle tira sa tête toute sanglante qu'elle avoit caché sous son gard-ènfant, et elle la roula sur la table où il étoit assis avec plusieurs de ses amis. Il est aisé de juger de ce qu'il devint à cette funeste vûe : elle se sauva dans un couvent, où elle devint folle de rage et de jalousie, et elle n'en sortit plus." *(Mém. de la Cour. d' Espagne*, part i. p. 108.)

bassy. On the 13th of July, the secretary of the Marques Balbases arrived, and brought official tidings, that Louis XIV. had agreed to give his niece in marriage to the King of Spain. His Majesty had awaited this intelligence with the greatest impatience, and he manifested the most extravagant joy at its announcement. He caused *Te deum* to be sung in one of the principal churches, and all the houses were illuminated with white wax flambeaux. Fireworks and bonfires were displayed in the streets, and one hundred and fifty knights of the first families in the kingdom rode along them, all night, on horseback, equipped in gaudy and fantastic dresses, and attended by trumpets, timbrels, and flutes. These amusements continued during three days and three nights. At the end of that period, a courier arrived from France with the contract of marriage. The ratification of it was speedily sent back from Spain, and this act gave occasion to new rejoicings and entertainments.

On the 9th of August the French ambassador made his public entrance into Madrid; and intelligence having arrived that the marriage had been celebrated by proxy at Fontainbleau, the King appointed the Duke de Pastrana and Infantado his ambassador extraordinary to the Court of Versailles. This nobleman accordingly set out, with great pomp and ceremony, bearing with him the nuptial presents; and at the same time, the ladies who were appointed to form the Queen's household, took possession of the apartments allotted to them in the palace.[1]

Amid all this public pomp and joy, there was one sad and desponding heart at Madrid. But Don John still maintained the appearance of good humour and gaiety. Madame d'Aulnoy saw him at Madrid in the month of May, while she was residing there with her kinswoman,

---

[1] *Mem. de la Cour d'Espagne.*

whom Don John frequently visited.   She had been extremely desirous of seeing him, but had been always disappointed, till one day, while engaged in painting a small
piece, a man came in whom she knew not, but whom she
easily distinguished to be a person of quality, from his
countenance and noble carriage.   He said that he intended to remain till her kinswoman returned home, and after
some little discourse he gave occasion to talk of Don
John, telling her that he doubted not she frequently saw
him.   The Countess replied, " that since her arrival, he
had often come to visit her cousin, but had never asked
for her."   " The reason of that," said Don John, " was
because you were sick with a fever."   " I was not sick,"
answered the Countess, " and I should have been very
glad both to have seen and heard him, for I have been
told both good and ill of him, and I have a mind to know
whether they do him right or wrong.   I have signified
my desire to my kinswoman, but she told me there was
no way to gratify me, for he was so devout that he would
not speak to any woman."   At that moment the kinswoman entered the room, and was much amazed to find
Don John there, as was also the Countess, who little
thought it was his Highness.   He told her several times,
that he knew not how to pardon her for the account she
had given of him,—that he was no bigot, and that he was
persuaded true devotion could not make any one rude and
uncivil.   Though Don John was at this time nearly fifty,
and was labouring under much distress of mind, the
French Countess thought him extremely handsome, very
well bred and witty, and of amazing quickness of mind.[1]

Early in July, however, Don John was seized with a
tertian ague, and, though he partially recovered, the disappointments which he now constantly experienced gradually undermined his health.   The marriage of his so-

[1]   *Voyage d'Espagne.*

vereign with the French princess he had never opposed,
regarding it as inevitable. But he looked forward to it
as the term of his power and greatness. The French
ambassador had manifested towards him a most unfavourable disposition. That minister had been at Toledo, to
pay his respects to the Queen-dowager, and, it was suspected, had held with her various confidential communications. It was generally believed, that, when the new
Queen arrived, she would unite her interests with those
of the Queen-mother, who would then, doubtless, be recalled to court. This impression strengthened the party
which was opposed to Don John. The prospect of his
fall alienated from him all the creatures of his prosperity
and power—particularly the King's confessor, whom he
had brought to Court from Salamanca, and, having raised
him to his present eminent situation, had relied implicitly
on his devotion to his interests. All who were yet attached
to the Queen-mother—all who thought themselves neglected since the commencement of his administration—
all who had felt the effects of his displeasure, or had a fa-
culty for intriguing, concurred in the insinuation, that
though Don John had not openly opposed the King's
nuptials, yet he had secretly laboured to prevent them.
These suggestions on a subject concerning which the King
was particularly sensitive, having made a considerable impression on his mind, the enemies of Don John next ventured to importune his majesty to recall those grandees who
had been banished from the capital soon after the removal
of the Queen-mother to Toledo. The Prince of Stigliano, the Duke d'Ossuna, and the Count de Monterey,
were successively permitted to return to court in spite of
his most strenuous opposition ; and the royal mandate for
the recall of the Prince of Stigliano was accompanied with
some disobliging expressions for Don John. He now
made a vain attempt to fortify his party by an alliance

with the Constable of Castile, whom he had treated with much arrogance in the days of his prosperity. He employed the Duke of Alva to propose a reconciliation, and a junction of interests. But the Constable, who saw through his motives, and no longer considered him either as a formidable enemy or valuable friend, replied, that his advances had now come too late.

In this situation, Don John was at a loss what part to take. He saw with alarm the powerful combination which had been formed against him ; he found the favour of the King gradually withdrawn, and the Queen-dowager deserted by his enemies. Although he had braved dangers, and supported disgrace, and though he was adorned by almost every accomplishment which could embellish private life, and render it delightful, he wanted sufficient magnanimity to renounce power, or relinquish a situation which he could no longer preserve. Depressed with chagrin and disappointment, he brooded over his perils and difficulties.[1] The mortifications he daily endured brought on a new attack of fever and ague ; and by the beginning of September he was so much reduced, that his physicians informed the King that scarcely any hopes remained of his recovery. On receiving this intelligence, the King, though he had almost resolved on his dismissal from the management of affairs, shed tears, and manifested the sincerest affliction. He immediately enjoined the Cardinal Portocarrero to acquaint Don John with his danger. On hearing these tidings of death, he showed but little emotion, and prepared for his end with the resignation of a philosopher and a Christian. He consoled all his friends with the greatest composure and presence of mind. " One has always lived long enough," he said, " who has nothing with which to reproach himself—I mean with regard to the relations of life, for as to my duty towards God, the

[1] Coxe, Mem. of House of Bourbon, t. i. p. 32.

time allowed for repentance can never be too long." He received the viaticum, and declared his last-will, by which he nominated the King his heir, and divided his jewels between the new Queen and his bitter enemy the Queen-mother, naming as his executors the Cardinal Portocar-rero, the Duke of Alva, the Duke of Medina Celi, and the President of Castile. He addressed a letter to a fa-vourite lady, and commanded Don Antonio Ortis, his chief secretary, to carry it to her in a little box of China-wood. He also gave orders, that, as soon as he expired, a cabinet filled with papers of the utmost importance, should be carried from his chamber into the private apart-ments of the King. In consequence of the illness of Don John, some of the public rejoicings which had been order-ed—particularly a great bull-fight, were delayed ; but though afflicted with excruciating headaches, he would not allow the postponement of a display of fireworks which were exhibited in the great court of the palace, close to his apartments. From the time the King heard of his extreme danger, in spite of Don John's earnest entreaties that he would not expose himself to the risk of infection from the fever, he was constantly going to the chamber where he lay, showing him every kindness and attention, and complaining, though perhaps with some deceit, that he was to be thus deprived of him, at a time when his presence and services would have been of so much im-portance. Don John, on the other hand, perhaps with equal insincerity, assured him that he would die content if he only survived to behold the Queen. In these, his last moments, he proved how much easier it is to give good advice than to practise it. He took the opportunity of one of the King's visits, to enter into a full detail con-cerning the state of public affairs—he exhibited to him their perplexed and declining condition—he pointed out the sources from which all these evils flowed, and the sole remedies which could prove effectual for their cure—he urged him to make a proper choice of a council, and to apply himself sedulously, by the help of its advice, to administer the concerns of his kingdom, and exhorted him, above all, to beware of listening to flatterers or unworthy favourites.

During the course of Don John's illness, it was frequently believed that he was at the last extremity, but he again revived, and exhibited such signs of strength as gave his attendants, from time to time, some faint hopes of his recovery. But the physicians, who were not aware of the chagrin which preyed on his mind, treated his complaint as a mere bodily ailment, and, by their injudicious remedies, subjected him to much annoyance, and perhaps accelerated his end. On the day before his death, he continued more than six hours in one of those faints to which he had been subject during the whole period of his illness. As he was believed to be dead, preparations began to be made for embalming him. He however revived and asked for some nourishment, of which he partook, but expired on the following day, which was the 17th of September, when he had reached the age of fifty. It was reported after his death, that he had been poisoned by the instrumentality of the Queen-mother; but the only poison was the care by which his mind was corroded. His body lay for three days on a bed of state, wrapped in those garments he had procured as the raiment with which he was to meet the new Queen on the frontiers. It was then carried, in a leaden coffin, to the Escurial, and deposited in a vault near that pantheon where repose the ashes of the kings and queens of Spain. His funeral was conducted with little pomp or attendance, and was accompanied only by a few private friends and the officers of his household.[1]

[1] D'Aulnoy, *Mem. de la Cour d'Espagne.*   *Voyage d'Espagne.* Leti, *Vita di Giovan. d'Austria.*

Don John had never been married, but he left an illegitimate daughter by a Spanish lady of quality. She was a person of exquisite beauty; but, soon after the death of her father, she became (reluctantly it is said) a nun of the order of Carmelites at Madrid.

Few men have been endued with such manifold acquirements as John of Austria. He was the bravest, the most accomplished, and most learned of his race. The small fortune of which he died possessed, was evidence of his integrity, and his bequest to the Queen-dowager, was a noble proof of his forgiveness and magnanimity. But though the subjection of the Neapolitans and Catalans may be justly attributed to his prudence and military skill, yet in the Netherlands and Portugal his military reputation had been clouded by defeat; the purity of his patriotism may be suspected in his persecution of the Count of Monterey, and in the measures of civil government, the resources he employed shewed that at least his talents were unequal to the distractions and the evils of the times.

With Don John expired the last rays of the genius of the Austrian dynasty ; and, after his decease, a species of dissolution took place in the government, which accelerated the decline of the monarchy. Yet the sickness and death of Don John were received with much indifference at Madrid, and he was scarcely talked of, the day after his demise. " Four and twenty hours after he was dead," says Madame D'Aulnoy, " I believe I saw, in different places, fifty persons of the highest quality, who did not so much as speak one word of this poor prince, though many of them had the highest obligations to him, and though he was undoubtedly possessed of great personal qualifications and virtues."

The eyes of Don John were scarcely closed, when the King repaired to Toledo, in order to pay his respects to his mother, who still continued to reside in strict retirement in the Alcaçar of that ancient capital of Spain. She received her son with much affection; they embraced each other, dined together, and had a long private conference. Before his departure, the King fixed the time when she should return to Madrid, and it may be believed that she gladly availed herself of this permission. On the day that had been appointed, the King proceeded to meet her beyond Aranjuez, on the road to Toledo. When she came up, he placed her in his own carriage, and conducted her in a species of triumph to Buenretiro. She remained there for some days, during which the King made her long visits, and usually took his repasts with her. All the Court paid her their respects, and after she had remained long enough at Buenretiro to receive their compliments, she retired to the residence of the Duke d'Uzeda, which she had hired, and where she remained for the rest of her days,[1]—the royal palace not being large enough to accommodate both the Queens. The joy on account of her arrival at Madrid, appeared as great and universal as it was two years before, when Don John returned from Saragossa and the Queen departed for Toledo, a wretched fugitive, followed by the execrations of the people. The Countess d'Aulnoy, who had visited her at Toledo, went to kiss her hand on her arrival at the capital. She looked more cheerful than she had done in the Alcazar, and said that she had not expected to come so soon back to Madrid, but that now it seemed as if she had never been out of it. Her maids of honour, who had been devoured by *ennui* at Toledo, were now in the full enjoyment of the most refined amusements of Madrid. During the visit, a giantess, who came from the Indies, was introduced. The ladies made this colossus dance, while she held in each hand

[1] Ortiz, *Compend. Cronol.*, t. vi. lib. xxi. c. 5.

two she dwarfs, who played on the castanets and the Biscay drum. Madame d'Aulnoy's Spanish kinswoman observed in the Queen-mother's apartment many articles which had belonged to Don John, and, among others, an admirable pendulum clock set with diamonds.[1]

About the period of Don John's decease, the ambassador extraordinary at Paris had informed the court of Madrid of the precise day on which the young Queen would arrive at Irun, a town situated on the Bidassoa, and the first on the Spanish frontier when crossing it from France by the way of St Jean-de-Luz. All those who had been appointed to the household of the Queen, proceeded in great pomp to the vicinity of that station, with the Dutchess of Terranueva and the Marques of Astorga at their head, in order to receive their royal mistress. So long as she remained in the French territories, she was under charge of the Duke of Harcourt, who acted as ambassador extraordinary from Louis XIV. One of the first persons who ventured to offer advice to the Queen, and to instil into her mind insidious principles, was a Theatin called the Father Ventimiglia, who advanced as far as Bayonne on pretext of paying his respects to her. He was born in Sicily, and was of an illustrious family in that island, being the brother of the Count de Prado, who had been governor of Palermo during the late revolt at Messina, and had been sent prisoner to Madrid in order to suffer punishment for some misconduct in the course of that commotion. The Theatin accompanied his brother to Spain in order to aid him with his talents and interest. He was a man equally bold and subtile, and so devoted to the interests of Don John, that his zeal led him to speak of the Queen-mother, even in his sermons, with little deference or respect. So long as Don John survived, he entertained the expectation of being appointed confessor to the new Queen.

[1] *Voyage d'Espagne.*

But though this hope perished with his patron, he resolved to obtain early access to her Majesty, in order to instil into her mind a suspicion and dislike both of the Queen-mother and the Marquis de Villars, the French ambassador at Madrid. To this he was instigated by a wish to injure those who had been the enemies of Don John—to revive, if possible, his party in Spain, and to form a Junta of Government which should be entirely dependent on the new Queen. His high birth, his prepossessing manners, and his knowledge of the French language, procured him frequent opportunities for interviews. In these, and in a plan of government he submitted in writing to the Queen's consideration, it is probable that those suspicions concerning her mother-in-law were first sown, which were subsequently productive of so much unhappiness and so many miserable intrigues at the Court of Spain. The Theatin who thus met Louisa d'Orleans in the first bloom of youth and beauty, delivered her funeral oration at Naples, ten years afterwards, in the church of Santa Chiara.[1]

The Queen left St Jean-de-Luz on the 3d of November, escorted by the body guards of the King of France. She proceeded to the wooden building in the Isle of Pheasants, which had been the house of conference at the treaty of the Pyrenees, and which, having been recently fitted up for her reception, now contained many handsome apartments, beautifully gilt and painted, and splendidly furnished with crimson damask. On her arrival at this temporary habitation, she attired herself magnificently, and partook of a collation which had been provided for her. She appeared, however, to be oppressed with a melancholy, which marked her deep regret at quitting, probably for ever, her native country. The Dutchess of Terranueva, at the head of a formidable band of ladies of honour, met her on the middle of the bridge by which she

[1] Gianonne, *Stor. Civile di Napoli*, lib. xl. c. 2.

reached the Isle of Pheasants. The Marques of Astorga
was waiting in a boat on the river, near the spot; and,
on being informed that the Queen was ready to receive him, landed, with a numerous train of gentlemen
and pages. On being introduced, he threw himself at the
feet of her Majesty, and, addressing her in the Spanish
language, presented two letters, one from the King his
master, and the other from the Queen-mother. The
Duke of Harcourt now announced, that he had the orders of his sovereign to consign the Queen into the hands
of the Marques of Astorga, who, after presenting to her
several Spaniards of distinguished rank, and, among others,
the Bishop of Pampeluna, reminded her that it was time
to set out on their journey.[1] She then embarked in a
barge which was beautifully ornamented, and was dragged
along the river by sailors in small boats. All the Spanish noblemen and knights discharged their pistols, and a
salute was fired by the artillery of Fontarabia. But the
eyes of the Queen were constantly turned to the French
shore, and her looks sufficiently testified the emotions by
which her bosom was agitated. Towards evening, she
landed in the vicinity of Irun, where a small and wretched supper, cooked and served up according to the Spanish
fashion, was placed before her. She expressed the utmost
surprise at the bad entertainment which had been prepared for her. She could hardly be prevailed on to partake of any of the ill-dressed dishes; and she was also
much disappointed at being compelled to sup in private,
instead of being allowed to eat in public, as she had been
accustomed during the preceding part of her journey.

Independently of her uncomfortable supper, the Queen
found herself in almost every other respect, placed in an
unpleasant situation. She was among total strangers, who
did not understand the French language; and, as yet, she
was almost wholly ignorant of the Spanish tongue. The

[1] *Noticia de la Llegada de la Reyna nuestra Señora à estos Reynos.*

manners and customs of the country were so different from those of France, that she could not be easily reconciled to them. Every thing was regulated by the restraint of the strictest formality and reserve. From her first entrance on their territory, the Spaniards supposed that she was to know all their ceremonies and fashions, as if she had passed her whole life at Buenretiro or Aranjuez. When they found she was not perfect in Spanish form, they compelled her, from the commencement, to its strictest observances ; and she could not stir without finding the gorgon eyes of the Dutchess of Terranueva fixed on all her movements.

It might have been supposed that, with a view towards her own interest, the Dutchess would have done all in her power to conciliate the Queen, especially as she had a great number of enemies, and had now lost her protector Don John, by whom she was raised to her present situation. But as there was hardly any precedent for a Camarera Mayor being dismissed from her employment, she probably regarded it as a thing for life ; and, in consequence, she followed a totally different course from that which it seemed most probable she would pursue. By acting the part of the Duenna, and being at all times a spy on the actions of the Queen, she ingratiated herself with the King. She studied all his caprices and jealous humours, and by insinuating herself into the confidence of the few French ladies who had accompanied her royal mistress, she obtained possession of some trifling anecdotes, from which she drew malignant conclusions, and speedily converted into poison the most innocent ingredients.

She also perceived that it was essential to her interests that the Queen should form no ties of amity or confidence with her mother-in-law, who hated the Dutchess as an old partizan of Don John, and would insist on her removal if she obtained any influence over her daughter. The

mind of the Queen had been already prepared on this subject, by the insinuations of the Theatin Ventimiglia.
She therefore listened with credulity to the assertion that
the Queen-dowager had never forgiven her as being the
cause of the rupture of the projected alliance with the
Austrian Archdutchess; that she would indulge the enmity she felt towards her in every possible way, and would
counteract her influence on every occasion. Even before
the Queen had quitted Irun, the Dutchess persuaded all
those who had access to her presence to repeat similar
sentiments, and also to prejudice her against the French
ambassador, as an ally of the Queen-mother, and an ancient enemy of Don John, to whom it was broadly hinted that she was indebted for her elevation to the throne
of Spain. Her Majesty was much agitated and perplexed by all these representations, as she was placed almost in
a new world, without experience, and with none on whom
she could depend for disinterested counsel.

The remainder of the journey from Irun to Burgos,
whither the King had advanced to meet her, was performed by the Queen, partly in her carriage, and partly
on horseback. She proceeded at a very slow pace, and her
progress was rendered peculiarly unpleasant, by the constant and violent altercations between the Duke d'Ossuna and the Marques of Astorga, concerning points of
precedence, and the respective places they were entitled
to occupy in the cavalcade. She had experienced stormy
and rainy weather all the way from Fontainbleau to
Irun: It was little better during the greater part of
her journey from that town to Madrid, and the roads
were in consequence so bad, that a carriage could with
difficulty pass.[1] At Vittoria, and the other towns through

[1] *Noticia de las Entregas de la Reyna Nuestra Señora*, in *La
Gazeta de Madrid*, 1679.

which her Majesty proceeded, she was entertained with
bull-fights, and some wretched dramatic exhibitions. As
she advanced, she received from time to time magnificent
presents, which were sent to her from the King and
Queen-mother, of diamond ear-rings, a watch, set with
diamonds, and bracelets of rubies. She also obtained special leave, by an order from the King, to eat in public—
an indulgence on which her heart seems always to have
been particularly bent, but which these formidable persons, the Marques of Astorga and the Camarera-Mayor,
would on no account allow without the royal permission.

The Marquis of Villars came to pay his respects to the
Queen at Bribiesca, and, though he had but a short interview, he did not fail to remark that she was much disquieted, and that she manifested a particular distrust towards himself. He was not aware of the cause; but as
he suspected that she had received some unfavourable impressions from those by whom she was surrounded, he
cautioned her against listening too readily to those suggestions which each interested courtier or attendant would
now be so eager to make. Her safest course, he assured
her, would be, to love the King, and to use every means
which might render herself beloved by him in return.
He counselled her to form a strict union with the Queen-
mother, and declared, that if she proffered amity, that
princess would entertain for her reciprocal sentiments of
affection. The Queen was prepared for this discourse:
It was such, she had been informed, as she might expect
to hear from the ambassador, and her suspicions having
been once excited, she unfortunately attributed political
and selfish motives to his whole conversation.

It was arranged that the Queen should arrive on the
18th of November at Quintanapalla, a small village about
three leagues distant from Burgos; and a plot was at the

same time hatched among the Spaniards, to prevent the
French ambassadors, Harcourt and Villars, from being
present at the celebration of the nuptials.   Accordingly,
while it was publicly given out that the marriage ceremony
would be performed at Burgos, it was privately settled that
it should take place at Quintanapalla.   The stratagem,
however, was discovered, and after much acrimonious discussion with the Dutchess of Terranueva, it was at length
agreed that the ambassadors should be allowed to assist
at the celebration, which, however, it was still resolved
should be held at this miserable village.

Her Majesty reached Quintanapalla on the day intended, and on the following morning, as early as ten o'clock,
the King arrived from Burgos, where he had been detained nearly three weeks by indisposition.   The Queen,
after having taken a look of him from the balcony of
the house, as he alighted,[1] went to receive him, dressed
in a Spanish garb, and met him when he entered her
antechamber.   It is said that she was strangely surprised at first seeing him; he wore a close short-bodied
coat of gray paragon—velvet breeches—stockings of raw
silk, and a gray hat; and his hair, which was very long,
was combed behind his ears.[2]   When she had recovered from her wonder, she attempted several times to kiss
his hand, and to throw herself at his feet.   But he prevented her, and saluted her in the Spanish manner, by
pressing her arms with his two hands, and repeatedly
calling her *Mireyna, Mireyna,* (my Queen, my Queen.[3])
As the King was totally ignorant of the French language,
and his bride knew little Spanish, they discoursed for
some time, without well understanding each other's mean-

[1] *Gazeta de Madrid,* 1679.
[2] D'Aulnoy, *Voyage d'Espagne,* t. ii.
[3] D'Aulnoy, *Mém. de la Cour d'Espagne.*

ing, when the Marquis de Villars, perceiving their embarrassment, took on himself the office of interpreter, and, it is said that, in his translations, he added much spirit and tenderness to the conversation of the King. . . . . At the commencement of the marriage ceremony, which was performed privately in the Queen's antechamber, the Marquis de Villars objected, that the Spanish grandees had stationed themselves on the right hand of the King, whereas, at Fontainbleau, when the nuptials were celebrated by proxy, this place of honour was yielded to the Spanish ambassadors, and should now be assigned to the French envoys. The Constable of Castile made some opposition to this claim; but it was at length sustained, and the Grandees ranged themselves behind the King, or on his left hand. As the Archbishop of Burgos was prevented from attending by indisposition, Antonio de Benavides, the Patriarch of the Indies, and Grand Almoner, pronounced the nuptial benediction. While mass was celebrating, a white riband, tied up into love-knots, was thrown around the King and Queen, and their heads and shoulders were covered with a piece of white gauze bordered by a silver fringe. When the ceremony was concluded, they dined in public, and the Marques of Astorga gave a magnificent entertainment to the household of both their Majesties; but, at the commencement of the third course, the unwelcome trumpets sounded the signal for departure.[1] The royal pair set out in the afternoon for Burgos, and travelled alone in their carriage, preceded by several Grandees of Spain dressed in the regal liveries. The King appeared all the while to be very attentive and gallant. On their arrival at the capital of Old Castile, a play was represented in the palace of its ancient monarchs, and brilliant fireworks were exhibited.

[1] *Gazeta de Madrid*, 1679.

On the following day the Queen dined at a convent of
Nuns called Las Huelgas, situated in the suburbs of
Burgos. At three in the afternoon she made a public
entrance into the city, mounted on a dark chestnut horse,
and dressed in the Spanish fashion. On this occasion
she appeared so lovely and engaging, that her new subjects were transported at the sight, and her figure was
contrasted most agreeably with that of the old Dutchess
of Terranueva, who made a most wretched show on her
mule. Next day there was a bull-fight, with which her
Majesty was much entertained, as the cavaliers displayed
great address and courage; and on the following morning there were horse-races, which were run by sixty
knights dressed in silver brocade.

Three days having been spent in these amusements, it
was considered as time to set out for Madrid. Before her
departure from Burgos, the Queen took leave of the
French gentlemen and ladies who had accompanied her
thus far on her journey. She parted from them with
many tears and obliging expressions, and she presented
several of them with her portrait set in diamonds. She
was allowed to retain in her service a few female attendants,[1] some household officers for her table, and a groom
who had charge of six English horses which she had
brought along with her.

[1] She would not have sustained much loss had she been deprived
of them all, if they were of the character which the Dutchess d'Or-
léans gives of Madame de Grancey, who had been what is called
in France the *Dame d'Atours* of the Queen of Spain, and now accompanied her to Madrid. "She was the Mistress of the Chevalier de
Lorraine," says the Dutchess in the correspondence attributed to
her, "and had never done any thing but sit at play with her lovers
until five or six o'clock in the morning, feast, smoke tobacco, and
follow, uncontrolled, her inclinations. When she attended the
Queen to Spain, as *Dame d'Atours*, she was locked up in the evening, and was in great grief about it."

Though accompanied by a numerous escort, the King and Queen were alone in the carriage on their journey from Burgos to Madrid. The distance between these two cities is only 40 Spanish leagues, or about 150 English miles; yet they stopped five or six nights on the way, sleeping at Lerma, Aranda de Duero, St Estevan de Gormas, Guadalaxara, and, lastly, Torrejon de Ardoz, which is only three leagues from Madrid.

It was yet too soon to suggest to the King any special ground of suspicion against the Queen; but the Dutchess of Terranueva had ample opportunity, during this long protracted journey, to foster in the mind of Charles those jealous sentiments which seemed, in that age, to be inherent in the breast of every Spaniard. She represented to his Majesty, whose confidence she had now completely gained, the evil consequences which had so often resulted from the freedom allowed to ladies in France. She hinted that the Queen was young, lively, and accustomed to gaiety; and she concluded every discourse with the maxim, that a woman is virtuous only so long as she has no opportunity of being otherwise.

The Queen-mother had arrived at Torrejon, the last stage from Madrid, in order to receive the royal pair. They all met with much apparent affection; and the young Queen, however much she had been prejudiced against her mother-in-law, assured her, on this occasion, that the sentiments she felt were those of unbounded respect and attachment. As there was not sufficient accommodation for her at Torrejon, the Queen-Dowager returned to Madrid in the evening,[1] but the King and his bride remained there all night, and proceeded next morning, (22d of December), to their capital in a coach, of which the curtains were left open, that they might be seen by all the inhabitants. They alighted at the church of Our Lady

[1] *Gazeta Ordinar. de Madrid*, 5th Dec. 1679.

of Atocha, where *Te Deum* was sung; and as the apartments in the royal palace within the city were not yet ready for their reception, they went in the evening to sleep at Buenretiro.

As soon as the Queen had arrived at this residence, the Dutchess of Terranueva, who wished to deprive her of all liberty, and to become herself, in her capacity of Camarera-Mayor, the sole arbitress of her conduct and actions, resolved that she should not be permitted to receive any visits till after she had made her public entrance into Madrid. Meanwhile the time passed heavily along, and the Queen, though possessed of the utmost sweetness of temper, waited with some impatience for the day of that ceremony, which she hoped would at least restore her to comparative freedom. For not only was she at present forbidden to see company, but was kept, for the most part, shut up in her apartment, except when she was brought out to witness the representation of long and tiresome Spanish comedies, of which she did not understand a syllable.[1] She had constantly before her eyes the morose and grim Camarera, who never smiled, and rarely spoke, except to rebuke her French vivacity, and to repress her still buoyant spirits.

The Marquis de Villars was aware of the harsh treatment she suffered; but was positively refused admittance to the Queen. At length, on a formal representation being made to the King, he was allowed one interview in private. The Marchioness de Villars, who thought she might accompany her husband to this audience, was driven from the palace gate by the Camarera-Mayor. Subsequently, however, the Queen-mother, who was occasionally permitted to see her daughter-in-law, remarking the deep

---

[1] The last theatrical representation she had seen before quitting France, was the *Phèdre* of Racine followed by the *Sicilien* of Moliere. (*Gazeta de Madrid*, 1679.)

melancholy in which she was now plunged, in consequence of continual restraint and, solitude, obtained leave for the Marchioness to visit her under certain limitations. Two caskets of valuable jewels, seasonably presented to the Queen-mother, procured for her the pleasure of going to a royal chase at the Pardo. This was the first time she had been on horseback since her arrival at Buena-tiro. The King killed a large boar in her presence, and afterwards permitted her to accompany him frequently to the chase.[1]

At length, the long expected day appointed for the Queen's public entrance into Madrid arrived. The preparations for this ceremony had been prodigious. Though Spain was in the last stage of poverty and decay, she was still well fitted to make a splendid appearance at solemn processions and bridal festivals. Her commerce and agriculture had perished, and her vast dominions were melting away; but the diamonds of India still remained, and sparkled as bright as in the days of Imperial Charles. On the morning which had been fixed for the commencement of the ceremonial, the Queen-mother repaired to Buen-retiro, which she soon after quitted along with the King. They went together to inspect all the streets through which the Queen was to make her progress, and which had been previously adorned with tapestry, sculpture, and triumphal arches. They then proceeded to a balcony on the house of the Countess d'Oñate, fitted up for the occasion with lattices, whence they were to view the procession. The Queen mounted her horse, which was a fiery Andalusian, about eleven o'clock of the forenoon. Her long hair fell loose over her shoulders and forehead. She wore a richly embroidered riding habit, and a small fardingal. Her hat was adorned with white, and carnation coloured plumes, and was tucked up on one side

[1] *Mém. de la Cour d'Espagne.*

lip or diamond clasp, whence hung the celebrated pearl called *Peregrina*, which was of inestimable value, and as large as a small pear. She bore on one of her fingers the King's chief diamond, which surpassed in size and lustre every gem in the world. But the grace displayed by the Queen in all her movements, particularly in the management of her steed, and the charms of her person, attracted far more admiration than the jewels, dazzling as they were, by which she was adorned. She was now in the first bloom and radiance of youth,—her aspect was mild and her mien graceful,—her eyes were black, large, and lively, —her eyebrows arched,—her lips rosy but somewhat thick, and her hair, which she wore in great profusion, of a dark chestnut colour.[1]

The drummers and trumpeters of the town, dressed in black and red suits, preceded the whole cavalcade; then came the Alcades of the Court,—the Knights of the three military Orders, in cloaks embroidered with gold, —the officers of the King's household in white robes and hats studded with diamonds, and the Mayordomos of the Queen. These officers, who were mostly Grandees of Spain, were all mounted on beautiful steeds, and were attended by their pages or grooms, in liveries of gold or silver brocade, mixed with coloured silk. The equerries of the Queen walked on foot immediately before her; the Conde de Villa-mayna, chief usher, was on her right hand, holding the horse's reins, and a canopy was carried over her head. The Dutchess of Terranueva, who was the worst[2] feature in the procession, was immediately behind her royal mistress, mounted on a mule, and dressed as a Duenna, with a terrific hat on her head. Eight of the Queen's maids of honour, some of whom were ex-

[1] Vera Tassis, *Noticias Histor. de la Enfermedad y Muerte de Doña Luisa d'Orleans Nuestra Señora.* Madrid, 1690. Folio.

[2] *Relacion del recibimiento y entrada de la Reyna en Madrid.*

tremely beautiful, and belonged to the noblest families in
the realm, next appeared, all covered with diamonds and
embroidery, and mounted on fine horses,—each with two
gentlemen of the court walking by her side. The Queen's
coaches, and several caparisoned horses, which were led by
grooms in magnificent liveries, went after them, and the
guards of the Lancilla brought up the rear. . .

On the walk of the Prado, along which the procession
moved in its progress into Madrid, there was an open
gallery constructed, in the different compartments of
which were blazoned the arms of all the kingdoms of
Spain. At the end of this gallery stood a triumphal arch,
painted with appropriate emblems, under which the Queen
passed from the Prado into the city. At this spot the
Corregidor and other municipal officers of Madrid, clothed in crimson velvet robes, and with caps, such as those
worn by the ancient Castilians, presented her with the
keys of the town, and brought along with them a rich
canopy, which they carried over her head during the rest of
her progress. The streets through which they proceeded
were lined with gilt statues, emblematic of all virtues and
blessings. In Madrid particular quarters of the city were
appropriated to different trades, and on this occasion displayed characteristic ornaments. Thus the street which
the furriers inhabited, was full of stuffed tigers and bears,
and that where the goldsmiths dwelt was set out with
little angels of pure gold and silver. The walls of all the
houses were fitted with balconies, from which hung the
finest tapestry ; and as the procession went along, the delighted people rent the air with acclamations. When the
Queen came in front of the balcony at the palace of the
Countess d'Oñate, she stopped in order to salute the King
and Queen-mother, who half opened the lattices to see
her. She then continued her progress till she arrived at
the Great Court of the palace of Madrid, which was sur-

rounded with young men and maids, who, crowned with reeds and water lilies, represented all the rivers of Spain. The King and Queen-mother, having come privately and more quickly by another road, were also waiting to receive her. The King himself assisted her to alight, and the Queen-mother, taking her by the hand, conducted her to the apartments which had been prepared for her reception. In the evening there were displays of fireworks, and the town was brilliantly illuminated.[1]

On the day after this public entrance, *Te Deum* was sung in the chapel of the palace, in presence of the royal family, of the grandees and officers of the Court, and all the foreign ambassadors. After dinner, the King and Queen went out together, for the first time, in public, to the church of Our Lady of Atocha. They were drawn in a chariot, built in the form of a triumphal car, and open on all sides, that they might be seen by their subjects. They crossed the great square in which the palace is situated, and passed along several streets, the balconies of which were crowded with ladies, who mingled their acclamations with the shouts of the multitude below. The grandees followed their Majesties in magnificent coaches, and with numerous attendants. As it was night when the royal pair returned to the palace, flambeaux were placed in the windows of all the houses, and the town was thus so completely illumined, that one extremity of a long straight street was visible from the other. But the best effect of lights was produced in the Plaça Mayer, where the lofty buildings had five rows of balconies above each other; to which, in all, more than 3000 flambeaux were fixed. For several successive days there was a continuation of all sorts of entertainments. Bull-fights, the chace, and theatrical amusements, followed each other with little

[1] *Mém. de la Cour d'Espagne. Voyage d'Espagne. Flores, Reynas d'España,* t. ii.

intermission.   Sometimes the King and Queen went to sup with the Queen-mother, at her residence in the mansion of Uzeda; while, at other times, she was regaled in the royal palace.   All the ladies of distinction had the honour of kissing the Queen's hand, and the members of the councils of state were admitted to her presence, to pay their duty and respect.   During the whole course of the entertainments and festivals, the grandees vied with each other in the splendour of their equipages, and the number of their retinue.   Several of them, during nine successive days, displayed nine different liveries, each more gorgeous than the preceding; and they sometimes carried their jealous competition so far as to overset each other's coaches on the streets.   A bull-fight was about this time exhibited, which surpassed in magnificence all former festivals of a similar description.   It was held, as usual, in the Plaça Mayor.   The houses in this square, which was the largest in Madrid, were fitted out with balconies on every story.   These were covered with embroidered carpets, and were crowded with persons of the greatest dignity and highest offices, and ladies in the richest attire.   The balcony appropriated to the King and Queen was larger than the others, and stood in the centre of one side of the square.   There were also seats on the ground, rising, as in a theatre, one above the other till they reached the balconies in the first stories of the houses.   By the King's directions, a collation of sweetmeats and *liqueurs* was presented to all persons of distinction.   Before the fight began, the square was filled with *cavalleros*, richly dressed, and mounted on fine horses.   Each was distinguished by a scarf or knot, of the colour supposed most agreeable to some mistress, to whom, if he discovered her in the balconies, he paid obeisance.   When the place had been cleared of these knights, the alguazils, clothed in white garments, and with plumes of feathers in their hats, entered the square, and introduced the cavaliers who intended to join in the combat. Six, who were dressed as Turks, Moors, or Armenians,[1] presented themselves, and thus entered the lists in the picturesque garbs of various nations. All these knights first came under the King's balcony, and asked permission to fight. The Duke of Medina-Sidonia, who was one of the number, had the good fortune to kill two bulls with two thrusts of his spear. The Count de Kœningsmark, a Swede, who was another of the six,[1] was not so lucky: he was wounded desperately by a bull, when a fine Spanish lady, in whose honour he fought, stood forward in her balcony, and made several signs with her handkerchief to encourage him. Though forced to lean on one of his attendants, who held him up, he went forward, sword in hand, and gave the bull a wound in the head; and, before he was borne off, he bowed to the spectators, and kissed his sword to the Beauty in the balcony.[2]

It was the custom in Spain on great occasions either of congratulation or condolence, for the different kingdoms and provinces to send deputies to Court, in order to express their participation in the grief or joy of their sovereign. Some days after the public entrance of the Queen, his Majesty received several deputations, which were composed of the chief noblemen in their respective districts. On the day that the King gave these envoys audience, there was a great boar-hunt, in which a number of wild animals were killed. The Queen, who was an excellent horsewoman, was often foremost in the chace. The Duke d'Infantado, who, in the absence of the Marques of Liche, acted as the royal huntsman, conducted the Queen, as if accidentally, to a

---

[1] *Gazeta de Madrid*, 13th February 1680.

[2] Van Ap-Rhyss, *Description of Spain*. Flores, *Reynas d'España.*

delightful part of the forest. This sequestered spot was irrigated and refreshed by a number of streams and fountains. Under the shade of lofty and umbrageous trees, a canopy of cloth of gold was stretched out. The branches were thronged with monkeys, squirrels, and a variety of different sorts of birds. Boys habited as fauns or satyrs, with girls representing nymphs and shepherdesses, presented her Majesty with an elegant collation. She at first seemed pleased with the entertainment: But, whatever may have been the painful reflections which obtruded themselves, she appeared during the rest of the day to be absorbed in melancholy. Scenes, perhaps, of rustic cheerfulness and freedom, were unpleasantly contrasted in her mind with the gloom of her palace, and the restraints of royalty.

In fact, in changing her residence from Buenretiro to the palace at Madrid, the Queen obtained but little more freedom of society or enjoyment. After those days had passed over which were allotted to the tumult of her public entrance, and the concomitant rejoicings, the tenor of her life returned to its former dull and listless monotony. The Dutchess of Terranueva still continued her inflexible command, and the rules she enjoined were the most intolerable that could be prescribed. She would not even allow the Queen to look out from the window, which she pronounced to be utterly inconsistent with the dignity of the royal Consort. She was now, indeed, permitted to receive the visits of a few more Spanish ladies of distinction than formerly. But she scarcely as yet understood the language in which they spoke. There was no mutual friendship or confidence; all was respect, and state, and ceremony. Hence, she was not gay, though she seems to have lived in all the colours of the rainbow. One French lady of rank, who was at this time admitted for a short while to her presence, found her sitting in a small apartment, which was ornamentally painted and gilded, and the ceiling inlaid with mirrors. She was seated near the window, on a cushion of blue silk, interwoven with threads of gold. Her head was bare, and her locks separated from the middle, fell down gracefully, on both sides, to her shoulders. One lock, which was braided and strung with pearls, reached her zone, to which it was fastened by a diamond. She was attired in a habit of rose-coloured velvet, embroidered with silver, and her ear-rings hung down to her throat. As the Camarera-mayor was present, she durst not speak in French, which was contrary to rule, and she made but poor attempts to express herself in Spanish. She inquired eagerly for news from France,—asked to see any letters which her visitor might receive from that country; and, on her taking leave, ventured to express, in a whisper, her warm attachment to her native land.[1]

The royal nuptials, it was rumoured, were not attended with consequences worthy of the preparations which had been made on account of them; and Louis XIV, who relied on the virtue of his niece, soon became aware that, on the death of the reigning monarch, the succession would inevitably open to his own descendants, by his Queen Maria Theresa.[2]

[1] *Mém. de la Cour d'Espagne.*

[2] " Era el Rey," says the Marques San-Phelipe, " sin succession, y con fama (aunque no muy cierta) de inhabil à la generacion. Esto secreto, como era en sì, descubrió al Rey de Francia Marie Luisa de Borbòn, primera muger del Rey." (*Comentarios de la Guerra d'España,* t. i. p. 1.)

CHAPTER VI.

COURT INTRIGUES AND AMUSEMENTS.

To brisk notes in cadence beating
Glance their many twinkling feet :
Slow melting strains their Queen's approach declare,
Where'er she moves the Graces homage pay.
GRAY.

NEVER had the Court of Spain been so crowded and brilliant as at the time of the marriage of Charles II, with the Princess Louisa d'Orleans. Some grandees had repaired to Madrid, that they might shine amid the pomp of public spectacles ; but others frequented the Court in expectation of political preferment. The death of John of Austria had left the state without a minister, and brought forward a multitude of noble candidates for those high appointments which had been hitherto distributed among his creatures and dependents. Don John had expired at the moment when the King and the royal household were about to leave Madrid, in order to meet the new Queen. It was not expected that his Majesty should have nominated a minister at that period ; and political affairs after his return, were for a time forgotten, amid the tumult and rejoicings consequent on the royal nuptials. But when these were past, the attention of the Court and people was naturally turned to the formation of a ministry capable of conducting the affairs of state, which were, in the mean while, chiefly directed by Jerome Eguya, a low adventurer, of the political school of Valenzuela. He was not even a member of any of the great councils of state; but merely held the office of his Majesty's secretary, by a species of commission or delegation.

In her *Mémoires de la Cour d'Espagne*, the Countess d'Aulnoy has presented us with a most graphical delineation of the Spanish grandees who were at this time the chief candidates for that court favour and preferment which (as there was no longer a John of Austria, Olivarez, or Lerma, to engross the whole patronage) now lay open to those who were best entitled by their birth, talents, and address, to aspire to the lucrative or influential offices of the state. Of these, some might be dexterous intriguers, and well skilled in the arts by which weak minds are managed, or in the tricks by which the ascendency of rivals is depressed. But not one of them was in any view a statesman. They were all alike ignorant of the principles of government, of the sources of national prosperity, or causes of national decay.

The Duke of Medina del Rio-Seco, whose family name was Henriquez, and who was generally known by the title of Admiral of Castile, was descended from an illegitimate branch of the ancient monarchs of that kingdom. He was a powerful and wealthy nobleman,—his person was considered as the most handsome of the time in which he lived; and his highly distinguished mein was united with manners which, at the same time, were perfectly easy and graceful. Possessing a great share of wit and vivacity, he wrote, with facility, very elegant verses, and paid more attention to this amusement than to his domestic affairs. He was a libertine and voluptuary by temperament, and lived, as it is called, for himself. At this period he was inconsolable because he had reached the age of fifty-eight. But he was still surrounded by a number of mistresses, for whose sake he had greatly impaired his fortune. His Dutchess had been accustomed to see fifteen or sixteen of these favourites occupy the finest apartments in his palace.

Hitherto the Admiral of Castile had not paid his court regularly or assiduously, either to the King or any minister of state, being convinced that the restraint which such attendance imposes, cannot be compensated by the most extensive privileges of power or the richest gifts of fortune. He also mixed little in general society, being fond of retirement, and too fastidious in his tastes to relish general intercourse. He had passed his time, like a sensual philosopher, in the voluptuous seclusion of the most magnificent palace and most delicious gardens in Madrid, till the circumstances of the times, and the recent opening to the career of ambition, led him to sacrifice some part of his ease and leisure to the pursuit of objects which he never attained.[1]

The Prince of Stigliano, formerly Duke of Medina delas-Torres, was son of the Duke of that title who married the daughter of the Count Olivarez, and was prime minister at the time of the death of Philip IV. He derived the title of Stigliano from his mother, a Neapolitan princess whom his father had espoused after the death of Maria de Guzman. At this time he was about forty-two years of age, and was united to the daughter of the Duke of Alva. As he had belonged to the party of the Queen, he was forbidden to appear at court during the ascendency of Don John. Though not destitute of natural talents and capacity, he wanted knowledge, experience, and the habit of exertion. He had scarcely ever quitted the capital during his whole life, and passed an

---

[1] In his old age he became a devotee ; and, on the spot in his gardens where a theatre formerly stood, he founded a monastery of Penitential Nuns, called of St Pasqual or Las Monjas del Almirante. (Pellicer, *Tratado sobre el Origen de la Comedia*, parte ii. p. 94.) He lived till the year 1691.

indolent voluptuous existence in his palace and gardens
of Florida, near Buenretiro, which were adorned with
fountains and statues.   He was possessed of immense
wealth, and indeed was accounted the richest subject in
Spain, except the Dukes of Medina-Sidonia and Medina-
Celi. But though his annual income amounted to 120,000
ducats, or about L. 25,000 Sterling, and though he neither paid nor received visits, his affairs, from want of management and order, were in a state of constant embarrassment.   Such was his indolence and pride, that though
he had places and commissions to dispose of to the value
of 20,000 ducats a-year, he refused to affix his signature
to the requisite documents, saying that it was not suitable
to the generosity of so high a grandee to trouble himself
concerning so small a matter.[1]   In consequence, the
King filled up the offices, and received the profits for the
treasury.[2]

The Duke d'Ossuna was equally distinguished by his
good and bad qualities. He was remarkable for his acute-
ness of understanding, firmness of purpose and liberality;
he warmly loved his friends, and willingly aided them
either with his purse or influence.   But he was an implacable enemy, and had all that pride and fierceness which
spring from an overweening self-estimation.   Though
now forty-nine years of age, he still adored the fair sex,
and spared nothing to obtain their favour.

The Marques of Liche or Eliche, sometimes called
Marques of Carpio, was the son of the minister Luis de

---

[1] *Voyage d'Espagne.*

[2] He died without issue in 1689, and bequeathed all his Italian
estates to the King. (Ortiz, *Compend.*, t. vi. lib. 21. c. 6.)   His
younger brothers having predeceased him, he was succeeded in his
Spanish title and fortune by his paternal sister, who had married
the eleventh Duke of Medina Sidonia. (Vayrac, *Etat de l'Espagne*,
t. iv.)

Haro, and the title he bore was one which his father had inherited from the Count-Duke Olivarez. He has already been mentioned as having engaged, in early youth, in a conspiracy against his King, and having afterwards served him faithfully during the war with Portugal. In maturer years, his conduct and qualities betrayed the same inconsistency. At once liberal and avaricious, he displayed on some occasions the most disgraceful penury, and at others unbounded magnificence. He had a mansion near the palace, which was the finest private dwelling in Madrid, both as to extent of building and the articles it contained; and it would have been still more superb, had not Philip IV., who did not chuse to behold a rival to the royal residence in its immediate vicinity, restricted the execution of the original plan.[1] The Marques was plain, and even mean, in his personal appearance, but he was free from that indolence which characterised so many of the Spanish grandees; he was indeed so active, ambitious, and enterprising, that he was dreaded by the court, which usually contrived to keep him at a distance by employing him in foreign embassies.[2] His wife, who was a daughter of the Admiral of Castile, was one of the most distinguished beauties of the court. Nevertheless, he entertained a number of female favourites, and a saying by him, which has been recorded—that he would be the happiest of men if he had a mistress as handsome as his wife—marks the dissolute depravity of his disposition.

[1] Colmenar, *Annales d'Espagne*, t. ii. p. 132.

[2] He died Viceroy of Naples in 1687; and, according to Giannone, (*Stor. Civil.* lib. xl.) was the best governor sent there for many years. " A lui dobbiamo," says that author, " che non pur mentre ci governò si restituisse la quiete e la tranquilità, ma che in virtù di suoi buoni regolamenti vi durasse anche ne tempi di suoi successori."

His brother, the Count of Monterey, who has already been frequently mentioned, was more engaging in appearance, more prepossessing in manners, and more consistently liberal than the Marquis. He was not less ambitious, but was more prudent and cautious. During his government of Flanders, he had the good fortune both to obtain great popularity among the inhabitants of the Netherlands, and to give satisfaction to the Court of Madrid. But the reputation he had gained in the Low Countries, was somewhat tarnished by his unsuccessful prosecution of the war against the French in Catalonia. He had acquired the title which he bore in right of his wife, who was the heiress of the House of Monterey. She was a woman of a mean aspect; and, it was remarked as singular, that she should have fallen to the lot of the handsome brother, while the plain-looking Marques of Liche had obtained one of the most celebrated court beauties.

Of all the grandees, however, who at present frequented the Spanish Court, hoping to make glorious summer, the Duke of Medina-Celi and the Constable of Castile were considered as possessing the best claims to the office of *Privado* or first minister. Others gradually ranged themselves under the banners of these noblemen, and supported their pretensions with true party zeal. The court, and at length the nation, thus became divided into two separate factions, of which the Duke and the Constable were the leaders. The heads of these parties were nearly equal in birth and fortune, and in the dignity of their hereditary offices. But they were totally opposite in temper and disposition; and this difference in character, joined to the dislike produced by constant emulation, rendered ineffectual all the attempts of their mutual friends to reconcile them, and to promote their reciprocal interests by a political union.

At this time the Duke of Medina-Celi was forty-five

years of age. He was of a mild temper and insinuating
address, but he was too tardy and remiss for the execution of important enterprises. He had all his life been a
regular and assiduous courtier, and had manifested much
attachment to the person of the King. In a court where
the distinctions of birth and rank were reckoned essential
qualifications for the situation of prime minister, the Duke
derived considerable influence from his high descent—from
his own wealth as well as that of his Dutchess, who was
heiress of the house of Aragon de Cardona, and from the
dignified offices which he held of Great Chamberlain and
President of the Council of the Indies.

The Constable of Castile, who was of the ancient
family of Velasco, and also bore the title of Duke of Frias,
was about twelve years older than the Duke of Medina-
Celi. He was greatly superior to his rival in capacity,
intelligence, and experience : but his disposition was harsh
and austere, and his unyielding imperious temper had
frequently involved him in disputes with Don John, and
led him to reject the advances which that prince repeatedly made towards reconciliation. This disagreement
had naturally thrown the Constable into the party of the
Queen-mother, and he was now supported by her influence and that of her whole faction, while, on the other
hand, the remains of the party of Don John supported the Duke of Medina-Celi. The Constable, however, while he certainly aimed at the sole power in the
state, ostensibly proposed a Junta in whom the administration should be vested. The Grand Inquisitor, and
the Marquis of Mancera who understood something of
the routine of office, were to be conjoined in it with
himself : but he entertained no doubt, that, with these
colleagues, to whom he was vastly superior, both in talents and influence, he would in fact possess unlimited
sway in the government.

Of the two political rivals the Duke of Medina-Celi was supposed to be the most acceptable to his sovereign. By his calm demeanour and moderate conduct he had insinuated himself into the royal favour. He extended his influence gradually, and almost by imperceptible degrees —seeming always to aim at power rather in compliance with the wishes of his friends than for the gratification of his personal ambition.

While the parties of the Constable and the Duke of Medina-Celi were thus almost equally balanced, Don Jerome Eguya continued, in the mean while, to hold the reins of government. This minister soon perceived that his sole chance of retaining his influence depended on preserving an equilibrium between the two great political factions into which the nation was divided. The family of Eguya had been originally from Navarre, and his father was one of the principal attendants of the Duke of Turcis. In early youth he became the page of Don Pedro del Campo, at that time Secretary of State, and by his agreeable figure and winning manners, he soon insinuated himself into the favour of his master. On Don Pedro being displaced by Valenzuela, as not sufficiently subservient to his designs, he was appointed to discharge the duties of the situation which had been held by that secretary. With such a recent example before him, Eguya was careful not to split on the same rock; and being full of address and dissimulation, he preserved, by his ready compliance in all things, the favour of Valenzuela so long as it was worth retaining. As soon, however, as he discovered that Don John was at length likely to prevail in the political struggles which agitated the commencement of the present reign, he took the earliest opportunity of offering his services, and in consequence kept his place during the whole of Don John's administration. Though he had been one of the first to join his party

when his success became apparent, he was also the first
to abandon it when he perceived (and he saw those things
at a great distance) that Don John's credit was about to
fail. Acting now on the same principle by which he had
been guided in the time of Valenzuela, he entered into a
negotiation with the Queen-mother, to whom he proffered
his services, yet with signal ingratitude and duplicity he
frustrated her intentions for the recall of that exiled minister from the Philippine Islands. Though only performing the functions of Secretary of State without bearing the title, he had constant opportunities, amid all these
changes, of seeing the King, and discoursing with him
concerning political affairs; and he conducted himself
with such dexterity and address in conciliating the royal
favour, that his Majesty seems to have been unwilling to remove him, by placing either the Duke or the
Constable at the head of his counsels. Availing himself
of his situation and his frequent opportunities of access
to the King, he inspired him with distrust of both the
great parties into which the court was divided. When
he suspected that his sovereign was too favourably inclined towards the Duke of Medina-Celi, he recalled to his
remembrance the subjection in which he had been held
during the administration of Don John. He reminded
him of the persecution and banishment of the Queen, the
insults offered to so many persons of rank, the miseries of
the people, and those general disorders of the realm, which
he alleged were the inevitable consequence of abandoning
the government to the caprice of one individual. When
Eguya saw that these reminiscences inclined him towards
the Junta of government, which the Constable intended to
form, and place himself at its head, he inveighed against
this mode of administration, in which a number of ministers, with equal powers, embarrassed all affairs by their
mutual jealousies and contrarieties of opinion; he insi-

nuated, that though a junta might be suitable enough during a minority, his Majesty was no longer of an age to think of appointing governors over him, and that as the Constable must necessarily be a member of the Junta, the King would be retained, by his proud and domineering spirit, in a state of subjection, to which the former sway of Don John or of the Queen-mother would be comparative liberty.

By these, and similar discourses, Eguya, though a person of the lowest rank, and most limited understanding, contrived to balance the two parties of the Constable and the Duke. While he himself, in fact, directed all things, he had the art to persuade his master, that he was now, for the first time, an independent sovereign, but that he would again be reduced to subjection by the appointment of a prime-minister, or the formation of a Junta. From enjoying so much of the royal favour, and possessing the sole management of affairs, Eguya gradually began to form a third party for himself. Having the custody of the *Bolsillo*, or purse for fines leviable by the crown, of which he was not obliged to render any account, although they annually amounted to an immense sum, he had ample opportunities of extending his influence by means of private pensions and gratuities. He was also supported by the King's Confessor, and the Dutchess of Terranueva, both of whom conceived that the nomination either of a first minister or a Junta would prove injurious to their interests.

Meanwhile, the influence of the Queen-mother, which had been considerable ever since the death of Don John, began to be now on the wane. This she herself perceived, from her son's conversation and altered manner; but, being unwilling that it should also be observed by the public, she, in a great measure, absented herself from court, pleading her wish for retirement and repose, and her declining years.

The Constable of Castile was one of the first who discovered that her influence was decreasing and he was at
no loss to fathom the reasons of her retreat from court,
at which he felt much disquieted.   He had, in a great
measure, relied on her credit for success in his political
struggle with the Duke of Medina-Celi, and he now perceived, that if he wished to prevail over his rival, it would
be necessary to form new alliances and connections.   In
this situation, he turned his attention to Eguya, pretending that he would readily take a subordinate station in the
government under that secretary.   His overtures were favourably received, and he soon found himself united in a
close league with Eguya, the Dutchess of Terranueva,
and the Confessor.   To this coalition the Duke of Alva
was soon afterwards associated.

Eguya, however, had only listened to the propositions
of the Constable, with the view of balancing the influence
of the Duke of Medina-Celi, which, at that moment, he
believed to have the preponderance.   He early found a
pretext for dissolving this political connexion, in the imperious temper of his new ally, and he again sought to
awaken in the breast of the King his fears and distrust of
the Constable, who, on his part, soon penetrated into the
motives of the insidious Eguya.

The effect which this discovery had on the haughty
and violent temper of the Constable may be well conceived.   At the first meeting of the Council of State, of
which he was president, he arraigned the conduct of
Eguya with the utmost bitterness and acrimony.   He
represented, that the affairs of the nation were daily becoming more desperate—that Eguya, who alone conducted them, had neither natural talents nor experience in
business—that he ought to be strictly confined to the peculiar duties of his office, and not be allowed to interpose
in matters which far exceeded his capacity.   When he

had concluded his invective, Don Manuel de Lyra, who was secretary of state for the affairs of Italy, and had a private understanding with the Constable, presented a memorial to the council, in which he clearly showed the prejudice that the misconduct of Eguya had occasioned in the Italian department.

These complaints, however, were not attended with the consequences which had been anticipated. The King paid no regard to them, and the Constable soon after learned, that what little interest the Queen-mother might still possess, had been at least neutralized by the submissions and professions of attachment which the Duke of Medina-Celi had at length tendered to her. The Constable now perceived, that the political struggle in which he had been so long engaged, was entirely hopeless, whether for himself or the junta which he had planned, and that even if he should succeed in displacing Eguya, he would not be the successor to his power. He, therefore, resolved to take some credit with the King, and with his rival, by resigning all claim to a situation, to which, he found, it was in vain to aspire.

Accordingly, the first time that he had an opportunity of access to the King, he declared, that no person was more capable of serving him than the Duke of Medina-Celi ; and while using the utmost violence to his feelings, he expatiated, with apparent ease and cordiality, on the merits of his foe.

Meanwhile, the intrigues of the court, and the irresolution of the King concerning the appointment of a first minister, had deeply injured the best interests of the country. The influence of Eguya, who was destitute of talents, and accustomed only to the routine of office, aggravated the public disorders, and occasioned an almost total suspension in the machine of government. A general inac-

tion and lethargy pervaded each branch of the administration.   Every department became a scene of confusion,—
the measures brought before the Council remained unexe-
cuted, and the despatches submitted to the King never
passed through his hands,[1]—his constant answer to every
application being *Veremos.*

The disorders, however, of the state, and the indignant
complaints of the nation, as well as of all the foreign ambassadors, began to fill the mind of Eguya with alarm,
and to shake his confidence.   He now saw all the danger
of the situation in which he was placed; and it at length
appeared to him, that his sole chance of escaping popular
vengeance was, to induce the King to choose a prime
minister.   After much deliberation, he at last fixed on
the Duke of Medina-Celi, as more likely than the Constable to allow him to retain his subordinate situation
of secretary.   No farther obstacle now remaining to the
elevation of the Duke, he was promoted, by a formal
and regular decree, to the situation of first minister.
It was in general agreed at the Spanish Court, that the
King could not have made a better choice.   The good
qualities which the Duke possessed were of a popular description.   But all were surprised that a nobleman of his
wealth and independence, and of his quiet, indolent, disposition, should incur the toil and responsibility of directing affairs which were in a state of almost irremediable
confusion.   A total change in the system of government
would have been necessary to rectify evils which had accumulated so fearfully in the progress of ages; but there
was so little patriotism in the land, and so many of the
highest rank were interested in the continuance of abuses,
that it seemed scarcely practicable to effect an amendment.

[1] Coxe, *Memoirs of House of Bourbon.*

Those petty intrigues by which the Duke of Medina-Celi was at length installed in the situation of prime minister, are sufficiently contemptible; but their detail gives some insight into the manners of the age, and enables us to estimate the state of political morals.

As soon as it was known that the choice of the King had fallen on the Duke of Medina-Celi, all persons of distinction in Madrid—the officers of the crown, and the foreign ministers, crowded to pay their respects to the new favourite. On the day after his appointment, he repaired to the royal palace, accompanied by all his friends and relatives, to kiss his Majesty's hand. During the following day, on pretence of a slight indisposition, which was feigned to relieve him from the fatigue of ceremonies, he received visitors in his own apartment, and in bed. A Spanish grandee resting on his bed of state is a magnificent spectacle; he reclines in his collar, mantle, and feathered hat, and is generally decked out with all his diamonds. The Duke, as Grand Chamberlain of the King, reposed, on this occasion, in one of the chief royal chambers, which was splendidly furnished.

In the course of a few days he held a public audience in what was denominated the Hall of Rubies. He subsequently gave entrance there to the Pope's Nuncio, and the Venetian ambassador; but these two envoys were much dissatisfied at the manner in which the arm chairs were disposed, for they were so arranged that it was impossible to determine whether the place of honour had been assigned to them, or arrogated by the Duke to himself. And on their departure, he accompanied them only half way down the hall of audience, instead of attending them to the door. This neglect, as well as the dubious position of the seats, being reported to the French ambassador, he adopted all the necessary precautions previous to his own introduction. He sent to demand categorically from the Duke, that he should be received in conformity with the usage and precedents followed by Don Luis de Haro, in his interviews with the French ambassadors. He obtained, on this point, the most satisfactory assurances. The position of the chairs was altered, and that there might be no mistake or ambiguity in this momentous concern, they were all marked with the names of the dignitaries who were to repose in them.

The nation awaited, with the utmost impatience, the remedies which the new minister had undertaken to apply to the disorders of the state. But the diseases were too complicated, and too rooted in the constitution, to be easily eradicated. Though his intentions were good, the Duke was totally inexperienced, having never previously held any employment or office in the government. He was an admirable personification of the political genius of the Spanish nation. Inert and indolent, and uncertain what course to pursue, he never brought any thing to a conclusion. The most trifling matters were of as much difficulty to him as the most important; he was terrified by the prospect of long continued investigations which required perseverance, and he had as little inclination for those which demanded immediate despatch. Feeling his own want of experience, and being jealous of Eguya, who still continued Secretary of State, he brought forward other coadjutors, and endeavoured to lessen his difficulties by committing the deliberations of state to Juntas, formed for the occasion, of which one of the chief was a sort of finance committee. From such a motley administration emanated numerous plans, equally specious and impracticable. The public distress was aggravated, and the labours of such mock statesmen only served to expose the government to ridicule and contempt.

A depreciation of the copper coin from its present to a former value, which was one of the few measures carried into effect, was attended with the most fatal consequences. To correct the evils which this step had produced, the copper money was all called in, and the King promised to pay its real value in six months. But as this sort of coin was very abundant in the realm, and the people knew that the King could not fulfil his engagement, the intended remedy only served to aggravate the mischief, and to ruin public confidence. In consequence of the scarcity of bullion, the great families began to coin or sell their plate. Commerce was entirely at an end,—the shops were shut up,—scarcity and dearth followed the suspended circulation,—and the people were brought to such extremity, that, according to a proverbial expression of the nation, they were reduced to subsist on sunbeams.

In this posture of affairs, a merchant named Marcos Diaz, presented a memorial to the minister, wherein he suggested a plan, which he considered as calculated both to augment the revenues of the crown, and assuage the miseries of the people. He undertook to prove that the magistracy of Madrid, under pretext of reimbursing itself for money advanced to the late king, had levied immense sums, of which they had never rendered any proper account. He proposed that, after deducting the debt really due to them, they should be compelled to pay the surplus into the royal treasury, and that all similar embezzlements should be prevented in future. The memorial was favourably received by the Duke; and Diaz, thus encouraged, proceeded to give in other papers, exposing the means by which the royal revenues were so diminished and intercepted, that scarcely a tenth part found its way into the public treasury. Diaz, at the same time, agreed, on certain assignations of taxes being made to him, both to alleviate the imposts, and to advance considerable sums for the immediate exigencies of the impoverished state, as also for defraying the expenses of the royal household.

The Duke, who seems to have understood the Spanish character, was well aware of the danger to which Diaz exposed himself by such propositions. Those who subsisted on the plunder of the king and people, particularly the corregidors and municipality of Madrid, threatened him with assassination if he persisted in his plans, and menaces were even uttered against the King if he should be induced to countenance them. Accordingly, the Duke assigned Diaz apartments in the palace for his security, and recommended to him on no account to quit them. But having insisted for some purpose on going to Alcala, he was waylaid, on his road back, by assassins who beat him with sacks filled with sand. This barbarous treatment produced a vomiting of blood, accompanied by high fever, which terminated his existence soon after his return to Madrid.

The people, who had entertained sanguine expectations that, if the plan suggested by Diaz were adopted, abundance would succeed to their present misery, assembled round the palace, exclaiming that he had been poisoned, and demanding a full investigation, as he had suffered on account of his regard for their interests : and whenever the King passed along the streets in his carriage, the multitude followed him with the well-known and much dreaded outcry, " Viva el Rey y muera el mal govierno." An immense crowd attended the funeral of Diaz, and for some days after it, the streets continued to be so thronged and tumultuous, that the King durst not venture abroad. Every thing wore the aspect of a general insurrection : But the mob had no leader, and wanted resolution and concert among themselves. The disturbance evaporated in idle threats ; and affairs continued to proceed in the former train of rapacity, oppression, and peculation.

Though the finances formed the department of the state which most imperiously required attention and reformation, one of the first acts of the Duke's government, to the nation's utter astonishment, was the appointment of Carlos d'Arrebano, as President of the Council of Finance, though he had been long confined on account of the disordered state of his mind,—had but recently recovered his freedom, and never, even previous to his derangement, possessed any qualifications to fit him for so responsible a situation.   The Bishop of Avila, however, having been nominated to the situation of President of Castile, which is accounted next in dignity to the office of prime minister, had no sooner entered on its duties than he directed his care to the alleviation of the national distress, which he attributed to the numerous monopolies in the sale of all articles of provisions, and the insatiable rapacity of the farmers of the revenue.   But his efforts were feebly seconded by the Duke, who dreaded lest in co-operating with the President for the reformation of abuses, he should draw on himself the hatred of all those who enriched themselves by the spoils of their country ; and he had not sufficient patriotism or magnanimity to hazard his own power or influence for the public good.

The time of the minister seems to have been chiefly occupied at this period by a dispute with the French ambassador, who had recently been deprived of some highly valued privileges—one, an immunity from imposts leviable on articles that entered the gates of Madrid, and the other exemption from the visits of alguazils and other officers of justice in that quarter of the city which he inhabited.   In all such controversies with foreign ministers the Spanish Court was generally violent and ill-advised in the commencement, and meanly humble in its subsequent concessions.

The patronage of his office was also exercised by the Duke in a manner calculated to create dissatisfaction and disgust. The Marques of Villa-Manrique was appointed to the viceroyalty of Peru, through the influence of a lady of distinguished beauty, to whom the Duke was attached, and one of his own relatives, who had nothing but this consanguinity to recommend him, was nominated to the government of Mexico. It was also suspected that one of the great objects of all his political intrigues was to obtain high matches for his seven unmarried daughters.

In triumphing over the machinations of the Constable of Castile, the Duke had not entirely extinguished all hostile factions at court. Eguya, the Dutchess of Terranueva, and the King's confessor, Francisco Reluz,[1] still continued strictly united, and as their respective employments gave them constant access to the royal presence, they had contrived to retain a great share of their sovereign's favour and confidence. The Duke perceived that this triumvirate might one day undermine his power, and he therefore used every effort to dissolve it. He first tried to discard Eguya entirely from the government, but his attempts only procured for him a higher situation, and fixed him more firmly than before in the royal favour. He then determined, in order to remove the confessor from court, to appoint him to the bishopric of Placentia. The King's consent had been obtained to this change, and it was resolved to raise Father Boyona, a professor in the University of Alcala, to the vacant situation. But the Confessor exerted all his influence to remain. He refused the bishopric, and declared he should appeal to the nation if the minister drove him from his spiritual duties near the person of his sovereign. The Duke was at length obliged to relinquish this project likewise, and all his adherents were of opinion that he would

[1] Reluz had been Profesor of Theology at Salamanca, and became confessor in 1679.— *Gazeta de Madrid.*

have acted more prudently had he not ventured on such an open manifestation of his intentions, which had confirmed the enmity of one who was always near the royal person, and who would now doubtless exert all his power to alienate Charles from his new favourite.

For some time the Confessor dissembled his resentment, as he did not yet find himself sufficiently secure of the King's support to hazard an open rupture with the prime minister. But he did not forget his injuries, and as soon as he found himself more firmly established at court, he stimulated his allies, the Dutchess of Terranueva and Eguya to espouse his quarrel. The Dutchess, who hated the Duke, and despised his want of energy and spirit, spoke of him to the King in the most contemptuous terms, and Eguya, when he could find an opportunity, charged on him all the evils and disorders of the realm. But the machinations of the Confessor himself, though the most secret, were the most dangerous of all. He addressed himself to the religious feelings and scrupulous conscience of his Majesty. He represented to him the extremity to which the nation was reduced, and declared to the King, that if he did not feel in himself the experience and energy necessary to place public affairs in a proper train of management, he ought to confide them to the hands of a minister, who might render a faithful account of the charge committed to him, since God, who makes and unmakes kings, would one day exact from them a strict reckoning of the manner in which they had fulfilled their duties towards their subjects : And, finally, he announced, that unless a speedy and effectual remedy was applied to the miseries of the people, he would, in conscience, be compelled to refuse him absolution. In this last menace the Confessor had rather overshot his mark. Charles was thrown into much agitation, and revealed the cause of disturbance to his minister. The Duke listened to him with apparent concern, and replied with much address. He applauded the Confessor's extreme piety and upright intentions, but he insinuated that he was a priest of little experience or knowledge of the world, and that his limited capacity did not permit him to apply the rules of his faith to the differences in the situations of his penitents : For himself, he promised, if allowed sufficient time, to remedy all the evils of which the nation complained, and he undertook, in the mean while, to procure for his Majesty another confessor, who should not be quite so scrupulous on the subject of absolution as Father Francis Reluz. The King felt much relieved by this last suggestion. But before determining on the matter he resolved to consult Eguya. That crafty politician, though he had been so long associated with the Confessor and the Dutchess of Terranueva, rather wished, by this league, to preserve his own influence, and to control the Duke than to exclude him entirely from the government. He now began to dread, that if the Confessor and Dutchess succeeded in completely ruining their enemy, a minister might perhaps be appointed in his room who would be less favourably disposed towards himself, and he therefore judged that it was most prudent for him at present to sacrifice the Confessor to the Duke. Accordingly he confirmed the King in the disposition in which he found him, so that Father Reluz soon fell the victim of his own refined and overstrained policy.

In consequence, however, of the spiritual remonstrances which that Confessor had made to him, the King for a moment bethought himself of applying some remedy to the grievances of his people. He, accordingly, proposed to the Duke the establishment of a special Junta or council, whose attention and efforts should be chiefly directed to that object—and he nominated as members of this board the prime-minister himself, the Constable of Castile, the Marques of Balbases, the Inquisitor-general, and Don Melchior Navarra, Vice-chancellor of Aragon. The Duke did not offer any direct opposition to this scheme; and he seemed, indeed, for a time, to acquiesce in the proposal. But he gradually began to dissuade the King from persisting in the measure. He insinuated, that in such a council, jealousies and disunions must necessarily arise, which would rather contribute to retard than accelerate inquiries and the despatch of business. The plan was in consequence relinquished, or at least it was never carried into effect.

Soon after the removal of the Confessor, a combination much more formidable than that of which he had been the head, was formed against the prime-minister. All the Grandees of Spain hated Eguya, and many of them envied the Duke for the elevation to which he had attained. A party was formed against him, consisting of the Dukes of Veraguas and Pastrana, the Admiral of Castile, the Prince of Stigliano, the Marques of Mancera, the Counts of Monterey and Oropesa. These noblemen had frequent meetings, in which they canvassed the political conduct of the Duke of Medina-Celi. They discovered that he was indolent where labour and industry were required, that he was feeble where firmness was necessary, and obstinate when compliance would be wise and prudent. But though this league was formidable, from the rank and power of the individuals of whom it was composed, it was weak, in consequence of the disunion among them, and the diversity of motives by which they were guided. They were all, indeed, agreed concerning the wretched state of the kingdom, the incapacity of the prime-minister, and the necessity of his immediate removal; but they entertained very different views with regard to the means that should be adopted to procure his downfall, and with regard to the person who had the best claim to be his successor. Some members, indeed, of the cabal, particularly the Marques of Mancera, who was a creature of the Queen-mother, were altogether opposed to the appointment of a prime-minister, and recommended the nomination of a Junta.

The Admiral of Castile was one of the first to remark the diversity of interests and the want of mutual confidence which pervaded the cabal. He became satisfied that he had rashly connected himself with this incongruous and ill assorted party, and that he should infallibly ruin himself by longer adhering to it. He therefore not only abandoned the confederacy, but, as was generally believed, made a merit with the King, and the Duke of Medina-Celi, by revealing the whole plot, and the names of those who were engaged in it. At all events, the conspiracy was discovered, and many of its abettors were disgraced and punished. The first victim to the resentment of the minister, was the Count de Monterey, who was banished from court, and deprived of his employments : the Duke of Veraguas was a few days afterwards ordered to retire to his estates. The Duke of Pastrana with his brothers conciliated the minister, and obtained their pardon by following the steps of the Admiral of Castile, and revealing all those particulars of the conspiracy with which they were acquainted.

Thus the influence of the Queen and of the Queen-mother was now the only obstacle which interposed to prevent the Duke's unlimited sway over the mind of the King. That, once removed, the Duke trusted his power would become both wholly despotic and permanent. The Queen-mother's credit, as we have seen, had already much declined, and the Duke, with the assistance of Eguya, and the Dutchess of Terranueva, now contrived completely to annihilate it, by insinuating to the King that she had not forgotten, and never would forgive, the injurious treatment to which she had been subjected during the administration of Don John of Austria; and by reminding him of the sound maxim of policy, never to put faith in a reconciled enemy. Charles's good natural disposition, and his affection towards his mother, soon yielded to these impressions, and she was no longer allowed to present herself at Court, except on stated days of ceremony.

This amiable triumvirate next attempted to awaken the jealousy and suspicions of their sovereign against his young Queen, by calling his attention to trifling circumstances in her demeanour and conduct, which were calculated to serve their purposes. The mind of the King was thus in some degree alienated from her Majesty; and when she expressed her grief and vexation at the bad humour which he in consequence occasionally manifested, the confidents of the Duke insinuated to her, that it was the Queen-mother who had prejudiced her husband against her, by which device the two Queens were also kept at variance, and prevented from any such union as might affect the credit of the chief minister.

The disposition of the Duke, which at the period of his elevation was considered as open and candid, seems to have been gradually perverted by power, and by the practice of those intrigues which, in the want of higher qualifications, are necessary in order to preserve it. Intent on holding a despotic sway over the mind of his master, he represented all those who frequented the Court, or had access to his royal presence, as concealed enemies, or domestic spies, who entertained neither attachment to his person, nor zeal for his service. These insinuations were so much the more dangerous, from the Duke's previous character for sincerity, and the apparent candour with which he well understood how to cover his malignant suggestions. All whom he suspected of carrying on any com-

munication betwixt the two Queens, or promoting their
good intelligence, were also the objects of his peculiar displeasure. Believing that the French ambassador performed this friendly part, he so prejudiced the King against
him, that his Majesty was heard to declare he would rather
be engaged in open hostilities with France, than longer
receive from Louis such an envoy at Madrid.

For some time, the power of the Duke of Medina-Celi
was almost as absolute in the Court of the feeble Charles
as that of Lerma and Olivarez had been in the two preceding reigns. Like them, too, the Duke did not content himself with unlimited sway in all public and political affairs : he exercised a species of rule over private families, forming amongst them those marriages and alliances which he found conducive to his interests, and the
aggrandizement of his House. He made a trial of his
power in this way by the union of one of his relatives
Don Henriquez de Guzman, who was in indigent circumstances, and had nothing to recommend him, with Donna
Laura de Monçada, the only daughter of the Duke of
Montalto, who was then but fifteen years of age, and
was considered as the first heiress in the kingdom. She
was privately married, without the knowledge of any of
her family except her father, lest they should have made
some attempt to interrupt the ceremony. The Count of
Oropesa, uncle to the bride, and her grandfather the
Marques de Los Velez, were highly exasperated both at
the unsuitable nuptials and their studious concealment ;
and in this union, which the minister thought would cement his power, he probably first shook its foundations,
by incensing these two powerful grandees, particularly the
Count of Oropesa, who, in fact, ultimately succeeded him
in the ministry.

While the Court had been agitated by these intrigues,

the young Queen continued to lead a melancholy and monotonous life in the interior of the palace. But the King,
in spite of all attempts to injure her in his esteem, still
loved her with unabated affection. Amid the restraints of
Spanish formality, he was occasionally much delighted by
that simplicity and freedom of manner which she had
brought with her from France, and which she still, in some
degree, retained : But he could neither break through the
ceremonial which prescribed the mode in which the Queen
was to spend her time, nor relieve her from the formidable presence of the Dutchess of Terranueva.

The amusement in which she was most frequently indulged, was the privilege of accompanying the King to
the chase. His Majesty had presented her with a spi-
rited steed from Andalusia ; and a circumstance which
occurred one day when she had mounted it in the court
of the palace, displays, in a striking point of view, the ridiculous forms established at the palace of Madrid. The
animal having begun to rear, the Queen fell from her
seat, and her foot having been entangled in the stirrup,
the horse dragged her along. Charles, who saw this
accident from the balcony of one of the palace windows,
became motionless from terror. The court, at the moment, was filled with guards and grandees, but no one
dared to run the hazard of assisting her Majesty in this
peril, as it was a species of treason for any one to touch
the person of a Consort of Spain ; and, which one would
hardly expect, it is a more heinous offence to touch her
foot than any other part of the body. At length, two
Spanish cavaliers, Don Louis de-las-Torres and Don
Jayme de Sotomayor, resolved, at all risks, to save their
Queen. The former seized the bridle of the palfrey, while
his companion extricated her Majesty's foot from the
stirrup. Having rendered her this service, they went home
with all possible expedition, and ordered their steeds to be

saddled that they might fly from the resentment of the
King. The young Count of Peñaranda, who was the friend
of both, approached the Queen, and respectfully informed
her of the danger in which her preservers might be placed,
unless she interceded in their favour. His Majesty, who
had now come to the spot, listened to the entreaties which
she offered up to him, and a messenger, who was immediately despatched with a pardon to the cavaliers, reached
them just in time to prevent their flight into a foreign
land.[1]

The tedious Spanish comedies and the bull-fights
which the Queen was permitted to attend, were little to
her taste. At one of the latter exhibitions, she was so
much shocked in consequence of two of the combatants
having been killed on the spot, that she was taken violently ill. One public spectacle which she was this season compelled to attend, must have added gloom and horror
to her thoughts. On the accession of a new queen, it had
been usual in Spain to get up an Auto-da-Fe for her edi-
fication. In 1560, the Inquisition of Toledo prepared a
grand celebration for the entertainment of their young
Queen Elizabeth de Valois, daughter of Henry II. of
France, soon after her espousals with Philip II. On the
30th of May of the present year, the officers of the Inquisition had proclaimed, in the *Plaça Mayor*, to the
sound of trumpets and cymbals, an Auto-da-Fe for that
day month. Such a spectacle had not been witnessed at
Madrid for forty years, and was expected by all classes
with much impatience. On the appointed day, an immense multitude assembled at the spot, with the same
eagerness and preparations as if they had been repairing
to a solemn festival. The whole court was present,—the
King, the Queen, all the foreign ambassadors, and the

[1] Spanish writers deny the truth of this story, which is related
by Mad. d'Aulnoy.

Duke of Medina-Celi, who, by a hereditary privilege, carried the standard of the Inquisition, which is of red damask, with the arms of Spain blazoned on one side, and on the other a naked sword, with a wreath of laurel. The chair of the Grand Inquisitor, at this time Don Diego Semiento, was placed on a sort of tribunal, elevated high above the seat occupied by the King. An immense scaffold was erected in the *Plaça Mayor*, whereon from seven till nine in the morning criminals of both sexes, from all the different Inquisitions in Spain, ascended in succession. Their processes, and the judgments pronounced on them, were then read: Mass was performed, and while it was celebrating, the King took the oath by which he bound himself to protect the Catholic faith, to extirpate heresy, and support, with all his authority, the proceedings and acts of the Holy Office. By the time these ceremonies were completed, and all the sentences of the condemned were read, it was nine o'clock at night. Then commenced the darker part of the spectacle. Some malefactors, accused of sorcery, and who wore paper caps with scrolls on their heads, and carried torches in their hands, were publicly whipt, and were afterwards sent to the gallies. From the earliest ages, Jews had been settled, and had also been persecuted, in Spain. At the present sad solemnity, fifty Jews and Jewesses, convicted for the first time, and now penitent, were condemned only to long imprisonment, and to wear a yellow scapulary with a red cross, which is called the *sanbenito*. But twenty of their class had been sentenced to the flames, as relapsed or incorrigible. The zealots of the Catholic faith vehemently argued with these unbelievers, but none renounced their errors, and some Jews disputed on doctrinal points with the utmost self-possession and composure. A beautiful young Jewess, apparently not above seventeen years of age, who stood close to the Queen, appealed to her for mercy. " Will not your royal presence," she exclaimed, "bring some change to the lot prepared for me? Consider my youth, and remember that this concerns a faith which I have imbibed with my mother's milk." The Queen turned away her head, and gave signs of the deepest compassion; but she had no power to save her, or alleviate the horrors of her fate. After the sentences had been read, the King and his Court retired. The criminals condemned were then delivered over to the secular power: they were conducted on asses to a spot 500 paces beyond the gate of Funcaral, and there executed at midnight.[1]

It perhaps adds to the horror and iniquity of this spectacle, that many wealthy Jews were allowed, though their tenets were well known, to remain unmolested in Madrid; and even to hold employments at this period in the public departments of finance. When it was wished to make them disburse large sums, their lives from time to time were threatened. But they were spared if they possessed funds sufficient to satisfy the rapacity of the extortioner; or if they did not prefer their gold to life itself.

On the whole, however, the present *Auto da Fe* was accounted highly creditable to the monarchy. A minute account of the procedure was published to the world, with the approbation of the authorities, civil and ecclesiastical; and in the palace of Buenretiro an historical picture of this exhibition was hung up, in which the spectator, judges, and victims, were all represented.

The Queen had looked forward with some pleasure this year to the amusement of an excursion to Aranjuez, where it was the custom of the King and Court to pass a few weeks during spring, or the early part of summer. Some obstacles, however, of which the chief was the want of funds, prevented, during this season, the usual

---

[1] Colmenar, *Annales d'Espagne*, t. iv.

expedition to that delightful spot. Charles instead of it, went for a few days to the Escurial, accompanied only by the Duke of Medina-Celi, one of the secretaries of state, the chief equerry, and two other officers of the household. The day after his departure, the Queen addressed to him a very affectionate letter, and forwarded to him a diamond ring along with it. The King sent her, in return, some beads of a precious sort of wood, set with diamonds, enclosed in a little casket of gold filagree, into which he had slipped a note, containing these words, " Madam, it is a great storm of wind here : I have killed six wolves."

Besides the solitude to which she was condemned, the Queen experienced much inconvenience and mortification in consequence of receiving no adequate or regular pecuniary supplies. Five hundred pistoles a-month (about L 400, formed the regulated allowance, but six months sometimes elapsed without payment of a pistole, and she was in consequence obliged to borrow for indispensable necessaries—for those acts of charity which she was always ready to bestow, and for the expense of a few favourite horses which she had brought with her from France.

Meanwhile, the Dutchess of Terranueva continued her misrepresentations and persecutions. The King and Queen had, about this time, amused themselves with going to the College of Jesuits, to hear an Asiatic priest called Hissa, from the town of Mousul, perform mass in the Chaldean language. Her Majesty, who had a great curiosity, afterwards sent for him to the palace, and, among other questions which she put to him, by means of an interpreter, she inquired if women were as closely watched and confined at Mousul as at Madrid. All present were horror-struck at this unexpected interrogatory, and the Dutchess represented it in such a light to the

King, that for several days afterwards he manifested towards his consort the utmost coldness and reserve.

Charles, who detested every thing French except the Queen, was at little pains to conceal his dislike. All her Majesty's French domestics experienced the effects of his displeasure, and in consequence of the treatment they received, they, one by one, insisted on returning home, and left their mistress, at length, without a single attendant from her own country. Even the favourite dogs which she had brought with her from France suffered the effects of his Majesty's aversion, and were kicked down stairs with execrations, whenever an opportunity offered. This hint was not lost on the Camarera-mayor, who felt all her sovereign's national antipathies. The Queen had brought two parrots with her from Paris, which she loved much, and which were extremely beautiful. The morose old Dutchess abhorred them, because they talked in French, and she thought it would be a patriotic act to silence them for ever. Accordingly, one day, in the absence of the Queen, she ordered the parrots to be brought before her. Her proceedings were of the most summary description, and despite of the intercessions of the person who had charge of them, she twisted off their necks with her lank bony fingers, before the return of her Majesty. When she came back to the palace she asked for her dogs and parrots, as she was wont, in the absence of the King, and it was long before any of her domestics could take courage to relate the catastrophe.

At length the Queen, exasperated beyond all farther endurance, by the persecutions of the Dutchess, resorted to a measure, which it seems wonderful she had not earlier adopted. Having one day conciliated the King, by all the caresses and blandishments of which she was mistress, she declared that if she was dear to him, and if he had any consideration for her health and happiness, the odious Dutchess of Terranueva must be removed from her situation of Camarera-mayor. Such a proposition had never before been made in Spain, and the King, after a long silence produced by the amazement into which he was thrown, answered, that there was no precedent for a Queen changing her Camarera-mayor. Her Majesty, however, replied, that he had shown her so many marks of kindness, of which his predecessors had left no example, that she counted on obtaining this favour also. Charles then consented, but he warned her to be careful in her choice of a successor to the Dutchess, since any future change would be altogether impracticable.

The Queen conceived that it would be prudent immediately to communicate this arrangement to the Duke of Medina-Celi. But she dreaded lest she should be overheard by the Camarera, who was constantly listening at doors, and often concealed herself unperceived behind curtains, in the embrasures of windows, or the dark corners of large apartments. At length she contrived to inform him of it by the agency of a third party; and she at the same time assured him that she was desirous to be regulated entirely by his opinion and wishes in her choice of a new Camarera-mayor. She afterwards made an offer of the situation to the Dutchess of Medina-Celi: But she was pretty well aware that this proposal would not be accepted, and, accordingly, as she had anticipated, the Dutchess, with many expressions of gratitude, declined it on the score of impaired health and her numerous family. She ventured, at the same time, to recommend to her the Marchioness des Los Velez, as a proper person, from her birth and merit, to fill the high situation which was about to become vacant. This recommendation, however, had been given by the Dutchess of Medina-Celi without the knowledge of her husband, who was much displeased

at it, as he was in the interests of the Dutchess d'Albuquerque, on whom he had fixed as the new Camarera-
mayor.

Meanwhile, the King informed his favourite, Eguya,
of the promise which he had made the Queen to remove
the Dutchess of Terranueva. The secretary endeavoured
to divert him from this design; but finding his persua-
sions fruitless, all he could do was to give the Dutchess
timely intimation of her approaching downfall. No one
had yet ventured to communicate to her the intelligence;
but as she was gifted with much penetration in all matters that concerned her interests, she had already suspected it; and she had also for some time conjectured, that
if ever she was displaced, she would be succeeded by the
Dutchess d'Albuquerque, the Dutchess d'Infantado, or
the Marchioness de Los Velez. These ladies, in consequence, were peculiarly obnoxious to her, and she had
used every endeavour to depreciate them in the estima-
tion of the Queen. She said that the Dutchess d'Albuquerque had a peculiar hatred and prejudice towards the
French,—that the Dutchess d'Infantado was in a state
of complete dotage, and that the Marchioness was of an
insufferable pride and severity. These representations,
however, made but little impression on the mind of the
Queen, and she early disclosed, both to the King and
the Queen-mother, her disposition in favour of the Marchioness Los Velez. But this choice was not agreeable
to either; and both joined the prime minister in their
approbation of the Dutchess d'Albuquerque, who thus
united all the suffrages of the court, and was accepted by
the Queen as preferable at least to her present Duenna.

Don Pedro of Aragon received orders to communicate
to his relative, the Dutchess of Terranueva, this final resolution; and he was at the same time instructed to recommend to her, as all opposition would be fruitless, to

submit, with a good grace, and to give her removal, as
much as possible, the appearance of a voluntary resignation. The Dutchess said little to Don Pedro, as she
could not yet fully believe that the King, in whose favour
she placed her chief confidence, had consented to her
dismissal. This point she resolved herself to ascertain.
Having waited an opportunity of speaking with him as
he was about to sit down at table, she talked to him
for some time in a low tone which was inaudible to those
in attendance, and then, suddenly raising her voice so as
to be heard by all present, she demanded permission to
retire from court. The King at once replied, " that he
consented, and that she might depart whenever she chose."
This answer appeared to have been totally unexpected.
She seemed greatly disconcerted, changed colour, and
hastily quitted the apartment. She retired to her own
chamber where she regained her composure, and attended
the Queen at supper with as much apparent tranquillity
as if nothing had occurred. But her mind was in a state
of agitation and fury. She spent the whole night in
pacing her room with her two daughters, the Princess
of Monteleone and the Dutchess of Hijar. On the following morning she did not wait to take her leave till
the Queen had risen. With a countenance pale as
death, and her eyes sparkling with rage, she sought the
royal chamber while her Majesty was yet in bed. On
the Queen expressing some regret at their separation, she
haughtily replied, " that it was beneath the dignity of a
consort of Spain to lament the dismission of her Camarera
Mayor;" and then, without farther words or ceremony,
she abruptly quitted the royal presence. On her removal
being known in the palace, some of the ladies attendant
on the court came to offer their condolence before her departure. The virulent old woman paid no attention to
their compliments, but declared, in a sort of soliloquy

" that she would never again enter a palace where she had received so many bitter injuries and mortifications." She twice violently struck a small table which, was standing near her, with her fist, and then seized a beautiful Chinese fan, which she broke in two, dashed the fragments on the ground, and trampled them under her feet to atoms.

In order in some degree to pacify the exasperated Dutchess and recompense her for past services, the viceroyalty of Galicia, and afterwards that of Aragon was bestowed on her son-in-law the Duke of Hijar; and on this appointment she came, for the last time, in great state, to court, in order to express her acknowledgments.

As soon as the Dutchess of Terranueva had quitted the palace, the Dutchess of Albuquerque took possession of her apartments. The new Camarera-Mayor was at this time about fifty years of age, and was the widow of the Duke of Albuquerque, chief of the House of Cueva. She had one only child, who was a daughter, and was married to a cadet of the family. Though she was supposed to be endowed with much of that pride and haughtiness which had characterised her predecessor, she assumed, on her admittance to the palace, a totally different conduct and demeanour. She studied to be civil and obliging to every one, and expressed, on all occasions, the utmost deference and attachment to her royal mistress. Having a cultivated understanding and extensive information, she held assemblies, in her apartments, on certain days of the week, at which all in the capital, who had pretensions to learning, were cordially received, and which her Majesty sometimes honoured with her presence.

In fact, the Queen had considerably improved her situation, by the change which she had at length effected. The King, no longer under the influence of the old Duenna, and left to the natural kindness of his own disposition, now told her, it was his wish that she should partake of more amusement than formerly, and that she should walk out or ride whenever she found it agreeable. By the order and ceremonial of the palace, which had been observed without deviation for more than a hundred years, it was regulated that the Queen of Spain should retire to rest at ten o'clock in summer, and nine in winter; and on the present Queen's first arrival, it frequently happened, that from her forgetting the appointed hour, her women, while she was yet at supper, would, without saying a word, begin to undress her head, and pull off her shoes under the table, in order to hurry her to bed with all possible expedition. But now the King declared, that he had no objections to her sitting as late at night as she chose, provided that, according to his usual practice, he might retire to rest at eight o'clock in the evening. A few days afterwards, he resolved to change his own hour of going to bed from eight to ten o'clock, that more time might be allowed for society and amusement.

Soon after the appointment of the Dutchess Albuquerque, the Royal Family and Court proceeded to Aranjuez. This excursion, which had been postponed in spring, in consequence of the want of funds, had nearly been again delayed in autumn for a similar reason. The ministers, though aware of the deficiency, pretended for some time to make preparations for the journey. They then alleged that the heavy rains had tainted the air, and rendered the roads impassable. The King, however, in spite of these reasons, still persisted in his design of setting out for Aranjuez, and he did not know till the evening before the day which he had fixed for his departure, that he could not go, as no preparations had been made, or funds provided. He and the Queen were the only persons who had been left in ignorance of this detention. The ministers, a fortnight before, had intimated it to their friends, so

that the court, and, indeed, the whole town, were aware,
that the King would remain where he was for this season.   Their Majesties, particularly the Queen, were
highly and justly indignant at this procedure.   Their
complaints of being mocked and treated like children
having reached the ears of the Duke of Medina-Celi, he
was in great alarm for what might be the consequences
to himself.   In order to pacify the King, he immediately set about providing sufficient funds, to defray the expenses of a regal journey to Aranjuez.   He forthwith
sold a government in India, and two situations in the
state accomptant's office, and having thus raised a sufficient supply, the royal party set out for their delightful palace.   The Duke d'Uzeda, the Count Altamira, and some
other young Grandees, who were *Galans del Palacio*,
as they were called, disguised themselves as muleteers,
and in this garb they ran on foot, by the side of the coach,
which conveyed the Queen's maids of honour, to whose
love and service they were devoted.

  This excursion to Aranjuez was not productive of all
the pleasure and amusement that had been anticipated.
The month of September, during which it was undertaken, is usually one of the finest in Spain.   But, this
season, it rained incessantly, and the state of the atmosphere prevented the enjoyment of the walks and rides
along the banks of the Tagus and Xamara, which form
the chief delight at Aranjuez.   Whenever there was an
hour of fair weather, the Queen mounted her palfrey and
rode out, attended by all her ladies.   One of them was
unfortunately killed, in consequence of a fall from her
horse, which had run off with her, and this accident so
alarmed the King, that he would scarcely afterwards allow the Queen, during her stay at Aranjuez, to ride out
on horseback, and when she was permitted, he was con-

stantly despatching messengers after her, to inquire if she
had not fallen.

Immediately after the King's return from Aranjuez to
Madrid, he resolved on an expedition to the Escurial.
This, indeed, was the regular season for the annual visit
to that palace, and as he had succeeded in compelling his
ministers to procure funds for the excursion to Aranjuez,
he would not listen to any opposition to his present plans.
The storms, and the floods by which the country was in-
undated, prevented for some time the departure of the
royal party, but they at length set out, on the seventh of
October. The journey, however, was conducted on a
moderate scale of expense and attendance. Having got to
the Escurial, the King devoted his whole time to the
chase. Toils were set, which enclosed a vast extent of
forest; and on some days 200 stags and does were shot.
The Queen took little pleasure in this species of sport,
and seldom was present. When the chase was conducted in this manner, his Majesty had a numerous escort,
and was usually accompanied by the Duke of Medina-
Celi and the Marquis of Grana, the Austrian ambassador, who had followed him to the Escurial. But the
King preferred tracking the wild scenes and lonely forests
of the royal domains, either alone, or merely accompanied
by his equerry and huntsman. He delighted to find himself in perfect seclusion in these vast and gloomy solitudes
from dawn till evening, and was often long sought, without being found or heard of, by his attendants. And here
he first gave symptoms of that deep melancholy, and morbid love of solitude, by which, till death, he was so heavily
afflicted.

One might naturally conclude, that the mind of a prince
with this taste for rural retirement, could not be destitute
of some elements of moral and intellectual grandeur. But,
in the unhappy Charles, these habits proceeded not from

that elevation or refinement of soul which seeks a solitary communion with nature amid her noblest works, but indicated the morbid commencement of the hypochondriac affection which preyed on his latter years.

That taint, which broke out into absolute insanity in Joanna—which displayed itself in the premature dotage of the Emperor Charles—in the gloomy temperament of Philip II, and the imbecility of his son, but which had lurked or been subdued in the veins of Philip IV, exercised redoubled influence on the mind of his unhappy successor, who now cherished, amid the haunts of the Escurial, this hereditary disease.

I have often thought, that the wretched despondency and depression of spirits suffered by the Kings of Spain, both of the Austrian and Bourbon line, may not improbably have been aggravated by their autumnal sojourn at the " Gray Escurial." The austerity of that monastic palace, its convent, its cloisters, and its tombs, where each succeeding Monarch of Spain was doomed to lie, its dismal galleries and twilight halls, where, as some believed, still lingered the Shade of the gloomy founder,[1]—the sterile and desert mountains by which it was surrounded,—the dark elms,—the Ilex dells,—and ceaseless winds which howled over the heights or through the narrow passes of the Guadarrama, must have tended, in a bleak October, to thicken those feelings of awe and sadness which, though salutary, perhaps, to an enlightened and duly regulated understanding, may, in a weak and superstitious mind, have increased that hypochondriac insanity which the Austrian dynasty received as its fatal inheritance along with the Castilian throne.

---

[1] This belief still prevailed in the middle of the 18th century. " Les Moines et le peuple sont persuadés, que l'ombre de ce méchant homme vient toutes les nuits roder, gemir, hurler dans les cloîtres du couvent." (Langle, *Voyage en Espagne*, t. i. p. 41.)

On her return to Madrid, the Queen was allowed to participate in the gaieties of the capital. An entertainment, given to the King and the two Queens on the evening of St Andrew's day, by the Admiral of Castile, affords some idea of the style of fashionable amusements in Madrid towards the close of the 17th century. The host received his company in his gardens, where stood large marble basins, into which fountains of water continually played; and immense silver baskets were suspended around them, containing all sorts of viands, and every variety of flowers. In arbours, at the end of alleys, there were placed small tables of agate or rock of crystal, on which stood baskets, of the same materials as the tables, heaped with every species of fruit the season could supply; and from all the grottoes hung artificial grapes, made of amethysts, emeralds, and rubies. The two Queens, who came first, enjoyed for some time the walks and recreations of the gardens. As soon as the King arrived, the company entered the palace of the Admiral, where fifteen ladies and as many cavaliers, dressed in masquerade habits, entertained their Majesties by dancing the Moorish Sarabend. The royal party testified much delight at this festival; and the Duke of Medina-Celi, the Constable of Castile, and Don Pedro d'Aragon, hearing of the honour which they had conferred on the Admiral by accepting his invitation, begged that they might each receive a similar distinction. At the entertainments which they in consequence provided, they vied with the Admiral in the splendour of their festivities. Dramatic representations, music, fireworks, and magnificent collations, marked the joy and gratitude which the royal presence inspired.

At the *fête* given by the Constable, the King's dwarf Lovisillo, who came from Flanders, and is said to have been a beautiful creature, danced what was called the *paso*

Cailla, with a little girl whom the Queen had redeemed from slavery, and had brought up at court. They were both dressed as Indians, being covered with the feathers of birds of all different colours, and they held little tambourines in their hands, on which they played delightfully. At the subsequent entertainment in the palace of Don Pedro d'Aragon, the Queen, which she had never done before, danced in presence of the King, and acquitted herself with marvellous grace and elegance. She had previously learned, expressly for this occasion, the Spanish dances of the Canario and Saraband; and the King was so surprised, as well as delighted, that he exclaimed, " *Mi Reyna, Mi Reyna, eres la mas perfecta de todo el orbe !* " [1]

As winter advanced, their Majesties took great delight in seeing some Dutch and Flemish strangers skate on the ice of the ponds at Buenretiro, in the manner of their countrymen. A party of Spanish ladies in masks, having asked permission of the Queen, tried to imitate them ; but the ice gave way on their attempting to dance the Saraband with castanets.

It has been already mentioned, that the amusements of the court and the harmony in the royal family had been, in some degree, interrupted by the suspicions which the Duke of Medina-Celi, or his confidents, instilled into the mind of the King concerning his Queen, and the belief impressed on her, that the Queen-mother was the cause of this temporary alienation of his affections. Fortunately, one day while the King was engaged in the chase, the Queen-mother invited her daughter-in-law to a repast. They met with that degree of embarrassment which arises from a feeling of mutual offence struggling with the dignity of situation. But tears relieved them, and they soon gave vent to reciprocal complaints and re-

[1] *Mem. de la Cour d'Espagne.*

proaches of each having estranged from the other the affections of the King.   Explanation followed ; and, when they came to relate and examine all that had been said and insinuated, with the reports conveyed to them, both were convinced that attempts had been made to disunite them by the party opposed to their mutual interests.   A complete reconciliation was effected, and a compact formed to join their influence in order to destroy the power of the Duke of Medina-Celi.

The Queen-mother soon afterwards sent her daughter-in-law a watch set in diamonds, with a gold chain of exquisite workmanship, and in a letter which accompanied the gift, she expressed a hope that it might always mark for her happy and agreeable hours.   It was replied by the Queen, that her hours should be ever such so long as her Majesty continued her affection towards her.

CHAPTER VII.

MISFORTUNES AND HUMILIATION OF SPAIN.

Madrid fremit d'effroi, de honte et de tristesse.
                                        VOLTAIRE, *Henriade*.

THE history of Spain, for some succeeding years, can only be a picture of the various misfortunes which she suffered, and the bitter humiliations to which she was subjected.

As Spain was a despotic monarchy, the character of her king must be rated among her chief misfortunes. Charles was not disagreeable in personal appearance and manners. His figure was tall and straight, and though he had a wide mouth and the thick Austrian lip, he had a fair and delicate complexion, fine hair, and much sweetness in his eyes. Nor was his natural disposition in any way vicious or depraved. He was temperate, pious, accessible, and unstained by cruelty or any flagrant vice. But his intellectual qualities were of the lowest and most limited description. In boyhood, his education had been systematically neglected; and, as in his maturer years none of his courtiers or ministers found it to be their interest that he should be better instructed, he remained in the profoundest ignorance. He knew not even the names of the most important towns and provinces in his dominions; and, during the war with France, he often pitied the Emperor of Germany for the loss of cities which in fact formed part of his own territories. His amusements beyond the precincts of his palace,—the chase and the bull-fights, were healthful and manly, or justified, at least, by the predilections of his country. But when he advanced in years, and when superstitious melancholy assumed a more decided sway, he gradually relinquished these active diversions, and renounced all share in affairs of state. He immured himself, like an eastern despot, within the walls of his palace. Nor did he there pass his leisure in reading or the enjoyment of any rational society. And though he employed the fertile pencil of Luca Giordano, and other foreign painters, he had none of his father's taste or relish for the arts. He spent his time chiefly among dwarfs, with whom he was particularly delighted, and among strange animals of every description, which were brought to him from all quarters of the globe. Sometimes, too, he pleased himself with playing paltry tricks on his courtiers, which marked the littleness and frivolity of his mind.

Nor, as we have seen, were the palpable deficiencies of the monarch in any way redeemed by the abilities of the ministers whom he employed. They, on the contrary, not only proved themselves incapable of extricating the nation from its difficulties; but, by their crude incongruous measures, which were ill digested, and were speedily relinquished, to be succeeded by others as exceptionable, they plunged it in more overwhelming and more inextricable confusion.

The Spanish army, once so formidable under the command of Alva and Farnese, had dwindled away to a few thousand ill paid, and worse disciplined, soldiers. While England, Holland, and France were constructing and equipping formidable fleets, the navy of Spain was reduced to a few shattered gallies. The magazines were unprovided, the arsenals deserted, and the frontier fortresses ungarrisoned.

But the present state of the national finances was the worst feature in the political aspect of Spain. As far back as the time of the Emperor Charles, the debt had become enormous, and difficulties had often been found in the payment of the immense armies which that monarch maintained. At the close of the reign of his successor, public credit was reduced so low that the Genoese and other Italian merchants, from whom Philip II. had already borrowed largely, refused any farther advances. To remedy the immediate embarrassments and inconveniencies that resulted from the deficiency in pecuniary supplies, the Duke of Lerma raised the nominal value of copper coin, or silver alloyed with copper, to that of pure silver. In consequence of this absurd and dangerous expedient, a quantity of counterfeit copper money had been poured into Spain by the neighbouring nations, who received for it silver in return. This state of matters continued during the reign of Philip IV.; and silver too was then raised above its former nominal valuation. Suddenly the present King, as we have seen, issued an edict, which diminished by two-thirds the value of the coinage of the precious metals, and altogether suppressed the circulation of brass or copper money. Foreigners thus obtained, at an undue rate, the copper coin, in which there was a considerable mixture of silver. They also purchased up the fine gold and silver species, which had been so much reduced in value, and exported it with advantage to other realms. All this perhaps might have been attended with no permanent disadvantage amongst an intelligent and industrious people, but the sudden depreciation of the metals proved fatal in Spain.

The public treasury early felt the dangerous and never-failing consequence of tampering with the currency. The Spanish ministry was now continually harassed by the demands of foreign ambassadors, for debts which had been

long due to their masters.　A special messenger arrived
from the Elector of Brandenburgh, to seek repayment of
several large sums which had been advanced in loan to
the King of Spain during the French war.　The court
amused him for a long while with promises and the most
paltry remittances.　At length, however, he procured an
assignation to the value of 50,000 crowns in bullion,
which was shortly expected to arrive from America.　He
accordingly set out for Seville, in order to obtain it:
But the Council of Commerce in that town had already
received private instructions not to deliver over the bullion.　The German emissary returned to Madrid much
chagrined at his disappointment, and justly indignant at
the treatment he had received.　He renewed his appli-
cations, which all proved as fruitless as his former instances, and then, by order of his master, quitted the capital
of Spain, protesting in the strongest terms against the
breach of faith that had been committed, and threatening the Court with the resentment and hostility of the
Elector and his allies.　A gold chain, worth about 100
pistoles, was presented to him on the eve of his departure.
But he returned the paltry gift as an affront and insult
to his master.　The Elector afterwards carried his threats
into execution, and having hired a squadron of privateers,
overpaid himself by the seizure of a Spanish vessel, loaded
with treasure, which his ships encountered, at sea, near
Ostend.

The ambassador of the Seven United Provinces demanded a special audience of the King, in order to solicit
payment of a large sum, which had been due to them by
the Crown of Spain since the year 1675.　Charles gave
the usual answer of *Veremos*: but, in the evening he
sent for the Duke of Medina-Celi, to whom he said, that
he had never known of so much debt where there was so
little money to pay it; and he declared, that if this state

of embarrassment continued, he would shut himself up in his palace, and give audience to none of his creditors. The Duke contented himself with replying that matters would shortly assume a totally different aspect, and that, in the mean while, the Dutch were rich enough to wait some time longer for reimbursement.

An emissary of the Duke of Savoy had, for four years, solicited payment of the subsidies which had been promised, and were now due to that prince; but all his efforts to obtain a settlement proving ineffectual, he quitted Spain in disgust. The envoys of several other states took their departure for similar reasons, and those who remained only stayed in order to persecute the ministry with their claims, and to complain of the violations of faith to which the Spanish government was in some measure compelled by the deplorable state of its finances. The ambassadors of Spain at foreign courts were in consequence insulted or neglected, and privileges formerly conceded to their character were now withdrawn.

Nor were the claims of its own subjects better attended to by the Spanish government than those of alien princes. The troops deserted on the frontiers for want of pay, and at Madrid the soldiers of the royal guard repaired daily to the convents, and struggled there, with the crowd of mendicants, for a morsel of the charitable distributions doled out at the gates. Officers of the army and governors of fortresses quitted their duty and employments in order to urge, at Madrid, in person, those claims which they had hitherto in vain represented by letters or memorials. The Marques of Balbo, and several other Italian officers from Naples and Milan, who had been long at Madrid, attempting to procure payment of what was due for their military services, were obliged to return home without having attained their object: And no excuse was offered by the court for this conduct, except the extreme poverty in which it was sunk.

But not only was the Crown unable to satisfy these larger claims, or fulfil its more important engagements. Such was the inconceivable penury to which it was reduced, that it was found as difficult to procure 50 ducats as 50,000. Money could thus be no longer raised for the most pressing occasions, however trifling might be the cost. Couriers charged with urgent and important despatches, on affairs of state, were often unable to quit Madrid, for want of the funds necessary to defray the immediate expenses of their journies. Some officers of the royal household having waited for payment of what was due to them, as long as they could without absolutely reducing themselves to beggary, peremptorily demanded their dismission, and were only retained by force and menaces. All the grooms, however, belonging to the royal stables, who had not received their rations or wages for two years, contrived to escape from their service, and the horses remained for some time uncurried and unfed. A table, which had been kept up, at the King's cost, for the gentlemen of the bed-chamber, was now totally unsupplied; and money was even frequently wanting to defray the daily expenses at the board of a monarch who was Master of Mexico and Peru! The household of the Queen-mother, which had hitherto been maintained at its full establishment, now began to feel the effects of the general destitution. The rations provided for her domestics were withheld, and on lodging their complaints at Court, they were told, with a sort of Cervantic humour, that the royal coffers were now all standing open, and they might come to supply themselves.

The Marquis of Grana, who had recently been appointed the Austrian ambassador to Madrid, was much distressed at the misery of a court so closely allied to his master. He publicly declared, that it far exceeded any thing of which he had formed a conception, and that he would not have accepted so painful a situation, if he had believed that it existed to the extent he now discovered.

In this wretched state of penury, it will readily be believed that the court learned with the severest regret and disappointment, that a sum of 200,000 crowns which the Viceroy of Naples had amassed with the utmost difficulty, had been seized on its voyage by eight galley-slaves, who were part of the crew of the felucca in which it had been embarked, and who having taken possession of the vessel, sailed with their plunder to the coast of Africa. The Viceroy received an order from Madrid to replace the sum thus lost, by mortgaging the revenues of the royal domains in Italy, but no one would advance funds on such security.

Scarcity of money, dearness of provisions, and want of employment, produced discontents, and at length open insurrections at Madrid, and in other parts of Spain. The masons, who had been a numerous class of tradesmen in the capital, and were dying of hunger, began to rob and murder the wealthy inhabitants, in order to supply their more pressing wants. As their crimes remained unpunished, they soon increased in numbers and audacity. They at last assembled in great multitudes in a remote part of the city, and resolved to break open and plunder the houses of several magistrates, whom they accused as the authors of the present misfortunes. The shoemakers, about the same time, in consequence of some unpopular regulations concerning the price of their articles of trade, congregated in a tumultuous body in the court of the palace. They crowded under the windows of the King's apartments, and vociferated with all their force the formidable cry of " Viva el Rey y muera el mal govierno." As soon as the King heard them, he came to the balcony, and was in the utmost astonishment and alarm at beholding such an assemblage of people, whose numbers, too, were every moment augmenting. His Majesty sent for the President of Castile, who, by his orders, entered into a treaty with them—promising redress of all their grievances, and permission to sell shoes at whatever price they chose. The shoemakers immediately proclaimed this privilege, by sound of trumpets, in all the most public quarters of the city. Perhaps the concession thus obtained might be suitable enough in itself, but it was of evil precedent, and soon gave rise to demands by tradesmen, which were obviously unreasonable, and were enforced by renewed disturbances. The police was utterly inadequate for the protection of the inhabitants. Murders were committed in the face of day with impunity. Bravoes, with swords at their sides, or daggers in their hands, swaggered through the open streets and squares of the capital, disturbing the public peace, and setting at defiance the officers of justice. The more wealthy inhabitants almost daily received threatening and anonymous letters, enjoining them to deposit money in particular places indicated to them, under menaces of poison or assassination.

But, in fact, those usually considered as the more wealthy classes, were in no better situation than the lower orders. After having pledged their jewels and plate, they found themselves without effects or credit. In many quarters of the kingdom, such was the scarcity of coin, that, as a medium of exchange, cattle were given in barter for grain, and one sort of cloth for another. The bankers had no cash, and the merchants no merchandize. Some deputies, who arrived at Madrid from the Council of Commerce at Seville, represented that their once flourishing and populous city was reduced to one-fourth of the number of inhabitants which it had contained about fifty years ago. In several parts, indeed, of the kingdom, particularly in Andalusia, such was the misery, that many persons daily died of hunger. On hearing of this last consummation of wretchedness, the King was much affected, and declared to his minister, that such a state of things could be no longer endured. But, as usual, he received some general assurances of amendment, and the distresses, for the time, were no more thought of.

While the kingdom laboured under all these political and financial embarrassments, it was still farther afflicted by natural calamities, being ravaged nearly at the same time by the plague and an earthquake. The former scourge commenced its inflictions at Port St Mary near Cadiz. No measures of precaution were adopted, lest an alarm being spread, the sailing of the Indian fleet might be retarded; and, the proper means not having been used to arrest its progress, the disorder soon extended from Cadiz along the whole coast of Andalusia, and thence into the interior, as far as Seville, Cordova, and the province of Estremadura.

The plague had but just begun to abate, when the capital was alarmed by an earthquake, which, however, occasioned no great devastations in that city. But, in Malaga, its effects were most severely felt. So violent was the shock in that populous town, though only of a few moments' continuance, that walls and ramparts were entirely subverted. The sea was so agitated, that the vessels in the harbour were raised up twenty feet, and were strained as if they had endured a tempest. Fifteen convents were overthrown—about 1200 houses were completely destroyed, and as many were irreparably injured. A vast number of people were killed and wounded by the fall of houses, or were buried beneath their ruins. The survivors, fearing a repetition of the shock, fled in consternation to the country. But there too the ravages of this convulsion had extended, and many dwellings in the vicinity of Malaga had received such a concussion that they shortly after fell. A mountain of considerable height tumbled into the plain below. The earth opened in several places, and the water gushed out in such quantities, that desolating torrents were formed, and the rivers were swelled by them to a destructive height. The effects of this earthquake were also severely felt at Jaen, Seville, and Cordova, where many of the churches and ancient Moorish palaces were levelled with the dust.

While Spain was thus afflicted in the heart of her dominions, both by political distresses and extraordinary inflictions of Providence, her foreign possessions were not exempted from the general suffering. In Naples, a formidable association of 3000 banditti ravaged and plundered the country, and could neither be dispersed nor subdued by the viceregal troops. So completely, indeed, had the Viceroy lost all authority, that the soldiery not having received their pay, became mutinous, and, one day, 100 of their number, who were mounted, and fully armed, stopped him on the Strada di Toledo, and peremptorily demanded their discharge, or the arrears which were due to them.

Profiting by the unfortunate situation of the monarchy, the Moors expelled the Spaniards from every spot in Africa, except Oran, which they now closely invested. The Buccaneers, whose piracies, in the commencement of this reign, have already been detailed, still continued their ravages in the West Indies and South America. The Portuguese, also, took possession of the Isle of St. Gabriel, situated at the mouth of the Rio Plata, in the vicinity of Buenos Ayres. Though the right to this island had long been disputed, the Spaniards had now occupied it for more than a century. The Spanish commander at Buenos Ayres having united some Indians to his own

troops, sallied forth, and having surprised the fort which
the Portuguese had erected at St Gabriel, took its governor prisoner, and cut the garrison in pieces. On
this occasion, the Court of Lisbon behaved with a spirit
and firmness which was in all likelihood prompted by a
knowledge of the weakness of its adversary. The Portuguese ambassador at Madrid demanded an audience of
his Catholic Majesty, and insisted on reparation for the
attack on St Gabriel, by restitution of the island, with
the cannon and ammunition captured, and the punishment of the governor of Buenos Ayres. In answer,
the Spanish Court prepared a lengthened memorial, in
which they proved, that the Isle of St Gabriel was comprehended within the Spanish side of the line of deman-
cation which Pope Alexander VI. had drawn between
the territories of the two rival powers, and that the Spaniards had now held uninterrupted possession of the
island for more than a century. A copy of this manifesto was delivered to each of the foreign ministers resident at Madrid, and the Duke of Giovenazzo was sent as
ambassador from Spain to Lisbon, in order to treat concerning an adjustment of the existing differences. On
his first arrival, he made complaints, and demanded satisfaction for the injuries received. But he was explicit-
ly told from the commencement of his embassy, that the
pretensions of the Court of Spain could not be listened
to, and that the matter must be settled on the terms formerly required by the Portuguese ambassador. After
some slight opposition, the Duke of Giovenazzo acceded
to an accommodation on these humiliating conditions.
The Spanish ministry affected to be much displeased at
the conduct of their envoy, and with a view towards
saving the national honour, they pretended that the Duke
had exceeded his powers, and departed from his instructions. They, nevertheless, immediately ratified the trea-

ty, and, in thus yielding to an inferior Power, on a question where the point of right was entirely in their favour, they affixed the last seal, in the eyes of all nations, to the degradation of their country.

In this state of weakness and abasement, without an army or marine, Spain daily saw herself on the brink of a new rupture with the powerful monarchy of France, and was, in the mean while, from time to time, subjected to fresh humiliations, by its haughty and ambitious ruler.

The Spanish fishermen of Fontarabia, and the French of Andaye, had now, for some time, carried on among themselves a petty warfare, concerning the fishings of the river Bidassoa, which separates the two kingdoms. The governor of Fontarabia directed the cannon of the fort he commanded against the French, and destroyed some houses in Andaye. Being apprehensive of the consequences, the Spanish minister ordered him to rebuild the houses, and make every possible satisfaction to the injured French inhabitants. But both parties, on these frontiers, were at such a distance from the seat of government, that disturbances soon again broke out. Some regiments, stationed at Bayonne, spread themselves along the banks of the river, and several vessels moored themselves at its mouth to intercept the commerce of Fontarabia. Its inhabitants were thus prevented from going out to fish, and from committing their usual acts of hostility. The vessels then feigned to sail away, and leave the coast clear. The Biscayans immediately returned to their fishings, but the French, as soon as they had sailed back to their former stations, seized their boats, and made the fishermen prisoners. Intelligence of this attack having reached Madrid, the ministry exclaimed vehemently against such unjustifiable violence, and the infraction of the treaty of peace. But they confined themselves to

complaints, and the ambassadors of Louis informed them,
that they must, in the mean while, acquiesce in the decision given by those French commissioners who had investigated and settled all questions with regard to the
rights of fishing in the Bidassoa, and whose award, it need
not be doubted, was sufficiently favourable to the claims
of their own countrymen.

The aggressions of Louis, however, were not long confined to such paltry interests. As might have been anticipated by the allies, the treaty of Nimeguen, instead
of setting limits to the ambition of the French monarch,
afforded him opportunity to complete that plan for universal monarchy into which he had been flattered by
his courtiers and poets. Accordingly, while Spain, the
United Provinces, and the Empire, disbanded their su-
pernumerary forces, he still maintained his troops on their
full war-establishment. In the midst of profound peace,
he was at the head of a formidable army. His celebrated
engineer, Vauban, improved and strengthened the fortifications of Ypres, Lisle, Tournay, and most of the other
towns gained in the Netherlands. By the exertions of
Seignelay, the son of Colbert, the French marine was augmented; new ships were daily launched, and the arsenals
were replenished with additional stores. Louis, thus re-
doubtable, acted as if he had been already the sole sovereign of Europe, and all its other princes but his vassals.

By the Treaty of Westphalia, the Bishoprics of
Metz, Toul, and Verdun, had been ceded to France.
Several fiefs and towns which were anciently united to
them, but belonged to the House of Austria at the period
of the cession, were now reclaimed by Louis as pertinents
of these Sees. A judicial council, which he established at
Metz, having examined some musty records, and collected traditional information relative to the absolute rights
which the former sovereigns of such dioceses had enjoyed

declared, that these ancient dependencies of the Bishoprics now belonged to the crown of France; and on the
refusal of the Emperor and King of Spain to do homage
for their possession, they were, immediately, confiscated
and occupied by French troops. There were also several
disputes with regard to the extent of the territories and
dependencies of places which Spain had ceded to France
by the Treaty of Nimeguen. But the King of France
now settled all these controversies, by seizing on the
contested ground by force of arms. In this manner the
Spaniards were deprived of Chiney and several other important districts in the Netherlands. Louis at the same
time seized on the imperial city of Strasburgh; and by
an agreement with the Duke of Mantua, he took possession of Casal, which was one of the strongest fortresses in
Italy, and from its proximity to the Dutchy of Milan had
been always an object of great interest and jealousy to the
Kings of Spain. It was thus that Louis made more important acquisitions in short intervals of peace than during
long and sanguinary wars. A general terror now pervaded Spain—the United Provinces—the Empire and Italy,
at his lawless and arbitrary proceedings. But none of the
states who regarded Louis as their common enemy, took
any effectual measures to frustrate his grasping policy.
The Emperor was at present fully occupied with the revolt of his Hungarian subjects. Holland was employed
in the re-establishment of her commerce, which had been
severely injured by the late war. Spain and Sweden were
too feeble, and the provinces of the Empire or of Italy
were too disunited to oppose any barrier to French ambition; and this peculiar position of the European potentates paved the way for that brilliant career which for a
time rendered Louis so illustrious, but which ultimately
cost France so dear.

Notwithstanding the miserable situation to which she

was reduced, Spain, still faithful to the family alliance, resolved to aid the Emperor, who was at present engaged in a contest with his Hungarian subjects, and was, at the same time, threatened with an invasion by the Turks. The Spanish minister had trusted that he should obtain a supply for this purpose, in an immense treasure now daily expected from the Indies. But a furious tempest at this time swept the Atlantic, and five vessels of the fleet, which contained the greater part of the bullion, with 1200 persons, were lost at sea. To repair this disaster, the minister sold titles of nobility and honour. Lucrative offices of state had formerly been disposed of in this manner, and even governments and viceroyalties; but never, till the present exigency, had a minister ventured to barter, for a price, the rank of a Spanish grandee. The money obtained by this base expedient was faithfully transmitted to the Emperor, and proved so far beneficial to Spain, that, in return, his Imperial Majesty exerted himself to form a confederacy or defensive league, for twenty years, with Holland and Sweden, of which the chief object was, to guarantee the integrity of the Spanish Netherlands, in the event of Louis making any farther attempt to appropriate them. The King of Spain, at the same time, committed the military defence of these provinces to the Marquis of Grana, the Austrian ambassador at Madrid, from the want of any Spanish commander whose courage or military endowments qualified him to repel such an enemy as the King of France.

That monarch, however, was not to be deterred from his ambitious projects, either by leagues or menaces; and his intrigues and superior influence, in a great measure, frustrated the expectations of the new alliance. He successfully tampered with a formidable party in Holland, and, at the same time secured the neutrality of England, by remitting to Charles II. sufficient sums of money to supply his profusion, without being reduced to the necessity of assembling a parliament. In the empire, he found a partizan in the Elector of Brandenburgh, who, dissatisfied with Spain for withholding the arrears of his subsidies, employed all his efforts to prevent the German Diet from declaring war against France. But above all, Louis contrived to give sufficient occupation to Leopold, by fomenting the insurrection of his Hungarian subjects, and exciting the Turks to advance, with a formidable army, against Vienna, from which, on their approach, the Emperor was obliged to fly with the Imperial Family.

Relying on the effect of these intrigues and negotiations, it seems now to have become the object of Louis to accelerate the commencement of actual hostilities. Unreasonable as some of his former claims had been, the most unfounded of all was that he now made to the town of Alost in Flanders, which he demanded of Spain, on pretext that, from neglect of his instructions, his ministers had omitted to insert an article concerning it, in his favour, in the treaty of Nimeguen. However compliant Spain had shewn herself in other particulars, she peremptorily refused to deliver up Alost, and the King of France, in order to compel her, blockaded, and soon afterwards bombarded, the town of Luxemburg.

Every event now prognosticated the immediate renewal of hostilities, and however incapable Spain at this time was of sustaining a conflict, yet, being provoked beyond farther endurance by the insolent treatment which she received from her haughty enemy, she at length formally declared war against France. The great difficulty, as may be believed, was to raise funds in any degree adequate to meet the expenses of the approaching contest. In order to procure supplies, the minister reduced most of the pensions by one-half, and fixed the maximum of all pensions at 4000 ducats. He also attempted to get rid of the cost of tax-gatherers, by allowing towns and communities themselves, to collect the taxes imposed on them, and to remit the amount to the royal treasury. But this measure, which was intended at once to augment the public revenues, and to alleviate the burdens of the people, was found to be altogether impracticable in the execution.

The campaign opened nearly at the same time in the Netherlands and Catalonia. The French troops having entered Flanders, took possession of Courtray and Dixmude. To sustain this attack the Spanish Court solicited succour from Holland, in fulfilment of the defensive alliance which had been concluded with that republic. The Dutch accordingly sent garrisons into those towns of Flanders which were most exposed to the assaults of the enemy. But, mindful of their own interests, and the injuries they had suffered in previous conflicts with France, they would not venture to declare an offensive war, and soon after, notwithstanding the opposition of the Prince of Orange, signed a treaty of neutrality towards Spain and France. Luxemburg, which had been for some time blockaded, and was considered as almost impregnable, surrendered to Maréchal Créqui, whom the King supported with an army of 40,000 men, after a month's siege. France, however, did not push her conquests in the Low Countries, as might have been expected, nor avail herself of the most favourable opportunity that had ever been afforded her of completing the subjugation of the Austrian Netherlands. In fact, Louis, actuated chiefly by vanity, was often satisfied with only domineering over the neighbouring nations,—and he was besides apprehensive lest, by extending his usurpations too far, he might rouse the Dutch from their phlegm and apathy, and induce them to abandon the neutrality to which they had hitherto adhered.

While these events were passing in the Netherlands, a French army, which had assembled under the Mareschal Bellefonds, advanced through Roussillon to the frontiers of Catalonia. The force opposed to him in that district was unable, from its inferiority, to dispute his passage, and no farther obstacle intervening, the French troops confidently advanced to the siege of Girona. But the Spanish commander had thrown into that place the best part of his infantry, so that, when the Mareschal came to form the siege, he met with a far more obstinate resistance than he had anticipated. However, having occupied some out-works, and made a breach in the walls, he attempted to carry it by assault. His troops succeeded in entering the town, and had even reached the market-place, when they there unexpectedly encountered an immense mass of the armed population, supported by some squadrons of cavalry. Being also assailed by attacks from the houses, they fell into confusion, and were not only completely repulsed, but pursued with vigour to their camp.[1] After this disaster the Mareschal found himself obliged to retire towards the sea-coast, where, by the assistance of the French fleet, he made himself master of Palamos and some other small places.

Notwithstanding this partial success on his own frontiers, the King of Spain found that it would be impossible for him longer to prosecute the war against France. He had been totally disappointed of that succour from the Dutch, to which he had chiefly trusted in commencing hostilities. The King of England, though for the sake of some commercial advantages, he had recently concluded an alliance with the Court of Madrid, refused to engage in a contest with Louis, and he would not even permit the levy of some English and Irish regiments in his dominions for the Spanish service in the Low Coun-

[1] De Quincy, *Hist. Militaire*, t. ii. p. 51.

tries. The Emperor and the Germanic princes, though full of indignation and alarm at the conduct of Louis, could oppose no obstacle to his designs, at a time when they were assailed by the whole forces of the Ottoman empire. In the general neutrality or defection of the allies of Spain, Genoa alone had ventured to remain faithful to her interests, and had even concerted a plan with the Spanish ministry for burning the French ships in the ports of Marseilles and Toulon. Louis was not slow in preparing a formidable armament in the harbours of the Mediterranean, the command of which was given to Du Quesne, and which having sailed for Genoa, proceeded to bombard that city, on the republic refusing to grant the satisfaction for its past conduct which was demanded. Having been assailed with much effect, both by sea and land, the Genoese at length submitted to the conditions required of them, which were the reduction of the number of their ships, the renunciation of all their leagues or treaties with Spain, and the expulsion of the Spanish troops from every part of their territories.

Spain thus reduced to her own scanty resources could not have withstood for a single campaign the powerful arms of France. She implored the mediation of the Dutch, by whose intervention both Spain and the Emperor accepted a truce for twenty years, which was concluded at Ratisbon, and by the terms of which Louis restored Dixmude and Courtray, but retained Luxemburg, with almost all those places which he had appropriated as the dependencies of the three bishoprics. However unfavourable might be its terms, this accommodation was received with transports of joy in Spain, where it was seen that a war, in the present circumstances of the nation, might have terminated in the utter destruction of the monarchy.

Immediately after this treaty was concluded, the Duke

of Medina-Celi, whose weak administration had contributed to reduce Spain to her present abject state, and to deprive her of what little respect or consideration she had retained in the counsels of Europe, was driven from the high situation which he so unworthily filled. He had, as we have seen, disconcerted many intrigues, and disunited many factions and cabals which were formed against him. But he was at length compelled to yield[1] to the political party which was headed by the Count of Oropesa, and was now supported by the voice of the nation, the representatives of the nobility, and the influence of the two Queens. This intriguing politician, whose family name was Toledo, was allied to the royal family of Portugal, and indeed accounted himself next heir to its throne on the failure of the reigning house. The Count was about thirty-five years of age, when he succeeded in displacing the Duke of Medina-Celi from his post of prime minister. He was a man of agreeable person and countenance, of mild manners and insinuating conversation: he had an air of frankness, but was in reality close and reserved: he never spoke what he thought, and seldom uttered an opinion or sentiment but to mislead or deceive. He feigned to be pious and devout, and under an appearance of disinterestedness and moderation, he concealed an unbounded ambition.

The Count of Oropesa had been one of the earliest favourites of Charles II, and it was believed, that on the death of Don John of Austria he might, notwithstanding his youth, have been elevated through the favour of his sovereign to the situation of prime minister. But as he had formed at that time a very close political connexion

---

1 He retired to his Castle of Cogolludo, still retaining some of his honorary dignities. He was allowed to return to court about two years afterwards, and died in 1691, (Ortis, *Compend. Cronol.* Vayrac, *Etat. de l'Espagne.*)

with the Duke of Medina-Celi, he conceived that, under the existing circumstances, it would be ultimately more conducive to his interests to aid the Duke's promotion. He trusted, that, through the King's partiality, he might thus, for some time, possess power and influence without incurring responsibility or unpopularity. The Duke of Medina-Celi, however, was not a person to concede either to a friend or a rival an undue share of the patronage attached to his station. Hence the mind of the Count was soon alienated from the minister, but he still continued to enjoy a large portion of the confidence of his sovereign. The private marriage of Henriquez de Guzman, the unworthy relative of the Duke, to his niece Donna Laura, filled him with indignation against the minister, and produced an open rupture between them. At length, availing himself of the favour of his prince,—the jealousy excited against the Duke,—the discontents of the people, —and the bitter humiliation which Spain had suffered during his unfortunate administration, he succeeded in supplanting his rival; and, like so many former statesmen, he commenced his new government amid the plaudits of the people, and general anticipations of the instant reform of all abuses and the returning prosperity of the country.

Oropesa was certainly a man of greater firmness of mind, as also of more intelligence and industry, than his predecessor Medina-Celi; and at the commencement of his administration, he applied a temporary relief to some of the difficulties under which his country groaned, by again raising the value of the currency, which had been too much depreciated, and by the repeal of some oppressive taxes. But, as the income arising from these imposts had been mortgaged, their abolition raised a great, and not ill-founded, clamour among the public creditors, or *asientists* as they were called, who had purchased these securities at a high rate, and were now unexpectedly deprived of their subsistence. In order to pacify their just complaints, the minister provided a new fund by the suppression of pensions and some superfluous offices. But this excited an outcry among those who were more powerful. The country was still drained of its coin by annual subsidies to the Emperor; and, amid the rapid succession of foreign troubles and domestic wants, the royal revenue was absorbed far more quickly than it flowed in. Oropesa soon became as unpopular as any of his predecessors, and the kingdom scarcely languished less than during the ministry of the Duke of Medina-Celi.

There seems in fact to have been a remarkable deficiency, during this period, of men of talents in Spain. The Marques of Liche and the Count of Monterey, the sons of Luis de Haro, were probably the two persons of highest capacity in the kingdom. But the former being accounted a dangerous character, was always sent from Madrid as ambassador to some foreign court, and his brother, who was detested by the Queen-dowager, was ever suspected, and sometimes in disgrace. Nor had either given such indications of talent as could justify an assertion, that if called to the helm of government he would have placed his country in a better situation than it had been by the Count of Oropesa or the Duke of Medina-Celi. Rousseau, in speaking of his Spanish friend Altuña, says, " he was one of those lofty spirits whom Spain alone brings forth, but of whom she now brings forth too few for her glory." During the present critical period, however, Spain produced no such spirits at all, and she truly appears to have been in the state described by Sir William Temple, in his admirable essay on Popular Discontents. " There is yet one difficulty more, which sometimes arrives like an ill season or great barrenness in a country: some ages produce many great men and few great occasions; other times, on the contrary, raise great occasions and few or no great men; and that sometimes happens to a country which was said by the fool of Brederode, who, going about the fields with the motion of one sowing corn, was asked what he sowed, he said, I sow fools; the other replied, Why do you not sow wise men? Why, said the fool, *c'est que la terre ne les porte pas.* In some places and times, the races of men may be so decayed by the infirmities of birth itself, from the diseases or disaffection of parents,—may be so depraved by the viciousness or negligence of education,—by licentious customs and luxuries of youth,—by ill examples of princes, parents, or magistrates,—or by lewd and corrupt principles generally infused and received among a people, that it may be hard for the best princes and ministers to find subjects fit for the command of armies or great charges of the state; and, if these are ill supplied, there will be always too just occasion given for exception and complaints against the government, though it be never so well framed and instituted." It is seldom that the ingratitude of a people discourages the services of individuals; and it is more probable that no talent now existed among the Spaniards, than that it was withheld from the service of the state. But never, except in the Grecian republics, had the benefactors of their country been so requited as by the despotic monarchs of Spain. Nor was this ingratitude experienced by foreigners alone, as Columbus and Spinola, who had ventured all in the service of that country, but by its own sons and natives,—Gonsalvo de Cordova, Ximenes, Cortez, and Alva.

Notwithstanding the twenty years' truce which had been concluded at Ratisbon between France and Spain, the latter country still continued to be exposed to a continuance of all those insults and mortifications which, for many years past, she had endured from her presumptuous foe. Soon after the Count of Oropesa had entered on

the ministry, the harbour of Cadiz was blockaded by a
French fleet, to enforce payment of half a million of
crowns, the value of confiscated goods belonging to some
French merchants, who had traded to Mexico and other
parts of America, in defiance of the commercial prohibitions of Spain : And the fleet was not withdrawn till a
promise had been obtained of full and immediate satisfaction.　Soon afterwards, though in a different quarter, a
Spanish Admiral having refused to lower his flag before
some French vessels, was fired on, and after an engagement of three hours, was forced to submit to the humiliating ceremony required by the more powerful nation.

Amid all these mortifications, the Court of Spain learned, with the liveliest satisfaction, that one of the most formidable coalitions ever entered into in Europe, had at
length been formed against the King of France.　As
Louis still continued his aggressions in Germany, the
Emperor Leopold had anxiously watched an opportunity
to rouse the torpid spirit of the European States.　He
found an able coadjutor in the Prince of Orange, who was
animated against Louis by motives of personal and religious antipathy ; and at this time was peculiarly anxious
to find employment for the French arms on the Continent, that he might not be disturbed in the views which
he had formed towards the crown of England.　Availing
himself of the abhorrence excited in Holland by the persecution to which the Hugonots were now subjected by
Louis, he united all his countrymen, who had hitherto
been so much divided by factions, in a determined opposition to France.　Under the auspices of the Emperor
and the Prince of Orange, that confederacy was formed,
which was afterwards known by the name of the league
of Augsburgh, and which, besides these two potentates,
included, almost from its commencement, the King of
Denmark, the Pope, and the Elector of Brandenburgh.

So potent and numerous was the coalition thought necessary to check the ambition of Louis, who had attained a superiority not hitherto known in Europe. The power of Charles V. had been counterbalanced by that of Francis I. alone, and Henry IV. was a sufficient check on the policy of Philip II.; but now it required a combination of almost all Christendom to resist the designs of Louis.

At this important crisis, a dispute concerning the succession to the Palatinate afforded an opportunity of strengthening the confederacy, by uniting to it in one general association almost all the Princes of the Empire. On the death of the Elector-Palatine about this period, his territories were claimed by the Duke of Neuburg, in competition with the Dutchess of Orleans, sister of the deceased Prince, whose pretensions Louis prepared to support by an invasion of the Palatinate. These threatened hostilities, and the arbitrary measures adopted against several of their number by those Chambers of reunion which he had established at Brisach and Metz, excited the utmost alarm through the empire, and opened the eyes of its princes to the dangerous policy of Louis. To repel his aggressions, they raised a formidable army, the command of which was entrusted to the Elector of Bavaria[1].

As for Spain, though her envoys in the different courts of Europe had been assiduous in prompting a spirit of resistance to French ambition, and though she hailed with delight the new prospects which were opened up to her by this confederation of Augsburgh, she seems to have been struck with such awe and dread of the power of Louis, that she did not, for some time, venture openly to declare herself a member of the league, or to come into direct collision with France.

Meanwhile, the secret of the confederacy of Augsburgh

[1] Coxe, *Hist. of House of Austria*, c. lxv.

having transpired, Louis, with his characteristic energy and rapidity, marched an army of 80,000 men to the banks of the Rhine.[1] Before the close of the campaign, he captured Philipsburgh, reduced Spire, Worms, and other fortresses on that river; and, on pretext of supporting the claims of the Dutchess of Orleans, he overran the whole Palatinate. In these irruptions, by which he laid waste the whole country with fire and sword to the very heart of Germany, he met with little resistance. The troops of the Germanic body destined to act under the Elector of Bavaria, had not yet fully assembled, nor were they prepared to cope with the formidable enemy who had fallen on them so suddenly and unexpectedly. The forces belonging to the Head of the empire were still chiefly employed in Hungary and on the frontiers of Turkey, whence, however, they were now speedily recalled for the defence of the Austrian dominions.[2]

It was at this time that the half-expelled half-abdicated monarch of England sought refuge in France. Louis was well aware of the wishes of Spain for the success of the league of Augsburgh, and, indeed, of her intentions to join it whenever an opportunity might offer. But he availed himself of the revolution in England to attempt an union between himself and the King of Spain, on pretence of vindicating, by this alliance, the injury offered to the majesty of kings in the person of James II. Before hazarding this proposal, Louis had secured the influence of his niece the Queen of Spain, for whom the King's attachment and deference were daily increasing. Her

---

[1] It is said that Louvois, the war-minister, promoted and accelerated this contest, in order to diminish the influence of Mad. Maintenon, because he thought his own credit would be paramount so long as he engaged his master in the hazards and difficulties of war. (*Mém. de Feuquières,* t. i. p. 8.)

[2] Coxe, *House of Austria,* c. lxx.

attention to him during those frequent fits of sickness and hypochondriac melancholy, which began to verge on insanity, had so much endeared her to his heart, that it was now understood at Court that nothing would be refused to her solicitations. Her present counsel, however, in favour of supporting Louis and the exiled King of England, was clearly pernicious. In following it, Spain would have lost the only opportunity which had ever presented itself of curbing the power of France; and, if Louis, by aid of Spain, had prevailed over the league of Augsburgh, she would then have been destroyed at a more favourable opportunity. But the endeavours of the Queen were opposed by the Spanish ministry and all the ambassadors of the allies, who incessantly recalled to the recollection of Charles the recent injuries which he had sustained from the King of France,—they exaggerated the power and resources of the league, and held out to him the hope, if he joined it, of recovering all those rich and ancient inheritances of the House of Burgundy, which had passed into the hands of his bitterest foe. Policy, hatred to France, and the desire of revenge, sometimes drew the King into the views which were thus suggested. But in the next moment, his weak mind, influenced by the caresses and entreaties of his Queen, and the fear of displeasing her, as also by his habitual regard for legitimacy, and horror at usurpation and heresy, inclined him to espouse, at all hazards, the interests of the dethroned English monarch. During his whole life, Charles was rendered miserable by irresolution. But, on the present occasion, his unhappy mental struggle was terminated by the sad catastrophe of the death of his Queen, who expired, after an illness of three days, in the twenty-seventh year of her age, after she had reigned about nine years and three months in Spain.

Her Majesty had enjoyed uninterrupted good health till the close of 1688, when she was afflicted with the

small-pox; and she had afterwards some severe attacks
of disorders in the stomach, accompanied with Calenture.
From these, however, though much weakened, she partially
recovered, till, in the beginning of February of this year,
after too violent exercise on horseback, she was seized with
cholera morbus. During her short and severe illness,
she conducted herself with much fortitude and resignation, and shewed, in all her expressions and actions, an ex-
emplary piety. The Queen-mother frequently came to
see her : all ancient grounds of offence between them were
mutually forgiven, and she even asked pardon for any displeasure which she might have occasioned to the Dutchess
of Terranueva.[1]

The youth of the Queen, the suddenness of her demise,
the doubtful nature of her disorder, and the advantages
reaped from her death by a powerful political party, led
many to believe that she had been poisoned ; and suspicion fell on the Count d'Oropesa, and on Count Mans-
feldt, the Austrian ambassador.[2] It was alleged that the
latter had bribed two of her French *femmes-de-chambre*
to give her poison in raw oysters, and afterwards to
withhold from her the antidote which had been entrusted to their care.[3] Such was the ascendency she had at
last acquired over the mind of her husband, that he was

---

[1] *Vera Tassis, Noticias Historiales de la Enfermedad y muerte de
nuestra Señora*, Madrid, 1690, *folio.* It
does not appear clearly whether the Dutchess had been admitted to
see the Queen during this last illness, or if her Majesty merely
desired this gracious request of forgiveness to be communicated to
her.

[2] *Mem. de Torcy,* t. i. p. 7,

[3] *Correspondence of Dutchess d'Orleans.* "The Queen of Spain,"
says her stepmother, the second Dutchess of Orleans, "daughter
of the first Madame (Henrietta of England), died in precisely the
same way he did, and at the same age, but in a much more painful manner, for the violence of the poison was such as to make her

about to send for her half-brother the Duke de Chartres, who was afterwards the Regent Orleans, and was then fourteen years of age, to constitute him heir to the monarchy, and bring him up in the manners and institutions of Spain. The ministry, on the other hand, were devoted to the interests of the Emperor, who already began to look forward to the crown of Castile as an inheritance for his family. This was sufficient, in such a country as Spain, to excite suspicion : But nothing farther than suspicion existed, and no inquiry or investigation was made on the subject.

The Queen of Spain had been placed during her short life, in a trying, and not very enviable, situation. " A political queen," as a modern author observes, is " a sacrifice by which enraged governments and wavering allies are conciliated, or ancient amities confirmed. Excluded from the exchange of equal and reciprocal affection, the great charm of female existence, she feels keenly that pomp is not felicity, nor splendour content. With little to fear or to hope, with no object but a cold duty to a royal husband, she passes her life in the discharge of trifling and mechanical occupations, which renders her frivolous in her pursuits, and formal in her manners." But of all political Queens, the fate of Louisa d'Orleans was perhaps the most to be pitied. In aspiring to the hand of the Dauphin of France, her mind had been fixed, in early youth, on a higher and a happier lot. That affection which she secured from her husband, could scarcely, from such a man, have been in any degree flattering or soothing. The country, in the government of which she was

---

nails fall off." St-Simon (*Mém.* t. ii, c. 4.) maintains she was poisoned, but alleges it was through the instrumentality of the Countess de Soissons (mother of Prince Eugene), who was at that time in Spain, and was both an able and experienced practitioner in the veneficial art.

called to partake, was in a condition the most wretched and hopeless; she was excluded from all society with the natives of her own country; she had no children to amuse or interest her vacant hours of solitude, and, which perhaps was worse, she never could have indulged in the pleasing prospect of offspring.

Yet Louisa d'Orleans passed the dangerous period of life with untainted reputation, and with many claims to popularity and esteem amongst her subjects. Leaving, in the first dawn of youth, the most brilliant court in Europe, and entering the most gloomy, she bore the change with cheerfulness, and, except in the few first days of probation, without repining. United to a husband of the most despicable understanding and deplorable ignorance, and who possessed no qualifications which could win either attachment or esteem, she paid him, in all his fits of caprice or despondency, unremitting attention, and never was suspected of allowing her affections to stray to a more worthy object. From the beginning of her reign, she shewed the greatest sympathy for the distresses of the people; and, during her last illness, being informed that the citizens who had assembled at the gates of the palace, were offering up prayers for her recovery, she said, " that she was well entitled to this return of affection, as she would at any time have laid down her life to relieve them of the burdens they endured.[1]"

After the death of his Queen, Charles threw himself entirely into the arms of the imperial party, and confirmed his accession to the league of Augsburgh, by a matrimonial union with Maria Anne of Neuburg, daughter of the Elector Palatine, and sister of the reigning Empress, as also of the Queen of Portugal. This Princess, who was then in the twenty-second year of her age, after

[1] Flores, *Reynas d'España.*

having been long detained by adverse winds on the coast
of England, landed at length at Ferrol, accompanied by
a squadron of Dutch and English vessels. She immediately set out for the capital, and, on her way, was sumptuously entertained at the palaces of the different grandees
which lay on her route, particularly at Monforte de Lemos, the residence of the Count of Lemos in Gallicia.[1]
She was met by the King and all his court at Valladolid,
where the marriage ceremony was celebrated with much
sadness, as the mind of Charles was still mournfully occupied by the recollection of his beloved Louisa d'Orleans.

This new Queen was neither so much respected nor
beloved by the Spaniards as her predecessor. Though
not destitute of personal charms, she had not those graces
and that winning address which had rendered their former
queen so dear to them. They did not relish her implicit
submission to the decisions and influence of a Capuchin
friar whom she had brought along with her from Germany, and who too strongly reminded them of Father
Nithard. This priest, and a lady of her bed-chamber,
called the Countess Berleps, composed her whole council,
with the occasional addition of Henriquez, Count of Melgar, son to the Admiral of Castile, who had been recently
governor of Milan, and ultimately, by the Queen's favour and protection, was promoted to the dignity of prime
minister. The nation soon found out that she despised
them ; and the unpopularity of the new Queen was completed by the obstinacy with which she supported the
pretensions of her nephew, the Archduke Charles of Austria, to the succession to the throne of Spain.

This alliance, however, with a German princess, was
at present so far fortunate for Spain, that it confirmed
the vacillating King in his renunciation of all farther

_____
[1] Flores, Reynas d'España.

correspondence with the King of France, and in his ad-
hesion to the league of Augsburgh.

That confederacy received at this time a far more important accession than the support of Spain, by the establishment of the Prince of Orange on the throne of
England. James II. was the only prince of the first
rank who had not acceded to the league of Augsburgh.
His abdication, consequently, produced a great and in-
stantaneous change in favour of the allies, and secured
the independence of Europe. In consequence of that
auspicious event, the empire was encouraged to issue a
formal declaration of war against France. The German
princes had flattered themselves that the ambition of
Louis would have confined itself to the acquisition of the
Spanish Netherlands. But their eyes being now opened
to his arbitrary measures and dangerous policy, the Germanic confederates assembled their contingents, and advanced from every quarter towards the Rhine. Not less
active in negotiation than in arms, the combined princes
intimated their party, and concentrated their efforts by new
alliances. The King of Denmark, surrounded by their
states and territories, was obliged to desert his ancient
ally, and conclude a subsidiary treaty with England, by
which he engaged to furnish 8000 troops, in support of
the common cause. In all contests between France and
Austria, the alliance of the Duke of Savoy had been accounted of the utmost importance. Accordingly, on the
present occasion, every endeavour was used to secure the
aid of the most powerful of the Italian princes. But the
wily, intriguing, and selfish character of the reigning
Duke, Victor Amadeus II, and the engagements which
he was supposed to have formed with France, rendered
all circumspection necessary in concluding with him a
treaty, which, it was believed, he might afterwards be well

disposed to elude, if he considered that the evasion suited his interests. Maréchal Catinat was already with him at Turin, as ambassador from Louis, urging him to declare against the allies. In order to counteract his negotiations, the celebrated Prince Eugene was sent by the Emperor to Turin, on pretence of visiting his family, and paying his respects to his cousin, the Duke of Savoy. His dissimulation towards France was carried on to the last moment: But he privately concluded, through Prince Eugene, a treaty with the Emperor, by which he agreed to join the confederacy, on condition that he should be appointed Generalissimo of the forces destined to act against France in Italy,—that he should be allowed to retain whatever places he might conquer in Dauphiny or Provence, and that, so long as he kept an army on foot, he should receive monthly subsidies from England and Holland.[1]

The league of Augsburgh, originally formed between the Emperor and the Prince of Orange, being now strengthened by the accession of Spain, England, Denmark, and Savoy, assumed the name of the Grand Alliance. In its commencement, its principles were purely defensive, and the original contracting parties had held forth that their sole object was to preserve and enforce the stipulations of the peace of Nimeguen : but now the allies agreed that they should exert their whole force by sea and land against the common enemy, till Europe was restored to the footing on which it had been placed by the articles of the treaties of Westphalia and the Pyrenees. They engaged to procure the re-establishment of the Duke of Lorraine in his territories, and bound themselves by secret articles to support the Emperor or his heirs in the right of succession to the Spanish monarchy,

[1] *Mémoires du Prince Eugene.*

should Charles II. die without issue.[1] Finally, they agreed to make no truce or peace without mutual consent; and even entered into engagements to maintain a perpetual league against France after the conclusion of peace, for the purpose of watching and repressing the designs of that ambitious power.[2]

France now, for the first time, since she had become predominant in Europe, instead of being assisted by a number of allies or adherents, was left singly to combat an host of foes ; and Spain, though weak in herself, entered into the contest with her ancient enemy, supported by the whole of Christian Europe, except Sweden, Portugal, and some of the minor Italian states. Within the last few years, France had also been deprived by death of her illustrious warrior the Prince of Condé, and of Mareschal Crequi, who, for some time, had ranked among the first of her commanders. She had recently sustained perhaps a still severer loss in her wise minister Colbert, who, by the order and economy with which he conducted the finances, had enabled his master to support the most expensive wars, and to dazzle, with his splendour, both his own subjects and foreign nations. France, too, had at this time been somewhat weakened, and her resources diminished, by the revocation of the Edict of Nantes, which transferred to Holland or Germany near a million of the richest, the most intelligent, and the most industrious of its inhabitants,—while those Protestants who yet lingered in the realm were preparing to take up arms in Languedoc and the Cevennes.

[1] Targe, *Hist. de l'Avenement de la Maison de Bourbon au Trône d'Espagne,* t. i. c. 1, sect. 14.

[2] Coxe's *Hist. of House of Austria,* c. 65.

CHAPTER VIII.

RENEWAL OF THE WAR WITH FRANCE.

> Never ending—still beginning—
> Fighting still, and still destroying.
>
> DRYDEN.

THE King of Spain having now publicly joined the
Grand Alliance, and declared war against France in due
form, the campaign was opened nearly at the same moment in Catalonia and the Netherlands, and soon afterwards on the banks of the Rhine and the Po. Each
successive season, hostilities spread more extensively, and
became more destructive.

The contest, as we have seen, was commenced under
favourable auspices on the part of Spain. But the advantages obtained by the allies were scarcely commensu-
rate to the vast expectations they had formed. It is in
such emergencies that a great nation comes to know and
appreciate its own strength ; and it was quickly proved
that a powerful and compact monarchy, placed in a commanding position, with a government of sufficient energy
to call forth all the resources of the people, and an army
led on by able generals, will ultimately prevail against an
extensive confederacy of states distracted by internal dissensions, varying in interests, and forming a heterogene-
ous body, incapable of combining in one uniform plan of
operations.

With an army of 300,000 well disciplined troops at
his absolute disposal, the French monarch succeeded in

baffling the first and most dangerous attack. Holding
the allied powers at bay on the side of the Netherlands
and Germany, he directed his efforts against Spain and
Italy,—pouring his forces into the former country by
Roussillon and Catalonia.

In that dangerous province, the Court of Spain, in addition to a foreign invasion, had to provide against the
consequences of civil commotion. As soon as a war
with France appeared inevitable, the Marques of Leganez, at that time Viceroy of Catalonia, attempted, by
levying troops and raising subsidies, to place his government in a suitable posture of defence. But such was the
hatred he incurred among the people in consequence of
these exertions, that he was recalled on his own solicitation, and the Count of Melgar appointed in his room.
This compliance, however, of the Court in removing an
obnoxious governor, seems to have been attended with
evil consequences: For the peasantry, pretending that
their privileges were violated by quartering troops amongst
them (though it was for their own protection against a
foreign enemy), assembled in great multitudes, and attempted to seize the Duke of Villa-Hermosa, who had
been appointed General of the Spanish army destined to
act against the French on the frontiers of Catalonia.
The Duke, however, easily disengaged himself, and forced
them to fly to the mountains. There, in a sudden fit of
apparent contrition, they cut off the head of one of their
chiefs, and sent it to the Duke, promising the most implicit obedience for the future. This submission, however, was only a device on the part of the Catalans to
gain time ; for, having received assurances of succour from
France, they again took up arms, and assembled to the
number of not fewer than 30,000, under the command of
Antonio de Soler, who had placed himself at the head of
the insurgents : But, before he could receive any effectual

assistance from France, or form a junction with its army, he was attacked with unusual promptitude by the Duke of Villa-Hermosa, and so totally defeated, that this formidable insurrection was quelled by a single blow.

The Duke de Noailles, who was appointed to the command of the French army in Catalonia, commenced his military operations by the capture of the town of Campredon in that province, situated at the foot of the Pyrenees, on the river Ter. His army, however, being inferior to that of the Duke of Villa-Hermosa (who was now appointed viceroy as well as general of the province) and being worsted in an encounter with the Spanish troops, he retired into Roussillon with some precipitation, leaving his ammunition and artillery behind him. Campredon, which the Spaniards had in vain attempted to retake, was dismantled by him, and the French garrison withdrawn from it.[1]

Nothing remarkable occurred in Catalonia in the year 1690. In the following spring, however, the Duke de Noailles returned with augmented forces, and, before the Spanish army had fully assembled, he took Urgel in the Cerdagne, and seized some strong passes which opened up the way into Aragon, where his troops made several incursions. The Duke of Medina-Sidonia, who, in order to satisfy the popular clamour, had been appointed Viceroy of Catalonia, at first marched towards the French, as if with the intention of giving battle. He afterwards, however, drew off his troops, and invested Campredon, in which a small French garrison had been replaced. But though that town had been almost completely dismantled of its fortifications, he could not succeed in taking it, and soon afterwards raised the siege, on the appearance of the Duke de Noailles. The Count de Pignatelli, who commanded under him, was so disgusted by his imbecile con-

[1] Ortiz, Compend. Cronol. tom. Ib. lib. &c.

duct, that he retired with the best part of the army to
Barcelona. This compelled the Duke of Medina-Sidonia to follow him, and both parties appealed, in justification of their conduct, to the Court of Madrid, which had
no great reason to be satisfied with either.[1] The French
having also, at this time, the command of the Mediterranean, their admiral, the Count d'Estrées, availed himself of this advantage to bombard Barcelona for three
days. He then sailed to Alicant, and, though he failed
in an attempt to disembark, his bombardment occasioned
great damage to the city; and so incensed the inhabitants, that they could with difficulty be prevented from
massacring some French sailors who had fallen into their
hands.[2]

The complaints and alarm of the natives, both of Catalonia and Aragon, were soon heard at Madrid. A general council of state was assembled, in order to discover,
if possible, the causes of the weakness of the monarchy,
and to devise some plan for opposing the farther progress
of the French. The Duke d'Ossuna declared his opinion—that the King should immediately show himself at
the head of his army, in order to restore confidence to the
nation. Such an example by the sovereign, he maintained,
would immediately be followed by the nobility, grandees,
and knights of the military orders, who had never appeared in a field of battle since the days of Philip IV; and
he ventured to cite the example of Louis XIV, whose
presence in his army made every soldier a hero. The
opinion, however, of those flatterers prevailed, who declared that it would be better to lose the whole province
of Catalonia, than to risk the health and life of the King.[3]
From his natural timidity and irresolution, Charles was
glad to avail himself of the pretext founded on the uni-

[1] Desormeaux, *Abrégé Chronol.*
[2] Ortiz, *Compend. Cronol.* t. vi. lib. xxi. c. 6.	[3] Ibid.

certain state of the succession, in the event of his death, to concur in these sentiments.

About the same time, the King exhibited a new mark of weakness, in sacrificing his favourite minister, the Count of Oropesa, to the hatred of the Queen, and appointing in his stead the Count of Melgar, eldest son of the Admiral of Castile, and lately Viceroy of Catalonia. The Count was at that time a young man without experience; and though a favourite of the fair sex,—though with pretensions to literature superior to what was usual among Spanish Grandees, and though well qualified for managing a court-intrigue, he was incapable of conducting with wisdom the affairs of an extensive empire. In the instructions to his grandson, Philip V, on his accession to the Spanish throne, Louis XIV. thus delineates the character of Melgar, of which he, of course, had judged from the reports of his able residents and agents at Madrid. " The Admiral of Castile has a good understanding, speaks and writes well, affects a love of literature, and maintains four Jesuits, who are admitted to his table; but he owes nothing to study. He is esteemed a miser, and yet would appear profuse, entering into all kinds of expense, without taste, and without discernment, merely from vanity. He has never had any view but his own interest; he has consequently no friend. Loving his ease and his pleasure, he will probably be more intent to efface the impressions made by his misconduct, than to form parties in the state." [1]

The King, however, could not altogether dispense with the attendance of Oropesa, for whom he had the warmest attachment, and soon recalled him from the banishment into which he had been driven; and though the Count

[1] *Mém. de Noailles*, ap. Coxe's *Memoirs of Kings of Spain of House of Bourbon*, t. 1. c. 3.

of Melgar still retained the situation of first minister, he appointed Oropesa President of the Council of Castile.[1]

Melgar, who had been accustomed to see each new minister attempt to signalize the commencement of his government by the reform of abuses, did not fail to imitate the example of his predecessors. He suppressed a number of superfluous and hereditary offices, and put an end to all reversions of places or pensions.[2] That he might abate the envy to which high situations are exposed, he had the moderation or prudence to share the supreme direction of affairs with the Prince of Melito—the Duke d'Infantado—and the Marques of Villafranca. A new Junta, with the Count de Monterey at its head, was appointed to bring the finances under proper regulation. One of the first resolutions of its members, was to examine into the conduct of all such as had been entrusted with the management of pecuniary supplies belonging to the state; and that it might appear they were in earnest, the Marques of Gastanaga, who had been recently governor of the Low Countries, was no sooner arrived in Spain, than he was committed prisoner to the Castle of Burgos, and a note sent to him of the immense sums he had received, with an intimation that he must render an exact account of the manner in which they had been expended. It does not seem that these investigations were attended with any important results; but a considerable sum, to defray the exigencies of the war, was at this time obtained, by the seasonable arrival of the galleons from America.

In order to remedy the bad state of military affairs, and to raise troops wherever they were wanted, four lieutenant-generals were appointed by the King to have the superin-

---

[1] *Mém. de Noailles*, ap. Coxe's, *Memoirs.*

[2] " Nada adelantó con esto," says Ortiz, " pues era como una gota de agua en la mayor sed.

tendence in that department over all Spain.   But the
number was soon reduced to three, as the Count de
Monterey, who was included in this nomination also, soon
afterwards resigned.   It does not appear, however, that
their exertions were attended with any more benefit than
those of the Junta of Finance, as we find that the incapable Duke of Medina-Sidonia was still continued in
command of the troops in Catalonia. Though his adversary the Duke de Noailles was considerably weakened by
being obliged to send large detachments to reinforce the
army employed against the Duke of Savoy, he was unable to avail himself of that advantage. The French,
indeed, from the diminution of their numbers, were compelled to remain chiefly on the defensive during this campaign ; but they occupied such strong and well chosen positions, that no superiority could be gained over them.

To prepare for the following campaign, the King sold
the small district of Sabionetta, in the Milanese, to one
of the Italian princes. From the funds procured by
this alienation, and some other devices, an army was at
length formed in Catalonia, and again placed under the
Duke of Medina-Sidonia. But little could be expected
from any army which he commanded. The Duke de
Noailles invested Rosas by land, while the French fleet
under D'Estrées blockaded it by sea. Their operations
commenced by a bombardment, which having continued
for some days, and the governor having been dangerously
wounded, the place capitulated on terms. The French
general being again obliged to send detachments to re-
cruit the army in Italy, the remainder of the campaign
was spent in marches and counter-marches, and at the
close of it he retired with his troops towards Roussillon,
after leaving a sufficient garrison in Rosas.

During these domestic transactions at the Court of
Madrid, and military operations on the frontiers of Spain,

the war was conducted with spirit in the Netherlands,
but with little permanent advantage to the cause of the
Allies. At first, indeed, they gained some successes over
Mareschal d'Humieres, but Mareschal Luxembourg having been appointed to the command of the army in
Flanders, soon gave a new turn to affairs. Being joined,
without the knowledge of his opponents, by the Duke
de Bouflers, he advanced against the united Dutch and
Spanish army under, the Prince of Waldeck, and an
obstinate combat ensued at Fleurus, near Charleroy,
where, by a bold and decisive movement of his cavalry on
his left wing, he obtained a complete victory: For, being
covered from the view of the allies by a rising ground, the
French horse fell on the flank of the Dutch while they
were engaged in front with the infantry. The Dutch
cavalry fled at the first shock, but their infantry stood
firm, and performed signal acts of valour. Five thousand
were killed or wounded before they gave way; and as for
the Spanish infantry, Luxembourg declared, that they had
not behaved with greater courage even at the battle of
Rocroy.[1]

The Duke of Lorraine, the only general who could
have been opposed, with any prospect of success, to Luxembourg, had died about this time, in the flower of his
age. But William III, King of England, being now relieved from domestic dangers by his victories in Ireland,
had at length the power of directing his attention more
immediately to the affairs of the Continent. On his arrival at the Hague in 1691, he found himself surrounded
by the ambassadors of almost all the crowned heads in
Europe, and assumed, amid their sanguine prognostica-
tions of success, the command of the allied army. But
William's genius for war was seldom seconded by good
fortune. Luxembourg still maintained over him the su-

[1] Russell's *Modern Europe*, vol. iv.

periority which he had held in all previous encounters, and
which he exercised till his death. Mons was taken by
the French in 1691, and Namur in the following season ;
and in 1693 the allies were totally defeated in a pitched
battle at Neervinden.

Dismayed by all these disasters in the Low Countries,
the Spanish ministry resolved to carry into execution a
project, which had been oftner than once under consideration, for detaching, in some measure, these distant provinces from the crown of Spain. Letters were accordingly despatched, declaring the Elector of Bavaria hereditary governor of the Spanish Netherlands, with incom-
parably higher powers than had been bestowed on any of
his predecessors, and granting him payment of a large
monthly subsidy. Some writers affirm, that this arrangement had been entered into several years before, on the
marriage of the Elector with the niece of the King of
Spain ; while by others it has been ascribed solely to the
influence of King William's counsels. It seems not improbable, that after so long a delay, his Catholic Majesty
may have been at length determined to adopt this step
by the representations of the King of England, who knew
by experience the great difficulty, or rather impossibility,
of concerting operations for the defence of countries of
such consequence to the maritime powers, with governors
who were seldom continued in their situations above three
years, who were chiefly intent on improving their private
fortunes, and who could undertake nothing of moment
till they received instructions from the Court of Madrid,
where the best judgment could not always be expected
concerning affairs at such a distance.[1]

The conduct of the Duke of Savoy, Victor Amadeus
II, compelled the King of France to maintain an army
in the north of Italy. The present Duke possessed all the

[1] *Universal History*, vol. xxi. b. 19. c. 1.

subtle qualities of his crafty lineage. But Louis having at length penetrated through this prince's deep dissimulation, the character of Mareschal Catinat, as ambassador at the Court of Turin, was quickly changed into that of a general at the head of a numerous and hostile army. He summoned the Duke to deliver up his capital, and also Vercelli, into his hands, as pledges of his favourable disposition towards France. As the Duke at present was neither provided with troops nor money for defence, and as a refusal of this demand would have exposed both Savoy and Piedmont to certain devastation, he still attempted to gain time by negotiation till the arrival of the succours which he expected from Naples and Germany. But the King of France, aware of his object, ordered Catinat immediately to commence hostilities. The Duke of Savoy, having been joined by the Neapolitan auxiliaries which he awaited, and by Prince Eugene from Vienna, though unaccompanied by any German reinforcements, resolved to give battle to the French. Victor Amadeus, was a commander of much personal courage, and well skilled in that deceitful species of warfare which may be carried on with advantage in a mountainous and uneven territory. Relying on these qualifications and his knowledge of the country, he advanced, contrary to the advice of Prince Eugene, in quest of the French army to the vicinity of Staffarda, a place long memorable for the signal defeat there sustained by the Italians. The allied army had upwards of 4000 men killed and wounded, and the French only 300,—a disparity which proves that the discomfited army was drawn up in such a manner and on such ground that it was certain to be overpowered.[1] In consequence of this battle all Savoy, except Montmelian, submitted to a French corps detached from the main army, while Catinat in person rendered himself master of

[1] Voltaire, *Siécle de Louis XIV.* *Mémoires de Prince Eugene.*

Saluzzo in Piedmont, and of Susa, which commands the passes between that principality and Dauphiny. He then entered Savoy, and advanced to Montmelian, of which he rendered himself master after an obstinate siege.[1]

At length, however, there was a full muster of princes, generals, and troops at the foot of the Alps. The Duke of Savoy, the Elector of Bavaria, Prince Eugene, and the Marques of Leganez, Governor of Milan, commanded a motley army composed of Italians, Germans, Spaniards, and some French refugees. Towards the close of the campaign, Prince Eugene, who now began to display his great military genius, first turned the tide of success against the French. He compelled them to raise the siege of Coni, retook Carmagnola, and obliged Catinat to repass the Po. That general being now too weak to resist the augmented army of the allies, the Duke of Savoy entered Dauphiny, and sufficiently avenged himself of the insults which had been offered to him in his own dominions during the preceding campaigns. He ravaged the country, and reduced several fortified towns; but his own sickness, and that of his troops, prevented him from achieving more important conquests. His army having been considerably diminished by disease, and that of Catinat, on the other hand, increased by the detachments sent to him from the Duke de Noailles in Catalonia, he found it prudent to retire within his own territories before the winter snows should block up the passage of the Alps. Thither he was followed in the ensuing season by Catinat; and the Duke having invested Pignerol, a town in Piedmont, which half a century before had been made over to France, the Mareschal descended from the mountains, and seemed to threaten Turin. Alarmed for the safety of his capital, the Duke raised the siege of Pigne-

[1] Voltaire, *Siécle de Louis XIV.*   *Mémoires du Prince Eugene.*

rol, and advanced to the small river Cisola where it passes Marsiglia.   There the two armies came in sight of each other, and neither declined the combat.   The Imperial and Piedmontese cavalry, commanded by the Duke in person, composed the right wing of the confederates : the infantry, consisting of the troops of Savoy and those in the pay of England, were stationed in the centre under Prince Eugene; and the left wing was formed of Spaniards led by their native officers.   The French began the engagement by an attack on the Spaniards, whom they charged with fixed bayonets.   The left wing of the allied army was in consequence soon broken and thrown in confusion on the centre, which, as well as the right wing, sustained the combat with obstinacy.   Those divisions, however, were ultimately constrained to yield the victory to the French, who, though with no small loss on their own side, slew about 5000 of their adversaries.[1]   It is said that this was the first general action, in modern Europe, in which the attack was made by the bayonet and sword alone, according to the rapid manner of assault which was used in the Roman armies, and which recently has been so decisively employed by British valour.

Louis XIV, though now triumphant on all sides, offered peace at this time to the allies, on the same conditions which were finally accepted by them, three years afterwards, at Ryswick.   Though everywhere successful, he perceived that, in his contest with the confederates, he was, in fact, combating a hydra which was ever revived and renewed.   Though defeated at Fleurus and Neervinden, they had never been completely beaten.   King William, though always vanquished, made skilful retreats, and such was his unconquerable perseverance, that, though one battle might be gained, it always seemed necessary to fight another for the ascendency in the campaign.   The vic-

[1] Russell's *Modern Europe*, vol. iv.

tories were productive of more glory than advantage.
Formerly, Louis had conquered one-half of Holland and
Flanders, and all Franche Comté, without fighting a
general battle, when now, after the greatest efforts and
bloodiest combats, he could hardly force an entrance into
the United Provinces. While the conduct and perseverance of King William, in the north, opposed such obstacles to the progress of the French, the rising genius of
Eugene, in the south, began to recall to recollection the
days of Spinola. The death of Louvois, his celebrated war
minister, who died in 1691, deprived Louis of the only
statesman capable of directing the vast and complicated
system which he had himself created; and the armies,
since his decease, had severely felt the want of his vigilance and superintendence. Seignelai, the son of Colbert,
who had called the French marine into existence, and
long maintained it triumphant, at least in the Mediterranean, died about the same period. These illustrious
ministers were quickly followed to the grave by Luxembourg, who, though deformed in his person and depraved
in his morals, united the calm circumspection of Turenne
to the piercing genius of Condé. Neervinden was the
last and greatest victory he gained, and with him ended
that race of commanders who had rendered France the
terror of Europe. Villeroi, who succeeded him in Flanders, was unable to cope with King William, and the
French troops were now everywhere headed by that inferior class of generals who, in the commencement of the
following century, quailed before the arms of Marlborough
and Eugene. The despot, too, who had so long wielded the energies of France with such wonderful splendour
and success, found that he was gradually sapping the real
prosperity of his people, by his unbounded love of dominion, and his chimerical schemes of universal conquest.
Amid all his victories, Louis had the mortification to see

his subjects languishing in want and misery. The finances, no longer regulated by Colbert, were falling into disorder. Heavier taxes were imposed, but a smaller revenue was obtained. France was afflicted with a dreadful famine, partly occasioned by unfavourable seasons, and partly by the war, which had not left hands sufficient to cultivate the ground. Numbers perished from hunger, while the whole kingdom resounded with rejoicings and pæans of victory. At length the spirit of confidence, and that consciousness of superiority which had been the soul of the French armies, began sensibly to diminish. Their monarch, advancing in years, and apprehensive lest disaster should tarnish his former fame, now seldom appeared at their head ; and, on the whole, the glory and greatness of Louis, while they outwardly seemed at their height, were verging towards their decline.

The confederates, being sufficiently aware of all these circumstances, rejected the advances of Louis, and hastened their warlike preparations for the ensuing campaign. Having failed to treat with the allies in conjunction, Louis next attempted, by separate offers, to disjoin Spain from the coalition. In a council of state, the Duke d'Ossuna advised an acceptance of the French proposals, and indeed recommended peace on any terms which could be procured. But the voice of the Queen and her adherents, who were warmly attached to the Austrian interests, was in favour of a strenuous prosecution of the war.[1] The King, too, had received from his allies a detailed account of the propositions made to them on the part of France, in which there had been rather injudiciously inserted some insinuations with regard to the propriety of a settlement of the succession to his dominions. This was a topic on which Charles was peculiarly sensitive : indignant that his inheritance should be already a subject of speculation

[1] Ortiz, Compend. t. vi. lib. 21. c. 7.

and canvass, he addressed a letter to the States-General of Holland; in which he assured them of his resolution to carry on the war with vigour; and he expressed, with more confidence than became him, his reliance on a successor to the monarchy in a direct line.

On finding that his offers of peace were not listened to, Louis resolved to direct his chief efforts against Spain, in order that, by completely overwhelming her with his forces, he might detach her from the confederacy. In consequence of his orders the Duke de Noailles, with an army considerably reinforced, again entered Catalonia. In that province the incapable Duke of Medina-Sidonia had at length been superseded by the Duke of Escalona,[1] who was esteemed one of the wisest and ablest of the Spanish grandees. The scarcity of men, however, was now almost as great as that of money, and the factions which prevailed at Court, where even those who opposed the French interest were divided among themselves, did not a little contribute to frustrate some of the best concerted undertakings. Hence, though the Duke of Escalona had been assured by the Spanish ministers that they would enable him to take the field early in the season, with a force superior to that of the enemy, he was not furnished by them at the opening of the campaign with more than 15,000 men, of whom a great part were raw and undisciplined troops. The Duke, it seems, was a popular character in Catalonia, and as his

---

[1] He is sometimes called the Marques de Villena, which was his oldest title. The family name was Pacheco. Ortiz says he *succeeded* the Duke of Medina-Sidonia. But I see in Capmany's list of the Viceroys of Catalonia (*Memorias Historicas sobre la Marina de Barcelona*) that nobleman is marked as holding the situation till 1696. I presume, therefore, that Escalona only superseded him in the military command, and that Medina-Sidonia retained the civil government two years longer.

presence there was acceptable to the people, the ministry trusted they would aid him both with recruits and pecuniary supplies. But, after all the assistance which he received from them, his army was still quite inadequate for the protection of the province committed to his charge. He endeavoured, however, to defend the banks of the river Ter, though it was fordable in many places, against the Duke de Noailles, who, having entered the Spanish frontiers at the head of 30,000 men, now attempted to cross this stream. The Duke d'Escalona made an obstinate resistance, but the French at length succeeded in forcing the passage, after an engagement, in which the Spaniards lost upwards of 3000 men in killed and wounded, besides prisoners. Encouraged by this success, the Duke de Noailles marched to Palamos, which he invested, with the assistance of the French fleet, sent under d'Estrées and Tourville, to hover on the Spanish coast, in order to aid the military operations by land. On the eighth day after the trenches had been opened, the French carried the covert way and the half moon, whence they pursued the Spaniards, sword in hand, and entered the town along with them. Such of the garrison as escaped threw themselves into the castle, which being now closely attacked by the army on the land side, and from the sea by De Tourville, who had approached with the fleet, surrendered at discretion, with its garrison, consisting of 2000 men.[1]

The Duke de Noailles then laid siege to Girona, a place which had sufficiently strong fortifications, and a garrison which was numerous, but was unfortunately composed of new troops, who deserted the works when they were attacked, and, by their misconduct, obliged the governor to surrender the town, in less than a week from the time it had been invested. Ostalric was next car-

[1] Daniel, *Hist. de France*, t. v.

ried by storm, notwithstanding its sevenfold entrenchments, and Castel-Follit was taken a few days afterwards :
A French soldier had the curiosity to examine if one of
the outworks of this fort was numerously guarded.   Having found it altogether unprotected, he entered, sword
in hand, calling aloud on his comrades to follow.   With
five or six of his companions in arms, he broke into the
second entrenchment, which was full of troops, but who
were so confounded at finding themselves attacked in a
post believed to be inaccessible, that they fled with precipitation, supposing the assault to be general.   They gave
the alarm to the citadel, which was seated on a rock in
the shape of a sugar-loaf, but they were so hotly pursued
by this handful of men, which however increased, that
the French soldiers entered along with the fugitives, and
captured the citadel, with considerable carnage of its garrison.[1]   While the French had been occupied with the
siege of Castel-Follit, the Spaniards made an unsuccessful attempt to retake Ostalric, from which they retired,
on receiving information that succour was approaching.
The Duke of Escalona, unable longer to keep the field,
or relieve the besieged fortresses, shut himself up with
the remains of his army in Barcelona.

This succession of disasters spread terror to the capital, and even to the provinces most remote from the
theatre of war.   In Aragon and Navarre, where they
were more likely to be immediately exposed to the invasion of the enemy, the inhabitants, alarmed and exasperated at so many misfortunes, basely avenged themselves
by the destruction of private individuals of the French
nation, who were settled in these districts.   The Duke
of Escalona, however, repressed the popular fury by some
severe, but well merited, examples of punishment.

In this emergency the King ordered each grandee to

[1] *Mémoires de Saint Simon,* t. i. c. 22. ed. 1829.

raise, at his own expense, 300 men, and each knight of a military order to maintain one soldier during the campaign,—a tardy measure, when Catalonia was overrun, and the interior of the monarchy threatened. In order to procure funds, he borrowed money at 12 or 15 per cent.; and sold the viceroyalties of Mexico and Peru[1]. The Spanish government, however, was too much dismayed, and was now too conscious of weakness, to trust entirely in its own resources,—and assistance was earnestly implored from Vienna, London, and the Hague. A formidable fleet in consequence, under the command of Admiral Russell, sailed from the ports of England and Holland, and united itself in the Mediterranean with the miserable remains of the Spanish marine. The allied fleet consented to winter in the harbour of Cadiz, and its presence served in some degree to tranquillize the fears of the people, who had begun to apprehend the total and rapid subjugation of the monarchy.

The native army of Spain having proved totally insufficient for the defence of its territories, a resolution was adopted to bring in a body of German and Italian troops, in order to augment the forces in Catalonia. This plan, however, would have been impracticable, but for the opportune presence of the fleet of the allies, by means of which it was executed without difficulty. Fifteen thousand troops, chiefly Germans, arrived in Catalonia in the beginning of this year, under command of the Prince of Hesse-Darmstadt, at that time an indigent military adventurer, though a relative of the Queen, and afterwards highly distinguished in the war of the succession. The Duke d'Escalona was at the same time succeeded by the Marques of Gastanaga, who had formerly been Governor of the Low Countries, and had been imprisoned in the Castle of Burges, till he rendered an account of

[1] Ortiz, Compend. Cronol. t. vi. lib. 21. c. 7.

the sums of money expended by him in the service of the state.   It being found, after the closest inquiry, that he had conducted himself, during his administration, with the strictest integrity and honour, he was appointed, as a reward for his services, and a solace for the affront which had been offered him, to the important government of Catalonia.   On his first arrival in that province, he applied himself with indefatigable diligence to discipline the militia and the peasantry; and as the French had fortified and put garrisons in a great number of the conquered places in Catalonia, he contrived, by means of this irregular force, sometimes to block up one, and sometimes another town, cutting off the detachments and convoys which were sent to relieve them.   The Duke de Vendôme, the successor of Mareschal Noailles who had retired on pretence of bad health, but in reality from the enmity of Barbesieux, the French war minister, found matters in such a situation in Catalonia, that he judged it expedient to abandon and demolish all those smaller fortresses,—retaining only the more important stations of Rosas, Gerona, and Palamos, in which he still left powerful garrisons.   The allied army invested this last place, but was obliged to raise the siege on the approach of the Duke de Vendôme, whose force in the field had been considerably increased by the garrisons of those towns which he had abandoned.   After this discomfiture, the Marques of Gastanaga, finding it impracticable to struggle longer against the difficulties of his situation, or to bear with the haughty temper of his colleague, the Prince of Darmstadt, resigned his command, and was succeeded by Don Francisco de Velasco.   No Spanish general was allowed, during this period, to remain in his command longer than a year.   These frequent changes were far from being favourable to the success of military affairs, as each new leader adopted a different system of tactics, and a new plan of operations.   But, in fact, most of the Spanish officers of that age were ignorant of the first elements of the military art.   The soldiery and the people had no confidence in their skill or talents, and in all the departments of the government which had the charge of arranging warlike affairs, there was a total want of proper co-operation and foresight.   Nor had the expected advantages resulted from the employment of the foreign German auxiliaries; and their high pay absorbed the funds, which had been procured at enormous interest, or by the sale of the American viceroyalties.

Velasco had no sooner entered on his command and formed a junction with the Prince of Darmstadt, than he was defeated by the French General in the neighbourhood of Ostalric.   Louis XIV. now finding that he was likely to obtain an adjustment of differences with the maritime powers which were leagued against him, offered the Spaniards a suspension of arms in Catalonia.   The proposal, however, was rejected; and so far was the Court of Madrid from listening even to this limited offer of accommodation, that they considerably reinforced the army of the Prince of Darmstadt, and issued orders for repairing the fortifications of Barcelona, as also for fitting out a fleet in the Mediterranean.   While these instructions were executing slowly, according to the Spanish custom, the Duke de Vendôme took the field with a numerous army, attended by a fine train of artillery, and directed his march towards the capital of Catalonia.   At the same time d'Estrées and the Chevalier de Noailles appeared on the coast,—one with a large fleet, and the other with a strong squadron of galleys, so that the place was quickly invested both by sea and land.   The Prince of Darmstadt had contrived to throw himself into it with 12,000 of his German troops; and immediately after his entrance he armed all the serviceable inhabitants of the town.   The

French, having only 18,000 men, could not make a complete circumvallation of so extensive a city as Barcelona.
Provisions, ammunition, and fresh troops could thus at
all times be introduced within the walls ; and a communication was also kept up between the garrison and the
Spanish general Velasco, who, with a force of six or seven
thousand men, had encamped in the vicinity, at St-Felieu
on the Llobregat. A signal discomfiture of the French
was now confidently anticipated by the allies. But Velasco imprudently weakened his army, by advancing two
considerable bodies of troops still nearer to the town, for
the purpose of preserving his communication open. These
detached corps were attacked and put to flight by the
Duke of Vendôme, and pursued to their main army
which he took completely by surprise during the night.
The imprudent Velasco fled in an undress, and his whole
army was dispersed almost without resistance. This signal
success cost the French only 80 men, while nearly 3000
Spaniards were slain, or drowned in the Llobregat, at this
disgraceful route. After their flight the Spanish camp
was pillaged, and all the papers, baggage, and money, captured.[1]

The besieged, however, still continued to hold out in
Barcelona. After the mines which had been laid produced their effect, they still persevered in defending themselves vigorously at the bastions, having good entrenchments and ramparts behind them. At one of these bul-
warks seven desperate engagements took place before the
besiegers had established their footing. At last, the town
being laid so open that it would not have been prudent
to stand the hazard of a general assault, the Prince Darmstadt submitted to a capitulation. Monjuich, which had
not been attacked, was included in the conditions of surrender.[2] This siege, though it cost the French, during

[1] Reboulet, *Hist. de Louis XIV.* Daniel, *Hist. de France.* [2] Ibid.

the two months it continued, nearly 9000 men who were killed or died from the distempers of the climate, gave them the command of the whole principality, and enabled them to carry war into the heart of Spain.   Its feeble monarch, whose natural apathy rendered him insensible to distant failures, and whose extreme ignorance exposed him to constant deception, was panic-struck with a loss too near to be concealed or palliated.   The Aragonese, alarmed at the capture of this city, which they deemed impregnable, sent a deputation to implore his Majesty to adopt some measures for the defence of their province; and he was obliged to promise, in order to prevent them from abandoning their country, that, before the commencement of the ensuing campaign, he would himself repair in person to Saragossa.

While the Spaniards were thus unfortunate in Europe, their foreign possessions were the scenes of commotion, or were gradually wrested from their grasp.   They were at present in imminent danger of losing the last remains of their power in Africa—the Moors having repeatedly assaulted Oran, and closely invested the fortress of Ceuta, immediately opposite to Gibraltar.   For the security of these important stations, they were reduced to the humiliating necessity of imploring the assistance of the Portuguese, who supplied them with some regiments, on the express condition that they should be employed only against the infidels.   The Indians of Mexico, too, had recently revolted, and it was believed that, if they had been directed by any competent leader, the Spanish sway in that vast empire must have speedily terminated. It was in the present year also, that an expedition from France, aided by the Buccaneers of America, executed one of the most important enterprizes of the war.   On the suggestion of the Baron de Pointis, an officer of high rank in the French marine, a large armament was fitted

out in France, jointly at the expense of the crown and of
private contributors, for an aggression on the Spanish
settlements in the West Indies. The chief command
was given to De Pointis; and orders were issued to the
Governor of the French possessions in St Domingo, to
raise a force to assist in the expedition. The squadron
sailed from Brest in 1697, and after a prosperous voyage,
arrived at Cape Francis in St Domingo. In that government the French King's regular force was small, but
Cape Francis was the ordinary rendezvous of the Buccaneers, who usually assembled there about the season
when De Pointis reached it. These freebooters, formerly
so independent, had by this time been brought under a sort
of vassalage to the French governor of St Domingo.
They had regular commissions given them,—they were
called the King of France's subjects, and they paid a
tenth of all their prizes and booty into the public treasury. It would appear that, in this subordinate state,
these pirates had much degenerated, and that, while they
had acquired the vices of civilized life, they had lost those
redeeming qualities which, in former times, shed a "doubtful glory" along the track of the reckless Buccaneer. De
Pointis was joined by 700 of their tribe, and their vessels, which at this season usually lay unrigged, were repaired and fitted out : but the French commander was
much disappointed as to the number both of men and
ships, and still more as to the qualities of the Buccaneers, whom he found to be cowardly and disobedient,
intent only on plunder, and ignorant even of the sea coasts
and harbours.[1]

When the shares of the prize-money and booty to
which the Buccaneers should be entitled, had been settled, the expedition set out for Carthagena. A disem-
barcation was effected without much difficulty; and after

[1] De Pointis, *Account of Taking of Carthagena.*

the forts which guarded the entrance to the harbour
had been occupied, the town was at once besieged by
land and bombarded by sea.   At the same time, all
those passages were seized and strictly guarded by which
the inhabitants could have escaped, or sent off their treasures to the interior of the island.   The siege, which was
commenced with spirit, was conducted with skill and
perseverance, and, after it had been carried on about three
weeks from the first landing, the town capitulated, on the
conditions, that the inhabitants should enjoy all their
possessions except plate and money, and that the churches
and convents should be preserved from violence or plunder.

Subsequent to the surrender, there was a public collection made of the plate and coin, under the authority and inspection of De Pointis.   But this did not
save the city from private pillage.   The Buccaneers plundered merchandize and all sorts of stores on which they
could lay their hands: In a short time the plate disappeared from the churches—houses were forcibly entered and despoiled, and, in short, as much violence was
committed as if no capitulation whatever had been granted.[1]   De Pointis, however, the regular troops, and those
who, in France, had partly borne the expense of fitting out the armament, were grievously disappointed
in the amount of those treasures to which they were entitled by the articles of surrender.   In spite of the precautions which the French employed on their arrival, of
seizing the outlets to the country, many valuable effects
had been saved.   Though the expedition was planned
with secrecy, the inhabitants had received intelligence
from Spain (which was all that country could do for them)
of the meditated project, and of the probable time at which
De Pointis would reach St Domingo.   The natives had, in

[1] De Pointis, *Account of Taking of Carthagena.*

consequence, bestirred themselves before his appearance in their seas. All the nuns and women of quality had taken their departure, with their plate and their jewels, and, in the course of four days, 120 mules went out laden with gold, and retired to Monpos, a town about 40 leagues from Carthagena. A misunderstanding arose between De Pointis and the Buccaneers, with regard to those terms of agreement which were to regulate their participation in the plunder, and the freebooters, after embarking with him for St Domingo, returned to Carthagena, uncontrolled by a leader, and more than ever athirst for rapine. They demanded five millions of livres as the price of their departure without the perpetration of farther violence. It seems strange that they should have expected to raise so much money in a place so recently sacked. Nevertheless, by threatening their prisoners, by applying the torture to the more wealthy, and by ransacking the tombs, they, in four days, had nearly made up the sum required by them. Having completed this contribution, they set sail from Carthagena, on receiving intelligence that a fleet of Dutch and English ships of war had just arrived in the West Indies. This was the last exploit of the Buccaneers, and they are scarcely again heard of in history.

Had France preserved this important conquest, which was considered as the key to the New World, they might have subverted the Spanish empire in America. But plunder was the object of the commander De Pointis as much as of the freebooters, with whom he was leagued, and whom he so much contemned. The Buccaneers accused him of an unfair partition of the booty, and De Casse, the Governor of St Domingo, who had been all along his bitter enemy, charged him with misconduct during the whole expedition. An order was issued by the French government for an additional payment to the

Buccaneers, but it never was carried into execution,[1] and De Pointis succeeded in justifying himself from the accusations of De Casse. On his return he was favourably received at Fontainbleau by Louis, whom he presented with an emerald as large as his fist,[2] and assured his Majesty, that his sway had now extended to the farthest verge of the Western Hemisphere.

The different states who had been so long at enmity with France, now began to sink under the evils of protracted warfare. The whole course and termination of this contest rather gives us an impression of the weakness of the nations of Europe in that age. They took arms with confidence, but without a due foresight of obstacles, or estimate of their own resources. Their enterprises were above their force, and they soon discovered, that they would be reduced to a state of exhaustion. Now that the first impulse of resentment had subsided, each began to consult its own hopes, interests, or fears. The Duke of Savoy, robbed of his territories, and lured by the prospect of a matrimonial alliance with the Royal Family of France, set the first example of defection. The states of that prince, as we have seen, had been overrun and ravaged by a numerous French army at the commencement of the war. But Victor Amadeus was a prince of infinite address and resources, and had lost none of that skilful duplicity which had so long distinguished the House of Savoy. On a superficial view of his character, it might have been supposed that he was irresolute and indecisive. But the deep dissembler was ever guided by profound motives of interest, and only renounced his allies, when he saw, afar off, some advantage from the change.

During the whole course of his military operations, and

---

[1] Archenholtz, *Hist. of Pirates.*
[2] *Mem. de Saint Simon*, t. ii. c. 3.

his apparently strict alliance with the Austrians, he had
never altogether ceased to hold private communications
with the French, and such was his duplicity, that it was
not very clearly known whether he wished to gain the
battles which he fought. The Prince de Ligne has said
of him, that his geographical position prevented him
from being an honest man; and Prince Eugene accompanied him in his warlike expeditions, more in the character of a spy from the Imperial Court, than of a military associate. As a pledge of his sincerity, Eugene had
compelled him, in the year 1695, to undertake the siege
of Casal, which at length capitulated. He next proposed
that they should invest Pignerol, but the Duke, while he
feigned consent, daily opposed new obstacles, or contrived
pretexts for delay. At length, in order to escape from
the spies of the Emperor, by whom he was surrounded at
Turin, he undertook a journey of pretended devotion to
the Chapel of Loretto, in fulfilment of a vow, which,
he alleged, he had made, while sick of the small-pox, during the campaign in Dauphiny. Prince Eugene, who
knew that the pilgrim was no devotee, soon afterwards
learned, without surprise, that he had met at this shrine
with the private agents of the French and Venetians,
who were disguised as priests, and signed with them the
preliminaries of a treaty, which was made public soon after the Duke's return to Turin. By its articles, he
stipulated for the marriage of his eldest daughter with
the Duke of Burgundy, son to the Dauphin, and for the
restitution of all his dominions, including even Pignerol,
of which the French had been in possession for more than
half a century. Having now thrown off his mask, the
Duke was not long of following up his intrigues by active operations and by a junction of his army with that
of Mareschal Catinat, in order to form the siege of Va-
lenza. The allies, and Prince Eugene, finding them-

selves too feeble to resist this united force, evacuated Italy, and the Prince hastened to Vienna, where he informed the Emperor, it is said, that the only way to secure the assistance of the Duke of Savoy, was to get from him an open declaration of hostilities.[1]

The defection of the Duke of Savoy, who was considered as holding in his hand the keys of Italy, materially altered the plans and prospects of the allies. They were highly indignant at his treacherous conduct, and loud in their complaints of his breach of faith. Suspicion and alarm began to spread through the confederacy, and Spain, which had hitherto so steadily rejected all overtures towards pacification, was shaken by the danger to which Naples and the Milanese were now exposed. The capture, too, of Barcelona, had made a deep impression on the nation, and after that event the Spanish ministry appeared far more desirous than formerly to enter into terms of pacification. Louis, availing himself of this disunion, proposed conditions which seemed moderate, considering his recent success and former pretensions. Those negociations for peace, which had been already opened at the Castle of Ryswick, in Holland, under the auspices of the King of Sweden, were earnestly prosecuted. The interests of King William were at present somewhat different from what they had been, and he was now as desirous to dissolve the League of Augsburgh as he was once to form it. As merely Stadtholder, it was his chief object to combine all Europe against France. But he was now King of England, and nothing was wanting to the stability of his British throne but the recognition of his title by all the powers of Europe. Louis accordingly conciliated him by acknowledging the Protestant succession, and by sacrificing the interests of James II., which he had so long supported. He propitiated the Dutch,

---

[1] *Mémoires de Prince Eugene.*

by agreeing to restore his conquests, to renew their commercial privileges, and accede to the formation of a barrier for their security on the side of the Netherlands. Most of the powers consented that the recent treaty of Nimeguen should form the basis of that at present negotiating, but the Spaniards wished to revert to the articles adjusted at the peace of the Pyrenees. Finding, however, that such exorbitant pretensions could not be listened to, they restricted their claim to the restitution of all that had been conquered from them during the present war. At length, to the surprise and satisfaction of the Spanish nation, Louis not only relinquished his recent conquests, but even a part of those reunions and dismemberments which he had been allowed to retain by the treaty of Ratisbon. In consequence of these terms, the Dutchy of Luxemburg, the County of Chiney, Mons, Charleroy, Aeth and Courtrai, with all the towns which the French now occupied in Catalonia, were restored to Spain.

Though the Spanish monarchy had experienced so many disasters during the war, and was in such a hopeless state of national debility, this was the most advantageous treaty she had concluded for more than half a century. But Louis, while making such concessions, had already begun to entertain the most sanguine hopes that the succession to the throne of Spain would speedily open up to his own family, and hence that all he now restored would only contribute to increase the inheritance of his grandson, and augment the power of the House of Bourbon. It was also his interest, by an apparent generosity, to conciliate the minds of the Spanish nation, and by terminating hostilities, prevent that exasperation of feeling against the French which a longer course of warfare must have naturally produced. " He, therefore," in the language of a Spanish historian, " like a competitor at public games, cast down his former spoils, that he might run more agile in the spacious course."[1] Finally, he foresaw, that if the powerful league of Augsburgh remained united at the death of the King of Spain, the facility with which its princes would have combined their plans and their forces, must have proved fatal to his designs. The confederates would have redoubled their efforts, and contested in strict alliance the succession to the monarchy of Spain.[2] The chief opposition to the treaty was on the part of the Emperor Leopold, who, of all the Powers engaged in the coalition, had suffered the least from the war, and whose interest it was to retard the negotiations for peace as much as it was that of Louis to accelerate them. It was his obvious policy to nourish the hatred of the Spaniards against the French, by protracting the war, and keeping the two nations involved in conflict till the death of Charles II., who, he naturally conjectured, would not bequeath his inheritance to one who was destroying his people, intercepting the arrival of his treasures from the new world, and carrying a sanguinary contest into the bowels of his country. Being deserted, however, by all his allies, the Emperor at length found it necessary to accede to the treaty : and he, too, received favourable conditions, in so far as regarded the restitution of conquered territories. But one of the great objects and principles of the alliance, which was to secure

[1] San Phelipe, *Comentarios.* Para correr mejor el espacioso campo, se aligeró de los despojos de sús enemigos.

[2] It was generally supposed in Europe at the time, that Louis was actuated by these motives in granting such favourable terms to Spain at the peace of Ryswick, and it seems difficult to believe that he was not at least in some degree influenced by them. Voltaire, however, says, that this notion, probable as it may appear, is erroneous. The obvious interest of quickly possessing Spain, he alleges, had not the least influence on the treaty of Ryswick ; peace was concluded merely because all parties were weary of a war, which was not carried on with any definite object.

the Spanish succession in the house of Austria, failing the present King without issue, was altogether overlooked. Leopold, indeed, was desirous of a settlement; but it was answered on the part of France, that the adjustment of this delicate and important question, which involved such difficulties, would indefinitely retard, if not wholly break off the treaty, and that Europe could not remain in a state of war till it was determined. The King of Spain, who did not chuse to see his inheritance a topic of discussion, concurred in these views. As from his declining health, however, his throne was likely soon to become vacant, it would have been more prudent, and perhaps more conducive to the general interests of Europe, that an opportunity should have been taken during the negotiations of Ryswick, to have regulated the line of succession. But as the Emperor was unwilling to relinquish a tittle of his claims,—as the allies were not inclined to prolong the war for the sake of supporting them, and as Louis was firmly resolved not to yield his pretensions, all parties seem, by mutual consent, to have passed over the question in silence, and Leopold was finally compelled to conclude the treaty without the slightest allusion in any of its articles to the rights of his family.

Though not fully successful, Europe had no doubt gained by the league of Augsburgh, as France was obliged to restore a part of its unjust conquests, and was arrested in its progress to universal dominion. The balance of power became in consequence better understood, and the rights of nations more respected. Without this powerful coalition, Spain would have been blotted out from the list of kingdoms, and the political independence of the other countries of Europe would have been at an end. Louis, perhaps, could not have reduced them to provinces of France, or incorporated them with the monarchy. But he would have controlled and governed them by mandates

issued from the foot of his throne; he would have chain-
ed their activity and industry, or rendered these subservient to his own splendour and glory. The fear of France
would have become the rule and principle of action in all
the cabinets of Europe. Servile princes would have purchased, by blind submission, a temporary existence in its
most debasing form—like Spain itself and the princes of
the Rhenish confederation, in a subsequent age, when
the throne of St Louis was filled by an abler, but yet
more remorseless despot than the most ambitious of the
Bourbons.

By the disunion, however, which existed in the Grand
confederacy, and the impolitic precipitation with which it
was dissolved, the coalition was far from obtaining all the
objects it had in view; and it was evident that Europe
was again to become the theatre of a new war, derived
from the very evils which the league of Augsburgh had
been formed to obviate. Indeed it might almost have
been suspected, that in concluding peace, the contracting
parties at Ryswick wished still to leave an opening for
war. It was the King of France who obtained the
greatest advantages from the intrigues which his plenipotentiaries employed to accelerate the negotiations; for, as
soon as peace was concluded, all the confederate princes
disarmed, and Louis was the only sovereign who maintained his armies on their former establishment, with the
resolution to employ them, if necessary, on the first intelligence which he might receive of the death of the King
of Spain.

CHAPTER IX.

INTRIGUES CONCERNING THE SUCCESSION.—DEATH OF CHARLES II.

The winding sheet of Edward's race.
                    GRAY's *Bard.*

AT the conclusion of the treaty of Ryswick, the eyes of all Europe were fixed on Spain and its unhappy sovereign. Charles had no issue by his first Queen, the young and beautiful Louisa d'Orleans, and he had now been married a second time above seven years without any prospect of children. It is true that the King himself had as yet hardly reached the age of forty. But he was the child of the old age of Philip IV. by an union with his niece; many of his brothers and sisters had died prematurely, and he had himself been so feeble in infancy that it was scarcely expected that he should ever have reached the years of manhood. But his constitution became wonderfully confirmed about the time he attained the age of twenty. Of late, however, he had suffered frequent attacks of severe illness. From childhood, in consequence of some organic defect, he experienced great difficulty in masticating, which, by causing him to swallow his food almost whole, occasioned indigestion and frequent vomitings.[1] His mind, too, was a constant prey to a corroding melancholy, which appears to have been in a great measure produced by the most ignoble and womanish su-

[1] Vayrac, *Revol. d'Espagne,* t. 5.

perstitions. About a year before the conclusion of the treaty of Ryswick, he had been seized with a tertian ague of a virulent description. During its progress, there were brought to him the relics of St Isidore and St Iago, which remained six months in the palace as pledges of his safety, and were then carried back to their convent by a procession, in which the King walked barefooted.[1] From this dangerous illness he only partially recovered, to continue during the remainder of his life in a pining state of bodily and mental imbecility, that rendered him a very fit representative of the declining monarchy which he governed. On his convalescence, he ordered all the prisoners in the kingdom to be set at liberty; he daily submitted to acts of the most degrading penance, and believed that he was under the influence of incantation or sorcery.

It was evident that such a man could not long survive, or, at least, could not long be capable of discharging the duties of sovereignty. All minds thus became engrossed with the subject of the succession. Though it was known the King had been long galled by the idea that he only held in his hand a barren sceptre, and that now he could not listen to the topic without shuddering and horror, the subject was discussed not only in foreign countries, and in the city and court of Madrid, but in the presence and hearing of the King himself. Charles thus became the victim, through the frail remnant of his life, to the selfish attempts of foreign powers to parcel out his dominions, and the sport of those contending parties which agitated his court. During these years, he merely retained sufficient intelligence (and it required no great penetration) to see through the interested motives of those by whom he was surrounded; and thus to be rendered more wretched by a painful consciousness that there were none in whom

---

[1] Ortiz, *Compend. Cronol.* t. vi. lib. xxi. c. 7.

he could confide, and that his importance in the monarchy
depended solely on his supposed right to its disposal after
death.   Each party, too, gave him exaggerated accounts
of the machinations of the other to appropriate his succession.   By these cruel disclosures, he was held in a
state of constant agitation, and was not even permitted
to end in tranquillity the few and evil days which Heaven
had marked for him.

The King of France, the Elector of Bavaria, and the
Emperor of Germany—though all in name of a son or
other descendant—now openly aspired to the unwieldy
inheritance which Charles was about to leave.   It was
claimed by the royal family of France, as the issue of
Maria-Theresa, Queen of Louis XIV, and daughter of
Philip IV. of Spain.   But as it had been stipulated that
the crowns of the two kingdoms should not be worn by
the same sovereign, the Bourbon pretensions were urged
in name of the Duke of Anjou (second son of the Grand
Dauphin), at that time a youth of fifteen years of age.
Margaret, a *younger* sister of Maria-Theresa, was married to the Emperor Leopold; and her only daughter, having been united to the Elector of Bavaria, gave birth to
a son, the Electoral Prince, then in infancy, who was a
second candidate for the Spanish succession.   The Archduke Charles, the third claimant, was the son of Leopold
by a second wife ; but he founded his right on a descent
from the Spanish Infanta Maria, the daughter of Philip
III, and mother of his father Leopold.   His elder brother
Joseph resigned his pretensions in Charles's favour, lest
the European powers should conceive a jealousy at the
union, on one head, of the whole Austrian dignities and
possessions.

There can be no doubt that, in the ordinary course of
succession, the French descendants of Maria-Theresa had
the preferable title to the crown of Spain ; but the re-

nunciation of it at the treaty of the Pyrenees, when Louis
espoused the Spanish princess, opened a way to the claims
of the Bavarian Prince and the Archduke Charles. When
the Emperor Leopold married his daughter to the Elector of Bavaria, he had required from her also a renunciation for herself and family of all pretensions to the crown
of Spain, in order that her rights might not interfere with
those of his son, and her own half-brother the Archduke.
But a renouncement which had not been demanded by
the Spanish nation or sovereign, was less likely to be of
any avail even than the relinquishment which had been
exacted from Louis and his Queen.

Each candidate for the Spanish succession had his party
at the Court of Madrid; and never yet was a kingdom
involved in such a series of intrigues, or torn by such jarring political factions. In disputes concerning ministe-
rial power, or pre-eminence among subjects, the reigning
sovereign usually interposes his choice and restraint. But
Charles II. could now be scarcely said to reign, and all
consideration or respect for him was lost in the eager discussions concerning his successor. The Queen-consort,
who, in some measure from necessity, had actually held
the reins of government since her marriage, was at the
head of the Austrian faction, supported by her favourite
Count Melgar, and by a majority of the ministers.[1] When
the claims of the Bavarian Prince were first started, they
were favoured by the Queen-dowager: But she died
about the time of the peace of Ryswick, in consequence
of a disorder which she had improperly concealed, and
which appears to have been hereditary among the females

[1] The power and influence of Melgar were this year greatly increased, from the immense riches he obtained by his second marriage with the widow of Don Pedro d'Aragon, to whose great
wealth, amassed during his viceroyalty of Naples, she had recently
succeeded.

of the Austrian line.[1] After her decease, the party was headed by the Count of Oropesa, who, during his retirement, had been frequently consulted by the King, and had united with Melgar, at least in resistance to the French claims. A majority of the nation at large was favourable to the House of Bourbon.[2] But the only nobleman of rank and consideration at this time inclined to espouse its cause was the Count de Monterey, President of the Council of the Netherlands.[3]

The unsettled state of the nation, which, from the distraction of parties, was in an anarchy almost as complete as if there had been no reigning sovereign, induced the

[1] Flores, *Reynas d'España*, p. 953.

[2] *Mémoires de Torcy*, t. i.

[3] Coxe, *Mem. of Kings of Spain of House of Bourbon*, sect. iii. The Count of Monterey who has been so often mentioned in the preceding pages, became one of the members of the Council of Philip V. on his accession, but was never employed in a military capacity, as Louis XIV. said of him " that he knew no more of war than if he had never been governor of Flanders." He soon afterwards withdrew into private life, and lived to extreme old age. Captain Carleton, who had served under him in Flanders in the year 1672, saw him forty years afterwards at Madrid. " In a conversation," says he " with Father Fahy, the head of the Irish College at Madrid, some words dropping of the Count Monterey, I told him I heard he had taken orders and officiated at mass : he made answer it was all very true ; and on my intimating that I had the honour to serve under him in Flanders, on my first entering into service, and when he commanded the Spanish forces at the famous battle of Seneff, and adding that I could not but be surprised that he, who was one of the brightest *Cavalleros* of the age, should now be in orders ; and that I should look upon it as a mighty favour barely to have, if it might be, a view of him, he very obligingly told me he was very well acquainted with him, and that, if I would come next day, he would not fail to accompany me to the Count's house." They accordingly went at the time appointed, and found him stepping into his coach, but, on seeing them, he returned to his house. A good deal of conversation passed, and the Count seemed pleased

grandees and ministers to implore the King that he should take measures for settling the succession, and should, for that purpose, call together a general council. Don Josef Perez de Soto, one of the most celebrated Jurisconsults of the age, was admitted to this assembly, and he there delivered an opinion in favour of the rights of Maria-Theresa and her French descendants. He maintained that the renunciation exacted from that Princess was null and void, since Philip IV. had no title to demand it, nor could any deed of the Infanta invalidate the claims of her children, and alter the established law of succession. Besides, the abandonment of this just right could not be considered as legal and complete, never having been registered in the national assembly of the Cortes, and Philip himself having neglected to fulfil the treaty by not paying up the dowry of the Princess: The only rational object in the stipulation was to prevent the two first crowns in the world from descending on the same brow; but, as the Dauphin and his eldest son the Duke of Burgundy renounced all claim, there could exist no obstacle to the adoption of one of the younger grandchildren of Maria-Theresa. In spite of these arguments, the inclination of the King, which was known to be favourable to the Prince of Bavaria, procured a majority of suffrages in his favour. Charles, who considered himself authorized to dispose of his succession by will, accordingly executed a testament, in which he called the young prince, now seven years of age, to the universal succession of the Spanish monarchy, and in the event of its opening up to him while yet in minority, he appointed his father, the

when the Captain mentioned that he had served under him; and he added that there were few besides himself now living who had been with him in that service. The Count then took his leave, and went into his coach, after ordering some refreshment to be provided for his guests. (*Memoirs*, p. 316, &c.)

Elector of Bavaria, sole regent of the kingdom.   Charles, from his throne, announced this nomination to the Councillors of State, and Presidents of the Supreme Tribunals, informing them that, in his choice of a successor, he had been guided solely by motives of conscience and justice, and by the advice of the most learned and upright in his kingdom.[1]

The French ambassador complained of this nomination to the Count of Oropesa, as the King's confident.   The Count's reply was brief and dignified.   " His Majesty," he said, " had acted according to the opinion of the ministers of state and of justice, without affection and without fear : Louis had consented to the renunciation by his Queen the Infanta Maria-Theresa, and hence the right had passed to her younger sister the Infanta Margareta, grandmother to the Prince of Bavaria.[2]"

That young prince, however, thus chosen to be the founder of a new race of kings, was not destined to enjoy the crown allotted to him by the testament of the King, and the wishes of a large proportion of the Spanish nation. He died suddenly in the beginning of the year 1699, soon after the succession had been settled in his favour. This disappointment of paternal hope, and the advantages which his death procured for the other candidates, led the Elector to suspect that his son had been carried off by poison,[3] and even induced him to charge the French King with the diabolical act.[4]   On the other hand, the

---

[1] Targe, *Hist. de l'Avénement de la Maison de Bourbon.*

[2] San-Phelipe, *Comentarios*, t. i. p. 4.

[3] *Mémoires de Torcy*, t. i.

[4] Afterwards, however, when he entered into alliance with France, he threw his suspicions on the Emperor. " That star," he said, in a public manifesto, " which proves fatal to all who form an obstacle to the greatness of the House of Austria, carried off this young prince by a slight indisposition, by which he had been often attack-

report was believed and circulated in France, that he had perished in consequence of the machinations of the Austrian cabinet.[1]

The unexpected death of the Prince of Bavaria rendered nugatory a treaty which had just before been concluded between Louis XIV. and William III. of England, with a view to the partition of the Spanish dominions; by which, while Spain, the Indies, and the Netherlands, were to be retained by the young Prince, the two Sicilies were assigned to the Dauphin, and Milan to the Archduke Charles. The decease of the nominated heir to the Spanish monarchy, revived the pretensions of the Duke of Anjou, and the Austrian Archduke, to the *whole* inheritance, and plunged the kingdom in the same state of party discord from which it had just been relieved. New intrigues were formed, and new cabals agitated the Court.

It was the French King who gained chiefly by the removal of his Bavarian competitor. The Queen, indeed, with the Counts Oropesa and Melgar, (who, as we have seen, had lately formed a junction of interests), most of the other ministers and the King's Confessor, supported the Austrian pretensions. But the great body of the nation, and all those grandees who, during his life, had favoured the Prince of Bavaria, now declared for the Duke of Anjou. The high character which Louis held for talents and power, and the moderation which he had shewn at the Peace of Ryswick, both overawed and conciliated the minds of the nobility, and they became persuaded that he alone could prevent that dismemberment of the kingdom by the other European powers, which

ed without danger, before he was destined to wear the Spanish crown." (Targe, *Hist.*)

[1] Le Prince Electoral de Baviere mourût fort brusquement les premiers jours de Février; et personne ne doutat que ce ne fût par l'influence du Conseil de Vienne. (*Mém. de Saint-Simon*, t. ii. c. 18.)

they dreaded would ensue, if the Archduke were called to the succession.

The scale was now to preponderate either in favour of France or Austria, and both powers were unremitting in their exertions to acquire partizans and to spread their influence in the monarchy. Louis, however, appears to have acted with far more skill and address than his imperial rival. When the settlement in favour of the Prince of Bavaria had been first publicly announced, the Emperor expressed the utmost resentment and indignation. Accounts of his language and behaviour were transmitted by the Spanish ambassador at Vienna to Madrid, where they excited the greatest disgust. Louis, on the other hand, more prudent in his policy, if not more moderate in his ambition, appeared to the Spaniards to acquiesce in the answer which his ambassador had received from Oropesa.

After the death of the young Bavarian, the Emperor Leopold, trusting to his constant alliance and family connection with the reigning sovereign of Spain, seems to have relied implicitly on that monarch's favourable intentions; he reckoned on the Spanish empire as a certain inheritance, and scarcely thought it possible that strangers and enemies should be preferred to his son. He slighted the advice of the Queen, who, even before the death of the Prince of Bavaria, had strongly recommended that the Archduke should be sent to Spain, and that some German troops should be stationed in Catalonia,—assuring the imperial ambassador, at the same time, that the King would never declare any Prince his successor whom he did not first behold in a situation to maintain and support his title. The Emperor, however, instead of adopting such advisable measures, contented himself with procuring every office of trust and emolument for those who were known to be in his interests; and he obtained,

to the exclusion of the native grandees, the viceroyalty of
Catalonia for the German Prince, Hesse-Darmstadt; and
the government of Milan for the Prince of Vaudemont.
The Spaniards thus began to dread that, if the Archduke
should ever ascend the Castilian throne, he would manifest the same partiality to the Germans which the Emperor Charles V. had shewn to the Flemings, and which,
in spite of all its triumphs, had rendered his reign unpopular among the natives of Spain. It was also understood, that the Archduke entertained, and even openly
expressed a contempt for the manners and character of
Spaniards. This was so much the more galling to their
pride, as they must have been conscious that, in the present age, it was not unmerited. The known preference
which Philip II. entertained for the Spaniards over all
his other subjects, and his respect for their usages and
manners, made his jealous and tyrannic sway scarcely
unpopular; and had the Archduke displayed a portion of
the same esteem, it would have gone farther to have procured for him the crowns of Spain than all the excellent
qualities he possessed, and all the exertions of the powers
of Europe, who were so soon to be conjoined and arrayed
for his support.

Those measures, too, which the Queen adopted as head
of the Austrian party, in order to pave the way for the
Archduke's succession, tended to alienate the affections
and excite the jealousies of the Spaniards. They were
disgusted at the confidence she placed in foreigners, and
displeased that she had bestowed both the government
of the Milanese and the viceroyalty of Catalonia on German princes. It was in vain that she now attempted to
revive those ancient feelings of rivalry and hatred which
had so long existed between the French and Spanish nations,—it was in vain that she endeavoured to inspire an
apprehension, that all Europe would declare against Spain

if its crown was transferred to a branch of the House of
Bourbon. On the contrary, the whole conduct of the
Queen and her German favourites, led the Spaniards to
dread that those evils and disorders which now prevailed would be increased and multiplied if an Austrian succeeded. For never had such rapacity or venality been
known, even in Spain, as was now practised by the Queen's
favourite, the Countess of Berleps, and her Confessor, the
Father Chiusa.

But the preponderance of the French over the Austrian interest, was at this time chiefly to be attributed to
the difference of characters in the envoys of the two nations at Madrid, and the superior management of the
French ambassador. The Count de Harrach, who was sent
as plenipotentiary from the Emperor, with general directions to act in concert with the Queen, and to prevail on
Charles to nominate the Archduke universal heir to his
monarchy, had received no instructions to gain over the
powerful Grandees, or conciliate the minds of the people.
His domineering spirit—forbidding deportment—and mis-
judged economy, were ill-calculated to sustain with propriety the part he had to act. He offended the Countess
of Berleps, the Queen's favourite, by attempting to check
her rapacity, and procure her dismissal, and he had even
the imprudence to quarrel with the Queen, who had been
hitherto the chief support of the Austrian interests.[1] On
the other hand, the winning manners, address, and liberality of the Marquis de Harcourt, whom Louis had sent
as ambassador to Madrid, in order to secure a party in
Spain, and counteract the Austrian influence, were well
calculated to gain a high-spirited nation, and eradicate
the prejudices fostered against France.[2] He had brought

[1] There were two Counts of Harrach, father and son, who, about
this period, were successively Austrian ministers at the Court of
Madrid. But their conduct and characters were similar.

[2] Coxe, *Mem. of Kings of House of Bourbon*, t. i. sect. 3.

with him immense sums from Paris, which he partly distributed in presents and gratuities, where he knew that these would prove useful. The Marquis lived, besides, at an enormous expense, and paid all tradesmen and artizans exorbitantly. He lavished the most profuse attentions on the ecclesiastics of the realm, and employed all the officers of his household in exposing to the Grandees the petty intrigues and misconduct of the German cabal, as also in exciting their dissatisfaction at the domineering and penurious spirit of Count Harrach. " The Austrian ministers," said the Count Mancera, himself a partizan of Austria, " will so mismanage, that, in place of the Archduke, we shall have some other prince proclaimed at Madrid—we shall swear allegiance to him, and if we have once sworn, no circumstance, no consideration, will make us faithless to our new king, even if reluctantly acknowledged."[1] The repulsive arrogance of Harrach, contrasted with the affability of Harcourt, produced their natural consequences, and gradually disposed all classes in the capital to a more favourable opinion of the House of Bourbon.

It was then that Harcourt first began to talk publicly of the rights of that family, and endeavoured to convince the nation, that their recognition could alone preserve the monarchy from dismemberment.

But, while the French party were thus triumphant through the nation, the Germans were still all powerful in the cabinet and court. And so closely besieged was the King by his consort and the ministry, that Harcourt had remained three months at Madrid before he obtained the first audience of his Majesty. When he was at length introduced, two gloomy lamps were so disposed in the apartment in which he was received, as not to permit him, during his momentary interview, to perceive the

---

[1] Coxe, *Mem. of House of Bourbon*, t. i. sect. 3.

marks of declining health in the countenance of the languishing monarch.[1] Harcourt was thus convinced, that though he had secured the favourable disposition of the people, it would be extremely difficult to profit by it, unless he could place round the King such confidents as might undermine, or at least counterbalance, the Austrian influence.

The Marquis of Balbases, who had been Spanish plenipotentiary at Nimeguen, and afterwards ambassador-extraordinary at Paris, for the marriage of the King with Louisa d'Orleans, was the first of the Grandees who entered into a confidential communication with Harcourt, instructing him concerning the errors and unpopularity of the Queen, and various court secrets.[2] Other Grandees and officers of state subsequently waited on the Marquis, to impart similar intelligence, and offer their services. His most important acquisition, however, was the Cardinal Portocarrero, at that time Archbishop of Toledo. Hitherto this prelate had not taken any active or decisive part in the question of the succession—and as yet his chief object had been to supplant Melgar and Oropesa, that he might himself enjoy the power and favour which these ministers at present possessed. But perceiving the precarious state of his sovereign's health, he now conceived ulterior plans, and looked forward to the place he might expect to occupy under a prince who should be chiefly indebted to him for the crown. From his birth, station, and consummate address, Portocarrero was well qualified to give the preponderance to whatever party he espoused; and by his boldness, policy, and successful machinations, the Duke of Anjou was ultimately raised to the throne of Spain. During one of those profound fits of depression and despondency, by which the King was frequently attacked, and which were now aggravated

[1] *Mém. de Torcy*, t. i. p. 35.   [2] Ibid.

by his deep sense of the miseries of the country, the Cardinal came to Court, on pretence of paying his respects
and duty to his unfortunate sovereign.   In an interview
which he obtained, and which the Austrian faction could
not have denied to the Archbishop of Toledo, Charles
unburdened to Portocarrero the afflictions he suffered from
the unhappy and unsettled state of the government.   The
Cardinal readily seized on an opportunity which opened
an access to the confidence of his sovereign, and soothed
him by insinuating that the evils which distressed him
might be remedied, provided the administration was no
longer managed by the Confessor and the Queen.   Portocarrero having subsequently consulted with his confidents, they were of opinion that the King, having represented his afflictions as matters of conscience, the Cardinal should begin with obtaining the dismissal of the Confessor.   As the priests and ecclesiastics, by whom he was
surrounded, had always exercised a wonderful influence
over the mind of Charles, this measure was of supreme
importance.   It was resolved that the present Confessor,
who belonged to the Austrian faction, and through whom
the Queen held the key to the King's conscience, should
be deprived of his situation.   The measure was carried
into effect with promptitude and secrecy; and Froylan
Diaz, a Dominican monk[1] from Alcala, was privately
summoned to Madrid to be installed in the vacant office.
He was introduced into the royal apartments, late in the
evening, while the King was listening to a concert of music.   Matilla, the present Confessor, was of the party,
and was familiarly conversing in the recess of a window

---

[1] Ceux qui de Dominique ont embrassé la vie,
Ont vu longtems leur secte en Espagne établie;
Et, de l'obscurité des plus humbles emplois,
Ont passé tout-à-coup dans les palais des Rois.
                                        Henriade, ch. v.

with the King's physician, who had been one of his fellow-students at Salamanca, when he was suddenly appalled by the apparition of Froylan Diaz, now ushered into the royal presence by the Count of Benavente, at that time *Sumiller de Corps*. Versed in the intrigues of courts, Matilla instantly understood what had occurred —he communicated it to the friend with whom he was conversing; and, rushing from the palace, betook himself to his convent of Rosario.[1] So privately had the intrigue been conducted, that the Queen had learned the secret from his Majesty only a few hours before the new Confessor was introduced into the palace. She was overwhelmed by the unexpected intelligence, but she dissembled her mortification, and gave her approval to the choice of the King.[2]

From this time Portocarrero, supported by the Confessor, and also by the Inquisitor-General Rocaberti, commenced a series of diabolical machinations, which must consign all who took part in them to the execration of posterity. The King's deplorable, and as it appeared, extraordinary state—one alike of pain, of mental vacuity, or sometimes even of only half consciousness—and those convulsive tremblings over his whole frame, with which he was periodically attacked once in the three or four days,[3] had given rise to a rumour that he was possessed by evil Spirits, and this report found very general acceptance amongst an ignorant and superstitious people. Availing themselves of this belief, Portocarrero and his ecclesiastical coadjutors persuaded the weak unhappy King himself, that he was under the influence of fascination and sorcery, and that in all probability those who ap-

[1] *Proceso Criminal Fulminado contra Froylan Diaz*, p. 38. ed. Madrid 1788.

[2] Coxe, *Mem. of House of Bourbon.*

[3] *Proceso contra Froylan Diaz*, p. 73.

proached him most frequently and nearly (meaning Oropesa, Melgar and the Queen) were the contrivers of those spells, from the pernicious effects of which he was so severely suffering. The Cardinal and his accomplices then convinced him, that, in order to be released from the power of the unclean Spirits, by whom he was tormented, it was necessary that he should be exorcised. Oropesa and the Queen did not venture to oppose this nefarious proposal, lest their resistance should increase those suspicions which had been already excited against them ; and the King himself, unable to withstand the impressions forced on his mind by his ecclesiastical advisers, submitted to the awful ceremony with agony and affright. The task devolved on a German capuchin, called Francisco Mauro Tenda, who was held to be very skilful in matters of sorcery,[1] and who performed the conjuration with every solemnity calculated to inspire horror into a timorous and bigoted mind. The King, appalled at the force and energy of the tremendous expressions employed in the practice of exorcism, became, after the conclusion of this superstitious rite, the victim of a melancholy more deep seated and overwhelming even than that under which he had previously suffered.[2] He grew restless and peevish, uttered dismal groans, and occasionally manifested symptoms of incipient mental aberration. But the French faction were disappointed in the hope they had entertained, that Charles, overcome by superstitious fears, would denounce, as the authors of his possession, the heads of the Austrian party, who, in fact, were the only demons they wished to exercise and expel.[3]

---

[1] Muy inteligente y practico en materias de conocer maleficios, y de lanzar demonios. (*Proceso contra Froylan Diaz*, p. 116.)

[2] " Per sacarle," says Ortiz, " los Espiritus immundos le iban sacando el espiritu vital."

[3] Llorente, however, in his History of the Inquisition, says, the

As the King's hypochondria, instead of abating, had become more profound subsequent to this conjuration, the Cardinal and his confidents induced their unhappy master, whose terrified imagination still brooded over the apprehensions of sorcery, to consult on his situation, a Dominican, called Arguelles, residing at Cangas de Tineo, in the Asturias, who was reputed to have a strong command over demons, and was said already to have successfully exorcised a nun.

The operations of the Inquisitor and Froylan Diaz, commenced by writing to request that the Monk of Cangas should inscribe the names of the King and Queen on a scroll, and laying them on his breast, should interrogate the spirits by whom he was moved, if any of the persons whose names were thus placed had been possessed. Arguelles replied, that the demon having been questioned in due form, declared that the King had been fascinated in 1675, when only fourteen years of age, by means of a decoction of dead men's brains,[1] administered to him in a cup of chocolate. The demon indicated clearly enough that this infusion had been given by his mother Mary Anne of Austria; and declared that her agents had, at the same time, by similar, but more powerful, means, destroyed Don John of Austria. The remedies prescribed were, to give him, fasting, a quart of oil, consecrated by the proper benedictions, to anoint his body also with that liquid, and to keep him strictly separated from the Queen. In answer to farther interrogation

sole object of the exorcism was to free him from the fascination of those who possessed the power, as the French term it, *nouer l'aiguillette*, and which as to Charles was truly what a French poet terms it—Un horrible et terrible secret.

[1] De los sesos de la cabeza, para quitarle la salud; y de los riñones, para impedirle la generacion. (*Proceso contra Froylan Diaz*, p. 91.)

from the Inquisitor and Confessor, whether the King had
been subjected to the influence of sorcery since the year
1675, it was answered that he had been bewitched on the
24th September 1694, by means of a dead body given to
him as an ingredient in his food. That this had been
administered by orders of one who eagerly desired to come
to Spain, and by the agency of a person called Maria, residing in the Calle-Mayor.

At this stage of the correspondence the Confessor complained from Madrid, that the answers were inconsistent,
and not sufficiently explicit, while, on the other hand, the
Monk, who probably thought he had designated the Austrians and the Queen as clearly as was safe for him, announced great obstinacy and rebellion among the devils
(*mucha y demasiada rebelion en los demonios*). Lucifer,
as he styled his demon, on being brought to the altar, had
shown a disposition to retract all his previous averments,
and was not even ashamed to confess that many things he
had already related were arrant falsehoods, and that the
only true or accurate information was to be procured in
the chapel of our Lady of Atocha.[1]

While, on the one hand, the Monk of Cangas was
pressed to employ stronger conjurations towards his demons, and while, on the other, he constantly referred his
correspondents to our Lady of Atocha, the Grand Inquisitor Rocaberti died, and the Dominicans having lost his
support, did not venture longer to continue their machinations.

The Queen, however, had come to a knowledge of
the proceedings at Cangas de Tineo some time before
the death of Rocaberti, and learning that she had not
herself escaped the calumnies of the demon, she resolved to be avenged on the confessor Froylan Diaz.
The vacant office of Inquisitor General was conferred on

[1] *Proceso contra F. Diaz.*

the Bishop of Segovia, who was a partizan of the German faction, and who now quickly satisfied the King that his pretended fascination and the conjurations which had been held, were the effect of the fanaticism and interested views of his confessor. That infamous impostor was in consequence driven from the confidential situation which he so unworthily filled near the person of his abused sovereign, and was denounced to the Inquisition for having placed his trust in demons, and having availed himself of their aid to discover forbidden secrets. Diaz, in his examination, threw the blame on the late Inquisitor Rocaberti, till becoming justly alarmed for his safety, he fled to Rome. But the Spanish ambassador at the Vatican, in consequence of instructions from the court of Madrid, got possession of his person, and having embarked him for Carthagena, he was confined in the prisons of the Holy Office of Murcia, where he was still lying at the death of the King of Spain.[1]

[1] It might be supposed that Froylan Diaz should have been absolved and released on the accession of the Bourbon family, for whose cause he had so severely suffered. But his case had become involved in a difficult discussion with regard to the respective powers of the Council of the Inquisition and the Inquisitor General, —the former having wished to quash all proceedings against Diaz, and the latter having instituted them on his own authority, placing, at the same time, in confinement those councillors whom he charged with partiality to the late confessor. (*Proceso Criminal contra F. Diaz.*) At length, in 1704, Louis XIV, though more remarkable in his declining years for bigotry than humanity, expressed a wish, in his admirable instructions to his grandson, then King of Spain, that the dungeons of the Inquisition should be cleared of their crowd of captives. The desire of Louis was a law to Philip, who forthwith commanded the Inquisitor General to place, within three days, all the documents concerning the case of Froylan Diaz in the hands of the Council of the Holy Office. That Board having instantly met, proceeded, in conformity with the understood will of the King, to absolve Diaz from all the charges which had been

Though the plot of the French party had not been attended with all the success anticipated, Oropesa and Melgar had at least been rendered objects of suspicion to a superstitious people, and it now became an easy task to excite against them such a clamour as would drive them entirely from the counsels of their sovereign. Availing themselves of a deficient harvest, and the misery occasioned by want of provisions among the inhabitants of the capital, Portocarrero and his emissaries insinuated everywhere that the scarcity was entirely owing to Oropesa, who, for his own advantage, had exported vast quantities of grain to Portugal, and had purchased up all the oil in Andalusia, that he might afterwards dispose of it at an exorbitant profit.[1] The starving and credulous populace readily believed that the partizans of Austria were the real authors of the calamities under which they groaned. Inflamed by the reports which had been spread, a clamorous multitude assembled one morning in the Plaça Mayor, where they assailed the bakers of Madrid and also those who brought bread into the capital from the neighbouring villages. The Corregidor having repaired to the spot with the city guards, and one of them having struck a woman selling herbs, who was among the loudest in her outcries concerning the dearness of provisions and the want of due weight, the exasperated mob began to throw stones and mud at the Corregidor and his escort, whom they put to flight.[2] Encouraged by this success, they proceeded, after committing various acts of

brought against him. Yet, perhaps, few inmates of the cells of the Inquisition less merited release or safety than Froylan Diaz. An impostor and fanatic of the most dangerous description, none better deserved to become the victim of an institution which priestcraft and bigotry had reared.

[1] San-Phelipe, *Comentarios*, t. i. p. 6.
[2] Targe, *Hist. de l'Avénement de la Maison de Bourbon*, t. i. c. 3.

outrage, to the front of the royal palace, demanding with outcries a supply of bread and the death of Oropesa. An ineffective police in vain attempted to disperse this concourse, which grew more fierce and violent from the fruitless opposition it encountered. The unhappy King, who was at this time in a truly pitiable state, both of mind and body, being overcome with terror, was uncertain what course to pursue. It was in vain the Countess Berlips attempted to appease the multitude by throwing some small pieces of money from the windows. Their fury increased every moment, and they now proceeded to attack the guard of the palace with an intention of forcing their way into its precincts. This attack was repelled, but the rabble vociferously required that the King himself should make his appearance. As the wretched sovereign was scarcely in a state to comply with their demands, the Count de Benavente, at that time *Sumiller de Corps*, having advanced to the balcony, called out aloud that the King was asleep. This assurance, instead of allaying, increased the commotion, and a shout burst forth, that he had slept too long and must now awake.[1] It was in vain to reason or remonstrate. Charles, pale and trembling, was at length brought forward to a balcony, supported by some of his attendants. As he was almost unable to articulate, the Count de Benavente announced to the enraged populace, in name of this shadow of a king, that they must have recourse to the Count of Oropesa, who had the charge of supplying the town with provisions.[2] On receiving this answer, calculated rather to keep up than subdue their excitement, the mob quitted the court of the palace with loud execrations, and rushed precipitately to the mansion of Oropesa. A billet hastily despatched from the palace by his colleague Melgar, warned the Count of

[1] " Ya mucho tiempo que dormia y convenia despertarse." (Ortiz, *Compend. Cronol.* t. vi. lib. xxi. & 10.)   [2] Ibid.

his danger before the arrival of the insurgents. His
house was fortunately next to that of the Grand Inquisitor, and having made an aperture in the wall, he and his
family escaped by this issue. There only remained some
soldiers, stationed at the gates, who, on the approach of
the mob, fired over their heads to deter them from farther violence. But one musket levelled lower than the
rest, shot a rioter dead on the spot.[1] The irritated crowd
quickly overpowered the soldiery, and burst into the mansion, where they in vain sought for its owner through the
splendid apartments, in order to sacrifice him instantly
to their fury. Disappointed in their hope of vengeance,
they pillaged the house, and then returned to the streets
ready for new and greater acts of violence. It was in
vain that the Corregidor of the city endeavoured to allay
the commotion by riding into the crowd with a crucifix in
his hand,—it was in vain that the Monks of St Dominic
carried about the Eucharist.[2] All such efforts were fruitless ; but the populace at length dispersed on hearing a report that 200 cavalry, sword in hand, and bearing loaded
carabines, were advancing to act against them.

After this alarm the King was induced, by the representations of Portocarrero, and the terror of a new insurrection, to banish both Oropesa and Melgar from his
court and capital. Charles, however, parted from these
ministers with much regret. In spite of all the Cardinal's machinations,—the exorcism and the late scene of
popular fury, he could never be induced to regard them
with dislike or distrust, though he now found himself
compelled to discard them from his counsels. The disgraced ministers experienced the deepest mortification,
and felt, that although the Queen still remained to sup-

[1] Targe, Hist. de l'Avénement de la Maison de Bourbon.
[2] Coxe's Memoirs, t. i. sect. 3.

port their views at court, a fatal blow had been inflicted on the Austrian influence.

Though the King experienced an internal dread and apprehension of the ascendency the Cardinal would assume on the dismissal of his rivals, he, immediately after the removal of Melgar and Oropesa, committed to Portocarrero and his faction the sole management of the affairs of the kingdom. Don Manuel Arias, a creature of the Cardinal, was appointed President of Castile in room of Oropesa, and Don Francis Ronquillo Corregidor of Madrid: the Prince of Hesse-Darmstadt retired to his government of Catalonia, and the German troops were discharged. Even the Queen, forcibly struck with the danger of the late popular insurrection, withdrew in a great measure from all concern in politics, on pretext of devoting her whole time to attendance on the King, whose situation was daily becoming more deplorable.

Leaving the Cardinal and his colleagues without control, the infirm and hapless monarch now shunned all the active duties of sovereignty: and if he at any time awoke from the state of listless melancholy in which he was usually plunged, it was only to receive the impression of the wildest and most sepulchral fancies. Enfeebled by disease—worn out by mental affliction, and harassed by those who importuned him to nominate a successor, he escaped from the capital in April 1700, and sought refuge in the cloistered Escurial. But in this gloomy retreat his melancholy became more profound and absorbing. Abstracted and desponding, he wandered amid the galleries and vaults of that stupendous and sullen fabric, spending his hours in chanting matins and vespers with the monks of the convent, or dirges to the memory of its founder. His behaviour here was not unlike that of his illustrious ancestor Charles V., for six months preceding his decease, when his spirit became depressed by timid

and illiberal superstition—when he employed his time in
chanting with monks the hymns of the missal, and celebrated before his death his own funeral obsequies.

Amid other gloomy superstitions the present King
had heard that the sight and contact of the mouldering
bodies of deceased ancestors would prolong the life of
their descendants, or at least induce the departed spirits
to intercede with heaven in their behalf. This strange
belief, and the morbid curiosity of disease, impelled him
to descend into the Pantheon, where reposed the mortal
remains of the Castilian monarchs. The ceremony of
opening the coffins was performed with all possible solemnity. He first unclosed that of his mother, whom he
had never greatly loved, but he long and earnestly contemplated the remains of his first Queen Louisa d'Orleans, which bore few traces of dissolution, and exhibited
a countenance scarcely less blooming than when alive.[1]
He at length exclaimed, " I shall soon be with her in
heaven,"[2] and recoiling from the niche which contained
her sarcophagus, rushed in horror from the aisle.

The effect of this visit to the awful dormitory of his
departed ancestors, and of the emotion he had experienced,
was deep and irremediable. Henceforth he viewed all
things as it were by the sepulchral light of the lamps of
the Pantheon, and death became the sole subject of his
discourse and contemplation.

After this fatal experiment the Escurial having become
to Charles a place fraught with horror, he quitted it on
the 4th of May for Aranjuez, where bull-fights, comedies, and cane-plays were exhibited in constant round
for his amusement. But neither could these diversions
nor the enchanting season of the year revive his exhausted spirits. The clear streams and fountains, and smiling

[1] Coxe's *Memoirs.*
[2] Ortiz, *Compend. Cronol.* t. vi. lib. xxi. c. 9.

gardens of the gay Aranjuez, were beheld with the same deep melancholy as the dark woods and sterile rocks of the Escurial. Ever brooding over the idea of dissolution, he found, even amid the most delightful scenes and objects, some analogy to the phantom that pursued him. Death, with all its train of dismal attributes,—

> The knell, the shroud, the mattock, and the grave;
> The deep damp vault, the darkness and the worm,

stood continually before his view, and rendered him insensible to all the attractive varieties of rural repose and tranquillity. In addition to other symptoms of malady, restlessness now goaded his enfeebled frame. After a month's stay at Aranjuez he again returned to Madrid, in the vain hope that the sadness which could not be dispelled by the rural delights of his sweetest palace, might yield to the bustle and glitter of the metropolis.

During the King's absence at the Escurial and Aranjuez, the Cardinal Portocarrero had completely overturned the system of government acted on by the Counts Oropesa and Melgar. The courtiers applauded the change, and condemned as abuses all that they had supported in the time of his predecessor. He rescinded the law by which gold and silver were permitted to be carried out of the kingdom on paying 3 per cent. to the treasury. In order to compensate for the loss of the profits which thus accrued to the state, the minister suspended payment of pensions, and he reduced the salaries of all civil and military appointments.

Amid these reforms, however, the chief attention of the Cardinal was directed to his favourite scheme of strengthening the French party in Spain, and securing the succession of the House of Bourbon. Several Grandees, who had formerly belonged to the Austrian faction, or had remained neuter, among whom the most distinguished were the Duke of Medina-Sidonia, the Marques of Villafranca, and the Count St. Estevan, were now gained over; and the King's German guards were disbanded, lest, on his death, they might feel disposed to rally in a body round the standard of a prince of their own country.

On the return of the King, who was in a more deplorable state even than when he had last quitted Madrid, and had now the appearance of a man of seventy years of age, though only thirty-eight, the Cardinal and his party were continually by his side, and exercised over him the same absolute and despotic sway that the adverse faction had exerted while in power. Their present aim was to compel him to execute a formal testament in favour of a French prince. In some of the despotic governments of Europe, the fundamental laws of the realm were insufficient, in the event of the extinction of the reigning family, to regulate the succession, which was in consequence left to the will of the last monarch of the race. In Spain, different rules were applicable in the kingdoms of which that monarchy was composed; and the Cortes, which was the only legitimate body competent to decide the question, had that assembly still preserved its original character and rights, could now no longer be considered as representing the nation. Having no direct heir to his possessions, the disposal of them was understood to be left to Charles, who, incapable himself of governing, was thus called to make a choice, affecting not only the interests of Spain, but involving the political relations of all the countries of Europe.

Strong, however, as was the sway of Portocarrero and his confidents, and weak as was the mind of the monarch, he could with difficulty be brought to the great object of all their importunities—the nomination of a French successor by testament. His natural diffidence—his dread that, by this final and decisive measure, he would have

to withstand the discontent, or even hostility, of the whole
Austrian faction——and the persuasion that such a step
would, in fact, be the termination of his own influence
and sovereignty, all rendered him desirous to defer this act
till the last moment.

The wavering and uncertain state of the King's mind,
and the inclination which he still felt towards the Aust
trian Family, in spite of all the maxims which had been
so strongly inculcated on him, began to render Louis
XIV. apprehensive that his well laid schemes might be
ultimately defeated. In alarm lest he should lose the
whole succession, and lest the rich inheritance should de-
volve on his natural enemies of Austria, he entered into
a second partition treaty, to be guaranteed by the King of
England and the Dutch, which was signed at London
on the 13th of May. By this new arrangement, the
Archduke Charles was to receive Spain, properly so called,
the Netherlands and the Indies, all which, by the former
partition-treaty, had been assigned to the now deceased
Prince of Bavaria. In return for the sacrifice of his
higher pretensions, the Dauphin was to obtain the two Sicilies,[1] and also the dutchy of Lorraine, if the Duke could
be prevailed on thus to transfer his own patrimony, and
accept the Milanese as indemnification. But it may well
be doubted, if Louis was sincere in this treaty, or if he
really intended that it should ever be carried into effect;
for among other provisions, it was stipulated that, if necessary, the contracting parties should, by force of arms,
prevent the Archduke from entering Spain or the Ita-

---

[1] San-Phelipe, however, says, that the two Sicilies were to be
given to James II., the abdicated King of England, and the Spanish possessions in America to William III. Nor, according to
this author, was Spain proper to be given in its full integrity to the
Archduke Charles, Catalonia and Navarre being assigned to France,
and Estremadura, with Galicia, to Portugal. (*Comentarios*, t. i.
p. 13, 14.)

lian dominions;—a compact which might easily have been converted into a virtual exclusion of the Austrian Prince from the Spanish throne.[1]

Charles was first informed of this treaty by Don Bernardo de Quiros, his ambassador to the United Provinces, who, having observed some private conferences at Loo, between the French emissary Count Tallard, and William III. of England, suspected their object, and obtained information concerning it from some deputies of the States-General, who were also parties to the negotiation.[2]

Notwithstanding his melancholy and listless state, the King of Spain was roused to the highest indignation, by the report of this intended partition of his dominions, and showed that he was not yet altogether indifferent to the honour and splendour of his kingdom. He expressed his feelings in the strongest terms through his ambassador at the Court of London, and such, indeed, was the vehemence of the language employed, that the Spanish minister was forthwith ordered to quit the British dominions. The Queen, about the same time, informed the King of the intimation made to her, that if she abandoned the support of the Austrian Family, she might hope, after the demise of her present husband, to be united to the Grand-Dauphin of France.[3]

The Emperor Leopold, who had neither been a party to this new treaty of partition, nor had given his acquiescence within the time allowed him, now peremptorily refused to accede to it. His expectations with regard to the Spanish succession had always been sanguine; and being now encouraged by the secret assurances of Charles, he openly declared that nothing less would satisfy him

[1] Coxe's *Memoirs.*

[2] Targe, *Hist. de l'Avénement de la Maison de Bourbon*, &c.

[3] San-Phelipe, *Comentarios*, t. i. p. 9.

than the Spanish empire in its present undivided integrity.

The intelligence of the proposed partition had not the same effect on the Spanish nation as on the King. Charles, indignant at the proposed diminution of the Spanish territories, became alienated from the French interests. But the nation at large, though alarmed at the idea of a dismemberment of the monarchy, were almost unanimously of opinion that this calamity could be averted only by calling a prince of the House of Bourbon to the entire and undivided succession. The grandees disliked the notion of a partition, which would have deprived them of their chance of the Italian governments and viceroyalties. At the head of this party of nobility, were the Duke of Medina-Sidonia and the Marques Villafranca, who, though supposed to have been once somewhat Austrian in their inclinations, preferred any thing to a partition of the empire, and were less anxious concerning the prince on whom the choice should fall, than that a selection should be made which might preserve their monarchy entire.

This feeling was most unequivocally manifested in a Council of State, which was a second time assembled to deliberate on the succession. Of twelve grandees consulted, ten, who were the Cardinal Portocarrero, the Dukes of Medina-Sidonia, Montalto, and Escalona, the Marqueses of Mancera, Fresno, and Villafranca, the Counts Montijo, St Estevan, and Monteleone, were of opinion that a Bourbon should be forthwith called to the succession. The Count of St Estevan, who opened the proceedings in a speech of considerable length, while he maintained the superior right of the Bourbon family, placed the issue chiefly on a question of expediency for the interests of Spain. The kingdom, he contended, had so much declined in power, and had recently fallen into so

calamitous a situation, that it had no longer strength to
defend or protect itself without the aid of a foreign power.
With unheard-of audacity, the maritime powers, he said,
had agreed to partition the monarchy, which could be saved
from this dismemberment only by interesting France in its
favour. The dominions of the German Emperor were too
remote to enable him to render speedy or effectual assistance, his treasury was exhausted, and he had no naval force
to protect the coasts or harbours of Spain from the aggressions and inroads of the maritime powers.[1] Two alone
of the Council, the Counts of Fuensalida and Frigiliana,
advised that the choice of a successor to the King should
be referred to the assembly of the Cortes, who might listen to the claims of the respective candidates, and determine according to the laws and constitutions of the realm.
The Faculties of Law and Theology of the kingdom, whom
Charles also consulted on the jarring rights of the rival
houses, concurred in the sentiments of the Council of Grandees, and unanimously decided in favour of the Bourbons
—provided due means were adopted to prevent the union
of the two crowns, which was the sole spirit and meaning
(as the divines and jurists argued) of the renunciation by
Maria-Theresa.

At length, to resolve his doubts, or rather, perhaps,
with a view of finding some high authority in favour of
his own inclinations, Charles determined to consult the
sovereign Pontiff, Innocent XII, as the father and head
of all Christendom. The Duke d'Uzeda, who was one
of the royal household, and possessed much of his master's
confidence, was selected for this delicate mission. The
Duke, endeavouring to decline an appointment which
would remove him from the royal presence and service,
the King observed, " You know I have no children, and
may shortly die. Have you not thrice held me as dead

Turge, *Hist. de l'Avénement de la Maison de Bourbon.*

in your arms? Do you not also perceive that, for the tranquillity of my subjects and the whole monarchy, I should think of chusing a successor? It is for this great work, for which I am answerable to God and to the world, that I would consult the Pope, and as it is necessary to keep the design secret, I have chosen you to serve me in so important a mission." He concluded with a remark which shewed that Portocarrero and the French partizans had already attacked the conscience of the King, and alarmed the weak and terrified monarch with the threat of eternal punishment, should he neglect to appoint a successor, or violate the rights of the legitimate heir. " Though partial," he added, " to my own family, my future salvation is dearer to me than the ties of blood.[1]"

Uzeda, accordingly, repaired to the Vatican, charged with copies of the opinions of the jurisconsults, and a letter to the Pope from the King of Spain, in which that monarch said he found such doubt in the rules of the Spanish succession, that he was unable to arrive at a fixed determination; and he therefore entreated his Holiness, that, having examined the case, and consulted with the Cardinals, he should advise him in what manner he might best regulate his conduct according to the constitutions of the realm and principles of justice. The Pope himself was wholly devoted to the interests of France, and the Cardinals, to whom the documents were referred by him, belonged to the same party. After affecting to consult and deliberate for forty days (which was longer than was safe in the precarious state of the King's health), Innocent prepared and despatched a report, in which he at length announced that he entertained no doubt that, after his Majesty's demise, the whole monarchy devolved by right on the Dauphin, but that his second son, the Duke of Anjou, ought to be called to the succession, in

[1] Coxe's *Memoirs.*

order to prevent the union of the two crowns of France and Spain. This report was accompanied by such an epistle from the Pontiff as he thought was calculated to influence the devout mind of Charles. " Being myself," he said, " in a situation similar to that of your Majesty, on the point of appearing at the tribunal of Christ, and of rendering an account to my Sovereign Pastor of the flock which has been entrusted to my care, it is my duty to give such advice as will not be a matter of reproach to my conscience at the day of doom. Your Majesty should reflect that you ought not to put the interests of the House of Austria in competition with those of eternity, and with that dreadful account of your actions which you must soon give before the King of kings, who admits no excuse, and is no respecter of persons. You cannot be ignorant that the children of the Dauphin are the rightful heirs of the crown ; and that, in opposition to them, neither the Archduke, nor any member of the House of Austria, has the smallest legitimate pretension. In proportion to the importance of the succession, the more crying will be the injustice of excluding the rightful heirs, and the more will you draw on your devoted head the vengeance of Heaven. It is therefore incumbent on you to omit no precaution which your wisdom can suggest to render justice where justice is due, and to secure, as far as lies in your power, the undivided inheritance of the Spanish monarchy to a son of the Dauphin of France." [1]

But neither the uniformity of opinion among his own subjects, nor the revered authority of the supreme Pontiff, could altogether still the yearnings of Charles towards his own kindred. The Queen, and the new Confessor who had been appointed in room of the hateful exorcist, being aware of the King's secret wishes, and perceiving

[1] Coxe's *Memoirs*, sect. iii.

in his mind more disinclination to the Bourbons than
they had anticipated, now suggested that the royal will
and pleasure were paramount to all rights or laws of
succession. The machinations of the Queen, secretly directed by Oropesa and Melgar, were renewed with redoubled effect. Military preparations were privately made
by her in Spain to add force to the expected bequest in
favour of the Austrian family, and permission was given
to receive the German troops in the Italian dominions of
the Spanish crown. By her perseverance the Queen at
length obtained from the King a mandate for the Duke
of Medina-Celi to proceed to Naples, and admit the
imperial troops into that kingdom, and she negotiated
with the Duke of Mantua for the reception of an Austrian garrison into his capital, in order to overawe the
Milanese. But all the efforts of her party proved ineffectual, and they served only to prolong the vain hopes
of the Emperor and the mental tortures of the irresolute
King. The Queen had been miserably deceived in her
choice of the Duke of Medina-Celi, as her confidential
envoy to Naples. That nobleman, before departing on
his embassy, had been convinced that the only mode of
saving the Spanish empire from partition was to seat a
Bourbon on the throne, and he therefore contrived to
frustrate or elude the orders of the Queen. The Duke
of Mantua also evaded his agreement, and so far from
receiving an Austrian garrison within his states, he entered into a close negotiation with Louis.

Meanwhile, the maladies of Charles, both physical and
mental, had so alarmingly increased, that no hope could
be rationally entertained that his life should be farther
prolonged. All parties were convinced, that now, if
ever, the last blow in the political contest must be struck;
and such of late had been the bitterness in the Court,
and such the disorders excited in the capital by the in-

cessant agitation of the topic, that an edict was issued at Madrid, prohibiting all discussion or conversation, whether public or private, on the subject of the succession.[1] This decree, however, was insufficient to restrain the eagerness of discourse. "Clamorous disputes," says Coxe, "were heard even in the antichamber of the dying monarch. Pressed on one side by the French, and importuned on the other by the Queen and Austrian partizans, the debilitated frame of Charles sunk under the struggle of contending passions, and a crisis in his disorder announced approaching dissolution. With a view still farther to stimulate his tender conscience, Portocarrero exposed to him his awful situation, on the verge of eternity, and persuaded him to receive the spiritual counsel of the most pious divines to assist his devotions, and prepare him to die with resignation. In the midst of those lugubrious ceremonies with which the Catholic Church appals the minds of the dying, these divines represented the danger of his soul, should he not dispose of his crown by will, and entail on his country, by this neglect the horrors of civil war. They held forth the vengeance of an offended Deity, if he suffered himself to be swayed by mortal love or hatred,—if he consulted the affections of that body which must shortly moulder into dust. The Austrians, they urged, were not the relations, nor the Bourbons the enemies of his soul; and it was his duty to conform himself to the opinion of the majority of his counsel, the disinterested advocates of justice, and the organs of the national voice."

The mental struggles of the King were terminated by this imposing and well-conducted scene. In presence of Portocarrero Charles subscribed his celebrated testament, in which more by compulsion and terror than by the spontaneous dictates of his own free will, he appointed Philip,

Belando, Histor. Civile d'España, c. 3.

Duke of Anjou, his universal successor. The Secretary
Don Antonio de Ubilla acted as notary,—the Cardinal
and Don Manuel Arias were the sole witnesses. Whether
it was the painful thought of disinheriting his family, or the
reflection that this act virtually ended his authority and
his reign, he performed it with manifest reluctance. As
he signed he burst into tears, exclaiming, " God is the
disposer of kingdoms, for they are his,"[1] and when the
ceremony was closed he added, with bitterness, " I now
am nothing."[2] After signing he fell into a long faint,
which made his attendants dread that this step, so re-
volting to his inclination, had accelerated the end of his
days.[3] There can be no doubt that, in subscribing this
testament, Charles acted according to the dictates of his
own conscience, and to the best of his feeble judgment,—
yet, as remarked by a native author, so widely does man
err—so little insight does he possess into futurity—so far
are the best adapted means from attaining their object,
that Charles left his subjects a cruel war, while believing
that he bequeathed them an everlasting peace.[4]

The contents of this document, the most important
ever executed in Europe, were carefully concealed from
the Queen and the Austrian party. But private information was communicated to the French Resident at
Madrid, and by him transmitted to his court.

After the execution of this testament the King's illness
daily increased, and every symptom announced a sinking
frame. A dysentery had now commenced—his limbs had
begun to fail—his pulse beat fainter, and he had solemnly renounced all projects of revenge or feelings of enmity,
which the noble author of the Succession War tells us is

---

[1] Dios es quien da los Reynos, porque son suyos.
[2] Ya nada somos.
[3] Targe, *Hist. de l'Avénement de la Maison de Bourbon.*
[4] San-Phelipe, *Comentarios.*

the surest symptom of approaching dissolution. Being now incapacitated from all business both by mental weakness and bodily suffering, he made a sort of abdication of the royal authority, and committed the whole government to Portocarrero, who immediately received from him the great seals of the kingdom. That prelate, with affected moderation and disinterestedness, proposed that the Queen should be associated with him in the regency. But the King, as he had now definitively called a Bourbon to the succession, refused, with much good sense, to accede to this proposition, lest her Majesty should again agitate and embroil the kingdom, by her intrigues, in favour of the House of Austria.

The King still languished till the 1st of November, a month from the day on which he had executed his testament; and at length, after having all his life trembled at the distant and shadowy phantom of death, he suffered, with admirable fortitude and resignation, its last tremendous blow.

His body, which was embalmed after death, was found to have been internally affected by many mortal and incurable causes of disease and dissolution.[1]

Thus, at length, terminated the long but inglorious sway of Charles II, in the 39th year of his age, and the 36th of his unfortunate reign. His character is written in the events of his clouded life. He was mild and conscientious,—suspicious and distrustful from diffidence in his own powers and talents,—timid, inconstant, and irresolute, from the influence of hypochondriac affections,—chaste from temperament,—ignorant from total want of instruction,—superstitious from habit and education;— he was utterly destitute of discernment, energy, or skill,

[1] " Sus entrañas se hallaron en parte canceradas, el corazon enxuto y seco sin sangre alguna," &c. (Ortis, Compend. Cronol. t. vi. lib. 21. c. 9.)

—he was but a ghost even of his grandsire Philip III, and in his premature decay, formed no unfit emblem of the declining kingdom over which he reigned.

Charles, indeed, was not wholly responsible for the state of degradation to which Spain was reduced when he closed his fatal career. The administrations of Lerma and Olivarez had prepared the way for a long train of losses, humiliations, and disasters; but the wavering and fluctuating counsels of Charles completed the ruin of his country.

Spain, which contained twenty million of inhabitants in the reign of Ferdinand and Isabella, had only eight millions at the close of the reign of Charles II. Moncada, an author at the beginning of the 17th century, estimated the population of its capital at 400,000; and Uztariz, who wrote immediately after the accession of the Bourbons, calculated it at only 180,000, so that it may be rated that it had diminished by one-half during the reigns of Philip IV. and his son. Except, indeed, from courtesy and custom, and the extreme interest excited by the question of the succession, Spain, at the end of the reign of Charles, would scarcely have been reckoned among the Powers of Europe. Her finances were in a state of most frightful disorder. The revenues of the crown were absorbed by those agents or farmers, on whom the urgent necessities of government reduced it to depend for supplies; and, at the same time, the people, both in the capital and provinces, were loaded with every species of extortion and monopoly. The ample treasures of the New World were still worse administered; the viceroys, after defrauding the crown and oppressing the subject, were suffered to return from their governments and to enjoy, with impunity, the produce of peculation. The harbours of Spain contained but ten or twelve rotten frigates,—the arsenals for the navy were neglected, and even the art of

ship-building had fallen into oblivion. Her army amounted to not more than 20,000 men, without discipline, pay,
or clothing. Her forts and citadels had crumbled into
ruins. Even the breaches made in the walls of Barcelona during the Catalan insurrection, continued open,
and at the other chief fortresses there were neither guns
mounted nor garrisons maintained. Such was the want
of vigour in the laws, and remissness in the officers of justice, that reins had been given to every species of licentiousness. The slightest rise in the price of provisions
excited tumult and alarm. Madrid had become the rendezvous of robbers and asylum of assassins, who haunted
even the palaces of the grandees or the churches,—unmolested and unpunished. Its squares and streets were filled with discarded domestics and famishing artizans, without occupation or the means of subsistence. Those establishments destined to maintain the respect due to royalty
had sunk into empty form, and were insufficient to protect the King from mortifying insults, both to his authority and person. The responsible ministry were without intelligence or skill in the science of government:
the real influence was in the officers of the household,—
the King's confessor,—the prelates, and the inquisitors of
the realm. The private and bitter jealousies of the grandees—the enmity of the provinces towards each other,
and the rigid adherence to ancient forms and usages,
however inapplicable to modern circumstances,—all con-
spired to prevent a cordial co-operation in any useful or
national object, and completed, in the last year of the
17th century, and at the end of the Austrian dynasty,
the picture of Spain.

Yet the sway, no doubt, of the imbecile Charles, may
have appeared more feeble from the contrast it presented
to the energy and skill of the other governments of Europe, which, at the close of this century, was ruled by

the ablest monarchs who had ever appeared, at one era, since the first rise of its States on the wreck of the Western Empire. The energies both of Holland and England were wielded by William III.;—Louis XIV. reigned in France—the prudent Pedro in Portugal—John Sobieski in Poland—Charles XII. in Sweden, and in Muscovy the immortal Czar.

CHAPTER X.

ACCESSION OF PHILIP V.—COMMENCEMENT OF THE WAR OF
THE SUCCESSION.

Du sein de Paris Madrid reçoit un Roi.
Henriade.

Under which King, Bezonian, speak or die.
SHAKSPEARE.

THE unhappy Charles II. was the last of the House
of Austria.   With him ingloriously terminated the male
posterity of the Emperor Charles, and the native line
which derived its descent from the ancient Gothic monarchs.

Though the import of the royal testament had been
privately communicated to Louis XIV, its contents had
not been publicly divulged, and were as yet unknown to
the Emperor or the Austrian faction at Madrid. Immediately, however, after the demise of the King, Cardinal
Portocarrero convoked the presidents of the supreme
councils, and the ministers of state, in whose presence
the testament was read.   This illustrious assembly was
agreeably surprised to find that his late Majesty had finally
acceded to the wishes of the nation, and had called to the
throne a descendant of their Infanta Maria-Theresa. On
the preamble, that the Infanta his sister had only renounced for her family the succession to the throne, in order that
the two countries might not be ruled by the same monarch, he nominated his grand-nephew the Duke of Anjou

X 2

his universal heir; and, in the event of that prince's decease without issue, he called to the succession the Duke de Berri, his younger brother; then the Archduke Charles of Austria, in right of his grandmother Maryanne, youngest daughter of Philip III; and, finally, the Duke of Savoy, as great-grandson of the Infanta Catherine, daughter of Philip II. It excited some surprise in the august assembly, that Charles or his advisers should have totally neglected the Duke of Orleans, brother of Louis XIV, and his son the Duke de Chartres, who, in the order of succession, ought to have preceded the Archduke Charles, as being the son and grandson of Anne of Austria, the eldest daughter of Philip III. This omission appeared the more singular, as the princes thus passed over were the father and brother of Charles's first and much-loved Queen Louisa d'Orleans.

As the public at Madrid were yet ignorant of the provisions in the testament, the courts of the palace were crowded with persons of all ranks, and its antechambers were filled with native grandees and foreign ministers, on the day on which it was known that the will was to be opened and read. Close to the doors of the apartments where it was submitted to the ministers and presidents of the councils, stood, in anxious expectation, the envoys of France and Austria. The folding doors being at length thrown open, the Duke of Abrantes issued forth to declare the nomination. A general silence having ensued, he advanced to Count Harrach, the Imperial ambassador, who was awaiting with undue confidence the announcement of joyful tidings, and maliciously embracing him, as if about to make the wished-for declaration, he said, " Sir, it is with the greatest pleasure that I now for my whole life—take leave of the illustrious House of Austria."

Charles had also provided that, until the new King

arrived from France, the supreme authority in the realm
should be entrusted to a *junta*, consisting of the Queen,
Portocarrero, the Duke of Montalto, the Marquess of
Villafranca, the Counts Monterey, Benavente, and Fri-
giliano, Don Manuel Arias, the Inquisitor-General, and
Presidents of the Councils of Aragon, Flanders, and
Italy. All things were to be determined by a plurality
of votes,—the Queen had only a single suffrage ; and, in
fact, the Cardinal possessed the supreme authority, as he
speedily evinced by prohibiting the return to Madrid of
his old enemy Oropesa, and banishing from it the Count
of Monterey, one of the members nominated to the Junta of Regency, and who, though one of the oldest sup-
porters of the Bourbon interests, had not proved himself
sufficiently subservient to the selfish views of Portocarrero.

A copy of the testament was immediately forwarded to
Louis XIV, with a letter signed by this Junta, in which
he was conjured to send the young Duke of Anjou forthwith to Madrid. Prayers were offered up in all the
churches of Spain that God should incline the heart of
the French monarch to accept the testament. In fact,
there was some apprehension that he might rather chuse
to abide by the partition treaty into which he had lately
entered with the maritime powers ; for, though the adoption of the testament was the most favourable to the interests of his grandson, the allotment in the treaty would
have contributed more to the aggrandizement of France.
This compact, too, had been so explicit and so recent,
that it was reasonably apprehended that Louis might
feel himself bound by its provisions. And, in fact, it was
not any attachment to the House of Bourbon, but the
patriotic dread of a people jealous for the grandeur of
their country, which rendered the Spaniards so anxious
that the Duke of Anjou should receive its succession

in its undivided integrity. Their fears, however, were entirely groundless. Louis had no hesitation or scruple on the subject. For the sake of form, indeed, and in order to give a colour to his proceedings, he summoned a private council to the apartments of Madame Maintenon, which was attended only by the Dauphin and some of the most confidential ministers. The question was canvassed at as great length, and with as much gravity, as if it had been a topic of serious deliberation. One member of the assembly alone, who spoke no doubt from concerted arrangement, delivered an opinion in favour of adhering to the treaty of partition. But all the other ministers urged the necessity of accepting the will; and the Dauphin, in a speech of great animation and eloquence, while he renounced the inheritance for himself, claimed the splendid prize as justly due to his family and lineage.[1] Louis listened with complacency to the deliberations, acquiesced in the result, and then, with his usual dignity, announced the resolution that had been adopted to his courtiers, his grandson, and the ambassador of Spain.

An answer having been returned to the *Junta* consonant to their wishes, the Duke of Anjou was proclaimed king at Madrid, by the title of Philip V, and the provinces quickly followed the example of the metropolis.

Meanwhile a vast number of Spaniards, impatient to see their future sovereign, had crossed the Pyrenees in order to pay him their obeisance in France. Some of them were present at the parting interview of Louis with his grandson, and heard the French monarch declare, that the Pyrenees should no longer separate the countries. Philip V, for such was now his recognised appellation,

---

[1] St Simon (*Mémoires*, t. iii. c. 2.) says, that this decisive harangue of the Dauphin (who, though usually sunk in indolence and taciturnity, could exert himself forcibly on great occasions,) fixed and determined the deliberations of the council.

set out from Paris, accompanied by his elder and younger brothers, the Dukes of Burgundy and Berri. On his route to the frontiers, he was met by the Constable of Castile, who offered to him homage in name of the Spanish nation, and then proceeded to Paris in the capacity of ambassador extraordinary to the Court of Louis.

As soon as Philip had reached the banks of the Bidassoa, which separates the two kingdoms, he prudently dismissed his French attendants, except the Duke of Harcourt, who followed him in the character of envoy to Madrid. He parted with his royal brothers on the Isle of Pheasants, where, half a century before, that memorable treaty had been so solemnly executed, which was for ever to exclude the House of Bourbon from the Castilian throne.

Philip entered his new dominions on the 22d January 1701. As soon as he had passed the frontiers, he despatched a messenger to Madrid, confirming the government of the Junta till such time as he should himself arrive at the capital. The King of France had recommended to his grandson to remove the Queen-dowager from Madrid, as by her residence there, she might still find an opportunity of forming cabals in favour of the Austrians. The late King of Spain had assigned her, by a codicil to his will, a suitable yearly pension, and had enjoined his successor in the monarchy to entrust to her the government of the Spanish Netherlands, or some district of the Italian dominions; or, if she chose to continue in Spain, to grant her the jurisdiction and sovereignty of the spot where she fixed her abode. The same messenger who carried a confirmation of the interim rule of the Junta, brought orders for her retirement, with the pension allowed her, to whatever town in Spain she might select for her residence. She lingered for some time at Madrid, but the constant mortification which she suffered

from Portocarrero and the Junta, induced her at length
to betake herself to Toledo, whither she retired before
Philip entered his capital.[1] The Confessor of Charles II,
the Grand Inquisitor, and the Count Oropesa, had signalized themselves too much by their determined opposition
to the French interests to meet with favour or forgiveness. Philip indeed dreaded they would excite a civil
war if permitted to reside in Madrid. The Inquisitor
was commanded to retire to his Bishopric of Segovia, the
Confessor was exiled to a distant part of the kingdom,
and Oropesa was ordered to continue in the banishment
into which he had been driven subsequent to the insurrection excited in consequence of the scarcity of provisions.

On his first arrival at Madrid, the King repaired privately to Buenretiro, where he remained nearly two
months, while preparations were making for a public procession into the capital, which he at length entered in a
species of triumph. Such a concourse of people to the
metropolis had not been witnessed in Spain for many centuries. Sixty persons were crushed to death during the
magnificent spectacle, and all bespoke the joy and eagerness with which the eyes of the multitude were turned
towards a new dynasty, and a new era in the grandeur
and felicity of Spain.

[1] The Queen was respectfully visited by Philip at Toledo, soon
after his arrival at Madrid. She continued in that city till the year
1706, when she imprudently took some part in favour of the Austrians on their entrance into that ancient capital of Spain. On pretence of protecting her from the casualties of war, she was removed
in that year to Bayonne. She was visited in that neighbourhood,
in 1714, by her niece Louisa Farnese, second queen of Philip V,
on her passage through France to her new kingdom. By the influence of this relative, she was brought back to Spain in 1739, and
passed a year before her death in Guadalaxara. (Flores, Reynas
d'España. Coxe's Memoirs, c. 22.)

Philip, at his first public exhibitions, rendered himself extremely popular amongst his subjects. His pleasing countenance, his youth, his affability, and bounty, won for the grandson of Maria Theresa the heart of every Castilian. While he gratified the national feelings by adopting a similar garb to that worn by the late sovereign, his youthful and animated appearance formed a pleasing contrast to the premature decrepitude and dismal aspect of that decayed monarch. He farther obtained their early approbation, by his apparent attempts to confer on his subjects some substantial benefits. With the assistance of Portocarrero, Manuel Arias, and the Duke of Harcourt, who alone composed his secret council or cabinet, he applied himself to the reformation of abuses. The people hailed with exultation the suppression of sinecures, and the abolition of a number of offices connected with the councils of the *Hacienda* or Finance, and of the Indies.

While thus favourably received in his capital and kingdom, Philip V. could depend on being protected abroad by his grandsire, at that time the most potent sovereign in Europe,—being at the head of 300,000 troops, admirably disciplined and inured to victory. Through the power and influence of Louis, he was recognised as King of Spain by most of the states in Europe. By the same mediation, he was enabled to sign a league offensive and defensive with the King of Portugal, as also with the Dukes of Savoy and Mantua. Those German Princes, who were jealous of their Imperial Head, tendered their support. The Dutch were overawed by a mighty French force, which was brought to their frontiers, ready to occupy their fortresses, and overrun their open country. Even William III. unable as yet to rouse the English to a sense of danger, and thwarted by his Parliament, as well as by foreign powers, was for the present reluctantly

compelled to acknowledge Philip as sovereign of the whole
Spanish empire.

Never was accession to a throne apparently more auspicious—never, on a superficial view, did any nation enjoy a fairer prospect of uninterrupted tranquillity and
happiness. But War and Discord ere now had yoked their
chariots, and were ready to commence their furious and
blood-stained career.

Though the Emperor Leopold had been foiled in his
intrigues to obtain for his son the peaceable succession to
the throne of Spain, circumstances at this moment enabled him to attempt its violent usurpation. He had recently triumphed over the rebellious Hungarians, and
concluded peace with the Turks. He had thus at his
disposal an army of 100,000 men unemployed ; he could
also depend on a considerable force being supplied by
those Princes of the Empire who were well disposed towards the House of Austria, and, what was of still more
importance than the formidable number of his troops, he
had now a Prince Eugene to command them. His treasury, indeed, was but scantily supplied ; but he trusted
to subsidies from William III, who, though unable, at
present, to engage in open war, beheld with dismay a
grandson of his inveterate enemy Louis master both of
America and Spain. Leopold, accordingly, issued a bold
and vehement remonstrance against the usurpation of the
Spanish monarchy by a Bourbon Prince, and he both
called in question the authenticity of the testament itself,
and the right of the deceased monarch to make a bequest of his inheritance, at variance with the obligations
of treaties and the acknowledged claims of his family.

After this protest had been issued, the Austrian ambassador withdrew from Madrid, and the Emperor commenced vigorous preparations to bring the dispute to
the test of arms. Levies were raised in every quarter

of the hereditary dominions, ministers were despatched to rouse the maritime powers, and troops were collected in the north of Italy.[1]

The Bourbon King of Spain might, however, have defied foreign coalitions, hád all his subjects continued faithful to their allegiance. Philip V, when he repaired to Barcelona to receive his Italian bride, the Princess of Savoy, had been induced, in the hope of a free gift or donative, to hold the Cortes of Catalonia,—a measure which had proved so fatal to Philip IV. Though the King confirmed and augmented the ancient privileges of the Principality, the Catalans were by no means conciliated by his condescension. They believed that the favours conferred on them had been bestowed because they were dreaded. From that time there was no end or limit to their demands and complaints. After much irritation between the sovereign and his turbulent subjects, a scanty contribution was reluctantly voted, which, in fact, never reached the royal treasury. So unpopular had Philip been during his stay at Barcelona, in consequence of mutual refusals and recriminations, that before he left the Province, the Catalans, though they had sworn fidelity to their new sovereign, had begun to consider whether they might not find some other prince less ready to ask donatives, and less scrupulous in granting enlarged immunities. They had been much attached to their late German Viceroy, the Prince of Hesse-Darmstadt, a man of courage and popular manners, who had been appointed by the influence of the Court of Vienna, and removed by Portocarrero. On embarking from Barcelona, he had not only intimated that he would speedily return, but return with another king of Spain.[2] These words had sunk deep into the minds of the Catalans, and, when irritated or thwarted, they remembered " another king of Spain."

[1] Coxe's *Memoires*, c. 2.   [2] *Hist. of War of the Succession.*

The very circumstance, too, that Philip had been so well received, and was still so beloved by the Castilians, towards whom they entertained a national antipathy, alienated from him the affections of the Catalans, and hastened the approaching revolution.

But even among the Castilians, the popularity of their French prince and their French government was on the wane. Such were the expectations which the Spaniards had formed of the Bourbon administration, that one of the French residents declared that, "should an angel from Heaven assume the reins of empire, the public hopes must be disappointed." Philip, decorous in his manners, unstained by vice, upright in his intentions, and obedient to tutelage, had at first won from all " golden opinions ;" but his character was one of insipid mediocrity, and I have often thought it singular what I see has been recently remarked, " that, born and bred in a foreign court, with French instructors and French courtiers around him, and the life of Louis, whom he so much venerated, before his eyes, Philip, when chosen to begin a new dynasty, should have so closely resembled, in character, the princes of the old. Like his Spanish predecessors, he was shy and secluded in his habits, almost mechanical in his regularity of hours—dividing his leisure between the chapel and the chase, and dotingly submissive to his wife." [1] At an age far earlier than it had seized the Austrian princes, a deep hypochondriac melancholy settled on the mind of the Frenchman, attended by its invariable concomitants, apathy and indolence. His Austrian descent, through Maria Theresa, seems scarcely sufficient to account for this phenomenon, especially as the French princes of the same blood are not known to have been affected by it.

But the unpopular government of Portocarrero was more injurious to the young King, than his own limited

[1] *Hist. of War of Succession.*

capacity and inactive character. That able, but selfish and overbearing, minister, had formed a cabinet completely subservient to his own views, and had seized on all offices of trust or emolument for his friends and dependents,— to whom he was as lavish as the worst of his predecessors. So far (although it rendered him unpopular) he perhaps proceeded wisely, as he might not otherwise have been able to maintain a fixed and permanent administration. But he acted most injudiciously in his continued perse-cution of the heads of the old Austrian faction, who were now willing to reconcile themselves to the existing go-vernment. Some grandees he dismissed from their situa-tions, and others he exiled. Sentence of banishment was confirmed against Oropesa;[1] and Melgar, now Admiral of Castile, distinguished by his exalted rank and princely fortune, was driven into defection by despair. Louis XIV., more sagacious than the minister, had said, in his counsel to his grandson, " that though it might be dan-gerous to place him in the highest situations, yet, in spite of the representations of the Cardinal, it would be pru-dent to take advantage of his apparent desire to justify himself towards his sovereign." Rumours were now dis-seminated that the testament of Charles II, if not actu-ally forged by Portocarrero, had been concocted by him, and afterwards subscribed by the King when deprived of consciousness. The multitude are ever prone to credit surmises, and reports of changes indicated an approaching convulsion.

The intelligence which was now spread over Europe, per-haps with some exaggeration, concerning the altered feel-ings of the Spaniards, and particularly as to the disposition

[1] Oropesa, during the course of the war of the succession, did not openly espouse the cause of the Archduke, but in 1706 he suf-fered himself to be taken prisoner by the allied troops at Guada-laxara, along with his son-in-law the Count de Haro.

of the province of Catalonia, gave hopes to all the powers
who dreaded the close confederacy between France and
Spain, and accelerated the formation of the grand alliance.
Though William III. had acknowledged Philip (his Parliament and a strong faction in England being averse to
war), he only awaited some act of aggression on the part
of France, which, by incensing his subjects, might enable
him to draw the sword. Louis, though he had shown
consummate skill and judgment in conducting all the intrigues concerning the Spanish succession, by no means
exhibited such sound policy in his conduct towards the
European powers after his grandson had quietly ascended
the throne. The impolitic recognition, at this crisis, by
Louis of the son of James II. as King of England, and
the hostile measures directed against the Dutch and English commerce, now afforded William the opportunity he
so eagerly sought. After great exertion, he succeeded in
engaging the governments of England and Holland, over
both of which he presided, in an alliance with the Emperor, who had already begun to fight his own battles in
Italy and Germany. As the public mind was scarcely
yet prepared for the decisive principles afterwards avowed
and acted on, the treaty was both limited in its objects,
and guarded in its expressions. The title of Philip was not
yet denied, nor the rights of the Archduke maintained.
At present, its apparent objects were to obtain satisfaction for the Austrian claims on Spain,—to rescue the
Netherlands from the grasp of France, and to provide security that the crowns of France and Spain should at no
future period be united on the same brow.

By the intrigues of the Count of Melgar, who had fled
from Madrid to Lisbon,[1] the King of Portugal was soon

---

[1] Melgar, though he always continued secretly attached to the
Austrian interests, had been allowed to return from his exile to
Madrid, and such were his talents for intrigue, that, while exciting

afterwards persuaded to join this confederacy, and by the proximity of his territories to Spain, was enabled to introduce the troops of the allies into the heart of the Peninsula.

It forms no part of my present plan or object to record the events of the celebrated War of the Succession, which agitated Europe for so many years,—deluged the Netherlands and Germany with blood,—desolated the finest provinces of Spain, and terminated in the loss of her fair Italian possessions. The incidents of that sanguinary contest have been already detailed in English history, more ably and more fully than I could pretend to unfold them : And, indeed, I fear the reader must have already tired of this long and almost uninterrupted record of hu-

discontent at home, and carrying on a correspondence with Vienna, he became, in some degree, a personal favourite with the Queen, and her confident the Princess Orsini. Portocarrero, alarmed at his increasing influence, named him ambassador to France; but Melgar, deeming that this appointment foreboded him no good, after travelling three days as if on his road to Paris, suddenly turned to the left, and made for the frontiers of Portugal. He was received with much distinction by the Court of Lisbon, whence he published a manifesto, declaring the pretended testament of Charles II. to be a forgery, and proclaiming his allegiance to the Archduke as his rightful king. While in Portugal, he applied himself, with much talent and activity, to forward the cause he had espoused. When the Archduke, however, landed at Lisbon, to attempt the invasion of Spain, he is said to have treated the counsels of Melgar with neglect and contumely. He served during one campaign in the united army, which invaded his country from Portugal, on the frontiers of Leon and Estremadura. But being totally disappointed in his expectations either of a rising among the peasantry, or desertions from the ranks of the Spanish army, he at length died in 1705, the victim of chagrin and disappointed ambition ; " a great man," says Lord Mahon, " if it were possible to be so without fixed principle ; and unfortunate chiefly from his own restless and aspiring mind. Had he been less able, he would have been more happy." (*Hist. of War of Succession.*)

miliations and disasters,—of the reign of worthless favourites,—the profligacy of courts,—the imbecility of kings,
—and the weakness of government.   But no age in history, even though its events be imperfectly sketched, is
altogether without its profit ; and the incidents of that
of Spain, during the 17th century, though they may not
be calculated to adorn a tale, yet point a striking moral,
by teaching us how great monarchies may become weak
and wretched.

At all events, there is no period, at least in modern
times, I could have chosen, concerning which so little has
been written, or of which so little is generally known :
And, in attempting to trace its outline, I have aspired no
higher than to mark out for the English reader a space
which appeared to me to have been hitherto left, nearly
a total blank in Spanish story.

CHAPTER XI.

RELIGION—GOVERNMENT—MANNERS AND CUSTOMS OF SPAIN
IN THE SEVENTEENTH CENTURY.

> What custom wills in all things should we do,
> The dust on antique time would lie unswept,
> And mountainous Error be too highly heaped
> For Truth to overpeer.
> *Coriolanus.*

Of all the nations in Europe, Spain seems to have been the least subject to change, in the character, or in the manners and customs of its people. These were nearly the same in the seventeenth as in the preceding century, and varied not greatly in the succeeding age.

But the influence of religion and the ascendency of the clergy predominated the most steadily and universally. These demand the first and chief consideration, being intimately blended with the whole system of public and domestic life in Spain during the seventeenth century; and whoever wishes to become thoroughly acquainted with the national character must study the national religion.

In the early ages of Christianity, opinions which were subsequently accounted heretical, particularly the principles of Arianism, had been widely disseminated and adopted in Spain,—a kingdom afterwards so distinguished by its adherence to the orthodox faith. It also appears that the ancient church of Spain had long maintained its independence, and had guarded itself against the interposition of the Roman See, or any other foreign authority ;[1] and it was not till the twelfth century that the realms of Aragon and Castile were led to adopt the liturgy and ritual of the Church of Rome, or subject themselves to its spiritual power. After they had submitted to this ecclesiastical vassalage, the early reformers, known by the name of Waldenses and Albigenses, spread into Spain from the south-western provinces of France. During the thirteenth century they had greatly increased in numbers and credit, and possessed[1] churches in various parts of Aragon and Catalonia, which were provided with bishops, who boldly preached their doctrines. The opinions they propagated soon became liable to persecution, but they were not finally extirpated in Spain till the middle of the fifteenth century.

These tenets, however, were destined soon to revive in a new and more formidable shape. The doctrines of Luther early became known in Spain, being introduced by some enthusiastic preachers at Seville and Valladolid about the middle of the sixteenth century.

It was in the interval between the suppression of the Albigenses and the first introduction of the Lutheran principles, that the Inquisition was regularly and permanently established in Spain. There had previously indeed been inquisitors, informers, and persecutors of sectarians, in all the provinces of Spain, but it was not till the close of the fifteenth century that it was confirmed as a national tribunal, by Ferdinand and Isabella. As it was thus instituted at a period when heretical opinions were but little prevalent, it is evident that its primary and original object was the extirpation of Mahometans and Jews; and Ferdinand, in its establishment, was probably less actuated by a blind zeal for religion than by a desire to appropriate the wealth of the Jews within his dominions, and by the belief that the destruction of the

---

[1] M'Crie's *History of the Reformation in Spain*, p. 13.

Moors, who were the great national enemies, would contribute to the peace and security of his Catholic kingdom.

But those flames which had been originally lighted to consume the guilt of Mahometanism or Judaism were kindled, under the sanction of Philip II., for the punishment of Christian heretics; and from that period, though the greater number of sufferers in *autos-de-fè* were still Mahometans or Jews, Protestants frequently atoned along with them. So energetic were the proceedings of the Inquisition during this reign, that before its close heresy was almost totally suppressed; and Spain continued free from schism during the whole of the seventeenth century. In that age, the Grand Inquisitor, who nominated his councillors, secretaries, and other subordinate officers, was appointed by the King under the sanction of the Pope. There were altogether about 200 Familiars belonging to the Institution; and, besides the Supreme National Council of the Inquisition, subordinate tribunals were established at Grenada, Seville, Murcia, and Cordova. The well-known association of the Hermandad, ostensibly established for purposes of police, was in the pay and employment of the Inquisition. This society, which was spread over all the towns and villages of Spain, strictly watched, and unrelentingly pursued, those who had fallen under the displeasure or suspicion of the Holy Office.

It is no part of my object, nor is it within my limits, to give a detail of the procedure of the Spanish Inquisition,—the slight information on which a charge was founded,—the uncandid examination of witnesses,—the complicated and iniquitous circumvention of the accused, by which they were often betrayed into fatal confessions, —the falsification of writings,—the bodily tortures which were applied, when deceit and artifice failed to ensnare the victim,—the mock provisions made for the defence of the prisoners,—the closing scene of condemnation to the flames or gallies, or the long protracted, if not perpetual, seclusion in subterraneous cells.

The instructions drawn up towards the close of the 16th century by the Inquisitor-General Valdes, for the guidance of the Holy Office, were nearly those followed during the 17th century, and are sufficiently arbitrary. It was ordered, that when a criminal was arrested, the Alguazil of the Inquisition should imprison him in so secret a manner as to prevent his being seen or spoken to by any one, or his receiving advice either verbally or in writing. When he had answered all questions concerning his employment, pedigree, or kindred, it was directed that he should be asked in general terms, if he had any knowledge of the cause of his imprisonment. At the end of the examination, in case the intention of the accused was not clearly proved, it is declared to be useful and proper that the Fiscal should demand the application of torture, though Valdes himself admits, that experience has proved that in this crisis, the accused say every thing which is suggested to them. Should the culprit candidly and seriously confess, the Inquisitors shall admit him to a Reconciliation, with confiscation of property conformable to law; he shall be clothed in a penitential habit; and be conducted to a prison called Perpetual or of Mercy.

An account given, in his Travels, by Lithgow, who was confined in the Inquisition of Murcia during the first year of the reign of Philip IV, may be taken as a specimen and example of the proceedings in the different provincial offices throughout the kingdom in the 17th century, and the mode of torturing their victims. During his stay at Malaga, an English fleet having appeared off the coast with suspicious intentions, he was arrested as a spy by the civil government, and some books of an heretical tendency having been found in his possession, he was delivered over to the Inquisition. " And, hereupon," says he, " the second day after Candlemas, the governor, the inquisitor, a canonical priest, accompanied by two Jesuits, one of whom was predicator and superior of the Theatin College of Malaga, entered my dungeon ; where being chair-set, candle-lighted, and door locked, the Inquisitor, after divers frivolous questions, demanded of me if I was a Roman Catholic, and acknowledged the Pope's supremacy ? to whom I answered, I was neither the one, nor did the other." The prisoner was then informed by the Inquisitor, that he was charged with having written, calumniously, against the blessed miracles of Loretto, and against his Holiness—Christ's Vicar on earth. After being exhorted to repentance, eight days were assigned for his conversion, and he was informed that the Inquisitor and Theatins would visit him twice a-day during that period. Accordingly, in this interval, the captive had to sustain the insidious arguments of his persecutors concerning purgatory, images, miracles, and transubstantiation, as also concerning the antiquity, universality, and uniformity of the Catholic Church. Arguments, menaces, entreaties, and an offer of 300 ducats yearly, having failed to induce the prisoner to swerve from his faith, he was condemned, as he informs us, " to receive, that night, eleven strangling torments in my dungeon, and then, after Easter holidays, I should be transported privately to Grenada, and there, about midnight, to be burnt, body and bones, into ashes, and my ashes to be flung into the air. Well, that same night the scrivan serjeants, and a young English priest entered my melancholy prison ; where the priest, in the English tongue, urging me all that he could (though little it was he could do), and not prevailing, I was disburdened of my irons, unclothed to my skin, set on my knees, and held up fast with their hands, where instantly setting my teeth asunder with iron cadges, they filled my belly full of water, even gorging to my throat; then with a garter they bound fast my throat till the white of mine eye turned upward, and being laid on my side, I was by two serjeants tumbled to and fro seven times through the room, even till I was almost strangled. This done, they fastened a small cord about each of my great toes, and hoisting me therewith to the roof of a high loft (for the cords ran on two rings. of iron fastened above), they cut the garter, and there I hung with my head downward in my tormented weight, till all the gushing water dissolved. This done, I was let down from the loft quite senseless, lying a long time cold dead among their hands; whereof the governor being informed, came running up stairs, crying, Is he dead? O fie villains, go fetch me wine; which they poured in my mouth, regaining thereby a slender spark of breath." He was also subjected to the torment of drops of water being allowed to fall gradually from the top of a chamber on the naked body, the pain of which, though at first inconsiderable, becomes, it is said, excruciating when prolonged,—producing the sensation that would be inflicted by some boring instrument. After sustaining a variety of tortures, Lithgow remained about six weeks in the dungeons of the Inquisition, during which time he was supported by a Turkish slave, who privately brought him some provisions; and, at the end of that period,.instead of being conveyed to be burned at Grenada, he was released by the interposition of the British consul and some English factors at Malaga.[1]

The internal horrors of the Inquisition may not, perhaps, be accurately known, but its *autos-de-fé* were public and avowed. During the 16th century, the persons burned alive, or condemned to minor penances, were

[1] *Travels*, part 10.

numerous, and the instances of absolution so rare, that one is scarcely to be found in a thousand cases.[1] From the commencement of the 17th century, acquittals became more frequent than formerly, and the *autos* were exhibited at more distant intervals.   The accession, however, of Philip IV. was celebrated by the *auto* of a Beata called Mary of the Conception, who, during the preceding reign, had deluded many by her pretended revelations, communications and ecstasies ; but had ultimately abandoned herself to unbridled debauchery. The charge, however, against her was, that she had entered into a compact with Satan, and fallen into the errors of Arius and Luther.   She appeared at the *auto* in the habit called the *San-benito*, and ˙having received 200 lashes, was sentenced to perpetual imprisonment.[2]

On the 4th of July 1632 there was a grand *auto* celebrated in Madrid, at which the King and Royal Family were present.   Fifty-three prisoners, chiefly Portuguese Jews, were condemned ; seven of whom were burned alive, and four in effigy.   They had held a species of Synagogue, where, as was alleged, they practised some Jewish rites, and had whipped, and then crucified or burned, an image of our Saviour.   A Jew-boy, in whose father's house the sacrilege was committed, having been missed during some days from school, and interrogated by his teacher, on his return, concerning the cause of his absence, answered, that he had been on guard at the Festival of the Whip.   The master gave information to the Holy Office, which, in consequence, watched the assemblies of the Jews, and literally caught them *in flagranti*, as they had just thrown the sacred image on the fire.   The house of sacrilege was demolished, and a Catholic church erected in its place.[3]

[1] M'Crie, *Hist, of Reformation*, p. 105.

[2] Llorente, *Hist. de la Inquisicion d'España*, c. 38.

[3] Ibid, and Ortiz, *Compend. Cronol.* t. vi. lib. 20. c. 3.   For an

Besides heresy and Judaism, the Inquisition also inquired into cases of magic, sorcery, and intercourse or compacts with evil spirits. At an *auto* held in Cordova, during the reign of Philip IV, among other criminals, Anne of Jodar was condemned for compounding powders or philtres, and forming representations of human figures in wax, for the purpose of injuring the persons modelled, or of producing towards them love or hatred.[1]

The Inquisition was originally established by Ferdinand the Catholic, in a great measure as a political engine, and had always proved itself a ready instrument of the atrocities of despotism. A tribunal, which wrapt itself up in impenetrable mystery—which was superior to every other in the kingdom—before which no laws or privileges could avail—which admitted of no revision or appeal—which came, as it were, in the place of a divine and invisible judge, could not but render itself formidable to the most refractory clergy, or the most powerful subjects. Hence the Inquisition was protected and nourished by Philip II. At the accession, however, of Philip IV. various circumstances might have convinced a wise or humane government, of the expediency of altogether suppressing the functions of the Holy Office, or at least limiting its powers to matters of sorcery and heresy, instead of permitting its cognizance of ordinary civil and criminal offences, in which it frequently interfered with the common judicatories of the kingdom—carrying its system of secrecy and oppression through all departments of the State. But Philip was too indolent to apply any effectual remedy to this evil. So far, indeed, from checking this extraordinary power of the Inquisition, he grant-

account of the *auto-de-fè* held in 1680, on occasion of the nuptials of Charles II. and Louisa d'Orleans, see above, t. ii. p. 203, &c.

[1] Llorente, c. 38.

ed, in 1627, express permission to Inquisitors to take cognizance of offences committed by contrabandists and illegal exporters of the copper coin of the realm, assigning to
them a fourth of all they might seize or confiscate.[1]
The Inquisition clashed in two different ways with the
ordinary tribunals of justice, 1st, By judging both in civil and criminal suits, which did not properly belong to
it; and, 2d, In reclaiming from the ordinary courts the
trial of all individuals connected in the most remote degree with the Inquisition, or demanding for them a total
exemption from punishment. This conflict, which had
begun as early as the middle of the 16th century, had
reached such a height towards the close of the 17th, that
a grand *Junta* was appointed by Charles II, for the purpose of settling these altercations and disputes, which
were constantly arising between the Holy Office and the
civil Jurisdictions of the realm, and which had occasioned
much inconvenience, by impeding the administration of
justice. In their report, the *Junta* declared, that the
inquisitors had, for a long period, used indefatigable exertions to extend their arbitrary dominion, and to deprive
of all authority those who were alone entitled to administer the law by the customs and institutions of the realm
—that there were no affairs, however foreign from their
own province, in which they had not interposed on the
most frivolous pretexts—that they denied their dependence on the power of the Sovereign—that there was no individual whom they did not treat as their immediate subject—that the slightest offence towards any of their familiars drew down their vengeance as much as a crime against
heaven,[2] and that no rule or moderation was observed
in the punishments inflicted. The houses, too, of in-

---

[1] Llorente, *Hist. de la Inquisicion*, c. 38.

[2] " I never knew a churchman," says Lorenzo, in Dryden's *Spanish Friar*, " if he were personally offended, but he would bring in
heaven by hook or crook into his quarrel."

quisitors, were formed into asylums for those guilty of atrocious crimes, by which means the authority of the magistracy and police had been enfeebled and brought into contempt. The *Junta*, however, did not venture to propose altogether to exclude the temporal jurisdiction of the Inquisition, and therefore suggested, that, in matters not ecclesiastical, and not relative to the faith or religion of the country, it should proceed according to the forms and laws observed in the common tribunals—that those accused of ordinary offences should be confined in the ordinary prisons, and not in the cells of the Inquisition—that, in cases where individuals had incurred the censures of the Holy Office, for crimes not connected with religion, they should be entitled to appeal to the royal councils, and complain as for an abuse of authority, and, finally, that it should be precisely fixed what class of persons were entitled to enjoy the privileges attached to members of the Inquisition. On this last point the *Junta* gave many instances of dispute between the ordinary tribunals and the Inquisition, when the former had attempted to take cognizance of offences committed even by the menials of an Inquisitor. In conclusion, the *Junta* recommended to his Majesty to adopt the most vigorous measures for the remedy of those evils which had existed for so long a period, and were yearly increasing. These salutary suggestions, however, of the Junta were never carried into execution, in consequence of the indolence of the King, and the intrigues of the Inquisitor-General Rocaberti, aided by the influence of Froylan Diaz his Majesty's Confessor.[1]

The effect of the Inquisition on the progress of the human mind in Spain during the seventeenth century has been the subject of much controversy. The reign of Philip II. when its power and tyranny were at their height, was unquestionably the golden age of Spanish

[1] Llorente, *Hist. de la Inquisicion d'España*, c. 39.

literature, and it seems too much to impute to the Inquisition the decay of learning and degradation of taste during
the time of Philip IV. and Charles II. But it had no doubt
an injurious effect on science and general knowledge. The
zeal of its ministers in proscribing all opinions at variance
with the interests of the Church of Rome or of the Spanish
clergy—their persecution of those who attempted to disse-
minate apocryphal doctrines, and their exclusion of foreigners and foreign publications, must have checked all liberal
inquiry, and impeded the culture of the understanding.
Spanish divines were themselves precluded from every
field of general discussion, or restricted exclusively to
the study of scholastic and casuistic theology. "Spain,"
says Raynal, "though not disturbed or wasted like
France by religious divisions, remained sunk in the profoundest ignorance. Religious disputes, though injurious
in themselves, at least exercise the mind; they lead man-
kind to reading and meditation, and induce them to study
antiquities, history, and the ancient languages. Hence
arises a criticism which is productive of solid taste and
judgment. They soon grow weary of the topic which
first inflamed them : the controversy is at an end, but the
erudition remains."[1] All books, though on general subjects, composed by Protestants, or translated by them, or
containing notes written by them, were strictly interdict-
ed by the Inquisition. A complete index of prohibited
works, with rules regarding them, was prepared in 1640,
by the Inquisitor-General Sotomayor.[2] In this list the
regulations are much more strict, and the condemned
books more numerous, than in former catalogues. All
persons were forbidden to import, print, sell or read, the

---

[1] *Hist. Philosoph.* lib. viii.

[2] Index librorum prohibitorum et expurgandorum pro Catholicis
Hispaniarum regnis Philippi IV., Antonii Sotomaior, Generalis In-
quisitoris, jussu ac studiis recognitus.

prohibited volumes under pain of excommunication : those who happen to possess them are to consign them to the Holy Office, and confessors are enjoined to inquire strictly at their penitents if they have any such in their libraries.   Booksellers and importers of works are to send catalogues to the Inquisition.   The writings of heretics, as Luther, Calvin, and Zuinglius are totally prohibited,— all controversial works of theology, Guicciardini's History of Italy, Rabelais, and all " *que tratan, cuentan y enseñan cosas d'amores :*" and though Latin versions of the Bible are allowed, it is prohibited in Spanish. " Como la experiencia," it is said, " aya enseñado que de permitirse la sagrada Biblia, en lengua vulgar, se segue mas daño que provecho, se prohibe la Biblia con todas sus partes, impresas o de mano, en lengua vulgar."

But, what was worse than a decline in taste or deficiency in knowledge, a change, it is said, was wrought by means of the Inquisition on the temper of the people.   From the dread of being watched by an invisible and vindictive power, reserve, distrust, and jealousy became the distinguishing characteristics of a Spaniard ; and by the cruel spectacles to which, in the execution of its sentences and decrees, it familiarized the people, this tribunal nourished a ferocious spirit.   Some writers have even attributed to the frequent recurrence of autos-de-fè the sanguinary habits of the Spanish soldiery, which first began to be manifested in the wars of the Low Countries.

The religious classes in Spain during the seventeenth century may be divided into the secular clergy, the monastic orders, and the Eremites or Anchorets.   The regular ecclesiastics are said to have been in this age more wealthy, numerous, and dissolute in Spain than in any other country of Europe.   The corruptions of the Romish clergy have formed at all times a topic of censure and declamation to Lutherans, and of sarcasm or anecdote to the satiric wri-

ters of their own faith. But it is impossible to ascertain
the extent (and that forms the whole question) to which
this corruption prevailed in Spain in the seventeenth century : and it would be difficult to affirm more, with cer-
tainty, than that, while there were some examples among
the Ecclesiastics of distinguished learning and piety, many
of their number were sluggish and sensual, like the Li-
centiate Sedillo, and many wretchedly ignorant like the
Canon Gil Perez.

Spain abounded more than any other Catholic country
in monastic institutions. It has been styled the land of
Romance ; but it might with more propriety be called
the land of

> —— Eremites and friars,
> White, black, and gray, with all their trumpery.[1]

According to a computation made by Gonzales d'Avila
in 1623, two years after the accession of Philip IV., the
Franciscans alone had 859 convents, and the Dominicans
about a third of that number.[2] These religious orders
increased in proportion to the decline of prosperity and
wealth. Nor is it wonderful, when the exterior world afforded no prospect of comfort, or even means of livelihood,
that so many should have deemed themselves happy to find
refuge in a cloister. In the one sex this retreat frequently
partook more of pride or prudence than of piety ; and in
the other it was often the effect of arts calculated to entice a weak enthusiastic mind, or of parental authority and
motives of family interest.

The immense number of monks and friars in Spain,
was a serious grievance during the 17th century. But
the evil was too deeply rooted in the soil to be easily eradicated. In a message to the Cortés of Castile in 1626,
Philip IV. laments the existence of such a multitude of

---

[1] Milton.   [2] Colmenar, *Annales d'Espagne*, t. iv. p. 45.

monasteries and convents,—he regrets that so much wealth should be daily abstracted from the secular to the ecclesiastical members of the state, whose exemption from all contributions weakened the strength of the kingdom ; and he expresses a decided opinion, that if the numbers, both of friars and secular clergy, were diminished, the lives of the remainder would be better regulated, and they would be more reverenced by the people.[1]

If in the early ages of Spain a spirit of poverty and disinterestedness prevailed in its monasteries, it was totally different during the 17th century. In that age the humble asylums of abstinence and mortification had increased to the grandeur and extent of royal palaces. They were frequently surrounded by ponds, orchards, and meadows; their granaries were stored with corn, collected from their tithes or lands, and their subterranean caves were filled with the produce of the vineyard. Even those orders which had vowed the most rigid poverty, such as the Observantins or third order of St Francis, procured dispensations from Rome, in virtue of which, they possessed rents and property, both in houses and lands.[2] The corruption of the monastic orders kept pace with the increase of their numbers and wealth. They broke through the rules prescribed by their founders, and relinquished that austerity by which, at first, they had acquired all their reputation.[3] At different times the kings of Spain at-

---

[1] Cespedes, *Histor. de Felipe IV*, lib. vii. c. 9.

[2] M'Crie's *Hist. of Reformation in Spain.*

[3] Ibid. In their ordinary and ostensible mode of living, however, and in the presence of strangers, the monks of some orders seem to have been sufficiently parsimonious and frugal. Labat, who was entertained at several of the monasteries of Andalusia, at the close of the 17th or beginning of the succeeding century, says, " the tables were spread with large cloths ; but for strangers, there were no plates, spoons, knives or forks, which the guests had to bring with them. The bread was white and excellent, and would

tempted to correct these abuses, but the monks and friars had always the influence or address to defeat whatever measures were directed against them.

The monastic orders sent forth into the world, from their cloisters, those itinerant and preaching friars who usurped the place of the regular clergy, and, by adapting themselves to the taste and understanding of their ignorant hearers, often earned not merely a subsistence for themselves, but brought back a share of their gains to the convent. The eloquence of the pulpit was the only sort of oratory for which there was scope in Spain, or which had at all flourished in the land. But the preaching friars, at least towards the close of the 17th century, were noted for their ignorance, as well as the bad taste and gross absurdity of their discourses. The object of the well known work *Fray Gerundio* by Father Isla, was to expose and check the pedantry and puerile conceits of these popular preachers, and by an exaggerated representation, eradicate from the Spanish pulpit the abuses which had crept into it. Though this book was not written till the middle of the 18th century, the vitiated taste which it was intended to correct and satirize, had commenced before the close of the preceding age. Cervantes himself could not boast of greater success in banishing the romances of chivalry, than Isla in shaming the friars out of the affected, and often profane, allusions or conceits

have been good if not flavoured with anis-seed, which gave it a medicinal taste. The first dish was a porringer of peas, the next stewed fish coloured with saffron, the third fried fish, which was excellent, and, lastly, a small plate of stock-fish. The dishes were of earthen ware, and the goblets of glass,—one of which was placed before each friar. The wine was contained in large leathern bottles with long necks. The priests and monks were supplied with it as often as they made a sign. But the novices were only allowed wine at particular festivals. (*Voyage d'Espagne, &c.* t. i.)

which, before his time, had been mistaken for sacred eloquence. This satiric novel contains a lively picture of the adventures of a novice whose parents, like many of the peasantry and rustics of Spain, were under the dominion of friars, and lavished their scanty incomes in alms and hospitality to itinerant members of the religious orders. Gerundio, in consequence, is early placed under their management, and tuition, and imbibes, from his various teachers, the most fantastic notions. " Let thy style," says one of his elder instructors, who formed the taste of Friar Gerund, " be always pompous, swelling, bristling with Greek and Latin, altisonant, and with as graceful a cadence as possible. Avoid, most sedulously, usual and common words, however proper, for if the preacher speak from an high place, and in a high voice, it is but reasonable that his expressions should be high likewise. Thou hast an illustrious model in the author of the *Florilegium*, and by studying his phrases alone, thou wilt form such a style as will overwhelm the audience with wonder and delight." Nourished by such precepts, Gerundio commences with puns and quibbles, then ascends to anagrams and acrostics, and finally mounts up to quaint conceits and Leonine verses. By the time he becomes friar, he is so hardened in folly and error, that the most powerful arguments against his false ideas of eloquence, urged by one of the most learned and sensible of his superiors, only serve to increase his perversity, and he continues to pursue his career with the highest popularity and most perfect self-satisfaction,—daily avoiding more and more all that is natural, and despising whatever is of easy attainment ; but for ever puzzling his brain to reach new heights of bombast, or to thread his way through the labyrinth of far-fetched conceptions.

From this work it appears that, in consequence of their education, the mouths of the Spanish friars were stuffed with Latin sentences they did not comprehend, and that their heads were filled with theological propositions which they totally misunderstood. The sermons delivered by them were generally such as are called *occasional*, which afforded them opportunities of seizing on trivial circumstances in their own situations or those of the audience, or of the place where the discourse was delivered, to found some far-fetched allusion to a scriptural, or, not unfrequently, a mythological coincidence. Ridiculous tales and pleasantries were often introduced for the purpose of amusing their hearers, and the whole sermon was clothed in language unintelligible and pedantic.. Some specimens of the discourses of Fra Gerundio are given in the work of Isla, and the accumulation they exhibit of strained illustrations of every text, are scarcely caricatured or exaggerated, if we may judge by an extract from a real sermon, quoted by Llorente, as delivered in the year 1671, in the church of the convent of Franciscans at Saragossa.[1] The subject was the ejection of a dumb devil by our Saviour, and the charge of the Pharisees, that he performed it by the power of Beelzebub. But the whole discourse consists of a string of coincidences and allegories, tending to the glorification of the Holy Office and the Inquisitors of Aragon, who were present on the occasion : Moses, it is said, was an inquisitor against his adoptive father, King Pharaoh, and got him drowned in the sea because he was an idolater,—he was an inquisitor against his own brother Aaron, when he consented to the fabrication of the golden calf. Therefore, when offence is committed against the Holy Office, no one should pay regard to the relationship of father or brother. Joshua was an inquisitor against Achan, in making him be burned for having purloined part of the booty of Jericho, which ought to have been delivered to the flames. Thus it is

[1] *Hist. de la Inquisicion d'España,* c. 39.

proved that heretics should perish in fire. But, farther, Achan was a prince of the tribe of Judah, which testifies that every heretic should be denounced, were he even sprung from the blood royal. The Apocalypse, which is sealed with seals, typifies the secret proceedings of the Inquisition, which are so impenetrable, that they seem to be closed with seven thousand seals, &c. &c.

There appears to have been a strong disposition in Spain to shun the duties of active and social life. Philip III, on his deathbed, exclaimed how much more happy he should have been had he passed the twenty-three years of his reign in a desert or hermitage.[1] The more complete the seclusion of life, the greater, as believed by some, was its merit; and the society, even of the convent or monastery, was considered as derogating from the sanctity of perfect solitude. Hence, besides the secular clergy and the monks or cœnobites, who lived together in the communion of the cloister, there were two other classes, who fled from the contagious vices of society, and sought in lonesome retirement the grace of superior holiness;— the anchorets, who inhabited some cell attached to a convent, though without any intercourse with the brethren; and the hermits, who fixed their solitary abode in desert and uninhabited situations.

Hermits sometimes resided in total solitude, but they were considered as entitled to the name and privileges of Eremites, though they inhabited a cluster of cells or huts in the same severe and desolate sojourn. The chief of these establishments were the declivities of the Sierra-Morena, and Montserrat, in Catalonia, whither all conditions of people resorted, as to a sanctuary and a shrine. These abodes seemed to exclude every comfort of life; the cells were placed at some distance from each other, and visiting or talking were strictly prohibited. The

[1] Vernulaens, *Annus Austriacus.*

time which was not occupied in penance or devotion, was employed in making a few simple articles of household utility, which they were permitted to exchange for provisions at the villages in the neighbourhood of their cells.

Such, at least, was understood to be the lives of these religious Solitaries.   But Boccaccio has not spoken more freely of the Italian monks and clergy than the authors of the Spanish romances in the *Gusto Picaresco* concerning the hermits and anchorets of their country.   If these writers may be believed, they were far removed from the abstinence and purity which distinguished. the original eremites of Thebais ; and the long beard and rosary often disguised the sensualist and the knave.[1]

There were *Beatas*, too, as they were called, or female devotees, who were held in high veneration in Spain, on account of their transcendent sanctity, and the communion they were supposed to enjoy with Heaven.   Philip IV. frequently consulted them, and listened to their revelations ; and, early in his reign, he visited, along with his queen and court, the coffin which contained the remains of the celebrated Beata, Luisa de Carvajal, and which was placed in the reliquary of one of the convents at Madrid.

But the Spaniards did not confine their adoration and reverence to their hermits and *beatas*.   The Roman Catholic saints were multiplied in Spain somewhat on the same system as the heathen deities had been in the ages of paganism ; and the worship rendered the saints was not far different from that which the Gentiles offered up to their false divinities.   The unchangeable nature of superstition, has in all times attributed our own passions and feelings to supernatural beings, and endeavoured to propitiate their favour, by flattering their vanity, or soothing their resentment.   In both systems of worship, fear,

[1] See *Lazarillo de Termes, &c.*

hope, or gratitude, a dream, a disease, or some convulsion
of nature, induced the credulous votary to enlarge the list
of his protectors. Each bodily disorder had a saint, who,
if duly invoked and propitiated, could mitigate or cure it.
Every city, every profession, every society of artizans had
its tutelar saint, on whose miraculous interposition the
utmost reliance was placed ; and this delusive confidence
often led to the neglect of those rational means which
tend to avert danger, or alleviate distress. In the commencement of the reign of Philip IV, immense importance was attached to the canonization of four old Spanish saints, St Ignacius, St Francis Xavier, Santa Theresa, and St Isidore the tutelar patron of Madrid. Their
reception into the kalendar was the subject of special in-
tercession by his Catholic Majesty to the Pope ; and the
Emperor, as well as the Kings of France and Poland,
were induced to interest themselves in behalf of St Ignacius.[1] The whole of the 12th volume of the *Obras Suel-
tas* of Lope de Vega, printed at Madrid in 1777, is filled
with an account of the festivals held in the capital in
1622 on account of the canonization of St Isidro, and
with two dramatic pieces represented on the occasion, entitled *La Niñez de San Isidro*, and *La Juventud de
San Isidro*.

But the most general devotion among the Spaniards
was that which they paid to the Virgin. It would be
difficult to express the veneration they entertained for
her, and the two precious gifts she bequeathed to man-
kind—the Scapulary and the Rosary. The Franciscans,
as is well known, maintained, in opposition to the Dominicans, that she was conceived without contracting the
stain of original sin ; and this doctrine of the immaculate
conception was the favourite tenet in Spain. As the Pa-
gan gods were multiplied by being worshipped as different

---

[1] Cespedes, *Histor. de Felipe IV.* lib. iii. c. 2.

deities, though in reality they were the same, so the Virgin was divided into distinct divinities, for almost every city and district in Spain. There was our Lady of Atocha, of Toledo, and Alcala de Henares. And little pictures, or images of these *Madonnas*, were worn by all ranks, as amulets, with the same faith and confidence which the Pagans reposed in talismans. But the Lady of Pilar in Saragossa was the greatest and most blessed of all the Virgins, and the chief object of devotion in Spain.

From the local authority of the Inquisition, the monks and the saints of Spain continued during the 17th century devoted to the See of Rome, with a blind submission and dependence. In a bull directed to Philip IV, concerning a controversy which had arisen at Seville, with regard to the immaculate conception, the King was expressly told, that he and his subjects were not entitled to examine this mystery, but that all the Faithful were bound to acquiesce in the authority of the Supreme Pontiff.[1] In the reign of Charles II. the Pope's Nuncio having disobeyed a mandate of the President of Castile, was amerced in a fine of 1000 crowns. Instead, however, of paying it, he excommunicated the President, who, next to the Prince Minister, was the chief officer of the Crown, and cited him to appear at Rome, to answer for his presumption. The King, with great difficulty, prevailed on the Pope to allow the case to be tried in Spain ; and the Junta appointed for this purpose condemned the President to be degraded from his high office.[2] During the same reign, about the year 1680, the Duke of Veraguas, Viceroy of Valencia (the province of Spain most infested with robbers and assassins) condemned to death an apostate Dominican Monk who had become a leader of banditti, and was taken with arms in his hands almost

[1] Cespedes, *Histor. de Felipe IV.* lib. iii. c. 2.
[2] Desormeaux, *Abrege Chronol. de l'Hist. d'Espagne,* t. v. p. 76.

immediately after he had perpetrated a murder. Though he was convicted of that and many other crimes on the clearest evidence, though he had abjured his monastic professions, and though the Viceroy had consulted some ecclesiastics, who approved of the sentence before it was carried into effect, such was the King's terror of incurring church or papal censure, that he appointed a Junta, with his own Confessor, and the Archbishop of Valencia at its head, which having investigated the conduct of the Viceroy, was of opinion that he had grossly violated the ecclesiastical immunities; and, in consequence of this decision, he was recalled from his government, and compelled to beg absolution from the Papal Nuncio.

On the whole, the ecclesiastical system which had been established in Spain, with such wide and prevailing influence, was little favourable either to the interests of true religion or of pure morality. In that kingdom the votaries of the Catholic faith thought that they marked their zeal for the divine service, and manifested their religious feelings, by the profusion with which they decorated churches,—the pomp and splendour with which they celebrated sacred festivals—the eagerness with which they sought and heaped up imaginary relics, and the frequency with which they told their beads and rosaries.[1] Those who led the most disorderly lives strictly observed

---

[1] " The Count de Charny," says Mad. d'Aulnoy, " who is a Frenchman, but the King of Spain's General of Horse in Catalonia, told me, that the other day being at mass, as he was saying his prayers by his book, a Spanish woman came and snatched it from him, and with great indignation threw it on the ground, saying to him, ' Let this alone, and make use of your beads.' It is strange to observe how fond they are of their beads; every woman in Spain has a pair fastened to her girdle, and so long that they almost touch the ground. They are perpetually using them in the street, —as they play at ombre—as they discourse ; nay, when they are making love, telling lies, or speaking evil of their neighbours."

every injunction of the church—lived surrounded with
relics, and bound themselves by useless vows of pilgri-
mage and penance. Yet all this proceeded not from hy-
pocrisy, but from mistaking the relative importance of
moral obligation and superstitious observances. This
was the creed inculcated not only from the pulpit but on
the theatre; and Calderon especially, the great dramatic
poet of the seventeenth century, and whom Sismondi
styles the bard of the Inquisition, has enforced it in many
of his comedies and *autos*. In the play entitled *Devo-
cion de la Cruz,* his object was to convince his audience
that a due respect for this symbol of the Catholic faith
was sufficient to excuse the commission of every crime,
and to ensure the divine favour and protection. Eusebio, the hero of the piece, is by profession a bandit and
assassin, but, preserving amid all his transgressions a
zealous devotion to the cross, he raises this ensign of the
church over the tombs of the victims whom he has sacrificed. His sister Julia, still more abandoned and ferocious than her brother, partakes with him the same superstitious reverence. Eusebio is at length slain in a
combat with a party of soldiers, whom his own father
conducts against him. But God recalls him to life, in
order that a saint may hear his confession, and thus secure his reception into heaven. His sister, on the point
of being apprehended and brought to just punishment,
on account of her monstrous iniquities, ardently embraces
a crucifix, which happens to be near her. That symbol
forthwith is elevated to the sky, and carries her along
with it into a heavenly and inaccessible asylum.[1]

Previous to their union, the monarchical power, both
in Castile and Aragon, was limited,—the Cortes possessing various rights both of taxation and legislation.

[1] Sismondi, *Hist. de la Litterature du Midi de l'Europe,* t. iv.

But Charles V, who was so powerful abroad, and had no longer, like his predecessors, any infidel enemies to contend with at home, dispensed, in all political matters, with the interposition of his subjects. Before his arrival in Spain from the Low Countries, his minister Ximenes, by flattering the *Comuneros*, without adding to their real consequence, had succeeded in breaking the power of the nobility. Charles pursued the line of policy which his minister had commenced, and now invaded the rights of the people. Irritated by the assistance which the commons had previously given to the attack on their immunities, the nobles either stood aloof from the contest which ensued, or sided with the Crown. The consequence was, that the *Comuneros*, after an enthusiastic struggle for liberty, were subdued. The Cortes and the chartered towns were stripped of their privileges, and the authority of the Sovereign became nearly absolute throughout the united kingdom. Under the sway of Charles's successor the constitution of the realm had degenerated into a pure and confirmed despotism. During the reigns of Philip IV. and Charles II. the liberties of Spain slumbered; and it appears singular that, in the course of that long period, the Spaniards were never once awakened by the voice of freedom. The reigns of both monarchs presented nothing but a series of misfortunes: their ministers were usually detested, the succession to the Crown was precarious, and neither prince possessed the personal qualities which command the fear or respect of subjects. Charles II. was in every point of view contemptible, and Philip IV, though endued with some of the virtues and many of the accomplishments of private life, was almost equally despicable as a sovereign. Perhaps the extreme imbecility of Charles, which was such as rendered him hardly amenable for his actions, may have moved compassion, and this sovereign was dear to the Spaniards, as

the last of a race of monarchs whom two centuries had
naturalized among them. Philip IV. was more culpable
than Charles, as he was not altogether destitute of talents; and it seems singular that, amid all the remedies
proposed for the evils by which the nation was afflicted,
some change in the constitution did not occur to the
people; for the insurrection of Catalonia was not an attempt at reform, but the uprising, without any definite
object, of a population goaded to despair.

During the whole of the 17th century, the supreme
power was lodged in the Prime Minister or Favourite,
who usually delegated a great share of his authority to
some rapacious but dexterous underling, raised by himself to unmerited eminence. Olivarez, or, according to
some writers, Luis de Haro, first checked the freedom of
debate in the councils, by introducing the system that,
on all important affairs, each member should give his
opinion in writing, which the minister himself afterwards
canvassed at leisure with the King. This destroyed the
mutual support and confidence which, in all boards and
councils, each individual derives from the concurring sentiments of his associates; and it was never clearly known to
the council itself, and still less to the public, what had been
the opinion of the majority of its members.

It was the *Council of State*, instituted in 1526 by the
Emperor Charles, which was the chief political council of
the nation; and deliberated on affairs of the highest importance—peace and war—alliances and truces—the nuptials of the king, or other members of the royal family.
Nominally at least, it disposed of the viceroyalties and
governments of the provinces subject to Spain, and also
gave advice to the king concerning matters which fell in
the first instance under the consideration of inferior councils. It usually met three times in the week, but could
be summoned more frequently, if the exigency of affairs

required. The King was its president, and the Archbishop of Toledo the assessor. Its number of ordinary members was not fixed; but it was generally composed of the Prime Minister, the Constable and Admiral of Castile, and some of the chief grandees of the realm, who had previously passed through the most important offices either in the civil or military departments. Such, indeed, was the dignity of this council, that foreign princes, particularly the Duke of Modena, became honorary members. The royal family were proud to be admitted into it, and in the time of Philip IV, his brother the Cardinal Infant on his reception presented each councillor with a valuable jewel, and the subordinate officers with massy golden chains.[1]

The *Royal Council of Castile*, though not the most important, was nominally the highest of all, and in speaking or writing, the King termed it Our Council. It was established in 1246 by Ferdinand III, King of Castile, surnamed the Saint, and consisted of a president, called the President of Castile, and sixteen councillors. Soon after its institution, it was divided into four chambers, each of which took cognizance of the different affairs appropriated to it. The King was frequently present at the deliberations of the Council, and after these were concluded, he usually retired with the president to consult on the various questions which had been propounded. This board, which met daily, had superintendence and jurisdiction over Castile, but in that name, besides Old and New Castile, there were comprehended the provinces of Leon, Biscay, and Navarre. It decided causes appealed from the Audience of Valladolid and other provincial courts, and had cognizance of the conduct of the corregidors of towns, and of judges and ecclesiastics with-

---

[1] Colmenar, *Annales d'Espagne*, t. iv. Vayrac, *Etat de l'Espagne*, t. iv.

in its jurisdiction. It also formed the only check on the papal authority in Spain, because, whatever briefs or bulls were issued from the Court of Rome, or whatever sentences were pronounced by the Apostolic Nuncio at Madrid, could be suspended by its power, and it sometimes did suspend them. Charles I. when in Spain, declared, that if his predecessor Henry VIII. had possessed such a royal council in London as that of Castile, he might easily have accomplished all the objects he had in view, without separating his kingdom from the Church of Rome.[1]

The president of this council held the highest rank in the kingdom next to the prime minister. He paid no visits; and even in his own mansion he took place of every person in Castile. It was customary for the ambassadors of crowned heads to send to beg of him an audience: he always replied that he was much indisposed, but that his sickness should not prevent him from admitting the visit; but however well he might be, he invariably received his guests while in bed.[2] This high officer was not generally a grandee, or even of illustrious birth, as it was thought he might become too powerful if he added the advantages of hereditary rank to such great official dignity.[3] When he lost his situation, of which he might be deprived at the royal pleasure, he still retained his rank through life, and was subjected to all those forms and restrictions attached to it.[4]

What was called the *Chamber of Castile*, consisted of a selection from the members who composed the council, and gave advice to the King on any subject referred by him to their consideration, particularly the granting pen-

---

[1] Zanetornato, *Relazione del Governo della Corte di Spagna.*

[2] Saint-Simon, *Mémoires*, t. iii. 8.

[3] Zanetornato, *Relazione della Corte di Spagna.*

[4] Saint-Simon, *Mémoires.*

sions, pardons, and gratuities, and the presentation to the situations of corregidors and alcades in the various towns and districts.

The *Council of War*, if we may believe some Spanish writers, was as ancient as the time of Pelayo, and the King was its president. The number of its members was not fixed : it met three times in the week, and was divided into several chambers, which separately assumed the direction of the marine, the artillery, the garrisons, and the fortresses of the kingdom.[1]

In the year 1602, Philip III. remodelled the *Hacienda* or *Board of Finance*, originally established by his predecessor under the name of *Contaduria Mayor*. In its new form, this board was composed of a president, eight councillors, and twenty-six treasurers or accomptants. It was divided into several chambers, the members of which laboured in all that related to the administration of the finances, the new imposition or augmentation of taxes, the exemptions from payment claimed by individuals, and contracts or agreements for the supply of the royal household or victualling the army. They also negotiated loans from individuals or foreign states, and issued the salaries of civil offices granted by the King. Philip IV. seeing that, though divided into four chambers, they were still overloaded with business, nominated the supplementary *Board of Millions*, which was so called, because it received the duties leviable on oil, wine, and vinegar, which annually amounted to an immense revenue.

The *Supreme Council of Aragon*, established in the time of Ferdinand and Isabella, met at Madrid. It consisted of three deputies from Valencia, three from Catalonia, and three from Aragon, with a president, who was usually styled Vice-Chancellor of Aragon. It exercised

[1] *Mém. de la Cour d'Espagne.*

[2] *Mém. de la Cour d'Espagne.* Vayrac, *État de l'Espagne.*

the chief superintendence of the affairs of these three provinces, as also of Sardinia and the Balearic Isles. At its
first formation, and for a long subsequent period, it was
also entrusted with the management of the concerns of
Milan and the two Sicilies. But Philip IV. established
a new council, which was called that of Italy, and consisted of six members, two for the Milanese, two for
Naples, and two for the Island of Sicily. Towards the
close, however, of Philip's reign, this recent council had
little employment, as the affairs of Italy were all regulated and determined by a private *Junta*, which met at
the house of the minister Don Luis de Haro.[1]

The *Royal Council of the Indies* was first established
by Ferdinand the Catholic in 1511, at the time when
the recent discoveries in America became an object of
consideration and value to the Crown of Spain. As the
conquests in the New World increased, Charles V. made
some additional provision for the advancement of business, and ordered that this council should consist of a
high-chancellor, a president, eight legal and four military
councillors; and, from that period, it advised with the
King on every matter that related to the Viceroyalties of
America and the East Indies, particularly navigation and
commerce. In its archives were preserved all maps,
charts, and geographical descriptions of the Indian seas
and regions, as also those works which had been, at various periods, contributed concerning the civil history and
the moral or political state of those immense foreign empires which Spain had founded.

Besides these regular or permanent councils, a number
of *Juntas* or extraordinary boards were also frequently
appointed by the King, from time to time, for the special
object of removing some temporary or pressing evil in the
state. Such were often nominated for the purpose of reme-

[1] Zanetornato, *Relazione della Corte di Spagna.*

dying the disorders which prevailed in the finances. The
Council of Regency, appointed by Philip IV. to act during the minority of his son, was likewise of this description.   Olivares, in order to control the authority and influence of the ordinary councils, established not fewer
than seventeen Juntas; but most of these were abolished
immediately after his disgrace.[1]

In fact, during the 17th century, the prime minister,
or favourite for the time, engrossed the whole power of the
monarchy.   Next to him the secretary *del Despacho
Universal*, through whose hands all despatches or representations to the King were transmitted, was supposed
to possess the chief interest and authority.   In consequence of his access to the royal presence, and his power
of awakening scruples of conscience in the breast of his
sovereign, the King's confessor was often employed as the
medium of court intrigue, and his suggestions frequently
contributed to the downfall of an obnoxious favourite.

The nobility, though their titles, honours, privileges,
and exemptions were scrupulously reserved to them, enjoyed, at least during the long administrations of Olivarez and Luis de Haro, but little political power or influence. The Admiral of Castile, whose high office was instituted in the middle of the 13th century, had possessed
for a long period the supreme superintendence of all maritime affairs; and, when he went to sea, he had the chief
command of the fleets.   But in the 17th century his
place had been reduced to a mere honorary title, which
was perpetuated in the family of the Dukes of Medina
del-Rio-Seco till the death of the last Admiral, known
in his father's lifetime by the name of Count Melgar,
who having espoused the Austrian interest during the
contest concerning the Spanish succession, died an alien
and an exile from his native country. The Constable of

[1] Siri, *Mercurio*, t. iii. 1.

Castile had originally the supreme command of the armies in absence of the sovereign, and a military jurisdiction over the kingdom; but, like the charge of the Admiral, his office had dwindled to a nominal title, which, though not strictly hereditary, had always been borne by the family of Velasco.

  And what in this age were the Cortes, those ancient guardians of the laws and liberties of Aragon and Castile —the Cortes who so often had resisted all exorbitant demands for pecuniary aid with equal prudence and determination—who scrupulously examined the accounts of the national expenditure, and often compelled the administrators of the public revenue to specify the mode in which they had employed the sums allotted to particular purposes—who made Ferdinand the Catholic swear, that the subsidy granted to carry on the war against the Moors of Grenada should not be diverted from its object—who, even as late as the time of Philip II, forced that despotic monarch to listen to their undaunted remonstrance against his prodigality, and presented a memorial, requiring that, according to ancient right, the laws enacted by them should be nowhere else repealed! How fallen were they from the ancient spirit of their fathers, in an age when they might have learned truer wisdom! The privilege, indeed, of unavailing representation was still open to them; and Philip IV. during the first years of his reign, sometimes assembled them in great state and form at Madrid, on pretence of discussing public affairs. He treated them, no doubt, with apparent respect, and always afforded them an exposition, nearly as full and detailed as a message from the President of the United States of America, concerning the condition of the monarchy, the military events which had occurred, and the alliances which had been formed.[1] But this very frankness shewed, that he ex-

[1] Cespedes, Histor. de Felipe IV. lib. iv. c. 5.

posted neither control nor contradiction. The last meeting of the Cortes, in the reign of that monarch, was in 1648, when they voted an additional Duty, corresponding to our excise, in order to enable their Sovereign to prosecute the popular war against Portugal.

The royal treasures and taxes of Spain, in the reigns of Philip IV. and Charles II. still annually amounted to about 20 millions of ducats. These consisted, 1. Of the Alcavala, which was a duty on every article sold within the realm. When first introduced by Peter the Cruel of Castile, it was a fifth of the price paid: it afterwards varied from time to time, and in the 17th century, it was a tenth of the purchase. 2. The sales of the Papal Bull, called the Cruzada, one-half of which were conceded by the See of Rome to the Crown, produced an immense revenue in Spain. It was requisite to purchase this Bull, in order to obtain the indulgence of eating those provisions which were otherwise prohibited during Lent; and the scarcity of fish at Madrid rendered it more productive than it would have been in any other capital of Europe. 3. The *Millones*, which was a sort of general excise on the sale of wine, oil, salt, vinegar, and other articles of provisions. There were also duties on the transmission of all commodities from one province of Spain to another. Besides these yearly taxes, the Crown possessed immense resources from its domains in Italy, and the bullion from the American mines. But though the nominal amount of these treasures was ample, the King did not receive into his coffers, as we have already seen, a fourth part of what was exported from America, or levied on his subjects in Spain. Much gold and silver being pillaged in Mexico and Peru, never reached Madrid. Large sums were mortgaged for payment of loans, chiefly advanced by the Italian Republics; and still greater were lavished on pensions and superfluous appointments. On the death of the Marques Ceralvo, in 1680, the King saved 70,000 piastres annually; and this at a time when there was not money sufficient to pay the troops, or even the officers of his household.

Even in the 17th century, the Spaniards were still a warlike nation (as appeared shortly afterwards in the contest for the succession to the Crown), but the military system was so wretched, that all the sinews of war were unstrung. The regular troops were diminished in numbers, ill clothed, ill-fed, and ill disciplined. The soldiers often robbed on the highways, or begged on the streets, or at the gates of convents. Labat even saw some inferior officers asking alms on the streets of Cadiz and in the garrison towns of Flanders, at the close of the 17th century: "Mais on doit dire," he adds, "à leur louange, qu'il n'y a rien de bas dans leur manière de demander : ils conservent toute leur gravité, et leur fierté ; et semblent plûtôt vous faire plaisir en recevant vôtre aumône que vous en avoir obligation." [1] The Spanish militia, which had once been numerous, had fallen away in consequence of the decrease in population, and were no better equipped than the regular army. "You seldom see," says a traveller in Spain of the 17th century, "you seldom see, in the whole regiment, a soldier who has more shirts than that on his back, and the stuff they wear seems, by its coarseness, to be made of pack-thread; their shoes are made of cord ; they wear no stockings, yet every man has his peacock's feather in his cap which is fastened up behind, and a rag about his neck in form of a ruff. Their sword oftentimes hangs by the side, tied with a bit of cord, and frequently without a scabbard. The rest of their arms is seldom in better order." [2]

At the close of the reign of Philip IV. there were only about six ill constructed gallies belonging to the Crown;

Voyage en Espagne, t. p. 167.

which were strictly Spanish, and about eighteen from Sicily, Naples, and Sardinia; though, in the reign of Philip II, Spain had contributed ninety vessels of war to the league against the Turks; and, of this number, the Neapolitan squadron alone consisted of thirty gallies.

It is Voltaire, I think, who has said, that in talking of the manners and customs of nations, it is always proper, for the sake of accuracy, to specify the period and reign referred to; and it will therefore be recollected that I now speak of the Spaniards as they were in the middle and end of the 17th century, the epoch of their lowest degradation, and not as they are at present, or as they appeared in their days of power and splendour, when the Emperor Charles regulated the destinies of Europe. Much, however, that may be said of the 17th century, is also, in a great measure, applicable to the 16th and 18th. In consequence of national pride,—the seclusion of the inhabitants,—their disdain of foreigners, and the little intercourse they held with them, less change occurred in Spain, either in manners or customs, than in most countries of Europe. The Spaniards prided themselves in adhering to their ancient customs, while other nations were throwing aside those antiquated usages which they found to be restraints or incumbrances. The Emperor Charles and his favourite ministers did not ingraft German or Flemish customs on Spain in the 16th century: nor were foreign manners introduced in the beginning of the 18th by a French monarch or his Italian queens; and it was not till after long sway of the Bourbons that some of the higher classes adopted those fashions in dress which prevailed in France at the Court of Louis XV.

But though the manners and customs of Spain changed but little from time to time, there had always been considerable dissimilarity in those of the different kingdoms and provinces of which the monarchy was formed. For a long period Spain had consisted of various Christian states, and the Moorish empire of Grenada.   Hence resulted a diversity in genius, temper, manners and customs; and this discrepance, though modified by the subsequent uniformity of government, by the more frequent communication between the inhabitants of different provinces, and the assimilation of general usages, left to each district a peculiar tinge, of which traces, more or less visible, might still be traced even in the 17th century. Madrid, too, was but a modern capital : It scarcely had sufficient metropolitan authority to stamp its fashions or customs on the rest of Spain ; and Seville, in fact, still continued to be the capital of the south of the peninsula.   What, therefore, may be true with regard to Leon or Burgos, may not always be correct as to Grenada or Barcelona.   " There are," says Bourgoing, in the last century (and his remark must be still more applicable to the 17th century, when the provinces had not been so long united), " there are such striking differences in manners, habits, and even external form, that the portrait of a Galician would more resemble a native of Auvergne than a Catalonian, and that of an Andalusian a.Gascon more than a Castilian."[1]

Manners and customs, too, in Spain were, of course, different in various ranks, and perhaps more so in Spain than in most other countries of Europe.   The system of social organization in the Peninsula, even at the present time, is not very well understood, and still less can we ascertain its relations in the 17th century. In order, however, to view it with any degree of accuracy, it seems necessary to consider it successively in reference to the King and his court—the Nobility—and the People.

It was perhaps from the Moors that the Spaniards were taught to regard their monarchs as somewhat more

---

[1] *Tableau d'Espagne.*

than human. Their widows could not marry any other
prince, however great. Their discarded mistresses were
compelled to withdraw to a convent, where no person was
permitted to see them: and it is related, that on Philip
IV. paying his addresses to one of the ladies of his court,
she replied to him, that she had no desire to become a
nun. His Majesty's horses could never be used by any
other person. One day, while Philip IV. was going in
procession to the church of Our Lady of Atocha, the
Duke of Medina-de-las-Torres offered to present him
with a beautiful steed which belonged to him, and which
was accounted the finest in Madrid ; but the King declined the gift, because he should regret to render so
noble an animal ever after useless. Philip who was most
anxious to preserve the regal dignity, always eat alone
and apart from his family, and seldom deigned to engage
in conversation with any officers of his household. With
their Queens, however, if all relations be true,. the Spaniards seem to have taken considerable liberties. The
Count of Villa-Mediana made an almost public declaration of love for Elizabeth, the first Queen of Philip IV ;
and Louisa d'Orleans, the Queen of Charles II, on her
return from religious festivals and public exhibitions, often
found amorous billets about her mantilla or fardingal.[1]

Every thing at court was conducted with much form
and regularity. " The Court of Spain," says Lady Fanshawe, who was there as the ambassador's lady in 1664,
" is the best established but our own in the Christian
world that I ever saw, and I have had the honour to live
in seven."[2] Even on the most ordinary occasions, as the
king going to mass, much state and ceremony were observed. The gates and doors of the palace were constantly watched by officers and porters, and by the old Spanish

[1] *Mém. de la Cour d'Espagne*, part ii. p. 4.
[2] *Memoirs*, p. 210. 2d ed.

halberdiers, called the Lancilla, which also attended the king along the streets, but rather resembled a burgher or civic guard than a military escort. The time of the royal family was chiefly spent at Madrid, or Buenretiro, in the immediate vicinity. But they had a spring excursion to Aranjuez, and one in autumn to the Escurial. The days for setting out and returning, and even the dresses which the royal party should wear, were all fixed in the court calendar. From the time of Philip II, it had been settled that the court should go some time before Easter to Aranjuez; and the length of the stay, the order of the journey, and its expense, which was fixed at 150,000 crowns, were written down in the books of Ceremonial. Casa del Campo, a hunting-seat to the north-west of Madrid, was also a good deal frequented by the last kings of the House of Austria. The days appropriated to religious rites, to bull-fights and the chase, and the precise hours at which their majesties should rise and go to bed, were all fixed.[1] The chase was the chief amusement and exercise of the last two monarchs of the Austrian line, particularly Charles II. The Escurial was the great scene of the stated royal hunts; but, from the ruggedness of the adjacent country, the stag-hounds could not be followed to any great distance, and the sports chiefly consisted in shooting, hawking, and *battues* of wolves and other wild animals. Dramatic exhibitions formed almost the only amusement in the interior of the palace. To these entertainments, in all their variety, Philip IV. was much addicted. There was a play almost daily at the theatre in Buenretiro, during the period of his residence in that palace, and he frequently attended the splendid scenic exhibitions which were got up for his recreation in the gardens and palaces of the grandees at Madrid.[2]

[1] *Mém. de la Cour d'Espagne*, part ii. p. 34.
[2] Pellicer, *Tratado sobre el Origen de la Comedia.*

Within the royal household the chief officer was the *Mayordomo-mayor*, or high steward. This functionary accompanied the court wherever it went; he stood by the King at public ceremonies or festivals, and on these occasions he had precedence of all foreign princes or grandees of the realm. He also stood by the King's chair when his Majesty was at table, but at other times he had, in the royal chambers, a velvet-covered seat to repose in. He enjoyed the privilege of entrance at all hours to the King's apartments, and had under his orders the other officers of the household, through whom he regulated the expenses of the table, furniture, medicine, and the general economy of the palace. By him was arranged all that related to bull-fights or other public games which the King attended; and to the Mayordomo foreign princes, cardinals, and ambassadors addressed themselves, on their arrival at Madrid, that he might fix the time for their presentation.

The *Sumiller de Corps* or Great Chamberlain, was one of the highest officers of Court, and as ancient as the foundation of the Castilian monarchy. In the seventeenth century his charge was one of great competition among the Spanish ministers and grandees, as no other gave such near and such frequent access to the royal person. On his appointment the *Sumiller de Corps* received the golden key, which gave him free admission at every hour to all the apartments in the palace. He wakened the King, and gave him, when he dressed, some part of his habiliments, and also presented him with the towel with which he washed his hands. He had the charge of the wardrobe, and the reversion of the royal vestments: When the King went abroad in his carriage, he was entitled to occupy one of the places along with him.[1] On such occasions the Grand Equerry rode on the coach-box. But

[1] Colmenar, *Annales d'Espagne*, t. iv.

when the King went on horseback, that officer put on his spurs and assisted him to mount. On public entrances into towns, the Equerry carried the sword of state before his master. He had also charge of the royal carriages, of which the Kings of Spain possessed an immense number. A gilt coach, lined with silk, was a common present to the King from a subject. Charles II., after looking at these gifts, set them aside in his coach-houses, where they were destroyed by dust and time ; and, while they were thus laid up, he drove about Madrid in a shabby vehicle, covered with green wax-cloth.

These superior officers had a vast number of inferiors, to each of whom particular departments in the household were expressly allotted. The gentlemen of the chamber, who were very numerous, were usually the sons of grandees; and it was their duty to wait in rotation on the King with the golden key at their girdle. They aided him to dress, prepared the royal table, carried to him the food, and handed to him the cup from which he drank. An usher of the chamber placed the dishes on the table, except when there was an *olla podrida*, which the chief cook had always the privilege of presenting in person.

The Queen's household consisted of the *Camarera-Mayor*,—some maids of honour, who were styled *Damas de Palacio*, and the *Menines* or pages, who were always children of the highest rank. Noblemen of the first quality in Madrid, professed love openly, and with the royal consent, to these *Damas de Palacio*. Such suitors were called *Galanes de Palacio*, and considered it as a high distinction to be so received, since it required much wit and many accomplishments to qualify them for this amorous service. Without aspiring to an union, they paid these ladies of the Court the most assiduous attention, and often ruined their fortunes by ostentatious expenses, incurred for their sake, particularly in

presenting·them with rich dresses or jewels. The only
return they asked to their passion was permission to sere-
nade them under the windows of their apartments, to
speak to them by means of their fingers, to accost them
on days of public ceremony, and to follow their carriages
when they went abroad. During an excursion of the
Court to Aranjuez, in the time of Charles II., the Dukes
of Montalto and Medina-Sidonia having no employment about the palace which gave them a pretext to accompany the royal party, sent their silver plate, as also
the cooks, butlers, and other officers of their household,
to Aranjuez, in order that their mistresses might fare
more sumptuously, and be more numerously attended :
they themselves following their coaches in the disguise of
muleteers.[1] When these ladies were married, with consent of their royal mistress, they received a considerable
dowry, and their husbands were generally appointed to
lucrative and honourable situations.[2] A match of this
sort was, as we have seen,[3] the first step to preferment in
the splendid fortunes of the Count-Duke Olivarez.

In the time of Philip IV. there were in all about 1000
persons belonging to the royal household, lodged within
the palace of Madrid, and of these about 300 were the
women in the service of the Queen and the·Infantas.
All of these were allowed rations and provisions ; and
although the officers and domestics of the household
were miserably paid, the expenses of their maintenance
became enormous. It amounted, it is said to 2,000,000
of crowns yearly, and the article of bread alone cost
60,000 ducats, as the Venetian ambassador, in the reign

---

[1] *Mém. de la Cour d'Espagne*, part ii. p. 119.   D'Aulnoy,
Voyage d'Espagne.

[2] Colmenar, *Annales d'Espagne*, t, iv, . .

[3] See above, t. 1. p. 27. .

of Philip IV, was informed by one of the mayordo-mos.[1]

, The *Grandees*, who formed the highest class in Spain, and whose rank was as ancient as the monarchy, were elevated above the rest of the nobility, by their privilege of remaining covered in presence of the king.   Those, however, who enjoyed this hereditary dignity were of three orders :—1st, Grandees who covered themselves at once before addressing the king ; 2d, Those who did so after they had spoken, but before they received their an-swer ; and, 3d, Those who were only permitted to cover when they had made their last obeisance and mingled with the crowd of courtiers.   The title of a grandee might be Duke, Marques, or Count, indiscriminately ; but he al-ways bore the ducal coronet, and was addressed by the appellation of *Excellencia*. In the ancient periods, both of the monarchies of Aragon and Castile, the privileges of the grandees were numerous and important.   They were possessed of castles and fortresses, which enabled them often to set at defiance both the sovereign and the laws. They nominated dependent judges in the villages and towns under their vassalage ; they levied tolls and imposts throughout their territories, and main-tained guards for their personal security.[2]   During the sway, however, of the Austrian princes, or at all events during the 17th century, these privileges had been much diminished. They still, however, retained many import-ant immunities.   By the right of *Mayorazgo*, grandees could not be compelled to sell their lands in order to pay their debts, and their creditors could only attach their rents and some of their moveable effects.   No grandee could be arrested for any crime whatever, without the ex-press order of his Majesty, who never issued it but for

---

[1] Zanetornato, *Relazione.*

[2] Laborde, *View of Spain*, t. v.

treason or some heinous offence against the state. Along with these more substantial privileges which still remained to them, the grandees had many advantages in points of respect and honour. They had precedence at assemblies of the Cortés,—at the proclamation of a new king, and at public entrances, over all secular dignitaries except the Constable and Admiral of Castile. One of their number was always chosen as proxy to espouse a new queen, and to receive or welcome the foreign princes who visited Madrid. When the king was on horseback they rode nearest to his person, with exception of the Grand Equerry. At bull-fights and other public entertainments, they occupied the places adjacent to those of their majesties. In the royal apartments they had the right of entrance as far as the picture gallery, which was adjacent to the king's chamber; and their sovereign, in writing or addressing them, called them Cousins German, (*Primo*). They alone had the privilege of driving four mules in their carriages on the streets of Madrid, and being attended by a larger retinue than the rest of the nobility: and when they entered garrison towns, a guard of honour was appointed for them.

Charles V. restricted, it is said, the number of grandees to sixteen families :—Medina-Sidonia, Albuquerque, Escalona, Infantado, Naxera, Alva, Arcos, Bejar, Medina del-Rio-Seco, Frias, Astorga, Aguilar, Benavente, Lemos, who were all Castilians; and the Dukes of Segorba and Montalto, as being descended from the kings of Aragon. These ancient grandees were all considered as of the first class during the 17th century. In that age many were raised to the dignity by creation, who ranked according to their antiquity.

In Castile and Aragon the *nobility* anciently went by the appellation of *Ricos hombres*; but that name at length became so general, that nobles of the higher

rank obtained, in order to distinguish them, the titles of
Duke, Marques, or Count. Though these (who were
termed *Titulados*) did not possess, at least since the reign
of Charles V, the high privilege enjoyed by the grandees,
of remaining covered in the royal presence, and were called *Pariente* by the king instead of *Primo*, they could
yet boast of some important immunities and distinctions.
They were exempted from many imposts, and from all
service in the militia,—they were not liable to confinement for debt, nor could their houses, horses, or arms, be
seized by their creditors,—they were permitted, on public
days, to kiss the hands of their majesties,—they were invited to certain court festivals, and were addressed by the
appellation of Señor.

The nobility, too, were chiefly, if not exclusively, admitted into the three great military ranks of knighthood
—St Jago, Calatrava, and Alcantara. These orders were
instituted by the ancient Gothic kings of Spain, as rewards and distinctions, to encourage their subjects during
the long course of warfare with the enemies of the Christian faith. Originally, each of the orders, like that of
Malta, had a grand-master who governed all its temporal
and spiritual concerns. In course of time these grand-
masters had acquired such wealth and power, as had nearly rendered them independent of the crown. Their
luxury, opulence, and pride, eclipsed the splendour of the
throne ; and their exorbitant pretensions, which struck
the boldest sovereigns with awe, often tended to the vio-
lation of the public peace.[1] From this perilous condition
the nation was rescued by the policy of Ferdinand the Catholic, who, at one blow, annexed all the grand-masterships
to the crown. Subsequently to this event, the affairs of
the orders were administered by a tribunal called the
Council of Orders, which took cognizance of all their tem-

[1] Laborde, *View of Spain*, t. v.

poral and ecclesiastical concerns—of their internal government—of the administration of justice in their territories
—of the convents, commanderies, prisons, and colleges. It
received the certificates of candidates, and pronounced on
their validity, and it proposed to the king fit persons from
the ranks of the nobility, to fill up vacancies in the commanderies, benefices, or offices of judicature.[1]

The nobility were a very numerous class in Spain ; but,
in the 17th century, their power and influence had been
destroyed by quitting their own castles and territories for
a servile attendance on court. Those who had once bid
defiance to their sovereign, now eagerly sought degrading
and almost menial offices about his person, and frittered
away their dignity and opulence in the splendour and luxury of the capital.

During this period the wealth and territorial possessions of some of the nobility and grandees had become
enormous. In France, agriculture is said to have been
recently injured by the too minute subdivision of inheritances. But in Spain a totally different evil prevailed in
the 17th century. By the *mayorazgo* (a species of entail) the eldest born of a family succeeded to the whole
inheritance on condition of transmitting it, on decease,
entire and undiminished to the next heir. There were
different sorts of mayorazgos. By some the succession
was restricted to male descendants ; but, in the chief families of the grandees, it opened to heirs-female on the
failure of males, who thus often transferred their ample
possessions into houses not less opulent,[2] while the col-

---

[1] Laborde, *View of Spain*, t. v.

[2] Baretti (*Journey through Portugal, Spain,* &c. t. iii. p. 172.)
mentions a Spanish law that no eldest born of a grandee could
marry the heiress of another ; but this law must either have been
enacted subsequent to the 17th century, or have been altogether
disregarded in that age.

lateral branches of their own, after remaining in a state of
indigence and obscurity, at length. died away and were
forgotten.

The luxury and expenses of the grandees, who were
possessed of this inordinate wealth, were productive of
little advantage, or perhaps were even injurious, to the
State and to other classes of the community. The late
diminution of coin in Britain has been attributed by
some to the increase of silver plate used for household
purposes. In Spain the enormous quantities of gold and
silver heaped on the side-boards of the Great, withdrew
much bullion from circulation. Almost every noble family could boast of an ancestor who had been viceroy in
Mexico or Peru, or in some other region of mines. Several grandees, it is said, had 1200 dozen of silver dishes and
as many plates, and a nobleman was thought very ill provided, who had not at least 800 dozen of dishes and 200
dozen of plates.[1] These were generally ranged on enormous and lofty sideboards, to which the menials ascended
by silver steps. The sideboard of the Duke of Albuquerque had forty silver ladders, and when he died in the
middle of the 17th century, six weeks were fully occupied in weighing and taking inventories of the gold and
silver vessels.

But the chief expenses of the grandees consisted in
their equipages and retinue. Their coaches and carriages
were numerous and magnificent, and the mules or horses
by which they were drawn beautiful. " Quien es este
Caballero y gran Señor," asks La Rufina at the Diablo
Coxuelo, " que pasa ahora, con tanto lucimiento d e la-
cayos y pages, en ese coche que puede ser carroza del sol ?
El Coxuelo le respondió : este es el Almirante de Castilla, terror de Francia en Fuenterrabia. Quien viene en

[1] Desormeaux, *Abregé Chronologique de l'Hist. d'Espagne*, t. v.
p. 80.

aquella carroza que parece de la Primavera? (preguntò la
Rufina).   Allí viene (dixo el Coxuelo) el Conde de Oropesa," &c, &c.[1]   When a grandee was offended by the
court, it was the custom, as a sort of defiance, to exhibit
himself daily on the streets of Madrid in a splendid
equipage, and accompanied by an immense retinue.

The prodigious number of those retainers called the
Servidumbre, who were maintained in every great household, formed a serious and ever augmenting evil in Spain.
" When a great man dies," says Madame d'Aulnoy, " if
he had 100 servants, his son keeps all he found in the
house, without putting any away ; when the mother dies,
her own daughter or her daughter-in law takes into her
service all the female domestics, and this custom holds
to the fourth generation, for they are never dismissed.
Sometimes, however, they are put into neighbouring
houses, where they receive their rations or allowances.
They come often to the principal house, but it is rather
to show that they are not dead than to perform any service.   I went to visit the Dutchess of Ossuna, who is a
very great lady, and I was amazed to see so many waiting women, for every room was full of them.   I asked
her how many she had.   She told me she had now only
300, but that very lately she had 500 more.["] A master
was not allowed to strike or inflict a blow on any of his
servants or pages.   There was not a scullion in the household but considered himself a hidalgo, and a blow would
have inflicted indelible disgrace.   But it was held quite
proper and correct for a master to run any of his domestics through the body, in a gentleman-like manner, with
a rapier.   Madame d'Aulnoy, while at Buitrago on her
way to Madrid, overheard the cook of the Archbishop of
Burgos say, on being reprimanded for some fault, that he

[1] Guevara, *Diablo Coxuelo,* 8.
[2] *Voyage d'Espagne.*

was of the race of old Castilians, who were as much gentlemen as the king, and somewhat more. " No puedo' padecer la rina siendo Christiano viejo,—hidalgo como el rey y poco mas." The vices of the numerous pages of grandees are the constant theme of the Spanish novelists who picture out the manners of the age. " When this hopeful son," says Donna Maria de Zayas, a novelist of the beginning of the 17th century, in her tale of the Miser Chastised, " arrived at the age of twelve, he was taken into the palace of the nobleman above mentioned in the capacity of page, in order that he might make himself master of those accomplishments deemed most necessary for the honourable discharge of such an office,—equivocation, thieving, lying, and all manner of meanness." Among the other attendants, were dwarfs, both male and female, who were in vogue during the whole of the 17th century.

Besides their domestics, the Spanish nobility often entertained in their houses a certain number of young ladies, under the name of *Criadas* or *Camareras*, whose parents (often themselves noble) could not well afford to educate them at home. These, who formed a part of the family establishment wholly distinct from the hired servants, were under the charge of the lady of the house, and were, for the most part, employed in embroidering in gold and silver, or silk of various colours—chiefly for shift-necks, and ruffles. But if left to their own inclination, they wrought, it is said, very little and talked a great deal.[1]

In the 17th century, the characters of the Spanish nobility were degraded and depraved. Even among the highest classes, the education of youth was miserably neglected. Of this we have seen a deplorable example in the instances of the Prince Balthazar, who was heir to' the monarchy, and of Charles II, who was actually king

[1] Laborde, *View of Spain.* D'Aulnoy, *Voyage d'Espagne.*

from his infancy. The stories of the Captain Rolando in
Gil Blas, and the sons of Montanos in the *Bachelier de
Salamanque*, present but too faithful a picture of the fatal
consequences resulting to youth from the neglect, indulgence, and caprice of parents. After the slight tincture
of learning which such schools as Alcala or Salamanca
could afford the noble Spanish youth, they were generally left by their parents, at the age of fifteen, to their own
guidance. A father seldom allowed his son to travel, and
suffered him to adopt what customs he pleased at home.
From this period of life he spent much of his time among
those courtezans called *amancebadas*, who in Spain were
more artful and intriguing, and possessed greater talents
and accomplishments, than in any other country of Europe.[1] Even the early marriages in which they were engaged by their parents, saved them not from these disgraceful connexions, of which mind and body early felt
the fatal influence. The fascinations of the Spanish ac-
tresses were peculiarly attractive. That amorous monarch
Philip IV. did not escape their allurements, and there
were few of the higher classes who could withstand their
arts and enticements : " Elles sont adorées des Seigneurs"
it is said in the Bachelier de Salamanque, " dans toutes
les villes par où nous passons. Par example, les actrices
de la troupe, qui est actuellement dans cette capitale dé
la province de Grenada, sont toutes parfaitement bien
établies depuis la plus belle jusque à la plus laide. On
diroit que les filles de théâtre ont un talisman pour plaire
aux hommes distingués par leur naissance ou par leurs
richesses."

The *Hidalgos* were an inferior class of nobility, who
had no particular dignity or title, as of Count or Marques, conferred on them, but they partook of many of the
privileges and immunities of the *Titulados*, and account-

[1] *Guzman Alfarache*, lib. ii. c. 6. and 7, lib. vi. c. 2.

ed themselves not less illustrious.   The *Caballeros* of Castile were those knights who served on horseback in the field, but were not expected to bring with them a train of followers.

The chief characteristics of all the upper classes in Spain during the 17th century (except, perhaps, in Biscay and Catalonia), were pride and indolence.   Their pride, however, was often displayed in a manner which, in this country at least, appears utterly ridiculous, and altogether remote from true dignity: " The Duke of Albuquerque," says Lady Fanshawe, " came to visit my husband, and afterwards myself, with his brother Don Melchior de la Cueva.   As soon as the Duke was seated and covered, he said, ' Madam, I am Don Juan de la Cueva, Duke of Albuquerque, Viceroy of Milan, of his Majesty's Privy Council, General of the Gallies, twice Grandee, the first Gentleman of his Majesty's Chamber, and a near Kinsman of his Catholic Majesty, whom God long preserve;' and then, rising up, and making me a low reverence, with his hat off, he said, ' these, with my family and life, I lay at your Excellency's feet.' " [1]

This pride, united with the most invincible indolence, prevented even the poorest hidalgo from earning his subsistence by any of the mechanic arts, or even by what were elsewhere accounted liberal professions.   Laborde, who is so favourable in his views of the character of the Spaniards, and their marvellous improvement since the change from an Austrian to a Bourbon dynasty, admits that " the invincible indolence and hatred of labour which prevails in their national character, has at all times paralysed the government of their best princes, and impeded the success of their most brilliant enterprizes.   All their own historians deplore the effects of this apathy, which has always kept them dependent on the industry of their

[1] *Memoirs*, p. 168.

neighbours, or at least behind them in improvement. The happiest ages of their monarchy have not been exempted from this evil, which seems to be at once the product of the climate and the administration."[1] The tardy and temporizing disposition of the Spaniards, is well exemplified in a maxim or proverb which prevailed amongst them in the 17th century, that one ought never to do to-day what may be put off till the morrow. "Seigneur," says Don Bernardo Castel-Blazo to the Corregidor, " vous sçavez que les Espagnols sont ennemis de travail; cependant quelque aversion qu'ils ayent pour la peine, je puis dire que j'encheris sur eux là-dessus. J'ai un fond de paresse qui me rend incapable de tout emploi. Si je voulois ériger mes vices en vertus, j'appelerois ma paresse un indolence philosophique : je dirois que c'est l'ouvrage d'un ésprit revenu de tout ce qu'on cherche dans le monde avec ardeur : mais j'avouerai de bonne foi, que je suis paresseux par témperament ; et si paresseux, que s'il me failloit travailler pour vivre, je crois que je me laisserois mourir de faim. Ainsi, pour mener une vie convenable à mon humeur—pour n'avoir pas la peine de ménager mon bien, et plus encore pour me passer d'intendant, j'ai converti en argent comptant tout mon patrimoine, qui consistoit en plusieurs héritages considérables. Il y a dans ce coffre cinquante mille ducats.' * * Que je vous trouve heureux ! lui dit alors le corrégidor."[2]

But, notwithstanding this indolence and tardiness of disposition, the Spaniard of the 17th century, when his pride was irritated, his anger provoked, or his jealousy excited, awoke in a moment from his apathy, and was capable of the most violent acts of vengeance. Keenly alive

---

[1] *View of Spain*, t. v.

[2] *Gil Blas*, t. i. livre 3. c. i. The incidents and characters in Gil Blas are both chiefly founded on Spanish originals of the times of Lerma and Olivarez.

to the sense of injury and insult, there were in Spain, as in Italy, certain personal affronts, and some contumelious expressions, that could not be otherwise avenged than by the blood of the offender.   " The Spaniards will keep a revenge for twenty years," says a traveller of the 17th century, " if they cannot sooner meet with a fit occasion to execute it ; and if they happen to die before they have obtained satisfaction, they leave their children inheritors of their resentments as well as of their estates : and the best way for a man that hath given an affront to another, is for ever to forsake his country.   I was lately told of a considerable man who, after he had lived twenty years in the Indies to avoid danger from another to whom he had given some mortal offence, and having understood that not only he, but his son, was dead, believed himself secure.   He returned to Madrid after he had taken care to change his name, that he might not be known.   But all this was not sufficient to save him from the grandson of the injured, who caused him to be murdered quickly after his return.   Sometimes they cause those to be assassinated whom they have offended, knowing well that if they do not kill, they will be slain themselves."

Conceiving that there were certain indignities for which it would be contamination to call the offender into the open field, but believing, at the same time, that these could only be expiated by blood, and deeming the life of the offender but a trifling consideration, in comparison with the reparation due to injured honour, the Spaniards of the 17th century accustomed themselves to the employment of hired bravoes as the instruments of their vengeance.   These assassins were usually from the province of Valencia, and are said to have highly relished their sanguinary trade.   Impunity encouraged and authorised such atrocities, for the privileges of churches and convents in Spain gave, at least for a time, a secure retreat to criminals. " The wretches," says Mad. d'Aulnoy, " who perpetrate these enormities, usually commit them, as near as they can, to a sanctuary, that they may have the less way to escape to an altar, which you often see embraced by a villain, with his poniard reeking in his hand, and himself besmeared with the blood of the victim he has murdered." [1]

Nor did such assassinations incur for the employer, or the instrument of his vengeance, any great share of public disapprobation. The most popular comedies were those in which a murderer was saved from the forfeit of his crimes by some sudden and miraculous interposition of Providence. Most of the dramatic heroes of this age have been forced to fly their native town or country on account of homicide. They are exposed, it is true, to the vengeance of relations, and the pursuits of justice. But they are favoured by public opinion, and are under the protection of the Faith. They save themselves from convent to convent, from altar to altar, and the priests, from their confessionals and their chairs, inculcate charity and compassion to a brother who has yielded for a moment to the vivacity of imagination.

These assassinations were sometimes committed in the boldest and most daring manner. Early in the reign of Philip IV, Juan de Tassis, Count of Villamediana, eldest son of the Count d'Oñate, an accomplished youth of twenty-one years of age, one day asked Luis de Haro, afterwards prime minister, but, at that time, a young man about his own period of life, to go an airing with him in his coach. To this Don Luis consented, and when they had arrived near that part of a principal street where it terminates at the gate of Guadalaxara, Don Luis stretched himself from the coach to give some directions to an attendant. At that moment the Count, who was leaning

---

[1] *Voyage d'Espagne,* t. 1.

on the other side of the vehicle, received a mortal wound by a dagger from the hand of one who had mounted on its steps. The assassin escaped before Luis de Haro or the attendants could come up with him, and he was never afterwards apprehended.[1] No inquiry was made, or suit instituted, nor was it ever known by whom the crime had been perpetrated, or what were the motives of the action. Even at his early age Villamediana had been distinguished by his verses and successful imitation of the fashionable poet Gongora ; and Quevedo attributes his murder to the vengeance which a dissolute life, a satirical muse, and a sarcastic tongue might readily excite. But an absurd and improbable story was subsequently prevalent in Spain, that he had set fire to the theatre at Buenretiro, in order that he might have the delight of touching the Queen's foot, while bearing her from the flames—that the Count was seen in the act by a page, who informed the Count d'Olivarez, and that he, in return, laid the proofs of it before his Majesty, who was so highly exasperated at the audacity of his subject, and at the desperate expedient to which he had resorted, that he caused him to be thus privately slain.[2] The boldness of the attempt, the impunity of the assassin, the total supineness of the police, an ambiguous phrase of the poet Gongora, that the hand was treacherous, but the impulse sovereign, and a warning said to have been given to him on the very day of his death, by the Confessor of Balthazar de Zuniga, the uncle of Olivarez, and at that time prime minister, afforded some countenance to the rumour, that Villamediana had fallen a victim to royal jealousy and revenge.[3]

Jealousy and love, which are said to have been the pre-

---

[1] Cespedes, *Hist. de Felipe IV.* lib. iii. c. 19.
[2] D'Aulnoy, *Voyage d'Espagne.*
[3] Holland's *Life of Lope de Vega*, t. i.

dominant passions of Spaniards during the 17th century, were frequent excitements to such acts of atrocious vengeance. In the early ages of Spain, these feelings partook of that chivalrous spirit which prevailed during the wars with the Moors, and which perhaps for some time survived the foundation of the Spanish monarchy. From the seclusion of the fair, and those obstacles derived from the jealous customs of the Moors, love had been converted into a species of warm and almost phrenzied devotion. It was associated with ideas of honour and religion, and the jealousy of lovers was but a generous rivalry to surpass each other in gallant and noble actions. Fiction generally presents but a highly coloured picture of the manners of the age, and it is in this period that we have stories of lovers expiring from the joy of meeting, or the grief of parting—surmounting almost insuperable difficulties—engaging in deeds of desperate valour, and devoting themselves to perils and death, not merely for the safety, but for some slight and temporary gratification to a mistress. But in the reign of Charles V. regular wars on the continent of Europe succeeded to adventures in Grenada, and encounters with the gallant Abencerrages: the conquests in America depraved the morals of the Spaniards; commerce and wealth subdued their chivalrous spirit, and the repose of an ignominious peace in the reign of Philip III. destroyed all that remained of warlike virtue, and romantic illusion. Hence, in the 17th century, the passions of the Spaniards were manifested by a train of intrigues and stratagems, in which Italian address prevailed more than Castilian love or honour. This was the period of jealous husbands and brothers—duennas—ingenious lovers—serenades and elopements—of all those amorous devices which have been so well portrayed in the novels of Cervantes, Zayas, and Montalvan, as also in the comedies of Lope de Vega, and Calderon.

How closely the delineations of the dramatist and novelist approached in this age to the occurrences of real
life, is well exemplified in an adventure of Sir Kenelm
Digby, when he and other noble youths of England resorted to Madrid, in 1623, during the abode of Charles
Prince of Wales in that capital.   He relates, that the
very night of his arrival, while returning home to his
lodgings from the English ambassador's with one of Lord
Bristol's family, whom he calls *Leodivius*, " a rare voice,
accompanied with a sweet instrument, called their ears to
silent attention, while with their eyes they sought to inform themselves where the person was that sung, when
they saw a gentlewoman in a loose and night habit, that
stood in an open window (supported like a gallery with
bars of iron) with a lute in her hand, which, with excellent skill, she made to keep time to her divine voice, and
that voice issued out of as fair a body, by what they could
judge at that light, only there seemed to sit so much sadness on her beautiful face, that one might judge she herself took little pleasure in her own soul ravishing harmony.   The three spectators remained attentive to this
fair sight and sweet music, Leodivius only knowing who
she was, who coming a little nearer towards the window,
fifteen men all armed, as the moon shining upon their
bucklers and coats of mail did make evident, rushed out
upon him with much violence, and with their drawn
swords made so many furious blows and thrusts at him,
that if his better genius had not defended him, it had
been impossible that he could have outlived that minute ;
but he, nothing at all dismayed, drew his sword and
struck the foremost such a blow on the head, that if it
had not been armed with a good cap of steel, certainly he
should have received no more cumber from that man."
After this exploit, Leodivius seeing how unequal would
be the contest, went back to the ambassador's house for

succour, leaving Sir Kenelm and his other friend to bear
meanwhile the brunt of the battle somewhat at disadvantage, since, besides the great disparity of numbers,
" the assailants had at the top of their bucklers artificial
lanterns, whose light was cast only forwards by their being
made with an iron plate on that side towards the holders,
so that their bodies remained in darkness, and they had
the advantage of seeing an opponent when he could not
see them." Sir Kenelm and his friend then began to remonstrate on this discourteous treatment, when one, who
seemed to be of the best quality among them by a cas-
sock embroidered with gold, which he wore over his jack
of mail, answered, with much fury in his manner, " Villain, thou hast done me wrong which cannot be satisfied
with less than thy life, and by thy example let the rest
of thy countrymen learn to shun those gentlewomen
where other men have interest, as they would houses in-
fected with the plague, or the thunder that executeth
God's vengeance." In spite of this rodomontade, Sir
Kenelm, after a long scuffle, " stepping in with his left
leg, made himself master of his sword, and with his own
did run him into the belly under his jack, so that he fell
down with a deep groan, that his life was at her last moment. The others by that time knew him to be their
master, for whose quarrel only they all fought, so that
they left Sir Kenelm, and all of them attended to succour their wounded lord. But all too late, for, without
ever speaking, he gave up his ghost in their arms. The
next day the cause of this quarrel was known, which was,
that a nobleman in that country having interest in a
gentlewoman that lived not far from the ambassador's
house, was jealous of Leodivius, who had carried his affections too publicly ; so that this night he had forced her
to sing in the window where Leodivius saw her, hoping

by that means to entice him to come near to her, while
he lay in ambush to take his life from him."[1]

The paltry pride and indolence, and even the jealousy
of the Spaniards, were injurious to the relations of social
life and the comfort of domestic arrangements. In the
country, the palaces of the grandees, in consequence of
the ambition of their owners to shine at court or hold servile offices near the person of the sovereign, were in a
great measure deserted, or were only inhabited by fallen
ministers—the Lermas and Uzedas—or those whom it
was found expedient, in consequence of their dangerous
characters or their hostility with the prevailing political
party, to banish to a distance from court. But in the
17th century, the castles of the nobility had scarcely yet
had time to fall into decay or disorder, and many stately
fabrics yet arrested the admiring gaze of the traveller.
Madame d'Aulnoy, who visited Lerma in 1679, says that
the palace which was built by the Cardinal-Duke, Philip
the Third's minister, " stands on the side of a hill, and
on the way to it you pass through a spacious place surrounded with arches and galleries. This castle consists
of four vast piles of building, which make a complete quad-
rangle of two ranges of porches within the court, which
are near as high as the roof, and hinder the apartments
from prospects on that side. The windows of all the
chambers look forward into the country. The apartments
are spacious and very finely and curiously gilt. There
are a prodigious number of them, and very richly furnished. Near the castle there is a great park, which ex-
tends itself along the plain, and through it runs a river
and several lesser streams. On the banks of the river
there are rows of large trees, and not far from thence a
wood, so that I believe in fine weather this is a delightful
residence." Like the Escurial and some others of the chief

[1] *Memoirs of Sir K. Digby*, p. 136.

palaces in Spain, there was a chapel and a convent adjacent, which communicated by a long gallery with the secular abode.

In the capital seven or eight streets were appropriated to tradesmen and artisans, while the other quarters were occupied by persons of some distinction, and in these there were no shops except a few, where pastry, sweetmeats, wine, and ice, were sold. Though the superior streets contained many large and magnificent mansions of grandees, they already presented to view some half-ruined houses of the indolent and impoverished Hidalgos.

The first floor of every house built in Madrid belonged, by law, to the king. The proprietor generally purchased it, otherwise his majesty sold it to whom he pleased. So ancient was this usage that, in the 15th century, there existed a council called the *Aposento*, which was directed to attend, on this point, to the interests of the crown. The houses of the higher classes at Madrid, though only built of brick and clay, were elegant and spacious. In the 17th century they were seldom higher than three stories. In most of these houses there were ten or twelve rooms (generally of an oblong shape) on a floor, sometimes twenty or thirty, and in the smallest six or seven. Sir Benjamin Keene, while the Resident at Madrid in the beginning of the 17th century, inhabited a house which had been built by one of the descendants of Fernando Cortez, and which, though it had been half burned down, was still capable of containing, with ease, 300 inmates.[1] Even the best and largest houses, however, were generally ill lighted. Glass being scarce, there were many which had small windows that were merely closed with lattices. At Madrid, and still more in the great towns in the south of Spain, the windows were purposely left small, in order to exclude the sultry and overheated air

[1] Clarke, *Letters concerning the Spanish Nation*, let. 19.

of the atmosphere.[1] Few of the houses in this age had chimnies. In place of them, a flat open brass pan called a *brasero*, containing charcoal, and usually raised, about half a foot from the ground, on a wooden frame, occupied the centre of the apartment. When the weather was cold, the inmates of the house and their visitors sat around its glowing embers, resting their feet on the frame by which it was supported.

Almost all the houses, even those on the smallest scale, had their summer and winter chambers, and some of the larger had rooms for autumn and others for spring. The winter apartments were high up, generally on the third story, and were inhabited from the beginning of October till the end of May, when they were deserted for the summer chambers. These, which were low down, were generally the largest and most commodious. Their floors were plastered and white-washed, or so well polished that they looked like marble. The walls were hung round with small mats, and on the top of these were hung pictures and mirrors. Cushions of gold and silver brocade were placed on the carpets. Cabinets, busts, and vases, were interspersed through the rooms, and at small distances from each other stood silver cases, filled with orange and jessamine trees. The household furniture, which was rich, though clumsily made, was frequently changed according to the season of the year. The winter beds were of velvet trimmed with the thick gold and silver lace called galloon. In summer there were no curtains nor ought else about the bed, except coloured gauze to keep off the gnats and other insects. In most of the rooms there were canopies,—the privilege of sitting under one being at that time highly valued, and assumed by almost every person of distinction. The mansions of the grandees, in consequence of viceroys returning home from

[1] Labat, *Voyage d'Espagne,* t. i. p. 160.

time to time laden with the curiosities and treasures of other realms, were filled with tapestry, cabinets, paintings, mirrors, and plate. Viceroys of Milan and Naples, or their descendants, had admirable pictures,—the governors of the Low Countries possessed the finest Arras, with which they usually decorated the winter apartments: the viceroys of Sicily and Sardinia had exquisite embroideries—those of the Indies precious stones, and vessels of gold or silver.

The summer apartments usually looked and entered to a court, on the pavement of which, water being thrown in the morning, left a pleasant coolness ; when dry, it was spread over with mats made of rushes, and sometimes dyed with a variety of colours. To the more sumptuous edifices gardens were attached, in which the family walked in the evening, and which were adorned with statues, fountains, and grottoes. Among the finest of these, in the middle of the 17th century, were the gardens of the Duke d'Ossuna and the Count d'Oñate ; but above all, those of the Admiral of Castile, called Florida, which were then in the outskirts of Madrid, but I believe are now built on, and comprehended within, the city.

In the early part of the 17th century, the master of the house had his table to himself, and the mistress with her children either eat altogether apart, or they sat after the Moorish fashion on the floor, over the carpet of which a cloth was spread. About the middle, however, of the 17th century, it began to be the custom amongst some of the greatest families in Spain to eat together.[1] It was not the custom of the Spaniards to invite their friends to feast with them at dinner, except on solemn and stated occasions, as the anniversaries of birth-days and weddings, or the promotion of some member of the family to a high or lucrative situation. These great entertain-

[1] Sir Richard Fanshawe's Letters, p. 81.

ments were given with immense displays of plate and embroidery. " I must not," says Lady Fanshawe, " pass by the description of the entertainment, which was vastly great, tables being plentifully covered for about 300 persons. The furniture was all rich tapestry, embroideries of gold and silver on velvet, cloth of tissue, both gold and silver, with rich Persia carpets on the floor. Very delicate fine linen on the tables, new cut out of the piece, and all things thereunto belonging. The plate, too, was vastly great and beautiful." But though it was not the practice to give dinner parties at home on ordinary occasions, it was much the usage to make pleasure excursions to the country, where at their villas the nobility provided collations for their guests. These collations, too, seem to have been the most ordinary entertainments in the capital: " The Princess of Monteleone," says Madame d'Aulnoy, " gave us a collation. Her women, to the number of eighteen, brought every one of them a great silver basin, full of dried sweetmeats wrapped up in paper, cut and gilt for the purpose; in one there was a plumb, in another a cherry or apricot, and so on in all the rest. There were some ancient ladies present, who, after they had eaten of these sweetmeats till they were like to burst, filled five or six handkerchiefs full, which they bring with them on purpose, and although they are well observed, yet no notice seems to be taken. Afterwards chocolate was presented, and every one had a china cup full on a little dish of agate set in gold, with sugar in a box of the same; one drinks it with biscuit or else with some thin bread as hard as if it were toasted, which they bake so on purpose. There are some who will drink six cups, one after another." With regard to the provisions in Spain, Madame d'Aulnoy says that the flesh was lean, dry, and black, but she speaks favourably of the bread, pheasants, partridges, and the hams from

the frontiers of Portugal, as also of the fruit and vegetables. Lady Fanshawe, who was in Spain only a few
years before Madame d'Aulnoy, gives a still more favourable account of eatables in Spain. " I find it," she says,
" a received opinion that Spain affords not food, either
good or plentiful. True it is, that strangers that neither
have skill to choose nor money to buy will find themselves at a loss; but there is not in the Christian world
better wines than their midland wines are especially, besides sherry and Canary. Their water tastes like milk;
their corn white to a miracle, and their wheat makes the
sweetest and best bread in the world ; bacon beyond belief good ; the Segovia veal much larger and fatter than
ours ; mutton most excellent ; capons much better than
ours. They have a small bird that lives and fattens on
grasses and corn, so fat that it exceeds the quantity of
flesh. They have the best partridges I ever eat, and the
best sausages ; and salmon, pikes, and sea-breams, which
they send up in pickle called *escabeche* to Madrid, and
dolphins, which are excellent meat, besides carps and
many other sorts of fish. The cream, called *nata*, is much
sweeter and thicker than any I ever saw in England ;
their eggs much exceed ours, and so do all sorts of salads,
and roots, and fruits. What I most admired, are melons,
peaches, burgamot pears, grapes, oranges, lemons, citrons,
figs, and pomegranates. Besides that, I have eaten many
sorts of biscuits, cakes, cheese, and excellent sweetmeats,
I have not here mentioned, especially manger-blanc ; and
they have olives, which are nowhere so good; and their
perfumes of amber excel all the world in their kind.[1]"
But however well supplied might be the table of the am-
bassadress with the veal of Segovia, Labat, who travelled
in Spain about forty years afterwards, informs us that
veal and lamb were not at all used by the Spaniards, as

[1] *Memoirs*, p. 208.

they considered it a want of prudent economy to destroy animals before they had reached perfection. Their beef, too, as we are informed by the same traveller, consisted entirely in bull flesh. " On sera," says he, " peutêtre surpris de ce que je ne mets que des taureaux, et point de boeufs dans la boucherie. Mais il faut sçavoir que c'est une pratique observée religieusement par toute l'Espagne (du moins, des gens très dignes de foi me l'ont assuré) on ne sçait ce que c'est que de châtrer des taureaux, ni de tuer des vaches, dont la chair pourroit être plus tendre, à moins que leur extrême vieillesse ne les empêche d'être propres à la generation.[1]" But, in fact, the Spaniards of that age eat little flesh except dressed up, their chief food being pigeons, pheasants, and their different sorts of ollas. The *puchero* was compounded of beef and chick peas, and a variety of other vegetables seasoned with bacon. The *olla podrida* was a richer and more expensive mixture of different sorts of meats and delicacies. In all such dishes pork was an universal ingredient. This arose from a desire to avoid a suspicion of Judaism, and a relish for bacon became a profession of faith and a test of orthodoxy. Most of the ordinary classes took their subsistence at cook's shops, which were established at the corners of streets. There, stood great kettles at which people got leeks, beans, and garlic, or a little broth, in which they steeped their bread.

Much has been said and written concerning the temperance and moderation of the Spaniards in the article of food; but on this point, Lithgow, who travelled in Spain early in the reign of Philip IV, draws a nice distinction. " The Spaniard," says he, " is of a spare diet and temperate if at his own cost he spend, but if given gratis he hath the longest tusks that ever played at table."[2]

But though it may have been possible to procure to-

[1] *Voyage d'Espagne*, &c. t. i. p. 255–6.   [2] *Travels*, p. 356. 2d ed.

lerable provisions in Spain, and though the cookery in
private families may have been excellent, the inns or
posadas, during the 17th century, were proverbially bad.
Throughout the Spanish provinces the lords and proprie-
tors of certain cantons or jurisdictions, farmed out the
right of erecting inns on their territories, and there was
thus no emulation, as there could be no competition within a certain district. " But I should tell you," says Mad.
d'Aulnoy, " how one is served at these inns, they being
all alike. When you come into one of them, wearied and
tired, roasted by the heat of the sun or frozen by the
snows, you see neither pot on the fire nor plates washed.
You enter into the stable, and from thence to your chamber. The staircase by which you go up is very strait,
and rather resembles a steep ladder ; you are then shown
an apartment hung with little scurvy pictures of saints :
the beds are without curtains ; they have only one cup
in the house, and if the mule-drivers get first hold of it,
which commonly happens, you must stay patiently till
they have done with it, or drink out of an earthen pitcher.
Though you arrive at midnight, you must send to the
butchers, the market, the tavern, the bakers, in fine to all
parts of the town, to gather wherewith to make a sorry
meal. They put what you would have roasted, on tiles,
and when it is well grilled on one side, they turn the
other ; when it is flesh they fasten it to a string, and so
let it hang on the fire, and turn it with their hands ; so
that the smoke makes it so black it is disgusting to look
on. I think there cannot be a better representation of
hell than these sort of kitchens and the persons in them."
This *venta* was in old Castile, but the Countess did not
find that the inns in any degree improved as she approached Madrid.

All Spanish writers, particularly the novelists, though
on most points jealous in what concerns the credit of their

country, confirm the truth of this picture, and bear ample
testimony to the wretched accommodation in the posadas, and to the villany of vintners.　They are represented as selling rain water discoloured with sloes, for wine,[1]
—giving mules' flesh in ragouts for veal,[2] and cats' for
hare.[3]　Gongora, in one of his satirical sonnets, thus
breaks out in vituperation of Spanish inns :—

> O Posadas de Madera,
> Arcas de Noe, adonde
> Si llamo al Huesped, responde
> Un buez, y sale una fiera ;
> Entrome (que non deviera)
> El cansacio, y al momento
> Lagrimas de ciento en ciento
> A diramallas me obliga,
> Non se qual primero diga
> Humo o arrepentimiento.

The knavery of Spanish innkeepers has been proverbial, and the unceasing theme of comic novels.　Yet
their dishonesty had not been universal.　Sir Richard
Fanshawe, while on a journey through Spain, " went to
bed for some few hours to refresh himself, in a village five
leagues from Madrid, and slept so soundly, that notwithstanding the house was on fire, and all the people of the
village there, he never waked.　But the honesty of the
owners was such, that they carried him and placed him,
still asleep, on a piece of timber near the highway, and
there he awaked and found his portmanteau and clothes
by him, without the least loss." [4]

In Spain, the fashions of dress, though they varied somewhat in the different provinces, appear to have changed

---

[1] Quevedo, *Fortuna con Seso.*　　　[2] Guzman Alfarache.
[3] Gil Blas.　It appears that travellers in Spain are still somewhat exposed to a risk of the cat.　(Southey's *Letters from Spain
and Portugal.*)
[4] Lady Fanshawe's *Memoirs*, p. 62.

but little. " After the expulsion of the Moors," says
Laborde, " the Goths and native Spaniards confounded
together, and forming but one nation, adopted also one,
costume. At the beginning of the 16th century it consisted of breeches of serge or cloth bound with garters,
and fastened up with points ; a doublet or vest with large
flaps, a cape and a hood ; a leathern purse at the girdle ;
a flat cap of wool or velvet; a round cloth hat or bonnet;
the ruff was added in 1522. This was the true Spanish
dress, which was continued till the accession of Philip
V, in the beginning of the 18th century. Hitherto the
Spaniards had known little of luxury in dress ; wool was
the material they employed, unadorned with gold, silver,
or silk. Philip II, who began to reign in 1556, was the
first who wore silk stockings, a pair of which were presented to him by the wife of Don Lopez de Paradilla,
who had knitted them. In the 17th century, the Spanish habit, without changing its form, became more rich,
and elegant. It was still short, with large flaps and
hanging sleeves, and covered with a frieze cloak. The
breeches were very tight ; taffety sleeves were attached
to the shirt, and all these parts of the dress were black ;
a *golilla* or white ruff was worn round the neck ; a dagger at the girdle, and a very long sword. By degrees
the dress came to be made of various kinds of silk fabrics
—as taffety, satin, moreen, damask, and velvet ; but it
was still black. At the same time a hat took place of
the cap, which was round, usually turned up in front,
and often adorned with a plume of feathers. The Spaniards had then two kinds of swords ; one called swords
d'Arçon, and the second *de Golilla.* The first, which
were shorter, and had a broader blade, were only used on
horseback. The second kind were long, narrow, and had
a basket hilt." [1]

[1] *View of Spain,* t. v.

The Countess d'Aulnoy, who, whatever may be her inaccuracy in other particulars, may be relied on for her accounts of dress and fashions, thus describes a young Spanish *Guapo*, or Spark of the 17th century. "His hair was parted on the crown of his head, and tied behind with a blue ribbon, about four fingers breadth, and about two yards long, which hung down at its full length; his breeches were of black velvet, buttoned down on each knee with five or six buttons; he had a vest so short that it scarce reached below his pockets; a scollopped doublet, with hanging sleeves, about four fingers breadth, made of white embroidered satin. His clock was of black baze, and, being a gallant, he had wrapped it round one arm, with which he held a buckler, with a steel spike standing out in the midst of it. This they carry with them when they walk on adventures during night. In the other hand, he held a sword longer than a half-pike, and the iron for its guard was enough to make a breast-plate. He had likewise a dagger, with a narrow blade, fastened to the belt round his back. He had such a strait collar, that he could neither stoop nor turn about his head. His hat was of a prodigious size, with a great band, larger than a mourning one, twisted about it. His shoes were of as fine leather as that whereof gloves are made, and all slashed and cut, notwithstanding the cold, and so exactly close to his feet, that they seemed to be pasted on. They had no heels. He made me, on entering, a reverence after the Spanish fashion—his two legs across one another, and lowly stooping, as women do when they salute one another. He was strongly perfumed, and was careful to tell me, that there were few courses of bull-fights wherein he ventured not his life."

The dress of women of distinction was not far different in the 17th from what it had been in the 16th century. At the Castle of Aranda, the Countess d'Aulnoy saw

a picture of Elizabeth, the Queen of Philip II, precisely
in a similar garb with that worn by the Countess of Lemos, whom she met with in her travels at least 100 years
after this portrait had been painted. The attire of ladies
of quality was very rich and magnificent, particularly in
gems and pearls. When the Dutchess d'Albuquerque
came to visit Lady Fanshawe, " Her Excellency had on,
besides other very rich jewels, as I guess, about two thousand pearls, the roundest, the whitest, and the biggest
that ever I saw in my life."[1] Cervantes, in one of his *No-
velas Exemplares*, thus describes the dress of a young
Spanish lady of rank in the beginning of the 17th century. " Being thus resolved, the next day they apparelled
Isabella in the Spanish fashion ; in a gown of green satin,
cut upon cloth of gold, embroidered with pearls ; wearing
a great chain of rich orient pearls about her neck ; having
a hatband of diamonds, and a fan in her hand, after the
manner of Spanish ladies. Her hair, which was full and
long, and of a pleasing colour, was sown and interwoven
with pearls and diamonds."

Any change that took place in ladies' dress during the
17th century, was in the Fardingal and Mantilla. Towards the middle of that century, the fardingal or hoop,
which had been previously worn of an enormous size, was
greatly diminished in its bulk, or only put on by court
ladies when they went into the presence of the King or
Queen. The mantilla or veil, the most interesting part
of a Spanish lady's attire, was placed on the head, and
was originally intended to hang over the back and shoulders. When the age, however, of Spanish intrigue commenced, the ladies frequently wore their mantillas crossed on their mouth and chin, so as to conceal their features, or only show the flash of a bright and beaming eye.
The mantilla thus worn, afforded an inexhaustible re-

[1] *Memoirs*, p. 170.

source for their plots to the dramatic writers of the period. But this pretext of modesty having concealed many
disorders, an ordinance was at length promulgated by the
Court in 1639, prohibiting any woman from wearing the
mantilla over her countenance.[1] It was expected, that
when the veil was thus removed from the face, the fair
would be more guarded in their conduct, as they would
run greater risks of being observed and detected by their
husbands and relations. It was as difficult, however, to
restore the mantilla to its proper folds, as it was afterwards found by the Bourbon kings to force the Spaniards to relinquish their cloaks and *sombreros*.

The private and domestic life of the Spaniards in the
17th century was somewhat monotonous, and not very
different from what it is described to be in the present day.
They generally rose about seven in the morning, and as
soon as they had got up, they drank some water cooled
with ice, and immediately afterwards chocolate. They
then went to church to hear mass or confess. The forenoon was spent by the ladies in embroidering, and receiving the calls of their acquaintances, whom they frequently presented with collations. Dinner was taken about
twelve o'clock, and after it was over, every one partially
undressed for the *siesta*, and lay down on beds which, for
coolness, were spread with leather skins. At this time
no one was seen on the streets,—the shops were shut, and
all trade or business suspended. About two o'clock in
the winter, and four in the summer, having dressed themselves again, they ate some sweetmeats, and drank either
chocolate or iced water. They then went abroad where
they thought fit, some frequenting the theatre, and others,
at least in summer, the public walks,—the Prado at Madrid, the Rambla at Barcelona, and what were called *Ala-
medas* in the other provincial capitals. The *Tertulias*,

[1] Ortiz, *Compend. Cronol.* t. vi. lib. 20. c. 4.

of which we now hear so much from modern travellers as
the common evening amusement in Spain, had not yet
come into vogue. When they returned home from the
public walks or the theatre, they retired to bed, and a
light supper was there served up to them by the He or
She dwarfs belonging to the family.

The Spanish people in the 17th century were inordi-
nately fond of all sorts of public spectacles and diversions.
In particular, they were much attached to the festivals of
the church, in which amusement was blended with devotion. An account has already been given of the celebration of the day of Corpus Christi.[1] Splendid as these exhibitions were at Madrid, they were still more magnificent and brilliant in the kingdom of Aragon, where de-
corations were varied without end,—where treasures were
displayed with the greatest pomp and abundance, and the
Naves and altars of the churches were lighted up with a
boundless profusion of torches and tapers.

Bull-fights are justly considered as the true national
pastime of Spain. It has been disputed whether they
be of Roman or Moorish origin; but from whatever nation derived, they have at all times intoxicated the Spanish people from the highest to the lowest ranks. The
taste for this amusement amounted to an unbridled passion among them. The lower orders often reserved the
money with which they ought to have supported their families to hire places at the bull-fights, and the women,
it is said, would rather have sold their last rag of clothes
than have missed the exhibition. There was scarcely a
town in the kingdom but had a large square for the purpose of bull-fights. So satisfied were the Spaniards of
the interesting nature of this spectacle, that, on the death
of Charles II. and accession of Philip V, the inhabitants
of Burgos humbly requested Louis XIV. to honour their

[1] See above, vol. i. p. 79.

town with a visit, and, as an inducement, they promised to gratify him with the national solemnity of a bull-feast.[1] But though the Spaniards were devoted to this amusement, the bull-fights in the 17th century were little different from those in the 18th, which have been minutely described by every modern traveller; and it is therefore unnecessary for me to paint the bravery or infinite skill and agility of the performers,—the fury of the bull,—the excitement of the spectators,—or the splendour and animation of the whole scene.

Although it has been disputed whether the bull-fights be of Moorish origin, there can be no doubt as to the *Juego de Cañas,* or Cane-play. It was derived from the oriental sport El-Djerid, which was the rehearsal of an encounter of light horsemen armed with javelins or darts. In this mock fight, as practised in Spain, two parties on horseback met. Each *cavallero* was provided with a certain number of canes, made of reeds, and about a yard in length. Being drawn up opposite to one another, they discharged their missive weapons, and then retired in exact order. Each next traversed the field, in order to take some enemy at disadvantage, and hit him with his cane, which those, who were well practised in the game, darted with great dexterity and force. In the various and unexpected turns, in the surprising address shown in pressing or eluding the adversary, and in the great variety of complicated yet graceful evolutions, consisted the pleasure and beauty of this entertainment. Being of a martial kind, it frequently accompanied or followed the bull-fights.

Running at the ring was also a Spanish amusement, particularly among the higher classes and at court. In this game a number of posts or columns were placed in a circle, from each of which a ring was suspended. The

[1] Coxe's *Mem. of Kings of Spain,* t. i. c. 2.

candidate for the prize, arrayed in knightly equipment,
gallopped round the circle, attempting in his career to
push his lance, usually decked with pennons, into one of
the rings and bear it away. Sometimes more than one
ring was thus snatched in his course by the triumphant
cavalier,—at other times an unsuccessful lance was shi-
vered on the post or column, so that there was much variety of skill and hazard in the enterprise. Charles I. of
England, as we have seen, distinguished himself while at
Madrid by his success and dexterity at this royal sport.

Fire-works *(fuegos de polvero)* were very common in
Spain, and formed a part of all public festivals and rejoicings.

Masquerades were also much in fashion in the large
cities of Spain, particularly in time of carnival. Crowds
of Masks then filled the streets, and all ranks were mixed
and confounded by favour of their various disguises. It
was an object of emulation to display the most elegant
and studied dresses; and the Masks often collected in
groups forming representations of various subjects of action, and frequently exhibiting a striking and picturesque
assemblage. "The city of Barcelona," says Laborde,
"was one of the capitals most distinguished for these exhibitions. The public walk called the Rambla, was covered with masks of all descriptions, and there were balls
called *de peceta* (because this small coin, worth about 10d.,
was the price of admission) which were crowded with
masks; all ranks frequented them without distinction,
and the appearance was brilliant. In the reign of Philip
V. a royal edict forbade this amusement."[1] There was
another species of amusement also called a Masquerade, in
which the courtiers and nobility of Madrid rode at night
through the streets in great numbers, mounted on the
finest horses, and attired in the garbs of various foreign

[1] *View of Spain,* t. v.

nations. They were preceded by trumpets, timbrels, and flutes, and the streets through which they passed were brilliantly illuminated with flambeaux, and coloured lanterns were placed in the windows of the houses. When they came to the end of their course, which was usually the royal palace or the Plaça-Mayor, they jousted with each other in frolic imitation of the ancient tournaments of chivalry. In that peculiar species of masquerade called the *magiganga*, the performers dressed themselves up as wild animals. Philip IV. was amused with an exhibition of this sort on the streets of Valladolid, on his way back to Madrid from the Pyrenees after the nuptials of the Infanta Maria Theresa with Louis XIV.

A *promenade* in the Prado must be reckoned among the public amusements of Madrid. This walk has long been famous in Spanish comedy and romance. The obscurity of the walks and inequality of the ground rendered it favourable to intrigue. Measures were there concerted to deceive the vigilance of duennas and the watchful jealousy of husbands. The walk, I believe, has undergone considerable alteration from time to time. In the 17th century it was the gayest and most splendid resort then in Europe. It was adorned with a number of shady trees, and its marble fountains imparted to the air that refreshing coolness so delightful in a southern climate.

The Spanish nation has always had a decided taste for dancing, and the greatest aptitude to excel in the art. All ranks, but especially the lower orders, were distractedly fond of it. In fact, from the earliest times, the Spaniards had been a dancing nation. The girls of Grenada and Andalusia (the *Terra Bœtica* of the ancients) leaving their own country, were wont to exhibit their native dances at Rome and other parts of the Roman empire, where they often captivated the hearts of

prætors and pro-consuls. Pliny, in proposing an entertainment to one of his friends, mentions a Spanish dance
as one of the proposed amusements. Martial[1] aims the
whole force of his invective against the wanton dances
of the *Terra Bœtica*, especially of the district of Cadiz,
and the voluptuous manner in which they were performed;
while Juvenal, with equal strength and spirit, describes
the style of dancing of the *Gaditanæ puellæ*, and de-
claims against it:

> Forsitan expectes ut Gaditano canoro
> Incipiat pruire choro, plausuque probatæ
> Ad terram tremulo descendant clune puellæ.[2]

In a note on this passage Gifford remarks, " that the
dance here alluded to is neither more nor less than the
Spanish Fandango, which still forms the delight of all
ranks in Spain, and which, though somewhat chastised
in the neighbourhood of the capital, exhibits at this day,
in the remote provinces, a perfect counterpart (actors and
spectators) of the too free, but faithful, representation before us. In a subsequent line Juvenal mentions the *tes-
tarum crepitas*,—the clicking of the castanets. These
were small oblong pieces of polished wood or bone, which
the dancers held between their fingers, and clashed in
measure with inconceivable agility and address. Holy-
day, who was in Spain, says he heard nothing but the
snapping of fingers; he was then unfortunate, I have
heard them often. The Spaniards of the present day
are very curious in the choice of their castanets. Some
have been shown me that cost five and twenty or thirty
dollars a pair. These were made of the beautifully va-
riegated woods of South America."[3]

[1] Lib. v. ep. 79.   [2] Sat. xi.

[3] Gifford's *Translation of Juvenal*, p. 380. According to others,
the fandango is of Negro origin, and was imported from the Havannah. (Swinburne's *Travels through Spain*, t. i. let. 29.) La-

Though it seems thus established that the fandango was a native dance, the Spaniards may probably have mixed in it some Moorish attitudes; and as Cadiz is supposed to have been a Phœnician colony, both the Spaniards and their Moorish conquerors may have derived their choral steps and movements from the wanton and pantomimic dances of the East.

The passion of the Spaniards of all classes for the fandango, was carried to a height which can scarcely be imagined. No sooner was the music to which it is danced heard in a village, or in a ball-room of the capital, than all became animated with delight, and their feet, hands, and eyes were set in motion. And so much was this the favourite entertainment, that it was not, as in most other countries, reserved for youth. The gravest matrons never considered themselves as excluded by age from this diversion, and grandmothers, mothers, and daughters were often seen joining in the same alluring dance. Townsend, in his Journey through Spain, says, " that from what he has himself seen, he is persuaded that if the music of the fandango were suddenly introduced into a church or a court of judicature, priests and people—judges, lawyers, and criminals—the gravest alike as the most gay, would quit their functions, and, forgetting all distinctions, would quickly begin the attractive dance to which they were thus incited."[1] This observation was probably suggested to the English traveller by a little Spanish dramatic piece, in which the Spanish clergy, in their zeal for the morals of the nation, propose the suppression of the fandango, and, in order to judge of its nature and ten-

borde says, that some of the provincial dances, the *Olla* and *Cachirula*, at once savage and voluptuous, remind us of the accounts given by travellers of the dances of the Negroes, and other African tribes. (*View of Spain*, t. v.)

[1] Vol. i. p. 332.

dency, order it to be exhibited before them. An Andalusian *Majo* and his mistress, dressed in the usual costume, make their appearance before the clerical tribunal. They take in their hands the crackling castanets, they raise their voices to the briskest notes, and commence the steps of the fandango. The venerable fathers for a time look grave ; but at length their hearts warm and their looks brighten, and, flinging aside their long hats and skull-caps, they skip and caper over the floor in all the ecstasy of the fandango.

No one, it is said, who has not seen them, can form a conception of the hilarity, nimbleness, and elasticity of the dancers of the fandango. It is usually performed by a pair, but they seemingly exert themselves less from partiality to a partner, than for the sake of the dance itself. It is executed either to the notes of the guitar alone, or to that instrument accompanied by the voice. " Both men and women while dancing," says Baretti, " give a double clap with their thumbs and middle fingers at every cadence, and the fandango is rather made up with graceful motions, and quick striking of the heels and toes on the ground, than with equal and continued steps. They dance close to each other, then wheel about, then approach each other with fond eagerness, then quickly retire and quickly approach again,—the man looking the woman steadily in the face, while she keeps her head down, and fixes her eyes on the ground with as much modesty as she can assume."[1] " The motions of the eyes and features," continues another writer, " mark the postures of this dance : the most lively expression of all the passions that agitate the heart are there exhibited,—fear, desire, and pleasure, are exhibited alternately, and in

---

[1] *Journey through Spain, &c.* letter 37. Baretti travelled in Spain, indeed, in the year 1760 ; but the fandango had not much changed at that time from what it had been a century before.

quick succession. Looks, gesture, attitude, and inflexions
of the body, bestow on them a still more lively and marked expression ; and such is the effect and impression, that
the spectator involuntarily imitates the actions of the performers."[1]   Though completely a national dance, and
prevailing all over Spain, the fandango was danced in its
greatest vivacity and perfection in the province of Andalusia ; and those who performed it on the stage at Madrid were usually dressed in the Andalusian habit.[2]

In good and genteel society, however, towards the close
of the 17th century, the *Bolero* began to be substituted
for the fandango.   This new dance was as lively as the
other, but less expressive, and wanted some of its voluptuous accessories. Like the fandango, it was performed by
two persons.   As danced at present, it is thus described
by a modern writer, and I believe it was not much different in the 17th century. " By way of prelude, *she* struck
her castanets in the air, and made a dignified bow, then
placing her right foot forward, with the point scarcely
touching the ground, she commenced, with the utmost
lightness, those steps which, by their pantomimic cadences
represent an invitation, a promise, a call, to the partner,
who, emboldened by her encouraging steps, advances with
ardour towards her, while she awaits his approach ; but
when he is on the point of reaching her, she escapes him,
and flies, leaving him mocked and confused.   He, half
angry, retraces his steps, to revenge himself in his turn ;
she then follows him, to entice him back, succeeds, and,
flying from right to left, flirts with him, till at last she
meets him, her body inclining forwards, her arms extended towards him, but her head turned another way, to hide

[1] Laborde, *View of Spain*, t. v.
[2] Breton, *L'Espagne et le Portugal, ou Mœurs, Usages, &c. de ces
Royaumes*, t. iii. p. 178.

the confusion produced by his triumph, and her right foot lightly raised, as if still threatening an escape." [1]

The *seguidilla* is the fandango or bolero, executed in the form of a *ballet* or figure dance. It is usually performed by eight—four men and four women, and at intervals each couple, in its own corner or department, goes through all the movements of these dances. " A Spanish female," says Bourgoing, " dancing the seguidilla, dressed in character, accompanying the instruments with castanets, and marking the measure with her heel with uncommon precision, is certainly one of the most seducing objects which love can employ to extend his empire." [2]

There are also a number of provincial dances, particularly among the lower classes of Spain, and all bearing more or less resemblance to the fandango. The three, however, which have been mentioned, the fandango, bolero, and seguidilla, are the national dances of Spain.

It seems singular that, while the light and lively French walked the grave and formal *Louvre* or *Minuet de la cour*, the slow and solemn Spaniard should have skipped the brisk fandango, which rather clashes with our notions of the dignified and lofty bearing of Castilians. It would appear, however, that nations often seek in their amusements some species of relaxation, which is at total variance with their usual habits and modes of thinking. In France, tragedy was elevated on her loftiest buskin ; while the Romans, universally accounted the most majestic race that ever appeared on earth, had little relish for the tragic drama, and were less delighted even with their pure though imitative comedy, than with the buffooneries of the Mimes' *Exodia*, and *Fabulæ Atellanæ*.

Of the public diversions in Spain, one of the most prominent was the drama. In the provinces, during the

[1] *Don Esteban, or Memoirs of a Spaniard.*
[2] *Tableau d'Espagne.*

17th century, the construction of the theatres was imper-
fect, and the stage was still in a half barbarous state. But
in the capital, under the patronage of an improvident
and ostentatious Court, nothing was wanting which could
contribute to the splendour and beauty of scenic decora-
tion. To this subject, however, I shall have an opportunity to recur, if I hereafter treat, in a subsequent volume, of the dramatic literature of Spain during the 17th
century.

INDEX.

END OF VOLUME SECOND.

CPSIA information can be obtained
at www.ICGtesting.com
Printed in the USA
LVHW081013220822
726552LV00009B/365